Securing the Revolution

IDEOLOGY IN
AMERICAN POLITICS, 1789–1815

Securing the Revolution
IDEOLOGY IN
AMERICAN POLITICS, 1789-1815

Richard Buel jr.

Cornell University Press | ITHACA AND LONDON

First published 1972 by Cornell University Press.
Published in the United Kingdom by Cornell University Press Ltd., 2-4 Brook Street, London W1Y 1AA.

International Standard Book Number 0-8014-0705-2
Library of Congress Catalog Card Number 74-38120

Printed in the United States of America by Vail-Ballou Press, Inc.

Librarians: Library of Congress cataloging information appears on the last page of the book.

For my father and mother

Contents

Preface

This book is about a special kind of politics created by the success of the American Revolution. It deals with the efforts of revolutionary leaders to consolidate their achievements after the framing and adoption of the new federal Constitution in 1787–1788. The Constitution provided only a partial remedy for the disorders that had plagued the nation's politics throughout the Confederation period. The establishment of a central government with formal powers which had been denied to the Congress under the Articles of Confederation promised some solution to the most pressing national problems: funding the war debt and gaining access to the European commercial empires. But at least equally responsible for the political turmoil had been pressures exerted on state governments by a people whose revolutionary experience had taught them how vulnerable the polity could be and whose revolutionary ideology made them profoundly suspicious of power. Although the new Constitution had been designed to remove the national government from the immediate reach of the populace, its power was still ultimately dependent on public opinion so long as it lacked a large revenue and patronage or a sizable military and judicial apparatus. Throughout the period treated here, the government was far more vulnerable to the people than it has ever been since.

Our early national politics was dominated by a disagreement originating in the leadership about how to secure the Revolution, given this state of affairs. Some believed that stability was best achieved by adjusting government to fit popular expectations; others, that government would never be safe until it was invulnerable to popular pressure, which duty required them to resist at every turn. Each opinion reflected an evaluation of republics in general that also influenced thinking about foreign relations. If the Revolution had been

ix

followed by a period of international tranquillity, the disagreement
in the leadership would very likely have focused on domestic matters
and would have been amiably compromised as the new government
showed itself competent to solve national problems. Unfortunately,
before any domestic stability had been achieved, the French Revolution and the international upheaval that followed it exacerbated the
quarrel among the nation's leaders. And the pressures exerted by the
great powers on the infant republic soon posed such dramatic strategic choices as to engage more and more of the people in this quarrel, thus making it possible for each faction in the government to
appeal for popular support against the other. In this fashion, the
first parties grew up.

Readers who are familiar with the literature on the politics of the
period will find some unusual emphases in my account. I have treated
the years 1794 to 1799 at greater length than any other period, and
have given considerably more attention to the 1790's in general than
to the years following 1801. Though foreign affairs necessarily dominate any discussion of the early national period, I have concentrated
more upon the effect of diplomatic events on public opinion than
upon the arcana of negotiations. Also, factions within each party receive only the briefest glance, and individuals are not developed as
personalities.

My approach has been shaped by the assumption that public opinion was the single most important ingredient in the politics of the
first party system. Therefore I have felt justified in treating the leading actors in this drama as the representatives of political principles
rather than as human beings in their own right, because that is how
the public saw them. Similarly, parties are here portrayed as more
homogeneous than they really were because they seemed so to the
people at the time, except for a brief period during the election of
1800. The same assumption underlies my account of foreign affairs.
And the asymmetrical organization of my argument proceeds from a
conviction that the struggle between the two parties for public opinion had been settled by 1800. After that, only some extraordinary
development could have returned the Federalists to power, and party
rivalry was reduced to relatively simple terms deserving less detailed
treatment.

Because of my emphasis on ideology and public opinion, most of this account is based on public sources, that is, documents to which the people had access, particularly newspapers with wide circulations, reports of congressional debates, diplomatic correspondence, and presidential addresses. To a modern reader, not accustomed to devouring the *Congressional Record* word for word, my stress on what was said in Congress may seem questionable. But it is my impression that these debates were a major determinant of public opinion, and that in an age when there was little distinction between culture and politics, an age with few other distractions for the average man, such accounts were widely read. Certainly the newspapers of the period, even the less prominent ones, devoted an unusual amount of space to them. For the same reason, private correspondence occupies a subordinate place in this account. People could not react to what they never saw. Though there were plots and intrigues, these rarely amounted to much without the support of public opinion, and attempts to manipulate opinion were usually exposed to the public by the opposition. Where I felt that the printed sources left a point in doubt, I have occasionally consulted manuscript sources. As a rule, though, the published papers of the leading actors in this political drama are sufficiently complete to make me feel justified in confining my references to them.

My use of the term ideology also needs explanation. Since it was coined at the end of the eighteenth century, this word has been applied to such a wide range of phenomena that its sense is now completely obscure. About the only thing its users agree upon is that it implies a coherent system of ideas. Among other meanings, it has acquired the pejorative one of "false consciousness" in defense of interests which cannot be defended in any other way. I propose to avoid such value-laden usage, taking the term to mean simply a coherent system of ideas consciously directed to the achievement of an ideal aim.[1] The ideal aim to which the men I write about were committed was the fulfillment of the promise of the Revolution. In the early years, this was for most a passive matter of resisting challenges to liberty as defined by revolutionary ideology. For the nation's leaders, however, it meant responsibility for choosing those strategies which would secure the full benefits of independence to the nation at large. This choice was controlled by two opposite views of republicanism, an experiment whose outcome in a country the size of

America was still in doubt. Some thought that it was in principle the best kind of government, while others thought that it was defective. These different assumptions produced correspondingly different sets of responses to a wide range of problems, so that the two groups found themselves in irreconcilable conflict. I have used the terms "Republicanism" and "Federalism" to refer to the ideology of each group, that is to their assumptions and characteristic responses.

Many good people and institutions have helped me write this book. Grants from the American Council of Learned Societies and from Wesleyan University, and a fellowship at the Charles Warren Center for the Study of American History, financed my research. The Dietrich Foundation's gift to the Wesleyan library of early American imprints on microprint made many important sources readily available. The staffs of Olin Library at Wesleyan University, Houghton Library at Harvard, Beinecke Library at Yale, the Massachusetts Historical Society, the Library Company of Philadelphia, and the American Antiquarian Society have been particularly generous with their help and hospitality. I am indebted to Mary Czaja, Rhonda Kissinger, and Dorothy Hay for typing various drafts of the manuscript. I am also grateful for the support and encouragement of Oscar Handlin, Jack P. Greene, James M. Smith, George A. Billias, Michael Kammen, and the late Douglas Adair. And I have benefited from the suggestions and criticism of Merrill D. Peterson, Gordon S. Wood, Roger H. Brown, David E. Swift, Jeffrey E. Butler, Donald Meyer, Louis O. Mink, Philip Pomper, and Gordon Marshall. Special thanks are due Bernard Bailyn, under whose guidance I began my work as a historian and who has given me not only careful criticism but also a standard of craftsmanship to which I could aspire. But my greatest debt is to my wife, Joy Day Buel, whose contribution to my work has been immeasurable.

RICHARD BUEL JR.

Haddam, Connecticut

PART I

DIVISION

It is now generally accepted that the first party system did not arise from the controversy over ratifying the Constitution. It grew out of divisions in the ranks of those men who had led the struggle to secure adoption by the state conventions and had been chosen by the people to implement the new government in 1789. During the first session of Congress, there was little sign that such divisions were soon to come. Despite sharp disagreements about specifics, both houses and the executive cooperated brilliantly in giving flesh to the skeleton of government. In seven short months they organized the executive and judiciary, established a national revenue, and proposed the series of amendments which would become the Bill of Rights. After these notable achievements, members were understandably reluctant to tackle the equally complex problem of framing a policy that would satisfy public creditors. So an exhausted House authorized the secretary of the treasury, Alexander Hamilton, to secure the necessary information and report to Congress on a plan for establishing national credit.

In January 1790, Hamilton duly submitted his comprehensive "Report on Public Credit" at the opening of the second session. The ensuing debate caused a rupture in the national leadership and set the pattern for the opposing alignments that were to dominate national politics for the next twenty-five years. The report urged not only that provision be made for the national debt and arrearages of interest but also that the debts of individual states should be assumed. To make this ambitious undertaking possible, Hamilton proposed that the effective rate of interest on the consolidated domestic debt be reduced from 6 to 4 percent. He hoped to gain the voluntary compliance of public creditors with this plan by waiving the government's right to redeem a portion of the debt at will in return for im-

1

mediate reduction of the interest rate on a good part of the principal. He assumed that creditors would find this attractive because interest rates were in any case expected to fall as the combined consequence of low rates in Europe and an increased supply of money at home produced by successful funding. Hamilton further proposed the institution of a sinking fund to purchase the debt at the market rate. This would help retire it and also raise its value to par so that it could become a source of fluid capital for the developing nation. He subsequently suggested that to make this capital the basis for a stable medium of national exchange there should be a national bank with the power to issue notes, three-quarters of whose capital could be subscribed in the funded debt of the United States.[1]

That party alignments should have formed over Hamilton's fiscal proposals seems reasonable enough in view of the economic interests at stake. Nothing appears more logical than that the representatives of states with large debts, together with individuals who either held securities themselves or were clearly associated with holders, should favor funding and assumption. By the same token, representatives of states which had already considerably reduced these obligations, or whose unliquidated debts had been engrossed by speculators, could be expected to oppose Hamilton's proposals.[2] Everyone acknowledged the economic character of the controversy, and this was later confirmed by the strikingly sectional character of alignments on such issues as assumption and the Bank. Representative Michael Jenifer Stone of Maryland was quick to attribute disagreement over the Bank to the geographical distribution of the Continental debt, remarking in Congress that because the greater part "has travelled eastward of the Potomac," and because the Bank would "raise the value of Continental paper" by making it receivable for the subscribed capital, the eastern states felt a "strong impulse of immediate interest" to support it.[3] Nor does it require much imagination to see that the measure added insult to the injury of the southern states, which (South Carolina excepted) had gone further than their eastern sisters toward retiring their debts but had gained nothing by assumption.

What appears simple in retrospect was nevertheless perplexing at the time. The framers of the federal Constitution and the national leaders who sponsored it held party politics in abhorrence and had expected their work to discourage it. In the convention and during the ratification controversy they had voiced their hopes that the Constitution would correct the tendency of state politics to disregard "the public good . . . in the conflict of rival parties." [4] They thought the enlarged dimensions of the national government would bring about this happy result by making it hard for a majority to coalesce except in the national interest.[5] In the Philadelphia convention some had expressed the fear that, regardless of the system's dimensions, if the choice were delegated either to the federal or state legislatures, or to the people at large, the presidential elections would be open to party influence.[6] The elaborate contrivance of the electoral college was intended to minimize this danger. By referring election of the executive "in the first instance to an immediate act of the people of America, to be exerted in the choice of persons for the temporary and sole purpose of making the appointment" rather than to "any pre-existing bodies of men who might be tampered with before hand to prostitute their votes," the framers hoped to frustrate "cabal, intrigue and corruption." They gave added effect to this precaution by requiring that "electors . . . vote at the same time throughout the U.S., and at so great a distance from each other." This would make it hard for them to combine, or for any outside power to influence their decision. Granted, it was also unlikely that there would be a majority for any one candidate, and there was a real danger that the House of Representatives, voting by states, would be subject to party influence. But complete security was unattainable, and the House's choice was at least confined to those candidates who had received the larger pluralities.[7]

Though in practice it was not long before the electoral college succumbed to political pressure as the contest for the presidency became the focus of the first party system, it is clear that the framers had never intended this to happen. They had made extraordinary efforts to keep presidential elections free of party influence. Yet the force of their desires has subsequently been questioned because of two circumstances. First, national parties did emerge, and except for a brief hiatus between 1816 and 1825 they have continued to be a standard feature of our political life. This has given rise to the theory that the federal Constitution, far from discouraging party formation, made it a necessity and that when the framers established a central authority able to enforce its decisions throughout the nation, they simultaneously created a need for a way to coordinate activities over large areas and influence these decisions.[8] What is more, various rationales for party current in Britain at this time were so used by American commentators throughout the 1790's as to suggest that it was gradually coming to be accepted.[9] And if any further explanation seems needed to reconcile the framers' declared intentions with their acts in the 1790's, it can be argued either that the factions and parties they disliked in state politics were different from those which emerged nationally, or that as practical politicians they knew when speculative ideals must give way to working necessity. This last theory is particularly attractive if one believes that the success of the Revolution created a generation of leaders sufficiently ambitious to sacrifice their scruples to the desire for power.[10]

Before the framers' intentions are so summarily dismissed, certain aspects of the first party system should be carefully considered. For instance, the national political coalitions that appeared in the 1790's could hardly be said to bear the mark of personal ambition. The men around whom these party alignments first formed all willingly retired to private life during the decade. It is true that resignation from office did not necessarily entail renunciation of power, and it is probable that Alexander Hamilton enjoyed as much if not more influence as a private citizen in 1795–1796 than he would have had as secretary of the treasury. But he was exceptional. Although the founding fathers were clearly concerned about how posterity would judge them, most realized that fame could only be pursued in subordination to the larger end of fulfilling the promise of the Revolution. Certainly the first parties gave short shrift to those suspected of pursuing personal power. Aaron Burr found himself isolated from the Republican leadership after he refused to break an electoral college deadlock, caused by the tie vote of 1800. In the same election, Hamilton was angrily attacked by other Federalists for his efforts to swing the electoral college against their own candidate, John Adams. The perception that personal ambition was counterproductive also had much to do with the restrained way in which James Monroe advanced his candidacy during the election of 1808, while James Madison's capacity for leadership was being questioned.[11] Indeed, the Republican party's collapse in the 1820's, when intramural competition for the presidency replaced traditional adherence to the authority of the caucus, might lead to the conclusion that a distinguishing feature of the first parties was their hostility to personal ambition.

As for the references to British theories that two-party competition tended to further the public interest, they must be examined in context if their significance is to be properly understood. Where I have encountered them, they are mostly being used for apology and reassurance.[12] It is true that this in itself shows ambivalence about party, but only in the sense that Americans felt obliged to rationalize what could not be prevented. If they had believed there was any choice, no one would have urged that parties be formed as a positive advantage. Eighteenth-century Americans had no grounds for concluding that such competition would lead to working compromise, or to any functional definition of the public good. Most of history, together with their own recent experience, suggested rather that party competition led to irreconcilable antagonisms, compelled reasonable men to abandon the middle ground for the extreme, and gave rash demagogues opportunities they would not otherwise have had to tamper with elections.[13] Nor were Americans reassured by the emergence of opposition parties in Britain. In his Farewell Address, George Washington had said that although in a limited monarchy one could look "with endulgence, if not with favour, upon the spirit of party . . . in those of the popular character . . . in Governments purely elective, it is a spirit not to be encouraged" because of "constant danger of excess." [14] Even those who did not agree with Washington that republics were more vulnerable to popular disorders than monarchies nevertheless saw that British parties were divided over place rather than principles, whereas each of the American parties accused the other of endangering the republic by driving it toward either monarchy or anarchy.[15]

There were two other aspects to the development of parties in the 1790's which made the national leadership even more afraid of them. First, it was disturbing that alignments on Hamilton's fiscal policy tended to parallel others on such diverse matters as the foreign policy of the nation and the powers of the federal government, in particular the executive. Everyone knows that after 1800 these divisions precipitated a secessionist movement among New England Federalists. It is

less well known that long before the conspiracy of 1804 northern
leaders talked seriously about secession to their southern counterparts
as well as among themselves. Even without this knowledge, it was
not hard to perceive what these divisions ultimately implied for the
union. That is why Washington declared it "a matter of serious concern, that any ground should have been furnished for characterizing
parties by *Geographical* discriminations." [16] In exacerbating the sectional character of alignments to the point where they threatened
division of the republic, the first national parties appeared a good
deal more dangerous than had the state party divisions of the 1780's.

Of equal concern was the international context in which party
divisions arose. From the start of the decade, it was evident that
Europe had entered a period of revolutionary instability. As time
went on, and the great powers with New World possessions were
drawn into war, it became increasingly clear that each of the belligerents would try to make the United States serve its interests and
damage those of its adversaries. The last thing needed by a new
and insecure nation confronting a warring world was a bitter disagreement among its leaders which might invite the intrusion of
foreign influence. "Columbus," writing in the *Columbian Centinel* in
1793, pointed to the dangers:

If the partizans of any particular faction, cease to rely upon their own
talent and services to support their influence among their countrymen, and
link themselves in union with an external power, the principles of self-
defence, the instinct of self-preservation itself, will suggest a similar connection to their opponents; which ever of the party [sic] nominally prevails, the whole country is really enslaved.

The leaders of the young republic believed foreign influence was
a much greater threat to popular government than to monarchies. A
foreign government would find it easier to bribe the people where all
men had power than to bribe a monarch with a proprietary right in
his kingdom. This, they reasoned, was why so many past republics
had been subverted from without.[17] In retrospect, it is clear that the
fear of foreign influence which permeated national politics in this
period proceeded less from historical or theoretical analysis than
from the lack of a secure national identity, the result partly of youth,
partly of a sense of weakness in relation to the great powers. What-

ever the reason, it did not have the effect of muting party strife, which seemed to grow more bitter as pressure from abroad increased during 1793 to 1815. Furthermore, as foreign policy became controversial, division was no longer confined to the nation's leadership but spread to the people at large.

There is need, then, for an explanation of the gradual separation of leaders and people into irreconcilable parties which does not deny or ignore that at this time in America's history such a phenomenon was held in strong abhorrence. It is especially necessary to account for the process of party formation having begun over an economic issue, for these are usually susceptible to compromise. It is true that such compromise is less likely where the economic equilibrium between classes and individuals has been violently upset,[18] and it might be said that revolution and the expansion which took place after 1786 had produced this condition in the United States. But the absence of a feudal heritage and the profusion of resources in America precluded the emergence of distinct class lines, at least among those enjoying legal equality. Even if they had arisen, there were no institutions through which one class could control another. Though some of the opposition to Hamilton's policies fed on the fear that he meant to set up class structures, the national government was so clearly incapable of controlling such a diffuse economy that this argument did not carry conviction. And it would not explain why Hamilton and Madison came to a parting of the ways over the fiscal issue. I grant that at the beginning of the 1790's there was not as much pressure against disagreement as there was later on, yet it still seems unthinkable that these two men, who had collaborated so effectively in securing ratification of the Constitution, should have gratuitously jeopardized their careful work over a mere economic issue on which a compromise could have been easily reached.

1. Fiscal Policy

Hamilton's fiscal policy became the initial focus of the first party system because it raised a question more fundamental than any clash of economic interests and one on which there could be no compromise: how to stabilize the republic and secure revolutionary achievements. It was this issue rather than money matters which set Hamilton in irreconcilable opposition to Madison and Jefferson. And that opposition in turn divided the members of the national government, making a breach in their ranks that would not heal until the first party system disintegrated more than two decades later. The key to the formation of the first national parties, then, lies in the development of Hamilton's first disagreement with Madison and Jefferson.

I

That there would be disagreement over fiscal policies first became apparent when Madison proposed that, instead of funding the domestic debt to current holders as Hamilton's plan suggested, "the present holders of public securities which have been alienated, shall be settled with according to the highest market rate of such securities; and that the balance of the sums due from the public, be paid in such proportion to the original holder of such securities." [1] Known as the policy of discrimination, Madison's proposal called for paying the interest and principal of the domestic debt according to the rate at which it had been contracted, that is, at 6 percent instead of 4 percent. If passed, this measure would have increased the revenue requirements for servicing the debt by roughly one-half. It would probably also have made assumption of state debts, which Hamilton thought politically essential to prevent the federal government from competing with the states, impossible in the immediate future. [2] Madison betrayed his hostility to assumption by proposing first that

8

it be tied to a final settlement of accounts between the states, and second that the government should assume state debts as they had stood at the end of the war.[3] The first proposal clearly reflected the hope of the southern states that assumption would not frustrate a final settlement from which they expected to emerge with advantage. The second, by reviving many debts already extinguished by the states, would have added substantially to the consolidated domestic debt and would either have forced federal creditors to accept an even lower interest rate or have made payment of interest uncertain. This group could certainly be expected to oppose assumption if it were adopted on Madison's terms.[4]

Hamilton felt outraged and betrayed by Madison's opposition. Writing to his friend Edward Carrington two years later, he said that he had accepted the post as secretary of the treasury "under a full persuasion, that from similarity of thinking, conspiring with personal goodwill, I should have the firm support of Mr. Madison, in the *general course* of my administration." Hamilton claimed to have believed that Madison shared his views on the inexpediency of discriminating between original and present holders of the debt because "an address of Congress of April 26th 1783, which was planned by [Madison] in conformity to his own ideas," had criticized this notion, and because subsequent reports had told of Madison strenuously opposing discrimination in the Virginia legislature. Certainly Madison had given no sign of having changed his mind about discrimination in October 1789 when Hamilton had solicited his ideas for establishing public credit.[5] As for assumption, Hamilton said that the issue had been raised before the Philadelphia convention, and that "in a long conversation, which I had with Mr. Madison in an afternoon's walk I well remember that we were perfectly agreed in the expediency and propriety of such a measure." When Hamilton found out that Madison intended to oppose him on both points, he asked for an explanation. According to Hamilton, Madison then acknowledged that he had changed his mind "but alledged in his justification that the very considerable alienation of the debt, subsequent to the periods at which he had opposed a discrimination, had essentially changed the state of the question—and that as to the assumption, he had contemplated it to take place *as matters stood at the peace.*"[6]

Hamilton was not impressed by this reasoning. Speculation in the debt had been going on continuously since the conclusion of the war: why then had Madison waited until 1790 to change his mind about discrimination? And Madison's proposal that "a vast mass of already extinguished debt" be added to the obligations of the federal government as a precondition of assumption seemed to Hamilton to work against his objective of confirming public order. He was willing to consider it, nevertheless, until he realized that it was politically impractical because it made federal creditors afraid that there would not be enough money to pay both the debts owed them and those owed by the states. Hamilton blamed Madison's extraordinary behavior and Jefferson's support of it on personal rivalry, an explanation which his friends were quick to second.[7] Others have subsequently observed that assumption was contrary to Virginia's economic interests. Madison himself said in the House that assumption would cost Virginia about $2,000,000 more than non-assumption, though this was premised on the belief that there would be no final settlement of accounts between the states. So it is tempting to see discrimination as an oblique way of attacking assumption, and Madison as responding to pressure exerted by his constituents. This seems the more plausible as he had been excluded from the Senate in 1788 and, despite his national prominence, obliged to work hard for election to the House of Representatives.[8]

Closer inspection casts doubt upon this account of the way Madison and Jefferson behaved. For one thing, if Madison was motivated largely by personal rivalry, why did he feel less personal animus toward Hamilton than Hamilton felt toward him? If we may believe Hamilton, Jefferson returned his dislike with interest,[9] yet if Jefferson were hungry for power why did he retire to private life in 1794, and why did Madison follow his example in 1797? For another, Virginia's economic interests were technically unaffected by assumption, because all the sums assumed by the federal government would be charged against the states in the final settlement of accounts. Though Madison had been sceptical that such a settlement would take place, during the debate on assumption, Congress agreed to a formula by which common charges were to be apportioned and appointed commissioners to pass on state accounts. This removed the principal obstacles which had hitherto obstructed a final settlement. The commissioners were also authorized to admit claims "according to the principles of general equity (although such claims may not be sanctioned by the resolves of Congress, or supported by regular vouchers)," and this together with an extension in the deadline for filing claims benefitted those southern states which had not observed proper accounting procedures.[10] Virginia's interests were further protected against the possibility that a final settlement might never be made by over-assumption of the debt in her favor. As Madison confessed, "in a pecuniary light, the assumption is no longer of much consequence to Virginia" because she would "pay no more to the general Treasury than she now pays to the State Trea[sur]y and perhaps in a mode which will be less disagreeable to the people." [11] If anything more was needed to reconcile Virginians to assumption, Hamilton's willingness to support Jefferson in establishing the nation's capital on the Potomac should have sufficed.[12]

Although Madison reluctantly acquiesced in the suggested compromise to keep the proponents of assumption from obstructing all attempts to fund the federal debt, he remained opposed to the measure itself, and Jefferson soon regretted having tried to break the deadlock in Congress by suggesting a trade-off on the residency issue.[13] The dislike which the future leaders of the Republican party felt for Hamilton's system had its origin in divergent ideas about a public debt. Despite disclaimers,[14] it was clear to everyone that both Hamilton and his supporters regarded the public debt more as an opportunity to be exploited than as a burden to the republic which must be removed as fast as possible. Not only was Hamilton willing to renounce the government's right to retire some of the debt for a period which Madison estimated as forty or fifty years, but the manner in which his supporters described the by-products of a successful funding was alarming. For instance, a writer calling himself "Tablet" wrote in the *Gazette of the United States* that "a National debt attaches many citizens to the government, who, by their numbers, wealth and influence contribute more perhaps to its preservation than a body of soldiers." Obviously, the Hamiltonians valued the fiscal system as a means of securing revolutionary achievements by making an influential creditor class dependent on the government.[15]

Madison and Jefferson were not happy about using a debt in this way. Their uneasiness may have been increased by the difficulties Virginia planters had suffered because of indebtedness to foreign merchants, but it derived from more than a simple confusion between private and public debts. In 1790 there seemed to be good reason for questioning that public debts were compatible with stable governments. That reason was the bankruptcy of one of Europe's greatest monarchies. Though it was not clear to what extremes of revolutionary fervor France would be driven by her financial crisis, no American had been better placed to see how it disrupted the *ancien régime* than Jefferson, minister to France from 1784 to 1789. Nor should France's bankruptcy have surprised any student of Adam Smith, and both Jefferson and Madison were familiar with the *Inquiry into the Nature and Causes of the Wealth of Nations,* republished in Philadelphia in 1789.[16]

Smith, the most influential critic of that English public finance which many Americans urged Hamilton to imitate, had invoked history to prove that funding schemes had a tendency to beggar every state adopting them by transferring revenue from the productive classes to pensioners who lived upon the industry of others. Smith also explained why a debt, once contracted, usually perpetuated itself and grew greater. He said that people were never willing to reduce the debt in peacetime at the same rate as they had been willing to expand it during war, because they would not accept additional taxes unless there was obvious necessity. In 1776, Smith had said that "the enormous debts which at present oppress . . . will in the long run probably ruin all the great nations of Europe." His prediction now seemed to be coming true with the start of the French Revolution.[17] And what had happened to France might surely happen to Britain next, given the dramatic expansion of her national debt. James Jackson of Georgia, who borrowed heavily from Smith for one of his speeches on public credit, exhorted his fellow congressmen to "take warning by the errors of Europe, and guard against the introduction of a system followed by calamities so universal."[18]

Nor were Madison and Jefferson impressed by the possible short-term tendency of public debts to stabilize regimes, for they shared in the belief that this means was incompatible with republican government. Richard Bland Lee spoke to this concern when he remarked that "in all the deliberations of the House, the nature of our Government should be attended to. It [is] a Government of the people, and nothing like a coercive principle [is] to be found in it."[19] A funded

debt divided the nation into two antagonistic interests and forced
government to tax the many for the few, so that, as Representative
Stone of Maryland put it, the new nation was placed "in the situation
of most Governments in Europe which do not depend for support
upon the love and confidence of their own citizens: but depend
altogether upon mercenaries who are sure of their pay." [20] If the
funded debt then expanded, as was very likely to happen in a republic where the people were hostile to taxation, it might eventually
become necessary for the government to "war on [its] own citizens to
collect it," abandoning republican principles in the process. Thoughts
such as these led Madison to remark in a letter to Henry Lee, "I go
on the principle that a Public Debt is a Public curse, and in a
Rep[ublican] Gov[ernmen]t a greater than in any other." Jefferson
was later to charge that "the ultimate object of [the fiscal system] is
to prepare the way for a change, from the present republican form
of government, to that of a monarchy." [21]

These attitudes toward a public debt did not lead to the conclusion that it should be repudiated. So blatantly unjust a policy would
have been as disruptive as oppressive taxation, and Madison, ac-
knowledging that the central government would never have authority
until it had made proper provision for its debts, urged that public
credit be established through "an experienced punctuality in the
payments due from the Government." [22] They do help, however, to
explain Madison's apparent inconsistency in responding to the secretary's proposals. Speculation was just one part of the story. At least
equally important was that the debt Hamilton proposed the federal
government should assume had been swollen well beyond Madison's
initial expectations. Assumption was not the only cause of this; there
was also the inclusion of indents (that is, scrip used in lieu of interest), which committed the government to treat arrearages in interest as principal. Given Hamilton's wish to bar the government from
retiring part of the debt for forty years, and given the hazards faced
by a small nation in a world dominated by larger powers, this made
it seem unlikely that the United States would be able to retire one
debt before it became necessary to contract another. Apart from
doubts about pecuniary advantage, then, Madison and Jefferson were
hostile to assumption because they did not wish unnecessarily to enlarge or perpetuate the debt. Assumption threatened to do this by

taking over state debts before a final settlement had ascertained their size. At the same time, by removing the pressure for final settlement, it removed the principal incentives for states to retire their obligations, so that the process would be prolonged. This is why Madison continued to have reservations about it even after Hamilton had guaranteed Virginia's financial interests.[23]

Madison's proposal that assumption should include compensation for "all debts which the states had discharged since the end of the war" seems at first to conflict with this, for by his own admission it would have added "⅓ more to the amount of the Debts." On a second glance, however, it manifests his other great concern, which was to establish public credit in some republican mode. The beneficiaries of his scheme would be states rather than individuals, and the states could ease the weight of taxation on all the people. Though the absolute size of the debt would have been increased, the burden would be more equitably distributed. The increase in federal taxes, which were largely indirect, would be balanced by a decrease in state taxes, which bore heavily on the poor. This removed one objection to a public debt by allowing all the people to participate in its benefits rather than the public creditors alone. Madison was not entirely satisfied with this plan, knowing that the more the debt was enlarged, the more likely it was to be perpetual. Nevertheless, he also realized that if public credit were to be established, the people had to be willing to pay. His proposed modification of assumption would at least have made the measure more equitable, reconciling it, "if anything can be supposed to reconcile it, to all the states." If there had to be a large debt, surely it was best to spread its benefits as widely as possible.[24] This would not preclude further adjustments in other parts of the funding system to compensate for the increments incurred. For instance, Madison's amendment might have led to the exclusion of indents from the funding system, a move for which there was some support in the Senate.[25]

In principle, Madison still preferred some means of reconciling the people to their part in establishing public credit which would not expand the debt at all. His discriminatory proposal was designed to do precisely this. It would have discouraged assumption, at least on the extravagant terms which Hamilton proposed; on the other hand it would have helped to popularize funding by including, in Richard

Bland Lee's words, "every class of citizens . . . in the distribution of national justice" and protecting the government against any charge that its policies would "aggrandize a few" rather than "accommodate all." [26] Though Madison had originally opposed discrimination, Hamilton's "Report on Public Credit" changed his mind about this too. But whereas Madison's reversal on the issue of assumption had been motivated largely by the amount that Hamilton proposed to fund, his espousal of discrimination was a response to the unpopularity of the debt. Though its size and its popularity were not unrelated, the speculative activity surrounding the release of the "Report on Public Credit" was particularly upsetting to southern representatives because it allowed northern agents to buy up the debt held by southerners at reduced prices before the secretary's proposal was known. [27] Madison undoubtedly decided that unless some attempt were made to compensate for these antics the public would turn against rapid retirement of the debt and perhaps even against public credit.

What needs explaining is not why Madison espoused discrimination, which had a certain popular currency at the time, but why his doing so antagonized the proponents of Hamilton's policies. The usual criticism of the scheme as inconsistent with establishing public credit is not plausible because Madison's proposal called for a more scrupulous honoring of the federal debt than did Hamilton's. Yet the degree to which the Hamiltonians were upset is suggested by the extreme charges of Fisher Ames that the measure would "shake Government," and of John Lawrence that it was treason against the Constitution. [28] In part these can be dismissed as the overreactions of men who had a financial or political stake in funding and assumption. They thought discrimination threatened negotiability of the debt and therefore its value as a currency substitute; they feared, too, that to make the original holders equal beneficiaries with present holders would alienate propertied, influential people from the government. Therefore they were reluctant to see the economic and political byproducts expected from a restoration of national credit sacrificed to abstract notions of justice and what they thought an erroneous assessment of public opinion. [29] Yet this alone would not have caused them to respond as violently as they did. Nor would Hamilton have been moved to say that his "respect for the force of Mr. Madison's mind and the soundness of his judgement" had been diminished by the proposal. Even Washington, who had not yet taken sides in the conflict, felt that "the subject was delicate, and perhaps had better never been stirred." [30]

Discrimination roused these widespread misgivings because the Revolution had made Americans unduly sensitive to taxation. As a result, attempts on the part of the federal government to promote fiscal responsibility risked the same popular resistance as had obstructed the establishment of public credit in most of the states during the 1780's and had even led to fiat finance in North Carolina and Rhode Island.[31] The risk was to some extent proportionate to the burdens assumed. If the federal government limited its own responsibility for the debt, the burden would be correspondingly light and the dangers of popular reaction less. On the other hand, if it undertook such an ambitious program as Hamilton had proposed, the demands of which might not be met by the yield from the impost, it was all too likely that the people would grow resentful. Though Hamilton was privately assuring members of Congress that the revenue from the impost would be sufficient for his proposal, few were convinced that this was true.[32] In the circumstances, the last thing his supporters wanted was to invite the agitation of special interests, angered by exclusion from a fiscal settlement. Many feared that Madison's discriminatory proposal would provoke this by putting one of the best-known leaders in Congress behind the notion that the original holders were victims of injustice, and would perhaps lead the people to reject all attempts to establish public credit. In other words, what had made Madison incline toward discrimination was precisely that aspect which most upset his opposition, its potential popularity.

This is not to say that Madison was playing the demagogue when he proposed discrimination. His insistence that the federal government pay off its obligations at 6 percent was hardly designed to court those who would have preferred some form of debt repudiation.[33] But then this was the last thing Madison wanted. He was just as preoccupied as Hamilton with establishing the authority of a government that had no coercive power, but was wholly dependent on the people's will, and whose political institutions were so new and untried that no one could be sure they would be obeyed. He knew that the government would lose all authority if it failed to establish its credit, and he also knew that the immediate interests of public creditors were directly opposed to those of the people, who disliked taxation so much that they might refuse to pay the debt. Indeed, this had already happened in Massachusetts.

Where the leaders of the future parties disagreed was on how to resolve these problems. The Federalists knew that the government was initially popular, but did not think this a secure enough base to rest upon permanently. They tried instead to use this popularity, together with the backlash from Shays's Rebellion, as an aid in pressing upon the momentarily acquiescent public a fiscal system which would give the government real power, or enough influence for stability.[34] The opposition thought that this was self-defeating because the favored few would be so far outnumbered by the excluded many. They were more inclined to believe that the public would support an equitable debt settlement, and wanted to establish federal authority by making it responsive to the aspirations and interests of the people.[35] These different approaches to the problem of making the republic stable proceeded from different visions of the nature of republican government which lay at the heart of the differences beginning to emerge between Federalists and Republicans. But this was obscured during the controversy over funding and assumption, appearing only by implication. The proponents of the scheme were anxious to avoid generating any more opposition than necessary; on the other hand, because Hamilton's critics agreed on the over-riding importance of establishing public credit, they were forced to compromise their dislike of a public debt. Madison described their objective well when he said it was "to shun . . . evils . . . without abandoning too much the re-establishment of public credit." [36]

II

The opposition's flexibility and willingness to compromise diminished when it came to the Bank of the United States. Then the disagreement which had lurked behind the controversy over discrimination and assumption began to come into the open. As the spirit of cooperation disappeared, there was a hardening of the divisions between Republicans and Federalists in Congress. There is no need to analyze congressional voting in order to assess the impact of the Bank on the opposition. This is plain in the unprecedented way Madison opposed it, not by reference to it as a policy so much as by questioning its constitutionality. Madison was not the first to take this approach. A month earlier, the Virginia legislature had led the way in questioning the constitutionality of assumption. It was largely thanks to Madison's efforts, however, that the doctrine of a strictly construed Constitution gained currency.[37] The significance of this can only be appreciated when we reflect that constitutional appeals were widely regarded as a means of rallying public opinion on extraordinary occasions. Given Madison's reservations about such a remedy, expressed in the *Federalist,* and the intricate sophistication of his argument, it is clear that he meant to appeal not so much to the people as to the President's veto power. But the tactical shift unmistakably heralded a change in national politics.[38]

Madison's case against the Bank rested on a narrow interpretation of the clause in the Constitution granting the federal government "the power to pass all laws necessary and proper to execute the specified powers" delegated to it by the people. He argued that "the essential characteristic of the Government, as composed of limited and enumerated powers, would be destroyed, if, instead of direct and incidental means, any means could be used." Madison urged that the Bank was in no sense necessary to any specifically denominated power vested in the federal government, but only convenient. He feared that its passage would establish "a precedent of interpretation levelling all the barriers which limit the powers of the General Government, and protect those of the State Governments." [39] The threat to the states posed by Hamilton's policies had already received some attention in the debate on assumption.[40] Its restatement by Madison, one of the principal architects of the Constitution, now brought it to the fore.[41]

In the nineteenth century, strict construction of the Constitution was to become the characteristic posture of southern leaders protecting slavery interests from federal intervention. It is tempting to see the origins of this in the 1790's, when alignments on Hamilton's policies were assuming a distinctly sectional character. Yet though southern leaders were obviously aware that a strong federal government would threaten slavery, the desire to guard a local interest against the central power was not all that moved the debate on how to interpret the Constitution. If it had been, a South Carolinian like William Laughton Smith, who was as anxious as anyone to safeguard slavery, would never have associated himself with the broad constructionists. Nor would James Sullivan of Massachusetts or William Maclay of Pennsylvania have been such enthusiastic proponents of a strict construction.[42]

Of greater importance at this time was uncertainty about the durability of revolutionary achievements. Those who had been foremost in the revolutionary movement and the struggle for the Constitution were peculiarly liable to such doubts. Not only were they aware of the bad historical record of republics, but they best understood the contingency of the events in which they had been leading actors. For instance, having made heroic exertions to rescue the nation from the "anarchy" of the Revolution in the immediate postwar years, and barely succeeding at that, it is not surprising if some of these men felt that the Constitution of 1787 was still vulnerable to antifederalism. In their certainty that if national affairs were again thrown into confusion the people might seek "shelter in the arms of monarchy for repose and security," [43] they were eager to establish a liberal construction of the national government's power. Unfortunately their efforts to protect themselves from the antiauthoritarianism generated by the Revolution stirred up fears of the opposite kind. Some men asked themselves if this might not lead to consolidation of power by the central government. The question was more than academic, for a government whose powers were not confined to specified common interests would be unlikely to rule by republican principles a country so large and diverse as the United States. There would be continuous pressure to sacrifice one sector's interests to those of another, which would create a government of force. In other words, a step toward consolidation was seen as a step away from government by consent.[44]

Yet the idea that the Bank of the United States threatened to reverse the Revolution still seems ridiculous. Compared to the Constitution, or to funding and assumption, it was a very small step on the road to consolidation. Though opponents argued that it illustrated some of the dangers inherent in a consolidated government by sacrificing the people's interests to those of a monied aristocracy,[45] such notions were heavily dependent on the prejudice that what the Bank gained the people would lose. Certainly the fear that it would strengthen the executive by providing a source of funds and patronage independent of legislative control seems exaggerated in view of the restrictions in the act of incorporation. These prohibited loans to the government exceeding $100,000 "unless previously authorized by law," and made violators of this provision liable for "treble the value . . . of the . . . sums which shall have been so unlawfully advanced." [46]

The alarm generated by the Bank among the opposition was real enough, though, and proceeded from two additional concerns. The first had to do with a notion which had been central to revolutionary ideology that the tendency of power to encroach on liberty might imperceptibly proceed to a point where the political equilibrium was irreversibly upset. And the very ease with which Americans had made the transition from monarchy to republicanism during the Revolution ironically contributed to their fears that the reverse transition might be equally facile. The second reason for concern was scepticism about the Bank's necessity. Though the Republicans had been resigned to accepting what they thought undesirable features of funding and assumption in the larger interest of public credit, the Bank was so blatantly unnecessary to this end that it cast a shadow of doubt over the whole fiscal system and made the Federalists seem more interested in its political by-products than in national faith.[47]

Save for the constitutional debate, however, no one would have guessed that it was a turning point. Only once was reference made to the ideological issues which were emerging over funding and assumption, and that was when William Branch Giles of Virginia claimed that the Bank posed a choice to Americans which would have far-reaching effects:

Two modes of administering this Government present themselves; the one with mildness and moderation, by keeping within the known boundaries of the Constitution, the other by the creation and operation of fiscal mechanism; the first will ensure us the affection of the people, the only natural and substantial basis of Republican Government; the other will arise and exist in oppression and injustice, will increase the previously existing jealousies of the people, and must be ultimately discarded, or bring about a radical change in the nature of our Government.[48]

Except for this, so much of the debate both in and out of Congress focused on the arid constitutional issue that it seemed as if members of the opposition, so far from being the demagogues the Federalists later described, were exercising conscious self-restraint. It is possible that they too thought an ideological appeal to the people might arouse uncontrollable forces which would be directed against the maintenance of public credit. The abandonment of all restraint after December 1791 would not disprove this point. Thanks to the nation's rapid growth, particularly southern expansion, the opposition had good reason to think that there was a remedy for Hamilton's encroachments which needed no exertion on their part.

The Republican leadership believed that the constitutional requirement for reapportioning representation after the first Congress in 1790 would help them in two ways. It would give more weight to areas opposing Hamilton's fiscal policies in the House of Representatives, and it would enlarge the House, making it more independent of Hamilton.[49] Admittedly, both gains could be pared away by raising the initial ratio of representation above 1:30,000. But public sentiment clearly favored the 1:30,000 ratio to enlarge the House, which had induced the First Congress to send a constitutional amendment to the state legislatures changing the wording of Article 1, Section 2. A simple prohibition against the number of representatives exceeding one for every thirty thousand would have become a constitutional requirement that this ratio be observed until the House increased in number to one hundred.[50] This gave the opposition hope that the system by which the first two congresses had been elected would prevail, and that opponents of the fiscal policy would be strengthened in the Third Congress. Admittedly they would still only control the House of Representatives, which would make it impossible to undo the damage already done, but at least they would be able to keep the secretary of the treasury under rein and guard against any further assumptions of debt.

A Federalist attempt to deprive the opposition of hoped-for gains by legislative tinkering with apportionment helped touch off a violent ideological assault on the entire fiscal system in 1792. That some such effort would be made first became clear in early December 1791 when the Senate rejected a House bill for apportioning representatives among the states according to the ratio of 1:30,000 in favor of one using the ratio of 1:33,000.[51] The House promptly refused to accept the amendment, and there was a legislative deadlock lasting until March. It was broken at last by a plan in which the number of representatives in the next Congress was to be calculated by dividing the total number of inhabitants to be represented by 30,000. The resulting figure of 120 was to be apportioned among the states, first by dividing 30,000 into the population entitled to representation in each state, then by allocating the eight representatives still unassigned to those states having the largest remainders.[52] Though the House was indeed enlarged, this gave the northern states (including Delaware) six additional members, while the southern states picked up only two representatives more than they would have had if representation had been determined for each state by dividing the number of those entitled to representation by 30,000.[53]

Washington promptly vetoed the bill, the only time he exercised this prerogative during his administration, on the grounds that there was no one divisor which would yield the allotments of representatives designated, and that eight states would have more than one representative for every 30,000 persons.[54] Unable to muster the necessary two-thirds majority, Congress passed an apportionment bill along lines initially proposed by the Senate providing that the ratio of 1 to 33,000 be observed. This trimmed the gains the opposition had expected in the House, and reduced its total size to eight fewer members than there would have been if the proportion of 1 to 30,000 had been kept.

The apportionment controversy would never have assumed the significance it did, had it not been accompanied by additional evidence that Hamilton could not be trusted and meant to usurp a power incompatible with liberty. In December 1791, he submitted a "Report on the Subject of Manufactures" to the Second Congress, recommending that discriminatory duties be laid on foreign manufactures which the United States could produce, and that domestic manufactures be encouraged by bounties.[55] This proposal drew opposition fire at once. It would require the raising of taxes which they thought already burdensome enough, and it seemed to be one more proof that the Federalists did not mean to be bound by constitutional restrictions on federal power. From a political standpoint, it looked like an extension of the monopoly system introduced in the Bank, which allowed the government to play favorites and the secretary of the treasury to create a dangerous personal interest.[56] Soon afterward, Hamilton submitted a new report on public credit recommending additional assumptions of the state debts, just as the opposition had feared.[57] It reached the House at the same time as a Senate proposal to grant bounties to the New England cod fisheries, a measure which the "Report on the Subject of Manufactures" had recommended for other industries.[58]

Hamilton's proposals in conjunction with the apportionment controversy inflamed the opposition's fear that republican principles were being set aside for the purpose of making the central government strong enough to be independent of the people. They began to suspect also that by expanding the debt the Federalists were on the verge of gaining a political advantage which could prove as irreversible as it would be dangerous to republicanism. This new threat seemed to them to justify the use of any means, even at the risk of unleashing forces which might permanently injure public credit, in resisting the secretary of the treasury. Consequently, at the beginning of 1792, opposition polemics against the fiscal system took on a stridency and an ideological character formerly lacking.[59] The distrust with which Republican congressmen viewed Hamilton can best be gauged by their opposition to a motion to reduce the domestic debt by refinancing as much of it as was redeemable at lower interest rates. The Republicans objected because this motion would give Hamilton authority to draft the plan, whereas many members felt his influence over the legislature should instead be curtailed. Their conviction that the House had become Hamilton's corrupt instrument approached certainty when Giles's motion to censure him in March 1793 was summarily rejected.[60]

III

From the start, Hamilton and his followers had feared the fiscal system's potential unpopularity. This was clear even before the "Report on Public Credit." In the very first session of Congress they had taken care to make provisions for public credit irreversible by appropriating permanent revenues to their service, thus putting it out of the House's power to revoke the revenue for funding without concurrence by the Senate and Executive.[61] Hamilton betrayed his own anxiety in his response to the Virginia Resolutions of November 1790, which had condemned assumption and the irredeemable quality of some of the debt. In a letter to Chief Justice John Jay, he exclaimed that "this is the first symptom of a spirit which must either be killed or kill the constitution of the United States," and wondered whether "the collective weight of the different parts of the Government [ought] to be employed in exploding the principles they contain?" [62] He showed more moderation in public, but the nervousness he and his partisans suffered from was still discernible when they equated opposition to the fiscal system with subversion of public credit and all government.

The Federalists were afraid of more than the potential hostility of a debtor majority toward a creditor minority. In seeking to compensate for some of the unstable tendencies in American politics, they were guilty of trying by a fiscal device to establish a center of power independent of popular control. One look at the critical reception accorded to John Adams's *Defense of the Constitutions of the United States* (1787) was enough to show the hazards of justifying any consolidation of power independent of the people. His book was intended less as a brief for the governance of the wise and good than as an essay on how to curb the danger of aristocratic usurpation in a republic. Adams had argued that if the natural aristocracy were set aside in a separate branch of the legislature, they might be more easily watched by the people and have fewer opportunities to harness popular power to bad ends. He had also pointed to the usefulness of a strong executive in forcing the aristocracy to identify with the people's interests.[63] But most people construed this as a plea for an aristocracy and the reinstitution of monarchy. Their suspicion of any forms of power not directly dependent upon them made this book a permanent blot on an otherwise distinguished political career.[64]

Federalist objectives were indefensible in terms of the dominant values of revolutionary ideology, which is why the movement into the opposition of Jefferson and Madison, two prominent revolutionary ideologues, was particularly disagreeable to them. It is the reason that Hamilton resented Madison's "holding up the bugbear of a faction in the Government having designs unfriendly to liberty . . . [when] it was a primary article in his Creed that the real danger in our system was the subversion of the National authority by the preponderancy of the State Governments." [65] It also explains why the Federalists were determined to dismiss the opposition's ideological assault as a cynical attempt to advance personal careers by appeals to the mob through their factional organ, the *National Gazette*,[66] as well as why ideological definitions of party differences came primarily from the opposition. Indeed, this dimension of the controversy is impossible to recover without turning to the Republicans. And there is no better ideological definition of the controversy than the measured and temperate analysis of that foremost Republican ideologue, James Madison.

In assessing Federalist policies for a series published by the *National Gazette* during 1792, Madison rejected the traditional classification of government into monarchy, aristocracy, and democracy, based on the allocation of the formal powers, and proposed instead to distinguish governments according to three administrative principles. The first, "operating by a permanent military force, which at once maintains the government, and is maintained by it," upheld most monarchies and military aristocracies. There was no danger of confusing it with a second, which derived its energy "from the will of the society" and operated "by the reason of its measures, on the understanding and interest of the society." This was the true principle of republicanism, easily confused with a third, which worked by "corrupt influence; substituting the motive of private interest in the place of public duty . . . [by] accommodating its measures to the avidity of part of the nation instead of the benefit of the whole," and thus enlisting "an army of interested partisans, whose tongues, whose pens, whose intrigues, and whose active combinations, by supplying the terror of the sword may support a real dominion of the few, under the apparent liberty of the many." [67]

Madison had succinctly expressed Republican fears about Hamilton's fiscal policy. In a subsequent essay, he went on to describe that policy's support, which he said came from those "who from particular interest, from natural temper, or from habit of life, are more partial to the opulent than to the other classes of society; and having debauched themselves into a persuasion that mankind are incapable of governing themselves . . . [believe] that government can be carried on only by the pageantry of rank, the influence of money and emoluments, and the terror of military force." Such men, he asserted, "must naturally wish to point the measures of government less to the interest of the many than of a few, and less to the reason of the many than to their weaknesses; hoping [that] by giving such a turn to administration, the government itself may by degrees be narrowed into fewer hands and approximated to an hereditary form." [68]

The Republican party, on the other hand, was made up of "those who believing in the doctrine that mankind are capable of governing themselves, and hating hereditary power as an insult to the reason and outrage to the rights of men, are naturally offended at every public measure that does not appeal to the understanding and to the general interest of the community, or that is not strictly conformable to the principles, and conducive to the preservation of republican government." [69] Because the antirepublicans were fewer in number, they would seek strength by ingratiating themselves with influential men. On the other hand, those who yearned to save the republic from such corruption would try to withhold the opportunity for a few to grow excessively rich and abstain "from measures which operate differently on different interests, and particularly such as favor one interest, at the expense of another." [70]

The Federalist attempt to make the fiscal system safe from political challenge in the Second Congress had provoked a response from the opposition which brought the ideological character of the controversy into the open. Essentially it proceeded from different assessments of republican government. The Federalists distrusted republics, fearing the dependence of public authority on popular whim, and tried to create sources of power and influence not immediately susceptible to public opinion. They valued Hamilton's fiscal program not just as a means of establishing public credit—there were clearly other ways in which this might have been done—but because it assured the government and particularly the executive of support from influential public creditors in the event of any contest with the populace. The opposition, on the other hand, had faith in republican government. They believed that public order in America would be best achieved, not by violating republican principles and popular feeling, but by showing scrupulous respect for them. They feared that the injustice of the fiscal system, with its disregard for the people's wishes, would excite violent opposition and prove self-defeating in the end. And they were not willing to sit back and let experience vindicate them, because this might allow their adversaries to discredit republicanism and usurp by means of popular acclaim a power incompatible with liberty.

2. Foreign Policy

The transformation of the fiscal controversy into an ideological dispute about fundamentals was not so damaging to the Federalists as one might have expected. Though it had divided the ranks of the leadership by 1792, this division had only marginal repercussions among the people at large. Nor was it likely that time would have worked against the Federalists. Those who had doubted the nation's ability to service the debts for which Hamilton had insisted it be responsible were to be reassured by a rapid economic growth which outran even his ability to assume new ones. Two decades of war scares culminating in three years of fighting never put full payment of the debt beyond possibility, and had the Federalists remained in power after 1800 they would have had several opportunities to spike opposition guns by taking steps in this direction. At the same time, Hamilton's success in constructing a popular fiscal system based largely on indirect taxes would have lessened the urgency some felt to secure it against political challenge.[1]

It is true that this success did not immediately reassure the opposition leadership. On the contrary, the system's popularity caused Republican polemicists to fear that the secretary meant to perpetuate the debt and enlarge the powers of the central government. They urged that it be replaced by a policy of direct taxation which would be sure to make an expanding debt unpopular before it became oppressive.[2] They tried by challenging the constitutionality of the carriage tax to forestall what they saw as Hamilton's policy of playing minorities off against one another, even though this exposed their motives to invidious construction.[3] Their deepest anxiety was that the fiscal system would become such a monstrous burden that eventually the government would have to use force to make the people bear it. Yet there were only two incidents in the 1790's which called

for repressive action by the government, and both could have been
ignored without much damage to the revenue. Indeed, the Republican opposition which formed in the early 1790's might have remained
a minor sect (such as the Tertium Quids became later) [4] had not the
fundamental issue in the fiscal system, the safety and stability of the
republic, been raised in a much more dramatic way by the question
of the nation's relations with the outside world.

I

From the very beginning, leading figures in the emerging parties
disagreed on foreign policy. At the opening of the First Congress,
Madison proposed a discriminatory tonnage duty on vessels whose
owners belonged to countries not having treaties with the United
States, and later advocated a discriminatory tariff along the same
principles for distilled spirits.[5] This was intended as both a response
to British restrictions on American commerce in the West Indies, and
an incentive to greater liberality on the part of France. Madison believed that such discrimination was desired by the people, and even
saw it as a means of confirming their loyalty to the new national
government.[6] To his surprise, the proposal encountered considerable
opposition in the House and was defeated in the Senate.

Opponents argued that the only effect of it would be to goad
Britain into commercial retaliation against the United States. They
admitted that British restrictions on American commerce were sometimes onerous, but pointed out that Britain compensated for this by
giving certain products of the United States an advantage in her
home market over those from other foreign countries.[7] Most important
in their eyes was the general dependence of American trade on Britain. Whereas Madison saw this dependence as undesirable and believed that it should be broken, by artificial means if necessary,[8]
they replied that Britain had achieved her dominance by being able
to supply the United States better and more cheaply than any
other nation in Europe. To provoke Britain's anger, they said, would
be to place America on a more precarious footing rather than a
firmer one.[9]

Madison and his supporters were not worrying about British retaliation. They were sure that a commercial war between the two
nations would hurt Britain more than the United States.[10] This con-

fidence stemmed from the belief that Britain's need for American trade was greater than America's need for British trade, because the United States supplied necessities to Europe whereas most of her purchases were luxuries. Though there were some English manufactures which Americans would have missed, they thought these articles could find their way into the country through a third party, and the inevitably higher price which would then have to be paid might have the desirable effect of reducing excessive consumption. Madison saw the propensity of Americans to overbuy British manufactures on credit as a liability which created an adverse balance of trade and subordinated American debtors to British creditors. He thought it in the national interest to discourage this and promote commerce with France, and was therefore not deterred by the threat of commercial war with Britain, which would accomplish at least the first of these objectives.[11] Madison did realize that yields from the impost, which had been the best source of revenue for establishing public credit, might be diminished. But in 1789 he was still more confident than his northern colleagues of the people's willingness to bear direct taxation. Throughout this period he thought the favorable balance of trade with the French empire would facilitate payment even if there were no British imports.[12] Nor did he believe Britain would embark on a policy of commercial war, however she might threaten, because to withhold her manufactures from the American market would be to encourage American manufacturers and perhaps jeopardize British interests permanently.

On the surface the controversy over commercial discrimination did not appear particularly significant, and certainly did not by itself herald the appearance of irreconcilable divisions in the national leadership. Though it led to the designation of opposing "British" and "French" interests in the federal government,[13] what separated the two seemed to be disagreement on tactics rather than anything fundamental. Admittedly the alignments were related to the economic differences between North and South. The representatives of staple-producing regions resented their subordination to British merchants and hoped to gain direct access to the continental market where most of their produce was ultimately consumed. They hoped the new federal government could achieve this end and were especially eager for it to act in 1789 because the beginnings of the French Revolution promised to weaken vested interests which had hitherto stood between American producers and access to the French market.[14]

Northern merchants, meanwhile, had found it hard to deal with French counterparts who were not willing to extend the long-term credits offered by British merchants. They felt the advantages to be gained by cooperating with the former mother country more than southerners did.[15] On the other hand every American thought it was desirable to have direct access to the West India market, and to equalize the terms on which American and British merchants traded. Nor would anyone have dismissed the possibility of using commercial retaliation against Britain to force a favorable commercial treaty from her. Differences in regional economic interests were far from irreconcilable, and those who opposed Madison's proposals seemed to be saying no more than that such a policy was not appropriate at that particular time.[16]

What most people did not know was that shortly after the congressional debate on discriminatory duties, Hamilton had made unauthorized overtures to George Beckwith, a British agent, for an Anglo-American commercial and political alliance, expressing regret at the tendency of Madison's proposal "to promote coldness and animosity between the two Countries." [17] It is possible to see this conversation, which was unofficial and hardly binding upon the government, as no more than an attempt to gain Madison's objectives through slightly different means. According to this view, Hamilton hoped to use the threat of discriminatory duties or perhaps the even harsher policy of excluding British vessels from American ports, to persuade Britain that a relaxation of her commercial restrictions would benefit both powers. At the same time it is possible to see Hamilton's suggestion of an alliance as a form of bait, though he well knew that the lively remains of hatred for the former mother country made a British alliance politically impossible at that moment.[18]

Yet there is evidence to suggest that though he was undoubtedly trying to manipulate the British, and though his aim was not immediately obtainable, the French Revolution made the substitution of an Anglo-American alliance for the Franco-American alliance a long-term objective for Hamilton. He often reverted to the possibility in his talks with Beckwith, hinted at it in a memorandum to Washington during the Anglo-Spanish war crisis of 1790,[19] and even dared to broach the subject before the full cabinet in 1792. Washington's strong rejection of the idea forced him to drop it for the moment, and friction between the United States and Britain in 1793–1794 thrust upon him the more pressing task of preventing the outbreak of war. Nevertheless, throughout the 1790's he remained committed to Anglo-American collaboration, even though worsening relations with France eventually made a formal alliance with Britain no longer necessary or even particularly advantageous.[20]

If Madison and Jefferson had known of Hamilton's confidential conversations with Beckwith, they would have felt as betrayed by him on foreign policy as he felt betrayed by Madison on fiscal matters. To suggest a political connection with the former mother country was to make a major departure from the principles on which the revolutionary leadership had conducted foreign policy during the Confederation period, when all believed the nation's interests would best be served by as great a separation as possible from European politics. Commercial needs did not permit total isolation, but commercial treaties need not lead to political association. What seemed to be important was avoiding entanglement in Europe's quarrels until the nation had grown strong enough to defend her interests by herself. The last thing the leadership wanted was a new war before they had solved the problems which had come in the wake of the last one. But if despite all precautions the nation should find itself pressed by a hostile power, that power would presumably be Britain, and the Franco-American alliance of 1778 would provide the needed help. Though most of the nation's leaders save Jefferson and Madison had grown disenchanted with the French alliance after the difficulties experienced in the peace negotiations of 1782–1783 and the disappointing nature of Franco-American commerce, everyone knew that France would never permit Britain to reconquer her former colonies.[21]

It has been customary to attribute Hamilton's preference for association with Britain to his desire for the success of his fiscal policy. Because 90 percent of the impost was raised on British imports, and because the impost had political advantages over every other kind of tax, good relations with Britain were bound to be more important to him than the friendship of France.[22] Jefferson quickly became aware of his reluctance to disturb Anglo-American commerce, and bitterly complained that the treasury's attitude toward Britain was "passive obedience and nonresistance, lest any misunderstanding with them should *affect our credit, or the prices of our public paper.*" [23] Clearly Hamilton's foreign policy had become subordinate to his fiscal policy, at least to the extent that he would sabotage all attempts to encourage the French relaxation of commercial regulations by granting them privileges denied to the British.[24] And nothing would be more effective in preventing the commercial war with Britain that had seemed to be foreshadowed by the reintroduction of Madison's discriminatory proposals in 1791 than a treaty which, by granting concessions to the United States, would have resolved one of the principal sources of friction between the two nations.

Yet Hamilton's concern for the fiscal system forced him to think about other threats than domestic political pressures. The greatest danger to his financial policies was war between the great powers. If the United States were compromised by association with France, she might find herself excluded from the benefits of British commerce. This was why Hamilton looked beyond the possibility of concluding a commercial treaty to a formal or informal political bond with Britain which would supercede the Franco-American alliance.[25] He soon saw that the revolutionary disturbances in France augured ill for the continuance of peace in Europe and that it behooved the United States to realign itself as quickly as possible with Great Britain. Independence from France did not in itself dictate dependence on Britain, but Spain's control of Louisiana put pressures on the infant nation which Hamilton thought could best be neutralized by an active collaboration with the former mother country.

As he saw it, the most troublesome unresolved problem in foreign relations was neither British retention of the posts, nor the exclusion of United States shipping from her West India colonies. The nation had no interest in expanding northward into Canada, and the security of the West Indian islands would in any case depend on the United States once the nation was stronger. Hamilton was also confident that postwar antagonisms would eventually be softened by the influence of shared culture and shared commercial interests, opening the way to reconciliation and the informal restoration of the first British empire. To him it was not the former mother country that threatened

the national destiny, but that power which controlled the navigation
of the Mississippi and could therefore command the loyalty of settlers in the West. Great Britain would be the most eligible ally here,
for France had a family compact with Spain which made it unlikely
that she would tolerate United States' seizure of the Spanish colonies,
let alone assist in it. Alliance with France would even obstruct the
acquisition of Louisiana if she ever became possessed of it again.[26]
Though the French Revolution was weakening the family compact,
Hamilton's desire to combine with Britain against Spain was not
diminished but increased by the vulnerability of Spain. It would be
all the easier to dismantle her American empire and use it to increase the power of the young nation.[27]

Hamilton's view of foreign relations, like his views on fiscal policy,
were colored by his opinion of the republic's weakness. He and his
followers believed that to impose discriminatory duties upon Britain
would invite a contest which would prove ruinous for a government
still not stable and mature enough to levy direct taxes upon its own
people. For the same reason he hesitated to have the United States
pursue an independent foreign policy, preferring alliance with another power and aggressive national expansion. During the Anglo-
Spanish war crisis of 1790 he pleaded the weakness of a nation "just
recovering from the effects of a long, arduous and exhausting war"
as a reason why Washington should not dispute the passage of British troops through American territory in the event of an attempt to
conquer Louisiana from Canada. He urged that instead of putting
Britain off with promises of further consideration, it would be better
to grant her rights of passage at once if she requested them in order
to prevent war breaking out through some accidental cause.[28] The
United States would have to grant parallel rights to Spain in order
to preserve the appearance of neutrality, but Hamilton knew that
these would be meaningless, so that his policy was a form of collaboration with the British. Certainly he would have preferred them
to turn to Latin and South America, leaving New Orleans to the
United States, for a British conquest of Florida and Louisiana would
encircle the new nation and threaten her independence more than
Spain had ever done. Nevertheless, Hamilton did not think Britain
would abuse her commanding position in the partnership because
the interests shared were so extensive that the British people would

not permit it. If she did, the republic could wait for a European war and a time of greater strength before settling accounts.[29]

Madison and Jefferson had more faith in the new republic. They were sure that the people would agree to direct taxation if necessary, and that the nation could survive the strain of a commercial war with Britain. Their response to the Anglo-Spanish crisis of 1790 shows that they were not afraid of pursuing an independent foreign policy. They knew as well as Hamilton did that securing the Mississippi was a vital national interest, but at the same time Madison agreed with Jefferson that the United States should use the prospect of war to make the belligerent powers bid for American neutrality. Though he would obviously have settled for less, Jefferson proposed that Spain be asked to grant independence to Louisiana and cede the east bank of the Mississippi, together with New Orleans, to the United States. In return, the United States would agree to maintain Louisiana's independence against Britain. The terms he asked of Britain were that she should fulfill the peace treaty and refrain from conquest on the southern flank of the nation.[30] When Washington asked Jefferson what he should do if Britain requested right of passage for her troops, Jefferson recommended silence. He too was against an outright refusal, knowing that the nation did not have the power to enforce it, but he firmly believed that the United States could not tolerate the British in Florida and Louisiana, and that "we ought to make ourselves parties in the *general war* expected to take place should this be the only means of preventing the calamity." [31] Even after the crisis had passed, Jefferson was still determined to press these strong terms upon Spain through diplomatic channels.[32] Clearly both Jefferson and Madison saw the United States as having much more independent power in world affairs than Hamilton believed she enjoyed.

II

The strong difference of opinion on foreign policy which had developed by 1790 between Hamilton on the one hand and Jefferson and Madison on the other would have been merely that, and not a focus of public controversy, had Europe remained at peace. Neither party to this disagreement would have been able to effect the change in foreign relations which each sought, for peace was too precious for an immature nation like the United States to risk tampering with. It is significant that the actions these three men advocated spoke for their sensitivity to the precariousness of the balance of power in Europe. The nation's political system did not share this sensitivity until the French Revolution had generated foreign and domestic problems which upset the status quo of Europe and weakened the capacity of the United States to remain detached from developments there.

It was not initially clear that the French Revolution would so affect the United States. The swift movement of events was at first an advantage. Late in 1791 the growing estrangement of Spain and France drove Spain to open negotiations with the United States on the subject of the Mississippi. Though the results were not encouraging, the fact that negotiations were held at all was enough to create the possibility of peaceful accommodation.[33] At the same time, the general uncertainty of European affairs made Britain act more temperately toward the United States. In 1791 she at last consented to establish full diplomatic relations with her former colonies. This was partly prompted by her fear of commercial exclusion. But her new sensitivity to threats she had shrugged off in 1789 had as much to do with European developments as with the growing power of the United States. Only in relations with France did the French Revolution not immediately improve the circumstances of the United States. In 1790 the reconstituted French government passed laws aimed at restricting the Franco-American tobacco trade. As France became ever more isolated in Europe, however, she mellowed toward her sister republic and by early 1793 looked on her as a confidential friend.[34] Though the United States remained peripheral to the European balance of power, the diplomatic instability of the Old World seemed likely to help her achieve peaceful resolution of her differences with the great powers.

The French Revolution also unified the American people, at least in the beginning. From 1789 on, informed Americans watched developments with eager curiosity. In general they liked what they saw, because it seemed in many ways to follow the American example. The Declaration of the Rights of Man in August 1789 and the new constitution in the following year clearly owed much to the Declaration of Independence and the American precedent of framing formal, written constitutions. There were isolated critical voices. John Adams in his *Discourses on Davila* (1790) had questioned the impulse of

French constitutional architects toward leveling all aristocratic distinctions, while his son in the "Publicola" letters of the following year charged that the National Assembly was still further away "from the spirit of democracy than the *practice* of the English House of Commons," calling it "an aristocracy without responsibility . . . limited only by a printed constitution subject to their own construction and explanation." [35] The Adamses in their turn found critics in the American press, but it is notable that these concentrated as much on attacking what they took to be endorsement of the British Constitution as on vindicating the French Revolution. In its early stages, this was not a subject for serious controversy among the American public. Almost everyone hailed it as a step forward; almost everyone was confident that occasional excesses would adjust themselves and the revolution prove a blessing to mankind. The few who dissented from this view kept their voices lowered, a piece of discretion which encouraged the belief that what little opposition did exist was the result of British propaganda.[36]

As time went on, Americans began to divide in their opinions on events in France. The cabinet shows the general trend in microcosm. At first only Hamilton had felt hostility toward the revolution, a hostility which was reflected in his early desire to liquidate the Franco-American alliance. During the Anglo-Spanish war crisis, he questioned that the United States could now count on French intervention in case of war with Britain. He warned that

the great body of malcontents comprehending a large proportion of the most wealthy and formerly the most influential class; the prodigious innovations which have been made—the general and excessive fermentation which has been excited in the minds of the people, the character of the Prince, or the nature of the government likely to be instituted, as far as can be judged prior to an experiment, does not prognosticate much order or vigour in the affairs of that country for a considerable period to come.[37]

Soon Washington himself began to have doubts. If we may believe Jefferson, his confidence in the outcome of the French Revolution was severely shaken by the king's flight in June 1791 and his capture at Varennes. Entertaining deep reservations about the modified constitution of 1791, he was not reassured by the subsequent turmoil which overturned it and led to the proclamation of the republic.

Though Washington remained ambivalent toward France throughout the remainder of 1792, any faith he ever had in her revolution was utterly destroyed by the trial and execution of the king, the tyranny of the Parisian mob, and the Reign of Terror. In 1793 the president was clearly convinced not only that it was a disaster for France but also that there was a danger of the same disorders rending the social fabric of the United States.[38]

Washington was not alone in this progression from friendly scepticism to abhorrence of French proceedings. The extreme intolerance shown to men of property and to religion, the violence surrounding the proclamation of the republic in 1792, and the execution of the king in 1793, seemed to many men to repeat the anarchy of the English Civil War and revived old doubts about the viability of any republican government. From the perspective of the twentieth century, this seems irrational. The monarchies of Europe, whose traditional authoritarian structures invited challenge, had reason to fear; but the United States surely had none. Her social system was new and enlightened, she had no *ancien régime* to call forth ideological assault, and, by no means the least of her advantages, she was at a safe geographical distance from France.[39]

The truth is that those who doubted the stability of a republican social order did so precisely because it lacked the customary attributes of European society. These men were not reassured by events in France after the monarchy fell. In the Terror they saw confirmation of their deepest doubts about the natural tendency of republican government, and in the slave rebellion on Santo Domingo they saw the logical outcome of the extremes to which France had carried republican ideals of liberty and equality. Critics continued to distinguish between the theory and the practices of the French Revolution and to condemn excesses as a betrayal of republicanism rather than its logical outcome. Yet the magnitude of the upheaval made a strong impression, and those leaders who were already uneasy about the prospects of republicanism began to fear that what was happening in France could happen next in the United States.[40]

The people who responded critically to developments in France were mostly from the elite and formed an increasingly isolated minority. For the majority of Americans were led to identify more closely and intensely with the revolution by the emergence of the republic. They firmly believed it to be an endorsement of the American experience, and dismissed revolutionary excesses as having been provoked by the treachery of emigrees and the king. When the abolition of the monarchy was immediately followed by an upturn in French fortunes at the Battle of Valmy, Americans hailed this as a promise of the brilliant future that would be enjoyed by all nations with republican governments.[41] Jefferson and Madison concurred in these general sentiments, and were encouraged rather than alarmed by France's abandonment of limited monarchy. Certainly this strengthened the argument for a Franco-American alliance, since a republican government would have more interest than a monarchy in preserving America's republicanism. And it enhanced the prospect for commercial concessions in the French empire, not yet as forthcoming as had been hoped.[42]

The full divisive impact of the French Revolution was not felt until the outbreak of a general European war in 1793 created difficulties with the belligerents that the federal government could not ignore. Though France had been at war with Austria and Prussia since April 1792, the effect on Americans had been negligible. But when France declared war on Great Britain, Spain, and the Netherlands on February 3, 1793, it was different. Not only were all the great maritime powers now at war, but also all the major colonial powers of the New World. This would have raised problems for the United States whatever the circumstances. Though neutrality would presumably be the course most likely to preserve the nation from harm while increasing her commercial growth, it would also create contention among the great powers. Each side would want to enjoy the benefits of American commerce at the expense of its adversaries.[43] Matters were further complicated by Britain's naval superiority to France, and by the Franco-American Treaty of Alliance of 1778, which bound the United States to defend France's West India possessions against her enemies. The outbreak of war between France and Britain put the French West Indies at the mercy of the British fleet, and made the United States liable to French requisition. What is more, by the Franco-American Treaty of Amity and Commerce of 1778 France was allowed to bring prizes into American ports, while the enemies of France were denied this right and forbidden to arm or provision there. So American neutrality was already compromised.[44]

Added to this was a more serious obstacle to neutrality. Their own revolution had made most Americans sympathetic to France and hostile to Britain. They saw France not as the nation that had threatened to sacrifice American independence during the peace negotiations of 1782, but rather as the faithful ally whose navy had made possible the victory at Yorktown. At the same time, the Anglophobia generated by the American Revolution had been maintained by Great Britain's refusal fully to execute the peace treaty. So the outbreak of war between Britain and France in February 1793, seeming to most Americans nothing more nor less than an extension of the struggle which had begun with the American Revolution, aroused all the old feelings against the first and for the second.[45]

Approval of France and hostility to Britain would have followed the outbreak of war between the two powers even if the Bourbons had still been on the throne. But it was particularly strong because the war in Europe raised an issue which transcended the old loyalties, that of republicanism versus monarchy. By joining a coalition of the leading continental monarchies, Great Britain seemed to be embarking on a crusade to destroy republican France so that the Bourbons could be restored. Who could doubt where American sympathies would lie in a life-and-death struggle between an isolated republic and a combination of monarchs? France acquired such imposing ideological stature in American eyes by her heroic stand against the First Coalition that some proclaimed the superior purity of her republican institutions even though these often differed markedly from those enjoyed by Americans.[46]

It is not surprising, then, that some Americans found it hard to restrain themselves from translating thought into action by civic demonstrations and even belligerent deeds. The intensity of pro-French sentiment could be gauged by the rapturous reception given Citizen Genêt as he toured the United States in 1793, and by American exultation at each fresh triumph of French arms. A French privateer bringing a British prize into Philadelphia, then the nation's capital, was hailed with cheers. Throughout the year, elaborate civic festivals in honor of France were held the length and breadth of the land.[47] And Americans often went well beyond such simple expressions of opinion. When Genêt arrived in the United States, many wished to join the French service and help fit out French privateers in American ports. Some even accepted commissions from him to conquer the lower Mississippi. They thought this was no more than adherence to the terms of the Franco-American treaties, for it was only what France and individual Frenchmen had done for America during the Revolution. Though Spain and Britain cried out against such action as a violation of American neutrality, many people thought the United States should do unto France as France had done unto her even at the cost of renouncing neutrality.[48]

These sentiments had considerable popular currency. The revolutionary leadership, however, knew that relations between France and the rebellious colonies in the Revolutionary War had been far different from those between the United States and the French republic in 1793. In the 1770's France, the oldest and most powerful nation in Europe, had been far better able to pursue her revenge on Great Britain than the United States was in 1793. She had also been reasonably sure that other European powers would cooperate in her design to limit British pretensions after the Seven Years' War, though she was prepared to go it alone if necessary to prevent a reconciliation between Great Britain and her colonies. The privileges she extended to the United States even before the Franco-American alliance of 1778 were in truth more becoming to an ally than to a neutral.[49]

The United States was not a world power in 1793, nor likely to be joined by other powerful nations if she espoused the French cause. She had every reason to avoid such conflict, being at last on the way to recovery from the effects of the Revolution. No one would have quarrelled with Hamilton's dictum that "if we can avoid war for ten or twelve years more, we shall then have acquired a maturity, which will make it no more than a common calamity." [50] The government's desire to resist the pro-French sentiment of the people was understandable, particularly since it knew from constant contact with the British minister what members of the public did not, that too much open partisanship for France might provoke the British into acts which would so anger Americans as to make neutrality impossible. Jay later wrote from London that British aggressions late in 1793 and early in 1794 were sparked by the assumption that war with the United States was inevitable.[51] At the same time, the administration was aware that the Franco-American Treaty of Amity and Commerce said nothing about permitting France to fit out privateers in American ports. The United States had only promised to deny those privileges to France's enemies.[52] And the cabinet had no difficulty in agreeing to restrict French rights under this treaty to the narrowest limit. French privateers fitted out in American ports were to be forcibly expelled, and after June 5 any prize taken by such vessels or by any French vessel within the jurisdiction of the United States must either be restored by the captors or the United States would pay for it out of sums owed to France.[53] The government granted France only one indulgence which was not required by treaty: the right to sell British prizes in American ports.[54]

The one part of the Franco-American treaties that could be strictly construed to compromise American neutrality was the clause in the Treaty of Alliance whereby the United States bound herself to guarantee French possessions in North America and the West Indies. This made it possible to argue that war between Britain and France necessarily meant war between Britain and the United States, and that therefore neutrality was not an alternative. Most of the national leadership saw from the start, though, that France was not likely ever to call upon the United States to honor this commitment. For one thing, the islands were not strategically important to metropolitan France. In the spring of 1793 it was even rumored that the National Assembly had consented to their independence. In any case, there would be no point in France insisting that this obligation be met. The United States had no navy with which to challenge British control of the Caribbean, and the only hope for the French islands was that American neutral shipping would be able to provision them. So no one was surprised when France relaxed all restrictions on the West India trade as soon as war broke out, thereby enlarging the privileges enjoyed by American vessels. Neither was the leadership surprised (though it was certainly relieved) when Genêt, arriving in Philadelphia, announced that he was not instructed to invoke the guarantee.[55]

III

On April 22, 1793, long before it was clear that the waiver would indeed be forthcoming, Washington issued a proclamation, later known as the Neutrality Proclamation. Warning Americans that acts contrary to the law of nations would put them outside the protection of the United States, it urged them to "pursue a conduct friendly and impartial towards the belligerent powers." It went on to say that Washington had "given instructions . . . to cause prosecutions to be instituted against all persons who shall, within the cognizance of the Courts of the United States, violate the law of nations, with respect to the powers at war." [56] This proved to be one of the more controversial acts of his presidency, which for the first time brought public censure upon him from those who would rashly have plunged the nation into a war with Britain [57] and eventually divided a cabinet that had unanimously endorsed the proclamation in principle.

Besides the offence it gave to popular sympathy for France, the proclamation was controversial because of its wording. Jefferson, who believed that it was beyond the president's power to declare that there would be no war and still thought the belligerents should bid for America's neutrality, insisted that the word "neutrality" be omitted so as not to give the impression that the United States would negate any special privileges due to France by treaty. Both Jefferson and Madison saw the difficulty in honoring the guarantee but thought it unwise to give a "hasty and harsh refusal before we are asked." Unfortunately Jefferson did not notice that Edmund Jennings Randolph had inserted into the final draft the term "impartial," which conveyed much the same meaning as "neutrality." So the president's proclamation went to the public in a form which allowed the construction that the administration would abrogate the alliance in order to maintain peace with Britain.[58]

Hamilton's "Pacificus" letters made it clear that the proclamation was so construed by some. In cabinet meeting he had questioned that Genêt should be received as ambassador from the new republican government of France without the qualification that the United States considered the Franco-American alliance "temporarily and provisionally suspended." He was promptly overruled by Washington, Jefferson, and Randolph; and Washington obviously hoped to conceal this debate from the public.[59] Yet Hamilton did not scruple to say in the public prints that the proclamation was "virtually a manifestation of the sense of Government, that the UStates are, *under the circumstances of the case, not bound* to execute the Guaranty." [60] This gave substance to Madison's inmost fears that it might conceal a "secret Anglomany." [61]

Hamilton was not suggesting that the United States should renege on all its obligations under the Franco-American treaties, but only those whose execution would make the nation a party to the European war. He added that the guarantee applied only to defensive wars and that France had been the aggressor in this one. Hamilton attached great importance to the French decree of November 19, 1792, "whereby the Convention, in the name of the French Nation, declare that they will grant *fraternity* and *assistance* to every people who *wish* to recover their liberty." He argued that this was "a general invitation to insurrection and revolution" and "amounted exactly to what France herself has most complained of—an interference by one nation in the internal Government of another . . . [which had] a natural tendency to disturb the tranquillity of nations, to excite fermentation and revolt every where; and therefore justified neutral powers, who were in a situation to be affected by it in taking measures to repress the spirit by which it had been dictated." If this were not enough to prove the point, he said the November 15 decree that France would treat as enemies all peoples who were "*desirous* of preserving their *Prince* and *privileged castes* . . . was little short of a declaration of War against all Nations having *princes* and *privileged castes*." Finally, he asked if an alliance contracted with Louis XVI was not abrogated by a revolution in the government and sought to minimize the necessity of gratitude toward France for assistance rendered to America during her own Revolution.[62]

Hamilton's "Pacificus" letters did not go unchallenged. Urged on by Jefferson, Madison responded with the "Helvidius" letters. Some reply was necessary, or Hamilton's heresies might gain currency for sheer lack of contradiction. Madison dismissed Hamilton's contention that France was the aggressor, pointing out that his evidence had no bearing on the relevant issue, which was "priority in the attack." Madison concentrated rather on the extent of the president's power to interpret treaties without reference to Congress. He accused Hamilton of pretending to defend the president's action while advancing principles "which strike at the vitals of [the nation's] constitution, as well as its honour and true interest." He objected to the monarchical implications of the claim that the executive had sole right to judge whether or not treaties were in force, or whether or not the ambassadors of a foreign nation could be received, pointing out that this encroached on the power of Congress to declare war. And he answered the suggestion that a treaty made with one government was not binding when another came to power by asking if Americans would have forfeited "their right to the guarantee of their territory" had their members of Congress been captured and executed by the British during the war. The audience to which Madison addressed himself was still the government elite, and his strategy was to separate Washington's proclamation from Hamilton's interpretation. He argued that it was a legitimate warning to the people not to precipitate a war until Congress had been able to decide what the nation's obligations were, but not a repudiation of the guarantee as Hamilton had urged.[63]

Opposition leaders had several good reasons for wanting to maintain the Franco-American alliance. One, which the public did not learn about until Genêt published his instructions, was that France was now willing to conclude a commercial treaty of the scope and liberality which southern leaders had long desired.[64] Another, and this no secret, was that a coalition victory over France could endanger the United States. Because the conflict was essentially ideological, the league of armed despots might turn on America next. Many Americans believed it would, for the very existence of a free republic challenged all despotisms. How else could existing alignments in Europe be explained? And what was more likely than that the European monarchies, flushed with victory over France, would seek to extinguish the last spark of that liberty from which she had caught fire? The incentive would be increased by Britain's desire to regain her lost colonies, always a possibility in these early years of our history. Spain and a restored French monarchy might even be willing to support her because the example of the American colonies having successfully rebelled against Britain raised a threat to their own imperial possessions. It could certainly be argued that a neutrality which assured the triumph of the combined European monarchies would ultimately endanger America as much as any precipitate entry into war. It was for this reason that many responsible men were anxious not to have neutrality confused with impartiality, and feared that the Neutrality Proclamation might be used against the French.[65] One writer even argued that the fundholders should support France because their stocks would be worthless if the coalition ever turned on America! [66]

The strategic questions raised by the opposition were answered. In two letters under the pseudonym "Americanus" beginning on February 1, 1794, Hamilton took up the matter of "how far *regard to the cause of Liberty* ought to induce the United States to take part with France." His argument contained predictable criticisms of the "excesses and extravagances" of the French Revolution and raised the inevitable doubt that the outcome would be liberty. But the bulk of it debated whether or not the United States could afford to remain detached. Hamilton maintained that it could, because American republicanism could be subverted by "nothing short of an entire conquest. . . . This conquest, with our present increased population, greatly distant as we are from Europe, would either be impracticable, or would demand such exertions as, following immediately upon those which will have been requisite to the subversion of the French Revolution, would be absolutely ruinous to the undertakers." He assumed that if the monarchy were restored in France it would take a large foreign army of occupation to keep it safe and that only England and Spain would have any interest in America, neither of which would want to establish an independent monarchy. After all, to place the United States under stronger government would pose an even greater threat to their colonial possessions. Nor were they likely to agree on a common course of action. As for the danger of reconquest by Britain alone, Hamilton was sure the English people would not stand for such a war.[67]

At this point the perception of threats from without was less important in dividing the government over the Neutrality Proclamation than concern for national advantage. For if Hamilton was right that the United States need not fear the coalition, there was certainly no immediate danger from France. She was finding it hard enough to hold her own in Europe without trying to wage offensive war three thousand miles away.[68] No one had to tell the leadership that a general European war would enhance the nation's bargaining position vis-à-vis the great powers and make more likely the resolution of outstanding differences. But their opinions varied on how to proceed, because the differing estimates of republican government which had formerly affected their views of the United States as a power now caused the leaders of each party to disagree on which belligerent would fare best in the European contest.

France's republicanism made Jefferson and Madison confident of
her ability to defend herself against the combined tyrants of Europe,
even in 1793 when her fortunes seemed desperate. Jefferson thought
the only real danger was famine. Otherwise France was now a free
country, and could depend on the loyalty of most of her twenty-five
million citizens as her antagonists could not. Britain looked considerably less stable than her adversaries to Jefferson, who attached
great importance to the precariousness of her finances. He thought
that because she had contracted an unprecedented public debt in the
American war, she could not resume hostilities against France in
the 1790's without risking national bankruptcy. This estimate certainly seemed to be confirmed by a wave of bank failures when war
first broke out. Jefferson gleefully reported to Monroe that the "beginning of the business was from the alarm occasioned by the war,
which induced cautious people to withdraw their money from the
country banks. This induced the bank of England to stop discount-
ing, which brought on a general crash, which was still going on."
Throughout the 1790's, opposition leaders confidently expected the
financial disintegration of Britain followed by the violent overthrow
of her monarchy and the establishment of a free and stable government.[69]

Hamilton and his followers, on the other hand, believed that Britain had a decided edge in the contest. Aside from his admiration for
her constitution, which was well known, he thought it boded ill for
France that she had "*singly* engaged . . . the greatest part of Europe, including all the first rate powers, except one, and [was] in
danger of being engaged with all the rest" at a time when her internal affairs were "*without doubt* in serious disorder." In the administration's private councils Hamilton had speculated that these
disorders would lead either to a military despotism or a monarchical
restoration,[70] but whatever happened he did not expect France to be
a republic for long. In his opinion, the French Revolution was far
from showing "the same dignity, the same solemnity, which distinguished the course of the American Revolution." Instead, "passion
tumult and violence" were "usurping those seats, where reason and
cool deliberation ought to preside." He warned the nation not "to
involve our Reputation in the issue," [71] for though he admitted that
France could defend herself against all Europe if she could maintain

internal order, events had convinced him that she would be torn apart by faction.[72]

Both the Federalists and the opposition desired British compliance with the peace treaty of 1783 and liberalization of trading restrictions but could not agree on how to achieve this. The Federalists did not think she could be brought to terms through confrontation, but hoped that if the United States refrained from open partiality for France the British ministry would make the concessions which both justice and the interests of British commerce demanded. They thought that coercion would fan the smoldering embers of resentment at Britain's defeat into a blaze that the ministry, secure in the possession of powerful European allies, would allow to rage unchecked.[73] At the same time they saw that war with Britain would force a French alliance, which would enfeeble the nation by drying up its source of revenue as well as increasing the danger that Americans would lapse into French ways.[74] Already the nation had seen the emergence of democratic and republican societies, too like the Jacobin clubs which had caused anarchy in France to be comfortably accepted.[75] Those who feared popular disorder and valued Hamilton's fiscal policy as counterposing the tendency toward it looked askance at popular agitation which might lead to war and the repetition of revolutionary anarchy. They retained a healthy respect for the stability of the British monarchy and feared to have the nation's destiny depend on so unstable and capricious an ally as republican France.

The opposition thought differently. Their belief that Great Britain's finances were precarious and that all monarchies, particularly the corrupt British one, were as vulnerable to revolution as the French monarchy had been, argued for a more aggressive policy toward the former mother country than "impartial neutrality." They saw no point in trusting to Britain's enlightened perception of her true interests, but thought she could and should be bludgeoned into concessions.[76] In its extreme form, this school of thought led to open public demands that the United States join France as an active belligerent, either formally or through volunteer programs, to ensure not only the settlement of outstanding disputes but also the survival of republican government in both Europe and America.[77] Even the more moderate critics of administration policies, knowing how unpredictable the fortunes of war always are, thought that Britain's instability offered a way short of war to comply with the Franco-American treaties and maintain the alliance as well as extracting concessions from her.[78]

They reasoned that her uncertain state would discourage the indulgence of resentment against the United States, and therefore they were opposed to an interpretation of neutrality which in effect canceled France's privileges under the treaties, either by denying the obligation or by admitting Britain to equal rights. Because they believed that France would triumph in the end, they thought national interest called for maintaining a partial neutrality under the terms of the Franco-American treaties of 1778. To show Britain favoritism would mean the exclusion of American produce from the French commercial empire when the war ended.[79] Furthermore, the moment seemed propitious for forcing trade concessions out of her. In January 1794, Madison reintroduced proposals for commercial retaliation and discrimination against her.[80] When the Federalists protested that to press Britain in such a way at such a time would mean war,[81] the opposition replied that this would further bankrupt her and hasten her political dissolution. War might be declared, but if it were, Britain would harm herself more than her opponent.[82] In general, the Republicans thought that anything they could do to promote a republican revolution in Britain was in the best interests of their own nation.

PART II

CONTAGION

Though men at the inner core of national leadership were actuated by their ideological assessments of republican government from the beginning, these concerns only gradually filtered down to the lesser figures in government. In the fiscal controversy, for instance, whatever motives Madison, Jefferson, and Hamilton may have had, many members of Congress and interested members of the public were obviously more responsive to economic factors than to the need to stabilize the republic. This was not necessarily because they were indifferent to revolutionary achievements or the need to make them lasting, but rather because they did not think that Hamilton's policies affected them one way or another. The European war changed things by raising issues so dramatic that no one could be oblivious to their implications for the survival of the republic, forcing an ever-wider circle of men to make strategic choices for ideological reasons. It was because of this that many men did not respond consistently to fiscal policy and foreign policy, though these issues were closely related in the minds of Hamilton and Jefferson. The same shift in emphasis was the reason why alignment at all levels of the political leadership began to harden after 1793. Except for a brief period after 1803, when a change in the character of one of the great powers, and in the strategic relations between both of them and the United States, allowed some political conversions, the political identity a member of the leadership assumed in the years 1793 to 1795 usually remained constant throughout the life of the first party system.

Ideological division eventually spread from public men to the people at large because, after Jefferson's resignation from the cabinet, the Washington administration committed itself to a policy of accommodation with Britain culminating in the Jay Treaty. It is not really surprising that a foreign policy issue rather than a domestic

51

one produced this development. Given the national economy's lack of integration and the general provincialism of people's lives, it is hard to conceive of a domestic issue which could have affected the whole nation simultaneously once the new government had been successfully implemented. But a foreign issue like the Jay Treaty, because it seemed to require mutually exclusive choices on which national existence depended, thrust upon ordinary men the same dramatic necessity as had come to preoccupy the leadership more and more, that of finding a way to preserve the achievements of the Revolution. Some saw these achievements as threatened by the treaty's betrayal of neutrality; some thought that the treaty was the nation's only hope for maintaining neutrality. Whichever view a person held, he was strongly inclined to see the sinister effects of foreign influence in those who thought differently. It was for these reasons that, despite a traditional aversion to party, parties were formed. While the republic was young and vulnerable to external pressure; while the great European powers remained at war, party politics seemed to be the only way to ensure that the nation would remain independent and the promise of the Revolution would be fulfilled.

The first party system emerged against everyone's will because the pressure of international events was added to the strains already created by a rift within the leadership about the stability of republican government. The political divisions which were then produced further deepened that rift by intensifying the fear that the nation was in danger, not only of succumbing to foreign influence, but also of internal dissolution. From the mid-1970's on, these divisions were decidedly sectional, with the northern states generally Federalist and the southern states Republican. There were exceptions. Until the second half of the 1790's, South Carolina resembled Massachusetts rather than its sister states, Georgia, North Carolina, and Virginia, while Vermont and Maine gave early proof of their Republican proclivities. The Middle Atlantic states were divided in allegiance, as was fitting to their position between the two extremes. But these were variations which did not affect the essential division between a Republican South and a Federalist New England, a division which increased the tension already created by the emergence of parties because it dramatized the possibility that the union might be sundered. No explanation of the extension of ideological alignments from the inner circle of the leadership to the populace would be complete unless it offered an account of the pervasive sectionalism in the first party system and of deviations from it.

3. Jay Treaty

It was not clear that foreign policy would become the focus of public controversy until well into 1794. Just as the majority of men were more concerned about their tax bill than about the ideological implications of the fiscal system, so they were more hopeful about the French Revolution as the precursor of a congenial world order than uneasy about it as a combination of danger and opportunity. Most people were wholly unresponsive to criticisms of the Neutrality Proclamation, objections to the coolness shown Genêt, and wild charges that the administration meant to precipitate a French war and a British alliance.[1] Such opinion as the proclamation did inspire was predominantly approving, as the large number of addresses supporting Washington bears witness.[2] Any doubt of its consistency with a full honoring of treaty obligations was quieted by Washington's reply to an address from the freeholders of Salem declaring that the proclamation did not violate "any political or moral obligation of the Republic."[3] Most Americans were still close enough to the Revolutionary War not to relish the prospects of another one. Moreover there was general agreement that if war must come the decision should be made by Congress rather than the executive alone, and the newly elected Third Congress would not meet until the end of the year. The facts were sufficiently obscure to most people, partly because communications from Philadelphia had been disrupted by the yellow fever epidemic in 1793, that they were content to wait and see.

It was the Federalist response to a crisis in Anglo-American relations which stirred up public opinion on foreign policy. The seeds of this were sown in mid-1793 when the British began acting on an Order in Council of June 8, 1793, and forcing American provision vessels bound for France to enter English ports instead. The resentment thus roused against Britain was further increased by the news that she had arranged a truce between Portugal and the pirate states of North Africa, permitting them to cruise against American vessels in the Atlantic.[4] But it did not reach explosive proportions until word came that, acting on an instruction from the Privy Council dated November 6, 1793, British warships and privateers had seized an estimated 350 American vessels in the West Indies.[5] Americans were angry enough about the detention of provision vessels bound for France, taking this as a violation of their neutral rights and an attempt to starve France into submission, but at least the cargoes had been sold in Great Britain and the proceeds returned to their owners along with the vessels. Now it seemed likely that both cargoes and vessels would be counted as lawful prizes by the British admiralty courts. The Rule of 1756, the only possible legal ground for such actions, stated that "a belligerent which in times of peace closes its colonial trade to foreign ships cannot in time of war open that trade to foreign neutrals, without making those neutrals liable to capture as enemy ships." But this clearly did not hold for many of these captures, for France had admitted American vessels to parts of her West Indian trade before the outbreak of war in February 1793.[6] Americans had not even been officially informed of the instruction until after its repeal, which induced the speculation that Britain had purposely concealed it in order to ensure the richest possible haul of American shipping.[7] So to most of them it looked like naked British aggression, demanding either the assertion of American sovereignty against Britain, or humiliating acquiescence in what amounted to the old colonial restrictions on trade with the foreign West Indies.[8] At the same time, the public tended to excuse French detention of American ships at Bordeaux as an act made necessary by the British orders.[9]

Then in the spring of 1794, when feelings were running highest, news arrived of a speech Lord Dorchester was said to have made to the chiefs of Indian nations allied with the British, a speech which many Americans interpreted as a declaration of war. Dorchester charged that the United States had violated the treaty of 1783 as it affected the Indians, and remarked that "from the manner in which the people of the United States act and talk near us, and from what I learn of their conduct towards the sea, I shall not be surprised if we are at war with them in the present year." In that event, he said, he would regard all encroachments on Indian land since 1783 as invalid, adding that the Indians would be in a position to establish a new line "by the warriors," and promising them all the "improvements and houses" of those who were not British subjects in the areas they conquered.[10] There had already been enough bloody warfare between the Indians and the white settlers for this speech to be taken as confirmation of a widespread suspicion that the British had fomented previous trouble and were now trying again.[11]

Added to the November 6 instruction, Dorchester's speech had the effect of reviving interest in Madison's commercial resolves and mounting support for belligerent action. Given the anger felt on both sides at the time, these measures might have touched off a war if they had been put into effect. The Federalists had good reason to be worried. They pleaded for restraint, at least until the nation's defenses were stronger, and to this end they proposed a series of measures to raise a standing army and create a navy.[12] But the public and many members of Congress were not to be satisfied by such cautious expedients as these, particularly since they touched on a fear of standing armies that had been kept alive by Indian warfare in the west. As a result, Federalist leaders found themselves faced with two proposals for retaliation made in the House in response to the people's anger at Britain's provocative actions. The first, put forward by Jonathan Dayton of New Jersey, called for sequestration of British debts until compensation was made for the illegal captures; the second, by Abraham Clark of the same state, proposed nonintercourse with Great Britain until the western posts were surrendered and compensation was made for illegal seizures.[13]

I

On one point there was no dispute. British acts toward the American republic at the end of 1793 and beginning of 1794 were provocative. Not even an arch Federalist like Fisher Ames could excuse "the insolence and injustice of the English. . . . The English are absolutely madmen," he wrote, and "not to be justified." [14] Nevertheless the Federalists did have an explanation for British aggression which affected the way in which they proposed to confront it. Ames asserted that it was attributable to the ministry's resentment of American "partiality to France. . . . Our gallicism hurts her pride, and she is heated enough to punish all the friends of her foes." Others added that this sentiment was not necessarily shared by most British people, nor did it reflect the true interests of both countries, which were to sustain a mutually beneficial commerce. They admitted that the Court was jealous of the growing power of the republic and not at all reluctant to embarrass Anglo-American commerce, but believed that its vindictiveness would be restrained by the interest of the British people in American trade. So they thought that in responding to provocation the United States should be careful to allow the British still to enjoy the benefits of commerce in order to "interest them in the preservation of our peace and . . . make them a counterpoise to any hostile designs their court might meditate against us." For these reasons, and because it was prudent in a nation threatened by war to preserve rather than destroy her sources of public credit, the Federalists continued to oppose Madison's commercial resolves even after news arrived that the British had been seizing American shipping.[15]

Though the Federalists still believed that war with Great Britain was an evil to be avoided if possible,[16] they were ready to concede that it might be forced on them. They were not as disturbed by this prospect as one might have expected, given their reservations about republican government. But they did see the people's support for the war as the one essential, for without it the government would be powerless. In an important letter to Washington, Hamilton said that in the event of war nothing was more vital than "the disunion of our enemies [and] the perfect union of our own citizens." He added, "Want of unanimity will naturally tend to render the operations of war feeble and heavy, to destroy both effort and perseverance. War, undertaken under such auspices, can scarcely end in anything better than an inglorious and disadvantageous peace. What worse it may produce is beyond the reach of human foresight." And because Hamilton thought perfect unanimity could be ensured only if the people believed war was unavoidable, he and most leading Federalists advocated that outstanding differences be negotiated with Great Britain while defenses were being strengthened. If it should appear that the government provoked a contest with Britain before the nation was prepared, the people would turn against it at the first reverse, no matter how pugnacious their feelings at the moment.[17]

The motions proposed by Dayton and Clark were in stark opposition to this policy. The Federalists argued that both would lead prematurely to war, precluding any possible advantage to be derived from negotiations with Great Britain.[18] Clark's motion for nonintercourse was the most provocative, being no less than a legislative ultimatum embodying the principle of coercion. It did not take much perspicacity to see that a government as proud and jealous as that of Great Britain, aided by a powerful confederacy, would "revolt at the idea of being guided by external compulsion." The Federalists also thought that nonintercourse would deal such "a sudden and violent blow to our revenue" as to "cut up credit by the roots." [19] The supporters of Dayton's motion for sequestration were careful to emphasize that it would not provoke war (though most of them regarded war as inevitable anyway) but would rather help to make the British people pressure their government.[20] Nevertheless, the Federalists saw it as a form of reprisal inconsistent with negotiation, and insisted on believing that southern war fervor arose from a desire to escape the burden of debts. They also feared that it would damage public credit in a subtler but equally devastating way by attacking private creditors and discouraging private capital from investment in the United States.[21]

Their best argument for negotiation before retaliation, however, was that Britain was ready now as never before to come to honorable terms with the United States. There were several indications that she was willing to abandon the ground staked out by the instruction of November 6, 1793. First it was superceded by a new Order in Council of January 8, 1794, which was clearly within the limits of the Rule of 1756 and which relaxed some of the "pretensions . . . Great Britain [had] in former wars maintained against neutral powers." Second, when Ambassador Pinckney in London asked Lord Grenville how the court interpreted the instruction issued on November 6, the answer he received implied that "no vessel would be condemned under that instruction which would not have been previously liable to the same sentence." Because the condemnation of American vessels had gone beyond the Rule of 1756, it seemed as if "the Court of Admiralty in the West Indies [had] contradicted the orders and intentions of the British Ministry" so that redress might be expected.[22] Most significant of all, the military advantage of the allies had been destroyed at the end of 1793 by the recapture of Worms and Speyer, and by the liberation of Toulon from the British. The coalition was on the defensive for the first time, and now the Federalists had good reason to believe the British would soften toward the United States. If the coalition should collapse, it was not in her interests to be at war with two maritime powers like the United States and France. And so long as it seemed that the peace could be kept, the United States was surely justified in postponing unnecessary wars and allowing itself time to grow stronger.[23]

These calm admonitions did not do much to soothe inflamed public opinion. The people were so aroused that vigilante groups in Baltimore were ready to prevent the export of flour to Great Britain even before a temporary embargo, designed more to protect American shipping than to retaliate, had passed.[24] Although sequestration was open enough to objections that it never came to an explicit vote, an amended version of Clark's motion passed in the House by a resounding majority of fifty-eight to thirty-eight, and the bill to implement it by fifty-nine to twenty-four.[25] There was even a chance that popular pressure would be strong enough to force its passage through the Senate. Indeed, in the end it was defeated only by the deciding vote of the vice-president. To forestall this and, one suspects, to save himself from having to veto a popular measure sanctioned by both houses of Congress, Washington took Hamilton's advice, appointing John Jay, chief justice of the Supreme Court, to be minister plenipotentiary to Great Britain.[26]

This appointment was controversial, to say the least. The opposition objected first that it undermined the independence of the judiciary. If the president could appoint a justice of the Supreme Court to a lucrative foreign post, judges might be prejudiced in dealing with cases brought under treaties that they had helped negotiate. Furthermore, the executive would have the power to influence the court in other matters. Finally, if a president could induce the chief justice to leave the country on such a mission he could avoid impeachment indefinitely, because the Constitution required that the chief justice preside over such proceedings.[27]

Besides violating the division of powers, Jay's appointment was questionable in terms of appropriateness. He was widely regarded as a leading member of the "British party" thanks to his role in the Federalist attempt to discredit Genêt [28] and his public espousal of certain unpopular opinions. He felt, for instance, that Americans owed their British creditors interest for debts outstanding from before the Revolutionary War even though British aggression had prevented their repayment, and also that the British were justified in retaining the western posts because America had violated the peace treaty.[29]

Yet Jay's identification with Great Britain could be an asset. Because he was more likely than any other American to be favorably received by the court, he might succeed where Adams and Pinckney had failed, and extract the desired concessions from the former mother country. This is one of the reasons why the congressional opposition ultimately gave way and joined the Federalists in waiting to see if Jay could arrange some accommodation short of war. The other was that news of Jay's appointment, made with the concurrence of two-thirds of the Senate, served notice that the executive was set on a different course from the House majority and decisively undercut further opposition initiatives in foreign policy.[30] The outbreak of disorders in western Pennsylvania, subsequently known as the Whiskey Rebellion, absorbed their energies through the last half of 1794 and made acquiescence certain.

II

The administration had neutralized congressional opposition. But public criticism continued, given new impetus by news received just after Jay's departure that British troops had occupied yet another fort in American territory. The opposition press poured out complaints that in refusing to respond to popular opinion the government was following a party policy. The divergence in sentiment between government and opposition was attributed not to honest disagreement about national interests but rather to a foreign influence working through the fiscal system, a charge which was vigorously seconded by the newly formed democratic and republican societies.[31] Thanks to the outcome of Jay's negotiations it gained still more authority with time, for the treaty gave the opposition enough evidence to sustain their wildest accusations. In the uproar that followed disclosure of its terms, Republican charges took deeper root than ever before in the public mind.

Evidence that the treaty was a party document intended to preempt the opposition's British strategy could be found in provisions that the United States would renounce the right to pursue policies toward Great Britain which had been considered by Congress in the first part of 1794. The sequestration of British debts proposed by Dayton was precluded by Article 10 of the treaty, in which both nations renounced either sequestration or confiscation of debts or property of the other. Clark's nonintercourse proposal was precluded by Article 15 which stipulated that no "prohibition be imposed on the exportation or importation of any articles to or from the territories of the two parties respectively, which shall not equally extend to all other nations." The same article undercut Madison's proposal to levy discriminatory duties against British commerce by providing "that no other or higher duties shall be paid by the ships or merchandise of the one party in the ports of the other than such as are paid by the like vessels on merchandise of all other nations." It also barred the United States from laying any additional tonnage on British vessels, at the same time as it conceded to Britain "the right of imposing on American vessels entering . . . British ports . . . a tonnage duty equal to that which shall be payable by British vessels in the ports of America." Finally, each country pledged itself not to levy a discriminatory impost on "any articles . . . [of] growth, produce or manufacture of the other" which would not equally apply to the same articles imported from other nations.[32]

If the Jay Treaty had been controversial only because it struck at all the policies of the Republicans, it might have irritated certain congressional leaders and made them even more determined foes of the administration, but it probably would not have helped them rally the people to their cause. It proved to be the focal point of opposition to the administration because it addressed itself to three issues central to Anglo-American relations in 1794. These were the nonexecution of the peace treaty of 1783; the violation of American neutral rights, particularly by the seizures made under the Orders in Council of June 8 and November 6, 1793; and the status of American shipping and commodities in the British commercial empire. And it resolved them in a way which seemed to affect national interests adversely.

Opposition leaders had been ready to acquiesce in Jay's mission because they thought there was nothing lost by trying to achieve what they took to be common objectives, satisfaction on the first two points and substantial commercial concessions won through negotiation. Circumstances undeniably favored such negotiation, particularly as Congress had already indicated what form of retaliation Great Britain should expect if she denied justice to the United States. By justice they meant compensation for unlawful seizures on the high seas and for the impressment of American seamen, as well as acknowledgment that the United States was entitled to indemnity for British violations of the peace treaty. These included the detention of the western posts, which had contributed to a bloody and expensive war with the Indians on the northwestern frontier, and the removal of Negro slaves with the British evacuation in 1783. These claims, if not the principles from which they rose, might in turn be used to bargain for substantial commercial concessions in the British empire.[33] Although some opposition members would have objected to any treaty with Great Britain,[34] the Republican leadership would have welcomed a relaxation of British commercial restrictions provided that no relinquishment of American rights was called for.[35]

This was the course the opposition had expected negotiations to take, but they were sorely disappointed. The treaty made no acknowledgment of the many injuries Britain had inflicted upon the United States; no mention of compensation, either for the removal of slaves or for the detention of the posts; and said not a word about impressment.[36] There was no clause in which the British explicitly abjured the power they had exercised under the hated Orders in Council. In Article 7, on compensating Americans for loss sustained "by reason of irregular or illegal captures," there was no definition of "irregular or illegal" and Americans were forced to seek a legal remedy before they could apply for compensation from the British government.[37] Then the commission which was set up to pass on American claims against Britain was matched by another authorized to certify British claims against American debtors, and the United States assumed responsibility for all private debts not collected because of legal obstructions in her courts, as well as for prizes seized within her jurisdiction. Jay had not only abandoned many claims but had also committed the United States to assume a swollen debt which it had not incurred.[38] The only concessions Britain made were a promise to relinquish the posts in eighteen months' time, an act which most Americans believed was already more than ten years overdue,[39] and allowance of a dubious right to compensation which might be more than canceled out by the counterclaims of British creditors.[40]

In the light of these unequal terms, which seemed to some like complete surrender to Britain, the treaty provisions barring sequestration, nonintercourse, and discrimination were far more than a personal slight to opposition statesmanship. It was bad enough that Jay had squandered American bargaining counters by renouncing valid claims and assuming responsibility for dubious ones, but his treaty would also have barred the United States from using the only weapons she possessed for bringing Great Britain to terms short of war. Sequestration took on significance because of twenty-five million dollars' worth of British debts in the United States that were infinitely more valuable hostages than the profits derived from Anglo-American trade. Though these profits amounted to six million dollars in cash each year, they could presumably be replaced by means of new trade circuits so that losses would be spread over a period of time. Sequestration, however, would have an immediate effect on British creditors, who probably wielded far more power over their government than those who would be threatened by unemployment if trade with America were interrupted. It was possible to argue that Article 10 bound both nations equally, but the opposition believed this apparent reciprocity merely dressed up the unpleasant truth that the Jay Treaty favored Britain at the expense of the United States. Everyone knew that, given the balance of trade between the two nations, British debts in America would always far exceed American debts in Britain. Thus by giving up an instrument of substantial power over Britain while Britain gave up nothing, the United States risked permanent subordination.[41]

The first ten articles of the treaty were, to put it mildly, a grave disappointment to most Americans. If only there had been substantial commercial concessions in the subsequent articles they would have felt less chagrin. Unfortunately these turned out to be as objection-

able as the first part of the treaty. Except for Article 13, which admitted American shipping to the British East India trade, and which
some thought would not so much liberalize British policy as withdraw
certain privileges which American vessels had informally enjoyed
since the outbreak of the European war,[42] the rest of the treaty
contained no commercial concessions worthy of the name. Though
Article 12 admitted American vessels under seventy tons to the carrying trade of the British West Indies, not even the Federalist majority
in the Senate would accept the humiliating terms on which this nig-
gardly concession was made, and the article was rejected. The seventy-
ton provision virtually excluded American vessels from the lucrative
timber trade. The provision requiring American vessels in the West
Indies to pay the same tonnage duties as British vessels in America,
put United States shipping at a competitive disadvantage because
British vessels paid no tonnage in home ports as Americans did. But
the principal objection to Article 12 was that the United States agreed
to "prohibit and restrain the carrying of any molasses, sugar, coffee,
cocoa or cotton in American vessels . . . from the United States to
any part of the world." This would not only have precluded Americans from re-exporting commodities grown in the French West
Indies, but would also have barred the export of native-grown cotton, fast becoming a major staple of the southern economy.[43] Instead
of winning concessions for American merchants, it seemed that the
treaty made concessions to Britain which would permanently exclude
Americans from lucrative enterprises. The equal admission of British
traders to the Indian fur trade was criticized as another instance of
the same principle.[44]

Jay's failure to win substantial commercial rights from Great Britain was not the opposition's only objection to this part of the treaty.
Their fiercest anger was reserved for the inexcusable way the treaty
surrendered American rights as a neutral carrier. In previous commercial treaties concluded with France, the Netherlands, Prussia,
and Sweden, it had been agreed that neutral ships would be allowed
to carry all enemy property except contraband and that "contraband"
would mean only military equipment, not naval stores. Article 18 of
the Jay Treaty made all French property in American bottoms subject to seizure, though by the Franco-American commercial treaty,
British property in American vessels was protected. Contraband was

defined to include all naval stores except unwrought iron and fir planks, and although the United States did not expressly concede that provisions were contraband she agreed to accept compensation in questionable cases when cargoes were seized by Great Britain rather than uphold her right to ship these articles as free goods.[45] Britain sweetened the pill by pledging to pay the value of the articles plus "a reasonable mercantile profit thereon, together with the freight, and also the demurrage incident to such detention." [46] Nevertheless, there was no denying that in principle this restored the powers she had exercised over American commerce in colonial days. So elastic a definition of contraband allowed Britain to compel all American commodities to be sold in British markets. It was true that, given Britain's naval superiority in the North Atlantic, such articles protected the immediate interest of United States shippers, but they did so by sacrificing their long-term interest in establishing the rights of neutral carriers.[47]

III

There was more in these concessions than commercial advantage or American neutral rights and profits. They also put France at a disadvantage. Opponents were quick to point out that many parts of the British treaty collided with the French one. They were not thinking only of formal contradictions, for supporters were right in saying that there were none given the "express stipulation, that no part . . . be construed to effect or impair any former treaty." [48] They were rather thinking of how Jay's abandonment of points established in the Franco-American Treaty of Amity and Commerce would affect France. The surrender of the principle that free ships make free goods penalized French commerce with her colonies, and America's refusal to insist that naval stores were not contraband, at a time when Sweden and Denmark were attempting to uphold both principles through armed neutrality, would help the British to establish naval superiority over France. But as one of the leading neutral shippers in the world, the most damaging concession the United States had made was that she would accept compensation for the seizure of commodities not necessarily contraband. It was not possible to argue that this clause favored France by encouraging American captains to risk the British blockade, because it did not specify blockaded ports.

Moreover, Britain had resumed seizing United States' vessels carrying provisions to France even before the treaty was ratified. Article 18 made America virtually an accomplice in the British attempt to starve France into submission.[49]

To most of the treaty's critics, its political and strategic implications were infinitely more important than any calculations of commercial gain or loss. More than anything else, they feared the consequences of the partiality it showed to Great Britain in the substance of its provisions and the circumstances in which it was concluded.[50] There was no denying that the government which had refused to negotiate a new commercial treaty with France in 1793 because the Senate was not in session had sent Jay to Britain in 1794 even though the Senate had not consented to his instructions.[51] A writer calling himself "Franklin" put this point bluntly, accusing the government of wooing "with a spaniel-like courtesy" an "enemy in a rapid career on the turnpike of destruction" while ignoring America's one republican ally.[52] Such behavior proclaimed to the world that "those nations who treat us worse, will share the greatest portion of our attachment," and invited further aggression. More alarming still, by giving "to Britain privileges which will put it in her power so materially to injure" the French, it incurred the risk of a rupture with France. The forbearance France had displayed with respect to the guarantee was unlikely to last, and the nation would be left to choose between either losing her as a friend who would help maintain American independence if need be, or fighting a war with Great Britain. If the first course were chosen, France might even decide to go to war against her betrayer.[53]

Opponents of the treaty were not the only ones who considered it in strategic rather than commercial terms. Its supporters also saw it as the only alternative to war with Britain on one the hand or national humiliation on the other.[54] While Federalist spokesmen continued to emphasize the treaty's advantages, such as the surrender of the posts and the promise of indemnity for property seized by the British, they had to admit that it had not produced all that Americans had hoped for. But they argued that it had removed the major causes of friction between the two countries and so averted a war which Hamilton believed would "arrest the present rapid progress to strength and prosperity." When the United States had achieved the stature of a world power, she could demand to be treated accordingly, but while she was still building herself up, to lower her expectations a little was surely no excessive price to pay for peace.[55]

This did not speak directly to the opposition's fear that a treaty so favorable to Britain might provoke war with France. Yet the Federalists said that it was not really inconsistent with independence and neutrality. They argued that it resolved outstanding differences with Britain "without violating any duty to France [and] without giving any preference to another," so that it was not a political alliance liable to offend the other belligerents.[56] And they insisted that accommodation with Britain was more consonant with American neutrality than the terms France appeared to be seeking. Though it was impossible to deny that France had offered generous commercial concessions and Britain had not, they used Genêt's published instructions to suggest that these concessions had the strings of offensive alliance against Britain attached to them. In exchange for France's removal of all restrictions on American commerce and for French naval protection, the United States would undertake to exclude British shipping from her ports. In other words, she would embark on a commercial war against Britain under French sponsorship. If anyone was still in doubt about France's intention to make the United States party to her struggle with Britain, the instructions showed that Genêt was authorized to commission Americans to prey on the commerce and attack the colonies of France's enemies.[57]

The spectacle of an aroused public opposing government policies and demanding that the treaty be rejected made the Federalists even more determined to support it, for they feared that if they were forced to back down on this, then more demands would follow. The public might next require a policy toward Great Britain which would almost inevitably lead to war, such as enforcement of the old rule that free ships make free goods.[58] Their feeling that the government lacked strength made the Federalist leadership eager to avoid war in general, but particularly war with Britain. They were convinced that the nation would be safer allied with Britain against France than vice versa. Britain's naval supremacy gave her more power to injure the United States. Moreover, war with Britain would destroy public credit by drying up the revenue at the same time as it increased the people's adulation of all things French. War with France, on the other hand, though in no sense desirable, would do no harm to the revenue and might help to temper the people's Anglophobia.[59] This is why the Federalists came to see the treaty as indispensable to securing their achievements, and part of the reason why they pursued ratification and implementation undeterred by any risk of war with France.[60]

The Republican opposition preferred war with Britain, if war there must be. For one thing, recent developments supported the belief that the British monarchy was precarious. For another, war with France would be so repugnant to Americans that it might provoke the people to revolt, but war with Britain would give them a welcome chance to pay back the humiliations which the former mother country had inflicted on them. All the old arguments that Britain would be at a disadvantage in such a war, first invoked during the debate on Madison's commercial resolutions, were revived and carried more weight now than before because the tide had turned against the First Coalition and weakened Britain's strategic position. Meanwhile the nation's response to the Whiskey Rebellion had shown that in any future war her adversaries would have to contend with a strong central government able to enforce its writ as never before. And considering the damage America had done Great Britain during the Revolution, when her government had lacked all its present advantages, it seemed probable that any British ministry daring to lead its people against the United States would not last long.[61] For these reasons, Republicans were not deterred from opposition by the threat of war with Britain.

IV

There was another dimension to the Jay Treaty controversy besides strategic choice. Acceptance or rejection might also seriously affect the nature of American society. Given the character of the European war, those who opposed the treaty felt they had good reason to infer that an administration which preferred this course to pursuing French diplomatic overtures must also prefer monarchy to republicanism. This led to the suspicion that though the British treaty was not a formal alliance, it was intended to serve as one.[62] Some went so far as to speculate that the administration had made a bargain with the British ministry by which it would "lend . . . aid for the support of our government" against its enemies in return for the right to plunder American trade, perhaps even to "engage America in a war with France." One form of aid might be the importation of "*supporters of our government* from thence" in the persons of merchants with large capital, whose residence in America was allowed by the treaty. Their influence "in a republic, where the population is thin, where wealth creates almost the only distinction, [and] where the sea ports give the tone to the politics of the country," joined with that wielded by holders of the public debt, would be controlling. Part and parcel of this scheme was the federal government's assumption of debts owed British creditors, which would increase "that debt which has already created an influence independent of the people." [63] Even without these specifics, the ideological implications of the treaty were obvious. If, as many feared, it was designed to provoke the French, the United States would have no choice but to ally with Britain, an alliance which would strengthen the monarchical party in America. [64]

The Federalists used much the same line of argument to convince themselves that the consequences of rejecting the treaty were subordination to French influence and French anarchy. If America's dispute with Britain were not peacefully resolved, the inevitable war would force the United States into a French alliance and partnership in her struggle against the rest of the world. They feared that "a numerous party among us . . . have been steadily endeavouring to make the United States a party in the present European war, by advocating all those measures which would widen the breach between us and Great Britain, and by resisting all those which would tend to close it." [65] Hamilton thought that such a war "would be conducted in a spirit which would render it more than ordinarily calamitous." He found abundant evidence that the pro-French party was "deeply infected with those horrid principles of Jacobinism which, proceeding from one excess to another, have made France a threater of blood." If war broke out, he believed men of this stamp would have the running of it. A nation so vulnerable to British attack could not hope to remain independent of French aid, and French aid would bring to power men of French principles. [66]

The treaty also raised a constitutional question which intensified the ideological doubts of both parties. This issue first appeared in the June 13 resolves of the town of Boston, which objected to the treaty "because it limits the Power of Congress delegated to them by the Constitution,—'To regulate our Commerce with foreign Nations,' —by prescribing conditions, and creating impediments to the exercise of that power." [67] Washington retorted that the Constitution had "assigned to the President the power of making treaties with the advice and consent of the senate." [68] Though he was careful not to say that the president and the Senate had the exclusive right to make treaties, critics of the Jay Treaty immediately replied that the Constitution would be undone if treaties could be put into effect without reference to the House. Robert R. Livingston, writing under the pseudonym "Cato," observed:

If the power to make treaties includes a right to regulate commerce, to raise money, to declare war, to appoint officers and settle their salaries, to establish new courts and new rules of jurisprudence, to place in other hands, rights reserved to the judiciary of the United States, to naturalize foreigners, to define and punish piracy and other offences against the United States . . . then the president and senate, by combining with a foreign nation, can invest themselves with all power, and congress and the judiciary must become useless.[69]

In other words, the opposition saw this as an argument for aristocracy and monarchy. And the Federalists, confronted by a Republican House which was threatening to deny funds for implementation, confirmed their fears [70] by arguing not only that the president and Senate possessed an exclusive jurisdiction over treaties but also that to challenge this power would be to destroy the government and bring on anarchy.[71]

Rhetoric about monarchy, aristocracy, and anarchy touched on ideological sensitivities that had been part of American politics since the Revolutionary War. These words could arouse real fear for the safety of the nation's unproven institutions, because Americans had experienced the realities for which they stood. Under the empire, they had known monarchy and the restriction of power to an elite few, while during the Revolution many had felt the unpleasantness of anarchy. But these evils were not always regarded with equal alarm. Immediately after the war, most people thought that monarchy and aristocracy posed greater dangers to the Revolution than the anarchy which was assumed to be temporary and self-correcting. The experience of the Confederation changed some people's minds, but even at the time of the ratification controversy, many whose political roles had been created by independence probably still held to the view that consolidations of power were more dangerous than the absence of power. Certainly antifederalist rhetoric assumed they did and tried to exploit their fear that the federal system would exclude them now as the imperial system had done before.[72] Not until the early 1790's was there any sign that the majority of people were starting to care more for stability than for liberty. Then the unusual ease with which proponents of Hamilton's fiscal policy were able to repel charges that it had monarchical and aristocratic implications suggests the beginning of a shift in emphasis. The Federalist achievement was the more impressive when we consider that those who had been hurt by British efforts to control of the imperial economy far outnumbered those who had been denied access to political influence.[73]

Several developments had combined to establish this trend. The successful consolidation of national authority in the early 1790's had given Americans their first chance to savor the comforts of stability. At the same time the contrasting horrors of the French Revolution gave new meaning to the threat of anarchy. But most significant of all, Americans were growing indifferent to monarchy and aristocracy as threats to liberty. In part this was because the memory of oppression was fading, and the imperial experience was second-hand knowledge for the rising generation. And in part it was people's desire to believe that the revolutionary demand for heroic achievement was coming to an end. When the Federalists said that opposition would disorganize government, they were addressing themselves as much to the people's weariness as to fears arising from the French Revolution or the memory of their own.

As a political group lacking a popular ideology and vulnerable to attack as betrayers of revolutionary ideals, the Federalists stood to gain from this long-term trend in postrevolutionary politics. The further the nation progressed from that unsettling experience, the less likely it became that the people would have violent ideological reactions to events. Had the Federalists been able to maintain this tendency, they might have succeeded in consolidating their power. But the Jay Treaty decisively reversed the trend by raising fundamental issues which would continue to be agitated until 1800. In doing so, it created a political climate in which the Federalists were at a permanent disadvantage.

4. Sectionalism

If the first party system originated in an ideological disagreement among political leaders which afterward gradually spread to the general public, what explains the sectional character of alignments? Not that any region was ever unanimous in its political sympathies: in every state there were factional disagreements within the leadership on both local and national matters. And as might have been expected from the increasing public involvement in politics, there was no area whose political complexion was invariable. For a brief moment in 1798–1799 it seemed as if Republicanism might die in the South, and in 1803–1807 New England Federalists seemed to be threatened with extinction. Such long-term changes as did occur, though, usually confirmed the sectional character of alignments. South Carolina's shift to Republicanism after 1800 ensured homogeneity with the rest of the South. In the North, Massachusetts, Rhode Island, New Hampshire, and Vermont flirted with Republicanism in the first decade of the century but cooled toward it in the second and eventually rejoined Connecticut to confirm the Federalist character of New England during the War of 1812. The Middle Atlantic states were less decided in their allegiance, but the Republicans gradually gained ascendancy in the larger states while the smaller ones continued to show Federalist proclivities. Yet these were minor deviations from a generally sharp division in national politics which Fisher Ames of Massachusetts noticed as early as 1790, observing that in contrast to the South, "the zeal for supporting the government and the strength, too, are principally on this side of the Hudson." [1]

Because regional economic differentiation corresponded roughly to the political divisions in the first party system, some historians have offered an economic explanation for its sectionalism. Stated in its simplest form, this argument asserts that New England was Federalist

72

because the commerce which predominated there was favored by the Federalist party, while the South was Republican because that party espoused its agrarian interests. The Middle Atlantic states shared characteristics with both regions, and consequently their loyalties were divided.[2]

Unfortunately for this explanation, many agrarians were Federalists while many merchants were Republicans. It is hard to attribute the strength of New England Federalism to commercialism once we know that the region's Republican leadership was as mercantile in orientation as its adversaries, while some of the staunchest supporters of Federalism came from isolated rural areas.[3] And it becomes less satisfactory to account for the South's Republicanism as the necessary concomitant of its agrarianism when we learn that in the 1790's the planters of the Northern Neck and eastern shore of Virginia were all Federalists, as well as inhabitants of the Shenandoah counties in the interior.[4] Southern mercantile centers were generally Federalist, and the Northern Neck and Valley counties of Virginia were the most commercial in the state, but in Maryland and Delaware this pattern was reversed. Although commercial Baltimore produced several Federalist leaders, it soon became the stronghold of the state's Republican party, obliging Federalists there to seek political allies in the rural, slaveholding counties of the south and east.[5] Similarly, in Delaware the most commercial county was Republican, while the rural southern counties were Federalist.[6]

That there were Republican merchants and Federalist farmers is not really surprising. Many of the issues which served as a focus when the first parties were being formed presented economic choices which contained elements of ambiguity, as the Jay Treaty shows. It is true that merchants who had been despoiled by the seizures in late 1793 had an economic interest in the treaty. But those who had suffered most by the Instruction of November 6, 1793, had been trading in the French empire, and may well have thought that the prospect of indemnity was not worth the risk of a war with France just when she was gaining the upper hand in Europe.[7] In raising the issue of war and peace, the treaty may have led a majority of merchants to conclude that collaboration with a power like Britain was more prudent than challenge.[8] Yet even collaboration had more than one side to it, as the controversy over the Embargo was to show some ten years later. Though the Embargo would injure commerce for a time, the long-term interests of American merchants would certainly not be served by cooperation with British efforts to control world commerce, which doomed their own to permanent, colonial subordination.[9] And if merchants came to disagree about the economic effects of certain measures, either because they had different interests or because they perceived them differently, no wonder if men of other livelihoods, with less immediate reason to look at each government measure in economic terms, were also in disagreement about them. Although the perception of economic interest did influence the politics of many individuals and some regions, it does not provide a comprehensive explanation for party alignments.

The same complexities hamper attempts to attribute sectionalism to the different military experiences of the regions during the war.[10] New England saw only sporadic action after March 1776, and that mostly favorable to the patriot cause. Even before Saratoga, British operations had been largely restricted to military objectives, and afterward it was clear that she had given up trying to conquer the North. As these hopes faded, however, she turned her attention to the South. Though she was no more successful, for the rest of the war the South suffered from the rape of the countryside by British expeditionary forces. Georgia and South Carolina were conquered for a short time, and the struggle became a vicious civil war in which no one was safe. In South Carolina it continued long after the surrender at Yorktown.[11] Though the French had failed the deep South in 1779, when the attempt to recapture Savannah aborted, southerners had to admit that the French army and navy had been essential to achieving Cornwallis's submission. It would therefore be possible to argue that the South inclined to Republicanism because she so vividly remembered the fight against Britain and the help brought by France, and because the European wars reawakened stronger feelings there than in the North.

While this was undoubtedly an ingredient in the sectionalism of foreign policy alignments from 1795 to 1815, there remain some awkward questions. Why should the leadership in that part of the South which had been most barbarously treated by Britain in the early 1780's be the most favorably inclined toward her in the 1790's? Why should the Federalist leadership of the northeastern states be pro-

British? Though northerners did not hate Britain as much as southerners did, the New England coastline had suffered from British raids throughout the war, and they were far from Anglophiles. They also knew how much the French had helped in winning the war, and to judge from the observations of foreigners, not to mention the celebrations of French victories, which took place in New England ports during the early days of the European war, they had not forgotten this in the 1790's.[12] Later, when France began to disgrace herself, particularly in the XYZ affair, New Englanders certainly did grow cool toward her. But this was also true of southerners.

Though an interpretation that emphasizes residual hatreds from the war speaks to the foreign policy orientation of the first parties, it has another serious limitation. In stressing grass-roots sentiment in the formation of the first parties, it ignores how much the national leadership took the initiative, particularly in the early phase, or how much political consciousness filtered from it down to the people, and from the metropolitan centers outward to the provinces.[13] It should not be forgotten that the character of American politics in the 1790's was still predominantly premodern; that is, many of the leadership assumed that they would be the principal force at work in shaping public opinion. Though the Revolution had proved that leaders who persistently defied the people's wishes could not hope to remain in power, and had briefly inspired a mass politics, most politicians regarded this as an anomalous interlude and looked to a gradual reversion to normality in the postwar period. The wide difference of opinion between leaders and led during 1793–1795 on the subject of accommodation with Great Britain showed that in many areas the Federalists still felt they had substantial discretion in choosing their course. It also suggests that during the formative stage of the first party system, the disposition of the regional leadership was often more critical than anything else in determining the political complexion of an area.

I

Focusing on the regional leadership seems at first to raise more problems than it solves. There was an obvious difference in their social characteristics that might explain their differing politics, but the relationship seems inverted. The aristocratic character of the southern leadership ought to have made them hostile to the French Revolution and strongly Federalist. More than any other group, southern planters had reason to fear the implications of events in France and their reflection in the rebellion on Santo Domingo. On the other hand, New Englanders, who had neither slaves nor a notably aristocratic social structure, should have been good Republicans hailing their French brothers with delight. Instead, Fisher Ames assailed southerners as "Frenchified" and "violent republicans," while the southern leadership regarded their New England counterparts as advocates of monarchy. The tension between the two parties was even increased by this incongruity, for each suspected the other of hypocrisy.[14]

Shays's Rebellion sheds some light on the anomaly. No New Englander would ever have written, as Jefferson wrote to Madison in 1787, that "a little rebellion now and then is a good thing, and as necessary in the political world as storms in the physical." [15] On the other hand, no one but a New Englander would have written, as "A Friend of Government" wrote in the *Columbian Centinel,* that "any attempt by an individual to lessen [the] respectability [of members of the government] or to alienate the affection of the publick" by insinuating "that the *General Government is pursuing measures, most destructive to the welfare and interest of the people*" threatened the country with "anarchy and confusion." In effect, this writer was asserting that any criticism of government was liable to destroy it.[16] The fear that libel would bring down government, and the accompanying desire to compensate for this by enhancing its dignity with high salaries and titles, may indeed have been produced in New England's Federalists by Shays's Rebellion. And the comparative freedom from such pressures that was enjoyed by southern leaders may have been the happy result of avoiding such disturbing upheavals.[17] Patrick Henry boasted in his state's ratifying convention that no country had been "so long without a rebellion" as Virginia, despite the burdens that the war had imposed upon her.[18]

Though differences in rhetorical and ceremonial emphasis may be attributed to Shays's Rebellion, it cannot be invoked as the sole cause of sectional alignment. As the first widespread insurrection in New England's history, it was certainly one reason why the northern leadership longed for a strong central government with power to repress such outbreaks. Yet this need was felt in the South too. The Revolution had proved that the presence of slaves was a handicap to southerners when they were obliged to defend themselves against foreign invasion, a factor which helped Federalists in South Carolina plead for ratification of the Constitution.[19] Even in peacetime there was always a danger of slave rebellion. It is possible to argue that the South had grown accustomed to the danger, and that having survived a revolution in which an invader tried to incite such rebellion, they knew now that the danger was not as great as they had formerly feared. But the experience of Santo Domingo could not have reassured them. Indeed the leading student of Negro slave revolts has found that "the dozen years following 1790 formed a period of more intense and widespread slave discontent than any that had preceded." [20] And if the fear of insurrection was the cause of New England's Federalism, Pennsylvania should have made the same response to the Whiskey and Fries's rebellions, and Virginia to her narrow escape from the aborted Gabriel's rebellion. But on the contrary, Virginia remained unshakably Republican, while in Pennsylvania the Republican party continued to gain strength.[21]

This is not to say that Shays's Rebellion had no effect upon political alignments in the 1790's, but that it was more symptomatic than causative. William L. Smith struck the proper balance when he observed to Edward Rutledge that "the influence the great body of the people in Massachusetts have in the state government & the insurrection of Shays co-operate to make these gentlemen great favorers of monarchy." [22] Smith's comment is one of the few contemporary efforts to account precisely for the anomalous distribution of ideologies that characterized the beginning of the first party system. By and large the problem was ignored while the leadership of each section trotted out pat explanations for the acts of the other. Southerners attributed the "monarchical" inclination of New England leaders partly to the influence of commercial interests dependent on British capital, partly to the inevitable lust for power of depraved men.[23] New Englanders in turn attributed the South's Republicanism to her people's reluctance to pay their heavy debts to British creditors.[24] Both theories were attractive because they tended to enhance the stereotypes that each region already attached to the other. I know of only one studied attempt to transcend this narrow view and

relate the ideological predisposition of regional leaders to their
social characteristics, and that was made by Fisher Ames. He tried to
analyze sectional antagonism in a letter written to George Richards
Minot in 1791. This letter, together with some comments in an earlier
one, provides a complex discussion of why the southern leadership
was so fervently Republican. It also inadvertently sheds light on the
Federalism of New England's leaders and confirms the insight of
William Smith.

As early as July 1789, Ames had denounced the southern nabobs
as "new lights in politics; who would not make the law, but the people, king; who would have a government all checks; who are more
solicitous to establish, or rather to expatiate upon, some high-sound-
ing principle of republicanism, than to protect property, cement the
union, and perpetuate liberty." [25] In 1791 he tendered this more
analytic explanation:

> To the northward, we see how necessary it is to defend property by
> steady laws. Shays confirmed our habits and opinions. The men of sense
> and property, even a little above the multitude, wish to keep the govern-
> ment in force enough to govern. We have trade, money, credit and in-
> dustry, which is at once cause and effect of the others.
>
> At the southward, a few gentlemen govern; the law is their coat of
> mail; it keeps off the weapons of the foreigners, their creditors, and at the
> same time it governs the multitude, secures negroes, etc., which is of
> double use to them. It is both government and anarchy, and in each case
> is better than any possible change, especially in favor of an exterior (or
> federal) government of any strength; for that would be losing the prop-
> erty, the usufruct of a government, by the States, which is light to bear
> and convenient to manage. Therefore, and for other causes, the men of
> weight in the four southern States (Charleston city excepted) were more
> generally *antis,* and are now far more turbullent than they are with us.
> Many were federal among them at first, because they needed some remedy
> to evils which they saw and felt, but mistook, in their view of it, the
> remedy. A debt-compelling government is no remedy to men who have
> lands and negroes, and debts and luxury, but neither trade nor credit, nor
> cash, nor habits of industry, or of submission to a rigid execution of law.[26]

Ames was still not free of the notion that southern leaders based
their politics on the desire to dodge debts, but he went considerably
beyond this in contrasting the disciplined lives of New Englanders

to the "turbullent" southern aristocracy, which had no "habits of industry, or of submission to a rigid execution of the law." Here he
was drawing an analogy between the political styles of Shays's rebels
and the southern leadership.[27] More than this, he was suggesting that
southern leaders would carry their opposition to effective government further than northern antifederalists, whom he believed "would
not be the least zealous to support the Union" if the crisis that he
foresaw were reached. Ames attributed southern extremism to southern strength: "Virginia, North Carolina and Georgia are large territories. Being strong, and expecting by increase to be stronger, the
government of Congress over them seems mortifying to their State
pride. The pride of the strong is not soothed by yielding to a
stronger."[28] The statement betrayed a fear, shared by northern
Federalists in general, that the political future belonged to the South.
But to New Englanders there was another way in which the South
appeared enviably strong. More important in shaping the ideologies
of the respective leaderships was the ability of the "few gentlemen"
who governed in the South to take their dominance for granted, or,
in Ames's term, to regard the government as their "property." This
contrasted dramatically with Smith's observation that the New England leadership felt insecure and threatened by the "influence of
the great body of the people."

Federalist leaders were understandably shy of drawing this difference to public attention, yet they bore indirect witness to it by
their loud and frequent criticisms of the southern leadership as lazy,
undisciplined, and in Ames's words riddled with "debts and luxury."
Ames's caricature became a northern stereotype of southern leaders
as corrupt, debt-evading, irresponsible gentry who could be conveniently summed up in the invidious word "Jacobin."[29] Though
there is some evidence that less prominent southern whites could and
did indulge a barnyard style of life, this was a grossly distorted picture of the aristocracy.[30] Virginian leaders like Jefferson and Madison
had attained standing by strenuously cultivating their talents, and
the economic adjustments that had to be made in the thirty years
after the Revolution required that even the wealthiest plantation
owner show entrepreneurial talent if he was to survive. But it did
reveal what northern Federalists thought made their southern counterparts different from themselves. They believed that land-owning,

slave-holding southern aristocrats could afford lax behavior because their social position was established by their property, whereas in New England there were few visible distinctions of wealth and family. Therefore, the leadership's position depended more on the less tangible claim of superior virtue and ability, which in turn rested upon ascetic discipline and the dedicated cultivation of talents.

The differences Ames hinted at were not just the product of over fertile northern imaginations. Their real existence was reflected in the contrast between the southern aristocracy's genial tolerance of different life styles and the antagonism with which northern Federalists greeted any behavior that implied a disregard for the attributes distinguishing them from the rest of the population.[31] Another striking illustration is the difference in sectional attitudes toward the code duello. In one, it was accepted as the distinguishing mark of a gentleman; in the other, it was utterly condemned. A leadership dependent on talent alone cannot tolerate a code of "honor" that might jeopardize its very existence. Honor of this kind is not a puritan virtue. It can be gained without rigorous discipline and prolonged application, demanding no more than the willingness to risk one's neck. It is the creature of impulse and chance, as open to the vulgar as to the wise and good, and the New England leadership despised it. When Thomas Blount challenged George Thacher, a representative from Massachusetts, Thacher had no hesitation in refusing. In the South, this might have cost him his reputation; in New England, it was matter for congratulation. New Englanders were not impervious to questions of honor, but believed they must be decided by public opinion rather than a bullet. Though on a few occasions New England congressmen did fight duels, this was never an accepted way of solving differences. In the North, Burr lost his reputation forever after he killed the most talented leader the Federalists possessed. But in the South right up until the Civil War the duel was a permissible indiscretion, if not a necessary part of a gentleman's background, even though society paid a price for tolerating killers among the elite.[32]

These facts could also be interpreted as showing that the southern leadership was not more but less secure in its identity, and that dueling became fashionable partly because social instability in the period between the Revolution and the Civil War created the need for a means of distinguishing the gentry. Certainly the duel performed this function, but it may well be that what was in question in the South was not so much elite rule as who was to exercise it. No elite not completely secure in its institutional foundations could tolerate such a mode of designation. Some more prominent southern leaders who were themselves distinguished for their talents did try to outlaw the custom, but the majority refused to see such statutes enforced because they would not part with so convenient a way of asserting superiority over the common man. It was different in New England. There the problem was less who belonged to the elite than whether those whose claim to membership rested upon talent would continue to wield the authority they believed themselves entitled to. Because New England Federalists thought dueling incompatible with preserving a social order dependent on their form of leadership, they condemned it unanimously and remained determined in their efforts to suppress it.[33]

II

If it is correct to say that the northern and southern elites were so differently situated in their respective societies, then their apparently anomalous ideological preferences begin to make sense. For if party affiliation depended on a judgment about the viability of republican government, it is not hard to see how this would be affected by a man's local situation. A sense of security in a leadership role would encourage faith in the republic, while the reverse would lead to doubt. It is beyond the scope of this study to discuss why the southern elite should have felt more secure than the northern elite. That is a complex subject worth a book in itself. But in retrospect, the different experiences of the elite in both regions as they tried to preserve and perpetuate themselves during the early nineteenth century show that there was reason for southern confidence and northern doubt.

In the North, Federalists experienced great difficulty in keeping the older settlements deferential to their pretensions. And for the most part, they failed to extend either their authority or their kind of leadership to the new western settlements where dissident New Englanders went in ever increasing numbers after 1780. The southern leadership could do both with apparent ease, and had a capacity for lateral extension which gave powerful testimony to its stability. The apex of Virginia's leadership continued to broaden throughout the eighteenth century. In spite of soil exhaustion, or often because of it, members of established families were willing to take up lands in the west, providing a natural leadership for the newer settlements. In the same way prominent Virginia families, like the Nicholases, the Bullitts, the Taylors, and the Breckenridges, were extended into Kentucky, while the Claibornes spread into Tennessee along with the Bentons and Blounts of North Carolina. This does not mean that the movement west did not make for greater social mobility in the Old South. Everyone knows the story of how Andrew Jackson began humble and became eminent. Such mobility as there was, however, tended to confirm the character of southern society by preserving the hegemony of the great plantation owners. Anyone on the rise usually copied their example and diverted profits into slaves. The possession of slaves then raised them above their poorer neighbors and gave them the advantage in competing for public honors, at the same time as it imposed solidarity upon all whites to gather for protection behind the plantation leadership.[34]

New England leaders had no such aids to self-preservation. Most of them were so dependent upon commerce that they could not migrate without forfeiting economic power. At the same time, diversified economic expansion was not congenial to the preservation of elite rule, because new areas of production had new and different interests and were determined to make their presence felt in politics. Sometimes expansion did strengthen the Federalist leadership because potential challengers were migrating to other states. This happened in Connecticut and Massachusetts, where already a large population was taxing limited resources. But more often, and particularly in states like New York and Pennsylvania, which still contained large unsettled areas, the long-term effect was to endanger the political hegemony of a restricted elite. Some commercial centers met the challenge well, but mostly because of their economic power. The South, on the other hand, had a simpler social structure that gave the region more flexibility. Economic uniformity produced few problems that could not be easily solved by the planters. Though the new cotton lands were often more prosperous than older areas, they posed no threat to the foundations of southern society because the old families and institutions had been extended into them. And the dependence of the elite upon slavery encouraged mutual forbearance and cooperation among themselves, as well as deference on the part of poorer whites.[35]

There were exceptions. In some parts of the South, the traditional elite was threatened by anomalous circumstances. In South Carolina there was a rift between the slaveholding planters of the eastern tidewater and the small, upcountry farmers who owned few slaves. The small farmers had gone to the uplands because they lacked the capital to turn seacoast swamps into rice-producing plantations. The large plantation owners had not followed because the region's principal cash crop could be grown only in the low-country tidal areas. Tension between the two sections was inevitable given their contrasting social systems. But it was heightened by differences in origin. The tidewater inhabitants had come from the cosmopolitan centers of the North Atlantic and retained close contact with them. The backcountry folk hailed largely from the interior of North Carolina, Virginia, and Pennsylvania. The cultural chasm between the two, described in Charles Woodmason's journal of his travels in the backcountry just before the Revolution, was made still wider by the colony's political institutions. The backcountry was virtually excluded from direct representation in the Commons House of Assembly and until the late colonial period was dependent on the tidewater even for the administration of justice.[36]

The immediate effect of the Revolution was to remove some of the grosser inequities by extending representation to the backcountry in the constitutions of 1776 and 1778. But the concessions made by no means altered tidewater planter hegemony,[37] which was not effectively challenged until the British invasion of the South in 1779. The prerevolutionary concentration of leadership along the coast and particularly around Charleston, made it vulnerable to British military operations in 1779–1780. The British occupation had disastrous results for most of the aristocracy, forcing them either to accept British protection in order to save their property, or to endure forcible removal to St. Augustine after the surrender of Charleston and the defeat at Camden. Those who escaped both fates, like Governor John Rutledge, were nevertheless obliged to rely on the backcountry for most of their political and military support. After the British had established their supremacy in conventional warfare, the patriot remnant turned to guerrilla tactics which, though brilliantly effective, were also more socially disruptive than the traditional way of fighting. For two years after the fall of Charleston, American military operations in South Carolina were often conducted by partisan bands under the leadership of Frances Marion, Andrew Pickens, Thomas Sumter, and Henry Lee. Attempts to raise larger, regular forces created financial problems and ultimately forced Rutledge to call an assembly in Jacksonborough, which confiscated the estates of collaborators. When three years of vicious civil war ended, South Carolina society was a shambles and the traditional structure of authority seemed broken beyond repair by the forced exodus of most prominent loyalists.[38]

Georgia, which suffered a similar fate at the hands of the British during the war, fared differently once it was over because the displaced were less able to resist the power of challengers. This was partly because they were less solidly established in the first place, and partly because the constitutional changes that accompanied the Revolution wholly altered the centralized character of the colonial government.[39] But when the South Carolina gentlemen who had preferred imprisonment and exile to collaboration returned home in 1782–1783, they made vigorous attempts to reassert their authority. They were not deterred by a grave economic crisis that led in 1786 to a court closing at Camden or by formidable political opposition, which drew its strength from two quarters: first, from the back-country leaders whom the war had brought to the fore and who played on local resentment of aristocrats who had failed the state in 1780; second, from the radical group in Charleston that resented repatriate attempts to restore damaged fortunes by alliance with Tory merchants. In the end, because the state constitution gave disproportionate power to the tidewater, the aristocrats succeeded in regaining much of their prewar hegemony, but their authority was not secure. Nor was it likely to become so as long as they were powerless to free the state from the burden imposed by the war debt. Any leadership that could not solve this, the principal postwar problem of its state, had reason to feel insecure.[40]

The South Carolina Federalists were an extreme example of a beleaguered aristocracy. But others in the South shared their plight, such as the slave-owning gentry of the southern and eastern counties of Maryland. They espoused Federalism because of the political challenge posed by the fast-growing commercial areas around Baltimore. Though their control of an undue number of counties, the unit of representation in the legislature, enabled them to resist this pressure, the threat to their power was unmistakable. The same was true in Delaware, where the rapid development and ethnic diversity of Newcastle County propelled the leadership of the two southern counties toward Federalism, though the construction of the state constitution confined the threat to elections for governor and congressional representative. Hamilton's fiscal policy was not an issue in either state, and party alignments did not emerge until mid-decade when the foreign policy dispute came to the fore.[41] It was very much the same in New Jersey. Hamilton's program was indeed controversial, but only because its first congressional delegation was composed of men personally interested in the fiscal policy. The state as a whole was not, and political divisions did not harden until after the neutrality controversy.[42]

By 1796 the Jay Treaty had arraigned Maryland backcountry and slave-owning Federalists against Republican commercial interests in Baltimore. Rural Federalists of the southern Delaware counties were similarly pitted against the commercial and industrial towns of Wilmington and Newcastle, and the static Federalist counties in southwest New Jersey were ranged against faster growing, more populous rivals around New York. What the Federalist leadership of these rural areas had in common with their commercial counterparts in New England, New York, and Pennsylvania, was that they all feared for their traditional status.

III

The theory that Federalism was the choice of those who felt insecure as leaders because of changes wrought by the Revolution sheds light also on the gradual transfer of power from Federalists to Republicans in the lifetime of the first party system. Neither party had ever appealed only to the elite. For instance, all who were alarmed by the speed of change, particularly in northern society, and many who were disturbed by the decline of the older religious sects, joined those whose interests were hurt by Republican policies like the Embargo in supporting the Federalists.[43] And some men, particularly in the Republican South, became Federalists primarily because their enemies were Republicans, that is, not so much for ideological reasons as for those of political identity and strategy. For one reason or another, they were alienated from the Republican coalition dominant in their state and sought to strengthen themselves in the only way they could: by alliance with external forces that had enemies in common with them. This was particularly true of the Cape Fear Federalists in North Carolina and the Federalists of the Valley in Virginia. To a lesser extent it was also true of those in the Northern Neck. Though they continued to supply more than their share of national leaders, their distinctive economy and the peculiar development of the region under the proprietorship of the Fairfax family made them a minority in their own state.[44]

In the same way wherever Federalism was the ideology of the established elite, the challengers became Republicans, and on occasion they were undoubtedly prompted by political calculation as much as by ideological conviction. When dissenting religious groups confronted a state-supported church, they aligned with its political enemies. Consequently, in an area like New England, which was the refuge of the remaining established churches, the Republicans could count on the support of many non-Congregationalists.[45] It would seem reasonable to have expected, then, that ethnic minorities would be predominantly Republican, particularly after the Federalist attempt to restrict immigration at the end of the 1790's. But the behavior of such groups was complicated by other factors. For instance, those who were more eager to preserve their distinctiveness than to assimilate often found themselves strongly in sympathy with the defensiveness of the Federalists. And though the Republicans were the principal beneficiaries of the immigration that followed the French Revolution, their identification with France at a time when all Europe was falling under her despotic sway was no help in winning over certain minorities already established, such as the Dutch in New York. In the long run, most national minorities did find it expedient to adopt Republicanism, particularly after Federalism became associated with disloyalty, but their presence did not decisively help either party in the period when these national coalitions were forming.[46]

Nevertheless, it was soon clear that Republicanism was infinitely more dynamic than Federalism, and that the espousal of one or the other in the 1790's was a good sign of who would or would not fare well with time. The unusual course pursued by the one Federalist leadership whose position improved as the first party system took shape, that of tidewater South Carolina, confirms this general interpretation. Conversion to or even acquiescence in Republicanism was rare because identification with Federalism as the ideology of the insecure tended to grow stronger with pressure. In the nation as a whole, the antagonism between Federalists and Republicans intensified throughout the 1790's, subsided briefly after the election of Jefferson in 1800, and re-emerged at the time of the Embargo. But in South Carolina, alignments began to soften with the Jay Treaty, grew confused in the election of 1800, and ended in 1808 with the state's Federalists being absorbed into a pervasive Republican establishment.

This was the more surprising since the early 1790's had seen a bitter struggle between the tidewater and the backcountry over representation. The census of 1790 had clearly shown that even though the capitol had been transferred to Columbia in the interior, the backcountry was still miserably under represented. With four times as many free citizens as the low country, it had less than a majority in both Houses. Charleston, with one-ninth of the state's free inhabitants, could elect one-third of the legislature. The tidewater argument was that the legislature should represent property as well as people. Backcountry spokesmen retorted that wealth had sufficient influence by itself, needing no special protection, and that even if wealth were to be made the basis of representation, they would still be entitled to constitutional reform. But while they lacked a staple economy dependent on slavery, the tidewater could not be persuaded. Planters feared that if farmers were given a majority in the legislature, they might seek to solve the state's fiscal problems by a discriminatory tax on two essentials of the tidewater aristocracy: commerce and slaves. And a requirement that any constitutional amendment must be approved by two-thirds of the legislature protected them even against the possibility of disagreement among themselves.[47]

The furor over the Jay Treaty, coming directly after the reapportionment controversy of 1794, should have been especially disruptive in South Carolina. In other states it certainly served to aggravate existing tensions. Here, however, it seemed to mute sectional controversy by distracting attention from it. One obvious explanation is that Article 12 of the treaty, which prohibited the export of cotton from the United States, was a threat to the economic interests of the entire state. Another was the intensity of anti-British sentiment surviving from the war. But equally significant was the radical improvement in the fortunes of the tidewater elite after 1794, brought about by the introduction of the cotton gin. By making possible the creation of a plantation aristocracy in the interior, this invention both promised to revive the state's economy and gave the tidewater elite the same potential for lateral mobility as the rest of the southern leadership had always enjoyed. In this way it ensured that with time the principal sources of antagonism between the two sections would be eliminated.

This did not take long, thanks to the reopening of the slave trade between 1803 and 1807, and the importation of almost forty thousand Africans during that time to meet the demands of the expanding upcountry economy. When formal reconciliation through revised representation was achieved in 1808, some parts of the state were still relatively free. But equitable apportionment was no longer a threat to the seacoast, for as South Carolina grew steadily more homogeneous, the planters were ever less liable to challenge. Because the implications of these developments had been clear from the start, the appeal of Federalist ideology had been muted and factional politics for personal advantage re-emerged here as it was disappearing elsewhere.[48] So the genesis and decline of Federalism in South Carolina both show that it was the ideology of those who felt their positions as leaders shaken by changes accompanying the Revolution.

Though in South Carolina the Federalists displayed less zeal than the Republicans in supporting their cause, this was not the usual pattern. Federalism may have been a symptom of elite insecurity, but the more typical response to this condition was heroic exertion. The superior dynamism of Republicanism was not the result of greater activity but of greater effectiveness in commanding mass loyalty. The Federalists labored under several disadvantages in this respect. The ideology of a threatened elite was not much of an asset either to challengers, on whom party growth should to some extent

have depended, or to recognized leaders trying to recruit public
support. It was not just that Federalists were anti-populist in out-
look, for they proved to be remarkably successful in making isolated
appeals to the people. More damaging because more visible were the
public postures Federalism forced its adherents to adopt, especially
the apparent liking for Britain and hostility to France. Most damning
of all was Federalism's sceptical view of republics, which brought
the value of revolutionary achievements into question. Republicanism, on the contrary, was admirably suited to the needs of challengers. They found its anti-elitism congenial; revolutionary loyalties
were stirred by its anti-British, pro-French implications, and best of
all it affirmed and exalted revolutionary achievements instead of
impugning them.

The capacity of Republicanism to assimilate both revolutionary
ideology and popular preferences goes a long way toward explaining why both Federalists and Republicans assumed the nation was
spontaneously Republican in sympathy and why, short of national
disaster, the Federalists were doomed to be the minority party after
1800. Yet the quality of the Republican triumph did vary, depending
on how local conditions favored challengers. In large states like
New York and Pennsylvania, where both the population and the
areas of settlement were expanding rapidly, there was so little hope
for the survival of elite rule that they had become irreversibly Republican by 1800.[49] The same forces were at work in Ohio, Vermont,
New Hampshire, and Massachusetts, all of which had become Republican within ten years of Jefferson's triumph.[50] Even in the smaller
states that were developing less vigorously, such as Connecticut,
New Jersey, Rhode Island, Maryland, and Delaware, Republican
challengers made considerable headway against their Federalist adversaries because the appeal of their ideology was increased by the
prestige that Jefferson's presidency conferred upon it. In Connecticut
and Delaware these advantages never proved decisive, though the
Delaware Republicans occasionally carried a state election for governor and representative.[51] But they produced a precarious Republican superiority in Rhode Island, and in New Jersey helped bring
to power Republicans who were dependent on the populous counties
of the northeast.[52] In Maryland, the Federalists accelerated their
own demise. Their efforts in the year 1800 to alter election procedures so as to give all the state's electoral votes to Adams was a

violation of state traditions which so deeply offended the voters as to cost the Federalist party their power.[53]

The natural advantages of Republicanism might soon have turned the Federalists into an embittered minority sect had not new international tensions and pressure from the belligerent powers after 1805 forced the United States to choose between humiliation and war. All the old doubts about the stability of republican government rose to the surface again, and surviving Federalists hastened to exploit them. In trying to meet the challenge without going to war, the Republicans did particular damage to their cause in states where they owed their power to commercial expansion. In New England, Maryland, and New Jersey, economic difficulties were blamed on Republican policies, and by 1812 these states had returned to Federalist control. Other factors also contributed to this. In New Jersey, for instance, Quakers in the south and west united with those who feared that war would make New Jersey a battleground again, as it had been during the Revolution. This coalition defeated the Republicans in 1812, though they quickly regained power in 1813. The Federalists were usually most successful in the older, more fully settled states. For instance, in Maryland they again exploited the overrepresentation of the rural counties, where Federalism remained strong because expansion in the Republican areas had been more intensive than extensive. This enabled them to regain control of the House of Representatives in 1808, though they could not achieve full control of the legislature until 1812 when the next election of the Senate took place. And though Vermont and New Hampshire had expanded considerably in the first years of the nineteenth century, their economies inhibited sustained growth and often attracted immigrants more interested in preserving traditional values than in material enrichment. Such conservative predispositions together with a decline in the founding of new towns after 1810 made these states once more congenial soil for a resurgence of Federalism. The only state where Federalism revived in the face of continued geographical expansion was Massachusetts, where the Constitution of 1780 was unusually sensitive in representing population, so that the Federalists could counterbalance the new settlements by sending full delegations to the legislature from the populous seacoast towns where they were still in control.[54]

PART III

PUBLIC OPINION

The first party system differed from its modern counterparts in that it was begotten less by the desire to win office through electoral means than by a fundamental disagreement about whether or not American republican government was workable and enduring. Each party believed that the other embodied a threat to revolutionary achievements, which had to be opposed. Not that the makers of the first national coalitions were innocent of electoral calculation, or the desire to capture and control the government; after all, this was essential to their larger ends. Nor is modern party politics wholly lacking in an ideological dimension. The difference is that for us, at least until recently, the significance of an ideology has had less to do with content than with function. Though it may help to maintain party integration through a sense of shared purpose, when it conflicts with the greater end of achieving power we expect it to be compromised.[1] But in the late eighteenth century, party was thought to be a dubious means of achieving power, only justifiable as an alternative to some greater evil.

Ideology performed a more important function in the first parties than merely convincing the members of each party that the other was a mortal antagonist. It also led to a fundamental disagreement about the place public opinion should have in the nation's politics, the Federalists being reluctant to give it any, while the Republicans wanted to enhance its importance. These differences might be dismissed as the result of chance, with the Republicans benefiting from an accidental congruence between popular prejudices and their own preferences in domestic and foreign policy, while the Federalists were the victims of a fortuitous conflict between popular expectation and a legitimate, informed estimate of national interest. Yet there was more than chance at work. The Republicans believed the mea-

91

sures of government should fit the expectations of the governed, because they had faith in republics. The Federalists believed rather that the social order was artificial, that contrivance was necessary to its preservation, and that the decisions of an elite must never take second place to the prejudice of the people. Perhaps personality was also a factor, for there were many Federalists who clearly enjoyed unpopularity. It was as if to have public opinion against them provided reassurance that they were indeed the wise and good, much as adversity reassured the Puritans that they were doing the Lord's will and so had roused the Devil's wrath.[2] One thing was certain: Federalist political instincts, whether ideologically or psychologically derived, were far more elitist than those of the opposition. And this difference not only affected the way each party saw the political process, but also determined its long-term strategy.

The view each party took of public opinion also dictated its distinctive style. In the early phases of the party system this relationship was generally straightforward. The Republicans had confidence in public opinion, believing that it would be on their side as soon as the people understood the issues. So they assumed that they could achieve their objectives by exposing the implications of Federalism and letting the people respond. In other words they were prepared to rely on a political style that did not demand especially heroic exertions. By contrast, the Federalists wanted to remain as independent of the people as possible in defining and pursuing their objectives, which forced them to adopt a manipulative style. This was necessary to preserve their power and implement their policies in a political system that was still sensitive to the people's expectations, thanks largely to opposition activities. And the unpopularity of their measures forced them to undertake ever more heroic maneuvers. The Federalists were not comfortable with this style, sensing that it was not compatible with their desire to keep the government free from popular pressure, but the only alternative seemed to be abandonment of their objectives.

5. Elitism

In the first phase of implementing the new federal government it was no more expected that there would be disagreement on the role of public opinion than it was that two opposing parties would arise. Every member of the First Congress knew that, despite the formal constitutional delegation of power, the federal government could not exercise any authority that the people refused to recognize and obey. All were keenly aware of popular expectation and eager to court approval by showing that the new government could solve problems that the Articles of Confederation could not.[1] Yet even in the first few months of its existence, the seeds of division could be detected in a dispute over priorities. When Madison tried to allay anti-federalist sentiment by proposing a series of constitutional amendments, part of which later became the Bill of Rights, some objected that organization of the executive and judiciary should come first. The public, they said, wanted implementation of the federal government more than changes in it.[2] Both sides claimed to have the support of public opinion, and in a way both were right. Madison admitted that "a great number of the community are solicitous to see the Government carried into operation," but he made the reservation that there was "a considerable part also anxious to secure those rights which they are apprehensive are endangered by the present Constitution." The difference was that some would hear only those who thought as they did, while Madison had a much more catholic ear for public sentiment and wanted to please as many of the people as he could.[3]

The fiscal system shattered any pleasant illusion that both parties had equal respect for public opinion. It may have been necessary to establish public credit even at the risk of unpopularity, but not to rush into an ambitious plan like Hamilton's before it was clear what the national revenue would bear. Not content with this, the Federalists next hastened to set up the Bank and use the backlash of Shays's Rebellion to create as many revenue sources as possible. Though the implications of these acts were not clear to the public at large, the opposition leadership saw very plainly what their adversaries were up to. And when in the Second Congress the Federalists tried to juggle the apportionment of representation so as to benefit the eastern states, it seemed to the Republicans that there was nothing they would not do to insulate themselves from public opinion. Not until foreign policy became publicly controversial did the people begin to realize that the Federalists had no intention of bending to their expectation. When they did, this increased the resolution of opposition elements which were springing up throughout the country. Yet the Federalists were undeterred, though they knew they might jeopardize their achievements by a head-on collision with an aroused public. Throughout the Washington administrations, they remained unwilling to compromise their policies for the sake of courting public opinion.

I

As opposition leaders became convinced that the Federalists meant to ignore public opinion, they began to see it as a means by which excesses might be controlled. Given the sectional character of alignments on the fiscal policy, they did not have the immediate power to influence a majority of the many sites at which the Federalists would have to be challenged if there were to be an electoral remedy. There was nothing for them to do but try to arouse public opinion, which was not only the key to effective use of electoral remedies, but might also provide a more immediate means of influencing the diffuse federal system. Appeals to public opinion had the double sanction of opposition ideology and revolutionary experience. Therefore when the opposition turned to public opinion in the 1790's it was not indulging vain fantasies. Madison wrote in the *National Gazette* of September 1792 that "the practice of making a common cause, where there is a common sentiment and common interest, in spight [*sic*] of circumstantial and artificial distinctions" was well understood.[4] And the more the Federalists tried to make themselves independent of

public opinion, the more the Republicans were attracted to it as a
weapon to use against them.

Yet as a remedy for Federalist encroachments, public opinion had
its limitations. How was its exact state to be gauged at any time?
Sometimes the public had no opinion on an issue. Then again, sometimes it was swayed by the very actions of government which the
opposition had hoped it would check.[5] Public indifference to the
federal government's conduct confirmed opposition fears that the
remoteness of representatives from constituents would license them to
act at will as it appeared they had in the funding issue. Two other
factors hindered the rousing of public sentiment to the degree of
unanimity achieved before independence on the subject of Great
Britain. First, the complexities of the federal system made the lines
of cleavage less visible than they had been during the controversy
over Parliament's jurisdiction. The colonists had then been refusing
to concede internal power over them to an external sovereign, a
distinction easily made. But the demarcation between the federal
government and state legislatures was difficult even to define, let
alone enforce.[6] Second, in the absence of any common external threat
it was unlikely that the country as a whole, given its vastness and
distinct regional interests, would have a spontaneous common
reaction to any given policy of the federal government. So long as
the central government avoided encroaching on interests that all
the people shared, it would be difficult indeed to rouse them to
vigilance.

Opposition leaders were not unaware of these problems. Madison
himself confessed that there were "cases where the public opinion
. . . not being fixed, it may be influenced by the government." He
acknowledged that this was more often so in a large country because
it was "less easy . . . to be ascertained and the less difficult to be
counterfeited. . . . The more extensive a country, the more insignificant is each individual in his own eyes," therefore the greater his
reluctance to challenge those who disagree with him. Both factors
troubled Madison. Nevertheless, he did not infer from the inde-
terminacy of public opinion that it should be ignored. He believed
that despite these shortcomings, governments were free only where
public opinion was "the real sovereign," that is, where it made a

continuous and active scrutiny of the state, not just on selective issues but on all important matters. Its capacity to do so depended in turn upon "whatever facilitates a general intercourse of sentiments, as good roads [and] domestic commerce, a free press, and particularly a *circulation of newspapers throughout the entire body of the people,* and *Representatives going from, and returning among every part of them,*" as well as a *"Constitutional Declaration of Right."* [7]

This explains the sensitivity of opposition leaders to the possibility that the postal regulations in 1791–1792 and the proposed stamp tax would interfere with newspaper circulation through the land. It explains the elaborate contrivances by which Jefferson and Madison installed Philip Freneau as editor of the *National Gazette* so that the public might have some alternative to the "monarchical" heresies in John Fenno's *Gazette of the United States.*[8] And it explains why they saw nothing wrong in such acts as that of the Virginia legislature when in November 1790 it resolved against the constitutionality of assumption and the irredeemability of the debt. Although this, the first of many Virginia resolutions censuring Congress, was met with the objection that a part should not act for the whole, Madison noted that "in proportion as government is influenced by opinion, it must be so by whatever influences opinion," and that nothing was more likely to become part of public opinion than a constitutional declaration by a state legislature.[9]

In the end, the press and legislative declarations of right proved disappointing as techniques for giving a focus to public opinion. The press remained predominantly Federalist, public opinion did not rise to the pitch expected by the opposition over the fiscal system, and Virginia's example of legislative declarations was either decisively rejected or ignored. Though several legislatures seemed ready to follow her lead in the matter of assumption, such determined opposition was generated by these actions as to neutralize their effect. The Pennsylvania Assembly's efforts to oppose the excise at the beginning of 1791 met with the same reception.[10] If anything, the legislative declarations were counterproductive, particularly the Virginia Resolutions of 1790, which Hamilton's Massachusetts correspondent, Benjamin Lincoln, said had produced "a good rather than an evil, by confirming the doubtful in the importance of a firm energetic head to the Union, sufficiently strong to control the whole." [11] If the opposition hoped to stir up public opinion against what they took to be threats to revolutionary achievements, they would have to find more effective ways than these.

II

Frustrated by the course the government was pursuing, some of the opposition did try another technique, that of corresponding societies dedicated to spreading political information. These had a precedent in the revolutionary committees which had mushroomed in the thirteen colonies during 1772–1775, and the men behind the attempt to establish them in the states in 1793–1794 undoubtedly hoped that they would be as contagious again.[12] They did not so much appeal to opposition congressmen, who already exerted maximum influence over public opinion through their visibility in the government, as to a secondary level of opposition leadership, men newly provoked by Federalist policies to make a first essay in national politics. Though some members of Congress did belong to local societies, there is no evidence that Madison and Jefferson, the recognized leaders of the opposition, sponsored them as they had sponsored Freneau's *National Gazette*, even though they defended the clubs against critics. The prestigious "mother" society of Philadelphia as yet included no politician of more than local reputation, though its president, David Rittenhouse, and James Hutchinson of the corresponding committee, were both renowned scientists.[13] The societies were further prevented from gaining in prestige because some of their most influential members left them as soon as they became controversial.[14] Yet during 1793–1795, as many as thirty-eight of them appeared on the scene, passing resolutions on both local and national matters. They became known as either democratic or republican societies.

Because their first appearance coincided with Genêt's arrival in America and the neutrality crisis, the Federalists persisted in seeing a sinister connection between the societies and French influence. This theory was strengthened by the degree to which they resembled the Jacobin societies of France and made foreign affairs their explicit concern. But the neutrality crisis did not generate the societies, though it provided the occasion and helped them proliferate. They would have emerged, even without the war between France and

Britain. The cause lay in the degree to which administration initiatives in both domestic and foreign policy violated popular expectation. "A Republican" later wrote that the public had been obliged "to associate, in order to compare and consolidate their opinions on those subjects, and, by publishing their sentiments, to convince their public agents, that the minds of the people were not with them in pursuing such measures." [15]

Nevertheless the Federalists were struck by the coincidence and firmly believed that the societies were vehicles of French influence. They had good reason to fear their opposition to the administration's neutrality policy. It was already under fire from France, and Genêt's antics showed that she was trying to influence the American government by appealing to popular sympathies. The Federalists were afraid that the societies might tip the scale toward a showdown between the government and the people and lost no time in denouncing them for trying to provoke a war with Britain in order to benefit France.[16]

If this had been the only objectionable feature of the societies, the Federalists would have been content merely to attack the measures they advocated. A more serious one was that they tended to "popularize" American politics and undo all that had been done by framing the federal Constitution to keep the leadership above the reach of popular agitation.[17] It was this fear that caused the Federalists to oppose not just the measures proposed by the societies, but their very existence, with a barrage of criticism intended to bring about their hasty end.[18]

Some of this criticism was candid about why the Federalists found the societies so disturbing. For instance, Nathaniel Chipman warned that the democratic societies would help to usher in the evils of simple democracy. He made this charge after the societies had tried to invoke his *Sketches of the Principles of Government* in their defense. He was obliged to admit that he had there advocated keeping the people informed about the actions of their government because representative democracy depended on public sentiment rather than force. But he denied that this justified societies, self-created for the "purpose of censuring the proceedings of government in transitu, of anticipating the deliberations of constitutional bodies, or dictating the measures, which those bodies ought to pursue." The issue here was the role of public opinion. Chipman thought it should be largely

passive and receptive rather than active and initiatory. He pointed
out that simple democracies had never worked because they were
invariably taken over by demagogues who exploited the people's
impatience and ignorance. Moreover, such governments usually
tyrannized the minority because "where all are immediate actors no
accountability can exist." [19]

The most forthright critics of the popular societies went on to say
that no government would be safe "until the legislative body is set
totally above the influence of a surrounding populace." [20] But this was
going too far, and others hastily added that they were not denying
all popular power, only suggesting that the people already did "all
they can do well—that is, they freely elect representatives and freely
censure or approve of their conduct—but never dictate or controul
them." If the people's power extended beyond these bounds there
would be no point in representation, which was designed to give them
exceptional leadership in the supervision of their public affairs.[21]
Even so qualified a criticism of simple democracy as this was risky
in American politics, for it might be construed as a denial of the
people's sovereignty and inflame rather than soothe popular passions.
Most who wanted to halt the trend of the societies avoided such
plain speaking and chose rather to assail them as usurpations of the
popular will, legitimately expressed through the people's representatives and the Constitution.

The Federalists stressed that the Constitution did not authorize
men to form clubs and "*set themselves* up as umpires between the
people and the government," while responsible to no one but themselves, and that those who wished to make the government more
democratic than the people as a whole thought it should be were
opposing the national will. Any "intermediate power or body . . .
between the people and their representatives," particularly one
dedicated to opposing government, might "defeat the intentions of
both." "Are they legally elected to enquire into the conduct of
public officers?" asked one indignant critic in the *Gazette of the
United States,* and did they "revert to the mass of the people . . . at
stated periods?" asked another. "A Friend of Representative Government" raised the question, Who are the people? "Are they a few
self-created, self-interested members of certain political clubs, or the
mass of citizens throughout the United States, who have chosen by a

fair and free election, Representatives to appear in their behalf, and act in their name?" "[N]o man, or *body of men*," wrote "Order" in the *Columbian Centinel*, "except such as are constitutionally appointed for the purpose by a majority of the whole people" could speak in the name of all. The societies could only claim to do so, said another critic, "when these men can show that a part is greater than the whole, or that a few individuals combined in party circles thro' the continent, are better entitled to regard, as the organs of the people, than the men elected by that very people." There would be a revolution, wrote one Federalist in the *Maryland Journal*, "whenever the *resolves of clubs* shall control the *resolutions of government*." This would be government by the minority, very likely accompanied by the disorders which had plagued ancient Rome and contemporary France.[22]

Some warned that such combinations, not delegated by the people yet claiming to speak for them, threatened the equal rights of citizens. Noah Webster, Jr., argued that

in a free country, each citizen, in his private capacity, has an *equal* right to a share of influence in directing public measures; but a society, combined for the purpose of augmenting and extending its influence, acquires an *undue proportion* of that general influence which is to direct the will of the state. Each individual member of the state should have an *equal* voice in elections, but the individuals of a club have more than an equal voice, because they have the benefit of another influence, that of extensive *private attachments* which come in aid of each man's political opinion. And just in proportion as the members of a club have an undue share of influence, in that proportion they abridge the right of their fellow citizens.

"Deodatus" wrote in the *Columbian Centinel* that "if part only of the citizens are formed into Clubs, and the others remain unassociated, the Clubs though a minority would have an over-ruling influence— and that excess of influence would be unfair, and utterly repugnant to the nature of an equal republican government." The areas favored by such an inequality would be those where it was easiest to form associations; for instance, the cities would enjoy an advantage over the country. Or so the Federalists said.[23]

The Federalists were trying to suggest that the societies were electioneering cabals of aristocratic usurpers. "Two hundred men," noted L. E. in the *Gazette of the United States,* "by clubbing together, can set at nought the vote of a citizen who minds his own business and joins no dark meetings.—They can over-rule the votes of two hundred dispersed citizens, who, not concerting together, how they shall vote, in fact lose their suffrages." Liberty, according to a writer in the *Minerva,* was not in danger from open aggression or an aristocracy of the rich, but rather from "designing men" who were a "secret aristocracy" and wanted places that others filled and that they knew they did not deserve.[24] The insistence of some urban societies on keeping their meetings secret sustained the implication that their plans would not bear inspection, and inspired taunting Federalist challenges to disclose their membership so that the public could use their talent.[25]

In their zeal to discredit the societies, the Federalists were not at all disturbed by the inconsistency of depreciating the members as nobodies at the same time as they branded them aristocrats.[26] Yet the term "aristocrat" was surely more appropriate to the Federalists. They were socially prominent, particularly in those areas where they waged the most determined war on the societies. They wished to assert their independence from public opinion, whereas the societies identified with it. For them to call the societies aristocratic was indeed the pot calling the kettle black, but they remembered how successfully this charge had been used against their pretensions to govern in the 1780's, and could not resist turning the tables now.[27]

It was equally hypocritical of the Federalists to accuse the societies of violating the freedom of elections. In theory, this freedom was designed to prevent minority domination and ensure that the wise and virtuous would be elected. The framers of the new federal Constitution of 1787 had intended among other things to upgrade the quality of men in public life by imposing large constituencies, which they believed would restore electoral purity.[28] William Beers of Connecticut summarized their reasoning in 1791 when he wrote that in all bodies "in which the weak and ignorant, those susceptible of influence, and of irregular passions have naturally the ascendant in point of numbers . . . [one could] augment the force of the wise, the uninfluenced and steady, and . . . divide and waste the strength of the opposite party" by enlarging the electoral districts. Though in small districts the best men might be overwhelmed by the superior

numbers of inferior men, over a large area they would be the only
ones able to unite for the same worthy object and so would over-
balance their less worthy brothers who would scatter their votes in
the pursuit of partial and personal interests.[29]

The theory was somewhat different from the practice. The men
who had framed and secured the ratification of the Constitution in
1787–1788 had no real intention of leaving the spontaneous workings
of free elections to elevate the wise and good to office. Though there
were rules of propriety designed to exclude lesser men, factional
rivalry within the regional leaderships led to considerable electioneering.[30] Patrick Henry's maneuverings forced Madison to engage
in this uncongenial activity in order to win a seat in the First
Congress,[31] and Fisher Ames's correspondence with George Minot is
larded with references to a Federalist "club" in Suffolk County
which played no small part in Ames's victory over the better-known
Samuel Adams. Ames's coterie seems also to have helped him win
repeated re-election and to have secured Harrison Gray Otis as his
replacement.[32] Nor were the societies innocent of this activity,
particularly in New York and Philadelphia where electioneering was
to some extent accepted because of a long tradition of electoral
competition.[33]

Nevertheless, most of them did not think this was their chief
function or even a legitimate one. They seldom nominated or
endorsed candidates in public, and some of their spokesmen condemned "[t]he practice in some States . . . [of conducting] elections
by 'self-created' . . . committees, corresponding one with another
throughout the state" as "unwise" and "very disagreeable in their
tendency." Their professed respect for the freedom of elections did
not, however, stop them pointing to electoral remedies and recommending their use for purging the federal government of as many
fundholders and British partisans as possible. They saw no incompatibility between one and the other. So at the same time as the Portland
Republican Society resolved in August 1794 that the people should
vote according to their own judgment, and "therefore any attempt
to corrupt and delude the people in exercising the rights of suffrage,
either by promoting the favor of one candidate, or traducing the
character of another, is an offence equally injurious to moral recti-
tude and civil liberty," they also censured their representative for

opposing Madison's resolves and urged that there be rapid rotation among the officers of government.[34]

On the surface, it seems remarkable that Federalist accusations of aristocratic electioneering by the societies did not meet with more countercharges of hypocrisy. There were occasional gibes. The opposition warned that the fiscal system was designed to weld the aristocratic monied interest together with merchants, manufacturers, and speculators "into political clubs, who would be interested in burthening the people with fiscal arrangements," and one Republican said that if the Federalists were really worried about secret combinations directing the choice of representatives they should have been more upset about "the paper combination" than about the popular societies.[35]

As a rule the Republicans eschewed such retaliation, particularly exposure of Federalist electioneering, in defending the societies. There were several reasons for their restraint. Conclusive evidence was hard to find, as most Federalist activity of this sort was covert, informal, and often relied on extended kinship connections.[36] Furthermore they were frequently as guilty as their antagonists, and, if an accusation should bring countercharges, the Federalists had superior resources for gaining the public ear. Therefore this form of attack would put the societies in the position of fighting the Federalists on their own terms. The opposition knew that the Federalists were not really disturbed by the electioneering potential of the societies. Their wide-ranging connections and superior influence gave them too great an advantage for them to be seriously worried about this. But they wished to associate their opponents with a publicly disapproved activity. Federalist interests would have been served if the controversy over the societies had focused upon electioneering, so the Republicans wisely decided that rather than contest this ground they would concentrate their forces on a more significant objective. This was to alter the national political scene from one where popular involvement was low and factional politics still possible into one where public opinion rather than intrigue would be the vital factor in elections. The Federalists would then lose their advantage.[37]

That is why the societies saw their principal function not as electioneering but as mobilizing public opinion. Their spokesmen turned back to the familiar categories of opposition ideology, assuming antagonism between rulers and ruled. Like their English predecessors, they saw a "natural tendency in all [governments] arising from the imperfection of human nature itself, to slide gradually into the lap of slavery." They attributed this tendency not just to the combination of the powerful but also to the "want of vigilance in the people," "too implicit a deference to precedent, and to the counsels of the celebrated and interested," and most of all to a "want of popular combination." [38] The societies assigned themselves the task of providing a remedy for this state of affairs by spreading information and encouraging political awareness. All the people could not watch the government all the time, so that in the opinion of the Baltimore Republican Society it was necessary to have select groups of men voluntarily establishing societies "to study the laws and constitution of their own and other countries, to watch the operations of government, and scrutinize the principles and conduct of men in power. . . . In times of public necessity [they] would sound the alarm, and, mixing among their fellow citizens, rouse them to a contemplation and sense of their danger." [39]

The need for such organizations in the United States was increased by the vastness of the nation and its ethnic and religious diversity.[40] How could the people act save through such societies? The German Republican Society commented that "[s]olitary opinions have little weight with men whose views are unfair; but the voice of many strikes them with awe. To obtain a connected voice associations of some sort are necessary, no matter by what names they are designated." And the New York Democratic Society added that there was "no better mode of expressing that voice, than by societies whose members are composed of, and mingle with, every class of citizens." [41]

The Federalists were not willing to accept the societies as instruments for mobilizing public opinion. When they addressed themselves explicitly to this claim (which was not often) they replied by professing complete confidence in the spontaneous workings of public opinion. "Order," writing in the Gazette of the United States, declared, "We want no clubs, or chimney corner combinations, to stand centinels for us," and said he was confident that at the first sign of corruption or abuse of power, four million Americans would unite to punish it. When the circular letter of the Democratic

Society of Pennsylvania urged that societies be formed throughout the nation, the citizens of Hanover County, Virginia, replied that the people were already able "by modes prescribed by that Constitution, to correct the abuses which may and will, from time to time, creep into this and *all other human institutions.*" Such organizations, they said, were only proper in *"monarchical and despotic* governments, where the correction of abuses or change of public men cannot otherwise be brought about." [42] The Federalists also argued that public opinion was better left to the spontaneous workings of a free press than abandoned to seduction by secret cabals tolerating only one point of view.[43]

The societies retorted that they had only become secretive when it seemed that this was necessary in order to protect themselves from their adversaries.[44] And they responded to the objection that the societies presented only one side of an issue by pointing out that the government's views were always sure of an airing in the press, and also by challenging the Federalists to form rival societies and engage in public debate.[45] This challenge was usually ignored because acceptance would have furthered the opposition objective of mobilizing public opinion.[46]

III

As goads for an apathetic public and aids to the formation of opinion, it is doubtful whether the societies ever justified the high hopes their founders had of them. They did not do much to bring about that confrontation between Federalist policies and the public which the opposition thought would be their best remedy. Far more effective than anything done by the societies, or even by Republican leaders in Congress, were the provocative acts of Great Britain and the Federalist response to them. Through astute maneuvering they were for a time able to avoid a collision between their policies and growing public concern about foreign relations. but once the terms of the Jay Treaty were released, they saw the very situation they had hoped to avoid looming before them.

Popular sentiment first focused upon Washington, whose signature was still required for ratification. One of the treaty's opponents confidently declared that "the president never will give his sanction to an irrevocable act, which he has the most convincing proofs of the great body of his fellow citizens viewing with hatred, horror and contempt." To do so, he said, would invite "commotions, which would not only be extremely dangerous to the community, but would probably be attended with his own political destruction." [47] It seemed to them that these cautions acquired added strength when the British resumed their seizures of American provision ships. They could not believe that the president would reward the British for these insults by signing so humiliating a treaty.

The evidence suggests that Washington was indeed hoping to bargain for the revocation of the order under which the seizures were taking place by withholding his signature.[48] But unbeknownst to the public, his hand was being forced by the British, who had captured, in the Fauchet correspondence, letters that implicated Secretary of State Edmund Randolph in an intrigue with the French minister. Though the British minister had revealed the correspondence privately to Secretary of the Treasury Oliver Wolcott, Jr., there was nothing to stop his government from making it public at any time. If Washington now refused to sign the treaty, he would risk the publication of these letters and expose his whole administration to a charge of French influence. Every effort made in the Jay negotiations to come to an understanding with Britain would be undone, and her government would have that excuse for war which the Federalists were afraid it wanted. Even before Randolph proved to be unable to defend himself at the full cabinet meeting where he was confronted with the letters, Washington had concluded that his only hope of keeping America neutral was to sign the treaty regardless of British insults.[49]

It now seems likely that Washington's assessment of public opinion would have led him in this direction in any case. That more people had spoken against the treaty than for it did not impress him so much as that opinions were harshly divided, while large blocks of the population had not spoken out on the matter at all. Long after he had signed the treaty, he still doubted "whether the great body of Yeomanry has formed an opinion on the subject." [50] Even if he had been disposed to heed public opinion then, he thought there was no way to discover what it was beyond the common knowledge that most Americans were pro-French. And the indications are that he considered this an argument for rather than against ratification. In a letter to Randolph, he had complained that "this government in relation to France and England may be compared to a ship between the rocks of Scylla and charibdas. If the Treaty is ratified the partisans of the French (or rather of War and confusion) will excite them to hostile measures; . . . if it is not, there is no forseeing *all* the consequences which may follow as it resp[ec]ts G[reat] B[ritain]." It could be said that the people should make the decision because then if there were a disaster they would be more willing to accept it as the result of their own preference. But Washington was worried about the effect public agitation against the treaty might "have on, and the advantage the French government might be disposed to make of, the spirit which is at work." He noted with alarm that it was "the interest of the French . . . to keep *us* and *G. Britain* at variance," and feared that if he gave way to public opinion in this, the nation would never again be independent of France.[51]

Realizing that he was on a collision course with public opinion, Washington declared his independence from it. In a reply to the selectmen of Boston, a reply which later became his circular response to all critics of the treaty, he said:

In every act of my administration, I have sought the happiness of my fellow-citizens. My system for the attainment of this object has uniformly been to overlook all personal, local and partial considerations: to contemplate the United States, as one great whole; to confide, that sudden impressions, when erroneous, would yield to candid reflection: and to consult only the substantial and permanent interests of our country.

He went on to say that when the Constitution had given the president the power of making treaties subject to the advice and consent of the Senate, it was "doubtless supposed that these two branches of government would combine, without passion [and with the best means of information], those facts and principles upon which the success of our foreign relations will always depend: that they ought not to substitute for their own conviction the opinions of others; or to expect truth thro' any channel but that of a temperate and well-informed investigation."[52] Washington's statement that he would not be bound by public opinion in making his decision about the treaty did not escape the notice of the opposition, and this had stirred up violent controversy even before the public found out that he had ratified it.[53]

When the people learned that the president had signed "during the continuance of the [British] orders, in the midst of numerous representations from the people in almost all parts of the United States," [54] their rage was boundless. The national mood found eloquent expression in the press. "A Political Watchman" in the *Jersey Chronicle* lamented that "the nation has been secretly, I will not say treacherously, divorced from France, and most clandestinely married to Great Britain: we are taken from the embraces of a loving wife, and find ourselves in the arms of a detestable and abandoned w[hor]e, covered with crimes, rottenness and corruption.[55] So great was the sense of betrayal that Washington became the object of a vicious personal attack. "Atticus" in the *Independent Gazetteer* observed that the "services of the president, during the revolution" would not "neutralize our indignation, at his having signed the treaty, *after the general sentiments of his country had been made known to him, in opposition to it.*" "Atticus" added:

Is gratitude to put a seal upon our lips under such circumstances? . . . Is the president to receive more reverence than our constitution, and more devotion than liberty? . . . [He has] substituted his will for the will of the people . . . he has thwarted the affections of the people, and in contempt of their attachment to the republic of France, and aversion from Great Britain, has deceived the one, and crouched to the other. . . . Are we to establish a political infallibility, and consecrate a political pope in our country? In signing the treaty, the president has thrown the gauntlet; and shame on the coward heart, that refuses to take it up. He has declared war against the people, by treating their opinions with contempt—he has forfeited his claim to their confidence, by acting in opposition to their will—and shall we not dare to speak our injuries, and proclaim our wrongs! . . . When *men* are substituted for *principles,* liberty is as much outraged, as when the *Deity* is supplanted by a *priest.*[56]

At first Washington's followers were not deterred by the outcry. Encouraged by his declaration of independence from popular sentiment, lesser Federalists were emboldened to launch a sustained assault on it in the public prints, which was much more explicit than anything they had previously hazarded.[57] They seconded Washington's reply to the Boston selectmen, arguing that the people were "without full knowledge of the whole subject and all its relations and consequences." [58] They attacked the way in which the town meetings had framed and passed their resolves, charging that large assemblages in the capital towns were often hastily called before there had been time for the people to receive and digest the facts about the treaty. They alleged that the "first impressions on the minds of the public were made by an abstract of the treaty which was published incorrectly," and Noah Webster, Jr., added that:

[T]here are strong suspicions that [this] was done with the insidious view of exciting improper impressions. The abstract was said to have been made from memory. This cannot be true. It is not in the power of a man, after the most careful perusal, to make out so large an abstract, without the help of notes, of twenty-eight articles of a treaty, without intermixing the articles in the sketch. This business must have been done with design; and it was inexcusable in any man to offer to the public a *sketch*, much more an *incorrect one*, of so important an instrument.

With no more information than this, said the Federalists, and sometimes without even a text of more than the first articles of the treaty, hostile resolves were passed at tumultuous mass meetings by a majority who were "incompetent to decide on the merits of so complex an instrument." [59]

The competency of town meetings was questioned on another ground in a satirical piece in the *Gazette of the United States* by "Fauxborg de St. Antoine." It purported to defend their haste in condemning the treaty as necessary to prevent "aristocrats" from influencing public opinion. Anonymous writers, discussing the treaty in newspapers, would only confuse the issue and the people, to the dismay of liberty:

By the unfair discussion above mentioned a cloud of darkness and obscurity will be thrown on the subject, the public will be divided, and unanimity, the glory of a democratic town meeting, will be frittered away to a small majority. . . . [But w]hen the debate is carried on in open town meeting the audience can see who support, and who oppose, whether they are whigs or tories, members of Congress or candidates; [and] weight will be given to their several candidates accordingly.[60]

The Federalists further complained that the meetings were organized by opponents of the treaty who dispensed with any legal qualification for voting, so that they were often boycotted by the best men. The point they were laboring to make was that because town meetings were not adapted for a full discussion of any subject their majority voice did not deserve to be heeded.[61] A correspondent in the *New York Herald* concluded that even if two-thirds of the people should condemn the treaty, it would not thereby be proved a bad one, and that it was much more likely in "an affair that concerns the intercourse between two nations, in which private intelligence may have a material influence . . . that the decision of the executive would be *right*, though directly against public opinion." [62]

To the hasty incompetence and irresponsibility of the town meetings the Federalists opposed the virtues of Washington and the treaty's supporters. They pointed out that the "Senate formed of men selected by the states from every part of this Union for their wisdom and patriotism, and as the guardians of their political interest in their foreign relations and named by the constitution as the advisors of the chief magistrate, recommended the ratification of the treaty." [63] "Federalist," the author of "Objections to the Treaty Refuted," declared that the senators as individuals "stand higher in the public estimation, as men of pure morals, sound understanding, industrious and steady attention to those duties, with which they had been entrusted" than anyone else.[64] The Federalists also pointed to the respectable minority of merchants and more temperate citizens who had petitioned for ratification. Few had the gall to argue that the "respectability" of the minority should carry more weight than the opinion of the majority, though Washington was accused of implying as much in his replies to supporting addresses from merchants. Such temerity only provoked responses like that of "Mentor," who asked sarcastically if "[o]ut of at least 40,000 independent citizens of the United States" who had expressed opinions on the treaty, one could not procure "a sufficiency of respectability . . . to outweigh that of 1,000 flatterers of administration!" [65] Nevertheless, the Federalists did not hesitate to question that counting noses was the best way to judge the wisdom of a policy, nor to argue that when Jay, Washington, and the Senate approved of the treaty, this was reason enough why those unable to judge for themselves ought also to support it.[66]

A writer calling himself "An American" was moved to ask:

[W]ould it not have been a crime against the principles of our sound constitution, against the principles of a true representative government, to have given up [Washington's] deliberate judgement founded on temperate

well informed investigation, as well as the advice of his constitutional
council chosen by the people, mediately or immediately, to the judgement
of any subdivisions of the people, who in the exercise of a clear right to
petition and address, chose to volunteer their advice? . . . [This] would
have been to have subverted the Constitution, . . . it would have been
creating a new power unknown to the constitution, unknown to the great
body of the people; speedily we should have seen these volunteer counsel-
lors exercising their petitioning authority over every act of government.
Jacobin clubs would have followed to regulate the government on every
important point; all who differed in opinion from these new governors
would have been silenced; terrorism would have been established; and
a Robespierre and a guillotine might have followed.[67]

This approach eventually proved to be more a liability than an
asset. In the first place, the Federalist attempt to impugn the authority of town-meeting resolves in 1795 exposed them to a charge of
inconsistency. "Atticus" was quick to point this out: "When the president's proclamation of neutrality appeared . . . it was thought
proper to convene town meetings in many parts of the states, to
approbate the measure. . . . If aggregate opinions were not improper at that time, by what rule of ratiocination will they be condemned now?" [68]

"Atticus" went on to say that to debate whether or not the officers
of a representative government should be bound by such opinion
raised a fundamental question: "Is ours a government of the people,
or of the officers of government?" [69] To the Federalist objection that
a part of the people could not speak for the whole, he replied: "If
the propriety or the right of many to give an opinion on public
measures is a questionable thing, the right of an individual must
altogether vanish." On whether treaties were beyond the competence
of town meetings to judge, he commented: "If the people had the
right to throw off their allegiance from Great Britain, if they had a
right to subvert the confederation and establish a constitution, will
their right be questioned to express disapprobation of an iniquitous
law?" And he concluded, "Who would be bold enough to say, that the
people have not the right to will their own happiness, under any
form of government, and under what laws they please?" Anyone
who did so would also have to argue that "instead of a republic, we
are an oligarchy." [70]

"Atticus" was right. The Federalists could not openly defend the position that magistrates should reject their constituents' views when these were made plain to them.[71] Nor could they deny that town resolves were legitimate vehicles for the expression of public opinion. The most they could do was question that the many town and country resolves upon the Jay Treaty were true expressions of majority opinion. They protested that not one town in a hundred had passed resolves either for or against the treaty, and that an "unqualified and unasked" minority in the capital towns should not be allowed to speak for the majority who lived in the interior.[72] Not that this led them to urge these silent men to speak up. They preferred the theory that their opinions had already been expressed through the president and the two-thirds of the Senate that had sanctioned the treaty, observing that the Senate majority included a representative from every state but two.[73] This attempt to dress up the power of the president and Senate in more flattering garb did not calm the anger that had been aroused by their elitist pretensions and the terms of the treaty. But they continued to insist on implementation even though they risked causing a rupture with France, for which they would have to answer to the people. In the end, they could bring themselves to compromise only the way in which they achieved their objectives, and not the objectives themselves.

6. *Style*

The Federalists had started out with a style to match their contempt for public opinion and their desire to keep the decisions of government out of the people's hands as far as possible. The administration's response to the war crisis in early 1794 was a perfect demonstration of it. Washington pre-empted congressional initiatives by appointing Jay, an act which closed the door on those provocative measures that an angry public hotly desired, and confined the settlement of outstanding differences with Britain to the president and the Senate, branches of the federal government less vulnerable to public opinion than the House. In 1794, Federalist congressmen had even defended this aloofness. Samuel Dexter urged the House to stand firm against public opinion because "We ought to judge that nothing will be popular which is not right." And in the congressional debate over Clark's motion, Zephaniel Swift boldly declared that "let the popular opinion be what it would, too much had been said about it. We are not to be influenced by such considerations, but are only to regard the public welfare." [1] Swift could be so emphatic because no one could deny that the nation's interests would best be served by peace, provided that satisfactory terms could be gained through negotiation. Once the terms of the treaty had been released, however, it quickly became clear that Federalist writings, which tried to justify defiance of public opinion, were simply increasing the people's angry abhorrence of it. So they gave up the attempt and tried instead to cool the popular temper, hoping that time would make the people and their congressional representatives more amenable to persuasion.

I

There was much to be said for such a strategy. For one thing, it was consistent with their wish to isolate themselves from public opinion. For another, circumstances favored it. The abrogation of Article 12 meant ratifications again had to be exchanged with Great Britain, and in consequence, the treaty would probably not be presented to the House for implementation until the beginning of the spring. Much might occur before then to the Federalists' advantage; indeed, it did, for the administration succeeded in making favorable treaties with the Indians, the Algerians, and Spain. The Spanish treaty in particular, because it opened the Mississippi to western commerce, so appealed to backcountry people that thereafter they supported the administration on the Jay Treaty.[2] Then the Federalists realized that once ratifications had been exchanged and the treaty made law—actions the president could take without consulting the House—opposition to the treaty would wear a different look. Unilateral abrogation of a fully ratified treaty would have more serious consequences than rejection of one still being negotiated, and the opposition would have to assume full responsibility, not only for throwing its benefits away, but also for any subsequent worsening in Anglo-American relations.[3] Moreover, such opposition could then be stigmatized as resistance to government itself.[4] The Republicans evidently understood this all too well, for in December 1795 Hamilton passed to Rufus King the rumor that Abraham Baldwin and Albert Gallatin had "made up their minds to consider the Treaty, if ratified by Britain, as *conclusive upon the H. of Representatives.*"[5] Lastly, the Federalists knew that Washington's popularity was still their trump card, despite the people's first hostility to the treaty. Throughout early 1796, they worked to magnify Washington's prestige, particularly through local celebrations of his birthday, so that his proclamation of the treaty would have the greatest possible effect.[6]

The treaty was promulgated on February 29, but Federalist belief that Washington would carry all before him when he issued the proclamation was rudely shattered. Though some opposition leaders were reluctant to challenge the president, Edward Livingston forced the issue on March 2 by moving that he be asked to lay before the House all documents relating to negotiation of the treaty.[7] When Uriah Tracy asked Livingston what the purpose of this was, he replied by expressing his "firm conviction that the House were vested with a discretionary power of carrying the Treaty into effect, or refusing it their sanction."[8] Though the Federalists knew "that a majority [was] prejudiced against the treaty," and though they would not have been surprised by attempts to pass resolutions in the House condemning it, they still expected the Republicans to appropriate the money for implementation because there would be "too much responsibility in deciding wrong."[9] Now, by raising the constitutional issue first, Livingston's motion had put them on the defensive. It was clear from the start that the motion would pass, and all who had been privy to drafting Jay's instructions knew they contained matter that would make the people more furious than ever.[10] So the executive would either have to release incriminating material or defy the House. If he chose defiance, the only possible justification would be that the making of treaties belonged to the president and Senate alone, that the House was bound to make appropriations for implementation just as the executive was bound to execute a law sanctioned by two-thirds of both houses of Congress, and that therefore it had no business with the papers. But in this there was a risk of reviving the previous summer's storm over the claims for exclusive presidential power in making treaties.[11]

Despite this dilemma, Federalists in Congress resolved to take up the constitutional challenge in the House. To have done otherwise would have been to concede this point forever to the opposition. And though there were hazards in this course, they were probably on stronger ground constitutionally than they would have been in any discussion of the treaty's merits. They could appeal to the formal wording of the Constitution, while the opposition would have to explain it away. They could also cast the opposition as "disorganizers" if they chose to obstruct the treaty. There was the risk that if they were badly beaten in the House on the constitutional issue, public opposition to the treaty would appear to be constitutionally sanctioned. But this would vanish if Washington supported the minority and refused the papers, as in the end he did.[12] Meanwhile the Federalists could continue to challenge the House's authority to express public opinion. They argued that it was not a true representation of the public will because when its members had been chosen the democratic societies had violated the freedom of elections. They said that the state legislatures which rejected the constitutional amendments proposed by Virginia in response to the treaty spoke more truly for the public mind, because, having been more recently elected, they were free of club influences.[13] At the same time, Federalists within the House extolled the representative character of the president and Senate.

So when Livingston's motion passed by a resounding majority of sixty-two to thirty-seven,[14] the Federalists in Congress did not despair. Though the majority was greater than they liked, its effect on public opinion was thought to be nullified by the president's firm refusal to surrender the papers. They remained hopeful of implementation until the middle of April,[15] when it was learned that an opposition majority of fifty-seven had decided to refuse appropriations.[16] What spurred the Republicans to this extreme is not certain. But there may be a clue in a resolve proposed by Samuel Maclay that given "the conduct of Great Britain, in persevering, since the Treaty was signed, in the impressment of American seamen and the seizure of American vessels (laden with provisions) . . . with such information as the House possesses it is not expedient at this time to concur in passing the laws necessary for carrying the said Treaty into effect." This suggests that the president's refusal to submit papers was thought especially provocative since the resolution acknowledged the British outrages were not new.[17] Such a resolve was not an uncompromising rejection. The treaty might still be implemented if certain conditions were fulfilled.[18] Nevertheless, Federalists like Oliver Wolcott, Jr., feared delay would serve no other purpose than "to alarm the British government and to set their privateers upon our commerce under an expectation of war." He angrily declared that "[T]he leaders of the party know that the British government does not conceive the treaty to be any great boon, and that unless we execute, they will not. They also know that by defeating the treaty, losses and injuries will happen, which will renew the animosities between us and Great Britain, and by which they shall profit." [19]

The prospect was alarming enough to prod the Federalists into a radical departure from their strategy of merely neutralizing public opinion. Hamilton immediately wrote a letter to King declaring that "[G]reat evils may result unless good men play their cards well & with promptitude and decision. For we must seize and carry along with us the public opinion; and the loss of time may be the loss of everything." Hamilton suggested a presidential protest containing the "reasons in detail against the claim of the House in point of Constitutional right," and stating "summarily but with solemnity and energy the danger to the interests & Peace of the country from the measures of the House." This protest would be seconded by Senate resolves, which would set the pattern for merchant resolves and petitions circulated through the nation.[20]

The elaborate plan was never put to the test. Instead, in an effort to gain six votes from those of the opposition who favored the motion for implementation that was then before the House, the Federalists decided "to risque the consequences of delay, and prolong the debates, in expectation of an impulse from some of the districts on their representatives." Chauncey Goodrich had already observed that both Gallatin and William Findley were under pressure from their constituents to vote for implementation, and that New Jersey was "becoming electrical, and expresses no small indignation against the pusillanimous conduct of some of their members." The Federalists were nonetheless pessimistic about this course of action because the towns, the only places in which it could work at such short notice, were "discontented and factious."[21]

Still, they were desperate enough to begin circulating memorials in the principal towns urging the House to vote appropriations. Needless to say, the opposition followed suit. Massachusetts, New York, and Pennsylvania in particular, witnessed a struggle prolonged throughout April and May between those for and those against the treaty, each seeking decisive authority for their claim to represent the public mind. It is noteworthy that the Federalists were better at competing with the opposition in the spring of 1796 than they had been in the summer and fall of 1795. Not only did they gather more signatures on their memorials, but also there were more memorials in support of the treaty than against it. And though the opposition tried calling town meetings to condemn them, this maneuver did not always succeed. In Boston the town meeting that had issued the first and most resounding condemnation of the treaty in July 1795 was captured by the pro-treaty forces in April 1796 and prevented from censuring the Federalist memorial. Though the *Independent Chronicle* accused the Federalists of packing the town meetings with country traders (in lines reminiscent of those once written by Federalists objecting to town resolves against the treaty), the opposition was certainly knocked off its accustomed perch. Even where meetings were held condemning memorials in favor of ratification—in New York, for instance—people were not deterred from signing them.[22]

It is not hard to see why the Federalists were more successful at harnessing public opinion in 1796 than they had been in 1795. For one thing, their new strategy implicitly acknowledged the legitimacy of public opinion. For another, many of those who first opposed the treaty had probably accepted it as *fait accompli* after the president's ratification. Finally those who were for the treaty had more at stake than those against it. The mercantile community, which stood to gain $5,000,000 in compensation for spoliations, was anxious enough for implementation to pay for it by private subscription if the House had refused appropriations. Their commercial connections gave these men greater facility than their opponents in circulating memorials and obtaining signatures. As one Republican in Congress observed, they had formed committees of correspondence to influence the House. Where their commercial connections did not reach, they could make use of the clergy, and in Massachusetts even county grand juries, in circularizing the towns. They could also gain the cooperation of those beyond their immediate group through their ability to affect provision prices. When the underwriters in the principal ports decided to stop insuring cargoes bound for foreign destinations, because there was a risk of war if the treaty were rejected, the price of provisions had dropped sharply. For many, particularly those in debt to the men circulating the memorials, this was a powerful persuasion to sign. The Republican press later charged that signatures had been obtained by resort to economic pressure, but this was only part of the story. The Federalists had also tried harder. They felt that they were on the verge of losing everything, while the Republicans had less to lose and more reason to be confident of victory.[23]

This flurry of extra-congressional activity eventually played but a small part in the House's final decision. For the assertion of the treaty's proponents that "if ever there was a public opinion well known, it was, that this Treaty ought to be executed in good faith," had been hyperbole for the occasion, and was more vulnerable than the Federalists would admit to the very arguments they had used against similar Republican claims.[24] The best they could do to support the superior authority of their own petitions was to charge that opposition to the treaty had been born of ephemeral passions fired by a mixture of prejudice, misinformation, French influence, and party intransigence. Fisher Ames said anti-British sentiment was so great that the public would have disliked any treaty, whatever its terms, and this claim seems to be confirmed by the "Franklin" letters which were published before disclosure of the Jay Treaty.

The Federalists argued that what counted was not the first angry voice raised in opposition, but the growing support for the treaty as shown by the memorials of spring 1796. They attributed this to the cooling of popular passion and the success of the Federalist press in replacing public ignorance with knowledge of the treaty's advantages. This in turn, they said, had encouraged the more respectable members of the community, those more aware of their interests than their passions, to express their opinion.[25] But these arguments in themselves could not be expected to affect the House visibly and dramatically. Nor did the memorials do much to change the minds of congressmen who had made them up on the matter. Only one member who voted for the treaty admitted that his constituents had governed him,[26] though several of its opponents may have absented themselves from the final roll calls because of popular feeling in their constituencies. Even so, this left treaty supporters facing a hostile majority in the House of Representatives, which seemed resolved, if not to obstruct ratification, at least to delay implementation until Great Britain ceased her depredations on American commerce.

In the end, the Federalists won by a tour de force of persuasion in the House. Running true to form, they put more emphasis on the uncertain but (so they claimed) disastrous consequences of rejection than on the positive advantages of the treaty. Opponents were quick to perceive this, and to charge that they were distracting attention from substantive objections by appealing to the fears rather than the reason of the House. Yet this very accusation, repeated often throughout the debate, shows that once the Federalists had neutralized the influence of hostile opinion their opponents were thrown on the defensive in spite of having a clear majority. So does John Swanwick's plea that the House should maintain its independence of the "many wise and virtuous and dignified men" among them in the government who supported the treaty. The Federalists did not have to win over every member of the opposition: it sufficed that they pry loose nine or ten of the most timid. And although the opposition vowed that they would not be threatened into ratification, and that the House had superior sources of information to justify a different course from the president and Senate, the result shows that a significant few were yielding.[27]

The Federalists rang many ingenious changes on the theme of the disastrous consequences that would follow if the treaty were not ratified, but the two they emphasized were foreign war and the internal dissolution of the state, proceeding from it as well as from the bitterness caused among all parts of the government by refusal to implement.[28] These were scarcely credible charges. The people would not allow the president and Senate to be at loggerheads with the House indefinitely, even if the Federalists were so irrational as to attempt to destroy the government because they could not get their way.[29] Madison also pointed out that apart from Britain's respect for her financial interests, now that the First Coalition was dissolving, for her to declare "an unprovoked war . . . on this country, would argue a degree of madness greater than under any other circumstances that could well be imagined." [30] Furthermore, if refusal to implement might bring about war with Britain, who could say that implementation would not bring about war with France? [31] The Republicans were not persuaded by Federalist arguments, and only one, Aaron Kitchell, seems to have taken seriously the threats of secession that were circulating in Congress.[32] Yet in the end the opposition crumbled. Three declared opponents of the treaty were absent from the final roll call,[33] and nine Republicans ended up voting with the Federalist majority. Most prominent among them was Samuel Smith of Baltimore.[34] He was joined by Gabriel Christie, Jeremiah Crabb, and George Dent, also of Maryland; by Theodorus Bailey and Philip Van Cortlandt of New York; by Frederick Muhlenberg and Andrew Gregg of Pennsylvania, and Kitchell of New Jersey.[35]

What caused the Republicans to yield was not simply unwillingness to be responsible for aborting a peaceful accommodation with a great power. Ten years later, the Republicans showed no hesitation in rejecting the Monroe-Pinkney treaty with Great Britain, even though this led to a decline in relations between the two countries for which the Federalists blamed them. If they had controlled the executive and Senate in 1796, they would undoubtedly have delayed implementation, at least until Britain had given satisfaction on impressment and seizures, confident of their ability to parry British hostility and any Federalist attempt to exploit it. As it was, the opposition had no choice but acquiescence, because they were unable to influence Britain's response to a suspension of the treaty, and there would then be nothing to stop the Federalists from pinning on them the unpopularity arising from the increasing British pressure that might be expected. Moreover, the Federalists were in a position to use their decisive control of the Senate to block appropriations for the advantageous Indian, Algerian, and Spanish treaties, or even to obstruct all government operations until either the House gave way or federal elections were held.[36]

On the other hand, if the Republicans accepted the treaty while making their reluctance manifest, and if Franco-American relations then degenerated, a public generally inclined to favor France would probably blame the Federalists and elect the opposition in their place.[37] This strategy was the more attractive to Republicans because while it gave the Federalists no excuse for carrying matters to extremes, it denied France nothing she needed to preserve her republicanism. In 1793–1794, when France had been in desperate straits, an alliance between Britain and the United States might have jeopardized her future as a republic. In 1796, France was no longer in military danger.[38] Madison was aware of the risks incurred by courting French hostility, but reasoning such as this undoubtedly made him try to persuade others to drop their opposition and settle for condemning the administration in motions like Henry Dearborn's, which warned that the treaty "may prove injurious to the United States." [39]

II

The Federalists succeeded in extracting a reluctant consent to the treaty from the House of Representatives, just as a few years before they had succeeded in reducing antifederalist majorities to minorities in the ratifying conventions of four key states. Their skill was in manipulating small, elite groups, and if they had been able to suit themselves they would have confined their activities to this sphere, leaving public opinion alone. They expected no positive return to themselves from it, and hoped only to circumvent or ignore it. They knew a republican government depended on public opinion for the execution of the law, but they assumed that it would also be the most powerful force which shaped opinion, and that so long as their rulers never went against their interests the people would defer to them.[40] Whatever else was needed in order to keep the people loyal they thought could be supplied through education. Fisher Ames wrote to George R. Minot in 1789 that "[s]ome are of opinion that ignorance produces loyalty. In 1786, it was found otherwise, and I believe it ever will be found, that the best informed among the people are the most governable." In another he looked forward to the time when "this country *will be* what China is, with this difference, that freedom and science shall do here, what bigotry and prejudice do there to secure government." He was not alone in these opinions, for many Federalists believed that education would teach the people to respect their superiors.[41]

This hope, which seemed to be justified by public response to the fiscal controversy, was shaken by the neutrality crisis. The people's enthusiasm for the French Revolution made it clear to the Federalists that they would have to take a more active part in shaping opinion than merely educating the public. Even before their foreign policy was subjected to any massive attack, their attempt to remain at peace with the belligerents was challenged in 1793 when Gideon Henfield, tried for enlisting on a French privateer, was acquitted despite the administration's obvious desire for a conviction and the opinion of the attorney general, together with the chief justice, that his action had been illegal.[42] Neutrality was an unusual issue because the act of one person could conceivably compromise a whole nation; nevertheless, Henfield's acquittal proved that it was not enough for the Federalists simply to ignore public opinion. Unless they were prepared to compromise with it, and on what they considered essentials they were not, they would have to try molding it to their liking. So they reluctantly began to develop ways of extending their methods of manipulation from the elite few to the general public.

It might seem at first that this made them no more manipulative than their opponents but merely indistinguishable from them. The Republicans had done their share of shaping opinion by means of the democratic societies. The Federalist party press, including such journals as the *Columbian Centinel,* the *Minerva,* and the *Gazette of the United States,* was matched by Republican newspapers like the *Independent Chronicle,* Thomas Greenleaf's New York *Journal,* the *General Advertiser* or *Aurora,* and the Richmond *Examiner.* And though the Federalists used their press not just to present their case but also to associate their opponents with unpopular causes or values, such as the Jacobin excesses of France, they would have seen little difference between this and what they considered the slandering of their motives by the opposition press.[43] Certainly both Federalists and Republicans placed equal reliance on public addresses and resolves.

Nevertheless, these similarities should not be allowed to obscure the markedly different styles that each party cultivated. That of the opposition was determined by Madison's belief that it was enough to awaken the people to their danger, diffuse information, and measure Federalist words and deeds against revolutionary and republican ideals. Despite passing frustrations, because they were confident that in the end the people would see things as they did,[44] they welcomed the prospect of an aroused public and put their faith chiefly in the power of exposure. The Federalists, by contrast, having no reason to assume that this would spontaneously work in their favor, were at a disadvantage. They had to be considerably more aggressive in molding public opinion for they were trying to instruct the people in "truths" to which they were not naturally sympathetic. And they stood in mortal fear that an aroused populace would be uncontrollable. As a result, every time they succeeded in persuading the people to take positive action, they themselves grew nervous and felt again the old desire to suppress popular politics. Because their objectives were both difficult to realize and inherently contradictory, they were forced to ever more strenuous exertions.

Yet to balance their strategic disadvantages, the Federalists had certain assets of their own. The greatest of these was control of the federal executive. Until the end of 1793, this was qualified by Jefferson's presence in the cabinet, but thereafter it became nearly absolute. They also enjoyed almost exclusive title to Washington's prestige, and both Federalists and Republicans assessed the value of this highly. Only Washington's declaration that he would not let public opinion sway his decision on the treaty had emboldened the Federalists to suggest that it should not have any effect upon government. And when he ratified the treaty, Massachusetts Federalists assumed that this would put a stop to all local opposition.[45] Not that Federalists in the cabinet were ever entirely sure what Washington would do. When they took their constitutional stand on the power of the House with respect to treaties, they did not act with complete confidence that he would support them by refusing to deliver the documents. Usually, however, they did not have to act before he did, and their commanding position in the government gave them a chance to make his opinions the same as their own. This capability served them well when they had to deal not only with Genêt's intrigues but also with a challenge to their power in the form of an insurrection.

III

Next to the people's enthusiasm for the French Revolution, the Federalists regarded the activities of the French ambassador, Citizen Genêt, as the principal threat to American neutrality. He had armed and commissioned French privateers in American ports, encouraged Americans to enlist on board these vessels, and enlisted others to seize Spain's possessions in Florida and Louisiana. Nor did the president's proclamation stop him; indeed, he continued his activities right under the government's nose in Philadelphia.

His most notorious escapade concerned the *Little Sarah*, a British armed merchantman seized by a French privateer illegally fitted out in Charleston. She had been brought into Philadelphia, renamed the *Petite Democrat*, and rearmed, apparently as a privateer. At the British minister's prodding, the cabinet sought to have the *Petite Democrat* detained until the president could return to Philadelphia and determine the government's policy toward such vessels. The Pennsylvania secretary of state, Alexander J. Dallas, asked Genêt to agree that the vessel would remain in Philadelphia until the president arrived, but Genêt refused. He made it clear that if there were any attempt to seize the vessel he would resist with force, and that he would not necessarily recognize the authority of any ruling Washington might make. Later, when Jefferson approached Genêt, he received verbal assurance that the vessel would not sail until the president's return. Jefferson followed this up with a written request, but a short time later the *Petite Democrat* departed.[46] After this open defiance, the administration resolved to have Genêt recalled.[47]

The administration might have let this suffice, but certain members of the cabinet, so Jefferson observed, were determined to go further. Hamilton's party, "sensible of the advantage they have got," was agitating for the government to appeal directly to the people, and though Jefferson hoped to prevent this he thought the president was interested.[48] In the end, Hamilton's object was achieved without formal action by the administration. Rumors were circulated that Genêt had threatened to appeal the president's concept of neutrality to the people, and an affidavit was published under the names of Jay and King testifying that this was true. It emerged later that neither of them had been witness to the reported exchange between Dallas and Genêt, and Dallas stated that the French ambassador had made no such threat but had only hinted that he might appeal to Congress.[49] Details were not significant, however. Even Jefferson agreed that Genêt had made some kind of threat, and documentary evidence of his impetuosity was to be found in his subsequent correspondence with the secretary of state and the president.[50] The point was that the people had learned of this, not from Genêt himself, but from the chief justice of the United States and the senator from New York. The Federalists had turned the tables on Genêt, and forced the people to choose between his interpretation of neutrality and that of their revolutionary hero and president.

The avalanche of addresses that descended upon the president during the late summer and autumn of 1793, pledging the people's support against foreign intervention and endorsing his neutrality policy, must have been gratifying to the Federalists. Yet they had misgivings about it too. Perhaps this was partly because they knew that they were trying to condemn Genêt for what they had effectually done themselves. The Republican opposition was quick to point this out and accuse them of inconsistency.[51] In his column "No Jacobin," Hamilton replied that the "right of appealing from the rulers of a nation to the nation itself . . . belongs exclusively to the members of that nation," and pointed out to the people that a foreign ambassador was challenging their president's authority.[52] But it was also because they regarded popular politics as both essentially distasteful and self-defeating. When Genêt was in New York City, Federalists had no choice but to counteract his presence by proposing public resolutions endorsing the president's policy. But Rufus King betrayed his misgivings when he complained that in principle this technique was "altogether wrong. . . . It was never expected . . . the government should be carried on by town meetings." [53] And on the eve of their appeal Oliver Wolcott, Jr., wrote to Noah Webster, Jr., that "as this is the first attempt of the kind which has been made, it is important that it should have such an issue as will render another improbable." [54] In other words, the Federalists hoped that their first resort to public opinion would also be their last.

Colonel William Willcocks, a member of Hamilton's New York City connection and a Federalist officeholder, wrote a widely circulated letter to accompany the Jay-King affidavit which illuminates the full Federalist design in appealing to the people. Of all Genêt's indiscretions to date, the worst had been the threat to resist detention of the *Petite Democrat* with force and his refusal to delay her departure until the president had decided upon her status. But Willcocks barely mentioned these. Instead he dwelt upon the threat of appeal to the people. "God forbid," he wrote, "that in this happy, free, and enlightened community, we, or our posterity, should ever see the day, that a mob, especially under the auspices of any foreign influence, or connivance, should assume the reins of government and dictate . . . the law of the land." But Willcocks was after bigger game than foreign influence. He went on to condemn all popular politics, arguing that government officials "virtually constitute, and *are the people,* by representation, freely and legally conferred." If the people objected to actions taken by their representatives, they had the power to speak, petition, and vote.[55] Nevertheless, "all acts of the people, in their individual capacity, assuming legislative, judicial, or executive powers, are incompatible with the authority constitutionally and freely invested, by them, in their representatives: And are null and void." He blamed Genêt and the opposition leadership for popular agitation over neutrality, remarking that "it is somewhat extraordinary, that the spirit of jealousy and faction, which showed itself heretofore with the greatest caution and decency, since the arrival of the French Ambassador has broke, with volcanic fury, threatening the President, the Secretary of the Treasury, and other officers, in its way, in short, the government itself, with annihilation." At the same time he accused Genêt of forming an alliance "with certain designing men to the southward." [56] This letter makes it clear that the Federalists hoped both to defend the nation's neutrality and to crush the opposition together with all tendencies toward popular politics. They were at one and the same time appealing to the people and asking them to stay out of politics.

The societies forced them into similar inconsistencies. At first the Federalists had thought that to dignify them with attention might only succeed in magnifying their importance, with the result that men who were deeply disturbed by them nevertheless refrained from direct attack, concentrating their fire upon Genêt instead. They thought that the societies had been quickened by his arrival in America, and would die when he was disgraced. This is probably why Willcocks did not mention them in his letter.[57] When they failed to disappear with Genêt, and instead proliferated even faster than before, the Federalists became alarmed and decided to take stronger measures. It is worth noting that the torrent of abuse directed against them by the Federalist papers was not in full spate until 1794. To some extent, this change of strategy was their response to Madison's resolves and the news of British depredations, factors producing a political crisis in which the influence of the societies might prove decisive. Their objections transcended the exigencies of the moment, however, and from 1794 on they were relentless in their efforts to wipe the societies out.

In pursuit of this objective, the Federalists made an even more heroic effort to manipulate public opinion. As in the Genêt incident, they were driven to adopt a strategy they did not really like by a serious challenge to their authority. This time it was the Whiskey Rebellion. The war crisis of 1794 had created a situation where the nation was faced with a loss of revenue through the interruption of foreign commerce just as defense expenditures were likely to rise, and this had impelled the government to enforce the excise in western Pennsylvania for the first time.[58] The result was an armed insurrection. Later, the Federalists succeeded so well in turning this episode to account that their critics suspected them of engineering it.[59] But it is hardly likely that a man who had so many doubts about republican government as Hamilton would have deliberately manufactured a rebellion in the midst of a foreign crisis. He was anxious to avoid war with Britain by negotiating with her, and no foreign power would respect the sovereignty of a government subject to challenge by seditious minorities. Moreover, the administration could not be sure that the people would support the government against the insurgents. Several days after Washington had called for troops, he wrote to a Virginia correspondent nervously enquiring if the state militia was going to cooperate with the government. And in some sections of western Maryland and Virginia adjacent to the Pennsylvania rebels, it soon became clear they were not.[60] Once the government did have the assurance that troops would be forthcoming, though, they made the most of the occasion with a show of force designed to prove that the federal government was master in its house, to discourage future rebellion, and to deter the British from aggression in the Northwest.[61]

They did not stop there, for the insurrection gave them a chance to strike at the hated societies. Long before its outbreak, Federalist critics had commented upon the similarities between these and the Jacobin clubs in France and branded them as hotbeds of sedition which imperiled the federal government. They argued that such organizations were only necessary when there were no legitimate remedies for oppression. A correspondent in the *Gazette of the United States* commented that:

Nobody will deny the usefulness of popular Societies, in cases of revolutions. The reason is obvious. By forming the people together into clubs, and giving to all those clubs, a central point of union, a bad government may be shaken down: for it has to oppose, not scattered and dispirited complainers, who may be kept under the harrow of the law, and demolished as fast as they show themselves, but it has to oppose an organized body, acting in phalanx, thus tyranny is pulled down because it is overmatched, and perhaps there is no other way to pull it down.[62]

In the American Revolution, for instance, popular sentiment had been organized through committees of correspondence, but there was no need for this in 1794, when Americans were enjoying the freest government on earth. If those who ran the societies should insist on their use even so, the result would be the same as in France where the Jacobin clubs had senselessly destroyed the constitution.[63] To dramatize this point, the Federalists asked their southern opponents what would happen if the slaves clubbed together.[64]

When the Whiskey Rebellion broke out, it seemed to be confirmation of these charges. Several of the societies were implicated, and one, that of Mingo Creek, had played a central part in fomenting the rebellion.[65] This put the societies on the defensive, as their spokesmen betrayed in the new tack they took toward critics. Earlier in 1794, they had interpreted rising criticism in the public prints as further proof that they were on the trail of some despotic conspiracy. The Pennsylvania Democratic Society thought it natural that "political associations which have for their object the restrictions of government within constitutional bounds, [would] excite the disaffection of those whose principles and measures are the subjects of enquiry and attention." [66] By the end of 1794, however, the societies had retreated into weak complaints that they were libeled instead of reasoned with. The martial tone of the Pennsylvania Democratic Society had become a whimper that influential men were unfairly using the insurrection to discredit it.[67] And this defensiveness was subsequently accentuated by the new Federalist tactic of governmental censure.

IV

Throughout 1793–1794, Washington had been concerned about the danger of westerners conducting filibusters against Spanish Louisiana, attributing such local attempts to usurp governmental authority to the subversive clubs spawned by Genêt. The Whiskey Rebellion at last impelled him to drastic action. After some hesitancy, he decided that in his annual message to Congress in November 1794 he would openly condemn "certain self-created societies" for fomenting the insurrection.[68] The Federalist-dominated Senate was quick to respond. In its reply to the president's address, the language was carefully chosen so as to condemn not only the societies directly implicated but all that had criticized the proceedings of government:

Our anxiety arising from the licentiousness and open resistance to the law in the Western counties of Pennsylvania, has been increased by the proceedings of certain self-created societies, relative to the laws and administration of the Government; proceedings in our apprehension, founded in political error, calculated, if not intended, to disorganize our Government, and which, by inspiring delusive hopes of support, have been influential in misleading our fellow-citizens in the scene of insurrection.

The Federalists were plainly maneuvering for a condemnation of societies by both houses of Congress in the hope that this, together with Washington's remarks, would decisively shape public opinion. An attempt to defeat this strategy in the Senate was a failure.[69] But in the House, where the Republican opposition was strong, the committee entrusted with replying to the president's speech did not even mention the societies. Thomas Fitzsimmons, a Philadelphia Federalist, then proposed an amendment that would have exceeded even the Senate's language in warmth:

As part of this subject, we cannot withhold our reprobation of the self-created societies, which have risen up in some parts of the Union, misrepresenting the conduct of the Government, and disturbing the operation of the laws, and which, by deceiving and inflaming the ignorant and weak, may naturally be supposed to have stimulated and urged the insurrection.[70]

This motion provoked a long and bitter debate in the House on the role of popular societies in the republic.

Defenders of the societies at once retorted that if anyone was guilty of self-created authority, it was the legislature in trying to condemn them. William Giles of Virginia was the first to argue in the House that it was "out of the way of the legislature" to criticize "particular classes of men." "Who can tell where they will stop," he asked. "Gentlemen were sent to this House, not for the purpose of passing indiscriminate votes of censure, but to legislate only." Giles warned the House not to interfere with the "delicate right" of associating and expressing one's opinions. Such interference was surely not necessary, for the societies were subject to all the normal restraints of the law, and "if the self-created societies act contrary to law, they are unprotected, and let the law pursue them. That a man is a member of one of these societies will not protect him from an accusation for treason, if the charge is well-founded." So long as they kept within the law, he concluded, the government had no business interfering with the societies in any way.[71]

The Federalists in Congress were not to be deterred from censuring the societies by this. Ames would hear nothing of the notion that the House had no such right, asking, "Are gentlemen who profess so much attachment to the people, and their rights, disposed to abolish one of the most signal, the character of this House as the grand inquest of the Nation?" It was the duty of such a body to expose all public abuses, he said, and could anyone doubt that the societies were a public abuse? [72] William Laughton Smith agreed that "the dissemination of improper sentiment [was] a suitable object for the public reprobation of the House." Realizing that his remarks could be construed as denying rights guaranteed by the Constitution, he quickly added that "he was a friend to the freedom of the press; but would any one compare a regular town meeting where deliberations were cool and unruffled, to these societies?" [73] The supporters of Fitzsimmons's motion said that they were not trying to deny the right of organizing political clubs. They agreed that men should be free to associate provided their associations served the interests of society, but added that "the power to violate the rights of others, and disturb the public peace with impunity, has been profanely called liberty. . . . Freedom consists rather in what it forbids than what it allows." In other words, congressional critics claimed that they were not condemning the societies for exercising the right to associate but for abusing it.[74]

The Federalists believed that the opposition also abused the freedom of the press,[75] but they singled out the societies for congressional condemnation because they were wary of antagonizing the newspapers when they already had their hands full. Because the Whiskey Rebellion occurred shortly after the most violent phase of the French Revolution, they could argue that more evil influence was exercised through the societies than through the press. In the *Gazette of the United States*, "Anti-Club" wrote: "While these attacks were simply the feeble efforts of scattered individuals, their malevolence was less to be dreaded than despised; but at this day when their inchoate projects have ripened into a regular system, strengthened by numerous combinations and spreading themselves all over the continent," they were more dangerous. Another critic asked what must "result from a combination of all the disaffected persons in a country, in pursuit of a favorite object—[Would it not be] continually strengthening by additions to its numbers?" Certainly Ames thought that "the credulous, the ignorant, the rash and violent, [would be] drawn by artifice, or led by character, to join these confederacies." Was there no danger that they would acquire more influence than the legitimate government, like the Jacobin societies in France? [76]

Spokesmen for the societies acknowledged that they banded together because they were composed of obscure individuals. But they vehemently denied that popular societies in the United States might ever have greater influence than the government, as in France. "Agis" in the New York *Journal* argued that the Jacobins had gained their ascendancy because there was no constitution, and because the people were not generally informed about "the distinction between private associations and general representation—between recommendation and legislation." This had made it easier for aristocrats to pervert the people's power and use it to serve their own ends. The clubs in France had also been coeval with the revolution, causing "a tide of popular prejudice and zeal in their favor, which might second even their extravagance; and the more so, because the national representation there have been much connected with the clubs, etc., and have generally shown them great deference and reverence." The American Revolution, in contrast, had been conducted by a Congress which continuously supervised affairs, to which "habit and prepossession must give at least all due advantage of popular confidence." Nor had anyone in the French government enjoyed anything like the prestige of a Washington. "What advantage then," asked "Agis," "in the scale of popularity, could recent political societies expect in opposition to such a government (even if they wished for any) in an enlightened country like this, further than from the conviction, that irresistible truth and reason must impress in every wise and virtuous breast?" [77]

The societies did not deny that the right of free speech could be abused, but they questioned that legislative censure was the appropriate remedy, and suggested that a jury representing the public at large would be a better means of restraining excesses.[78] They pointed out that the advocates of congressional censure were condemning in others what they proposed to do themselves. If the societies were wrong to encourage opinions critical of the government, surely the House was wrong to infringe upon the freedom of opinion by attempting to turn people against the societies.[79] Most Federalists denied that this was their intention, but said they meant rather to act as sentinels, the same excuse as the societies had used. Samuel Dexter protested, "We do not contend for controlling, or even animadverting, on the rights of opinion, or of publishing opinions. We wish only to call the attention of the public to the abuses of those rights, and the crimes such abuses have produced, (which endanger the existence of those rights, and liberty in general) in order that the people, knowing the evil, may themselves correct it." William Vans Murray thought it was the legislature's duty to erect "a warning beacon . . . [illuminating] the stormy breakers which lately threatened the public peace with shipwreck," and to invite the people "to adhere to pilots of their own choosing, and to charts with which they were acquainted." He "could not see any evil that was to result from an expression of the opinion of the House, by the proposed amendment," which did not interfere in any way with free speech or the freedom of the press. He thought that it was more likely "to excite a judicious and salutary inquiry among many respecting the just and true limits within which a virtuous and enlightened well wisher to our country would think it safe to exercise this right." [80]

All the more sophisticated defenders of the motion for congressional censure ended up presenting it in this way, as a device for stimulating discussion rather than for controlling opinion. They had good reason to do so. The Federalists were all too open to a charge that such censure was incompatible with republican government, for implicit in the motion was the question of whether or not the government was responsible to the people. A writer calling himself "Z" made this reply to the argument that Congress could censure societies because they had an "evil tendency":

Now if a government can suppress, or stifle free strictures, on the ground of their tendency, and are to judge of the tendency, all free strictures are at an end, and government may do as it pleases, abuse of all sorts may go on, and none dare to take measures for a reform. . . . No government can remain free, which has a discretionary controul over the right of examining and covering its proceedings; nor become tyrannical, when this right remains sacred to the people.[81]

Madison put it another way: "If we advert to the nature of Republican Government, we shall find that the censorial power is in the people over the Government and not in the Government over the people." Giles said it most succinctly. To James Hillhouse's quip that if "constituents made no scruple to tell Representatives of their faults . . . he saw no reason why Representatives might not tell constituents theirs," he replied briefly that "the public have a right to censure us, and we have *not* a right to censure them." [82] In effect the defenders of the societies had associated them with the basic principles of republican government.

The upshot was that the Republicans won the battle but lost the war. They were able to keep Fitzsimmons's motion from passing the House. No one could answer their argument that if the societies threatened government by encouraging freedom of enquiry and opinion, republicanism was impossible, for there was no other way in which rulers could be made responsible to the people.[83] But the Federalists had consolations. The censures of the president and Senate, added to the publicity given the debate on Fitzsimmons's motion, generated enough mistrust of the societies to subvert their influence, and early in 1795 they began to fade.[84] Their disappearance was undoubtedly all the easier because, if nothing else, they had succeeded in focusing public attention on the conduct of national politics. Many members of the societies surely construed the popular outcry against the Jay Treaty as a vindication of their efforts in 1793–1794. Though there were still a few societies when this agitation broke out, and though Federalists found it convenient to hold them largely responsible for the uproar against the Jay Treaty, most had become inactive and no such institutions were ever again to be significant in national politics.[85]

Nevertheless, the Federalists paid a price for their victory. Their manipulative technique had been exposed, and though they did not have to abandon it altogether, their options were narrowed in two ways. First, because the people had become conscious of their activity, they could no longer use this tactic as successfully as before.

Throughout the Jay Treaty controversy, for instance, they were plagued by charges that they were trying to control public opinion by proclaiming dangerous conspiracies against the government.[86] Second, any future attempt to use the legislature in this way would probably be self-defeating unless the Federalists had a clear majority in the House. Beaten at their own game, and faced with a new, more opposition-minded House in 1795–1796, they abandoned manipulation in favor of executive pre-emption. Though they could never entirely free themselves from the necessity of trying to influence public opinion, for the rest of Washington's administration their best efforts were directed to circumventing and rendering it powerless.

PART IV

CRISIS

The increasing importance of foreign policy issues in American politics after 1793 had been a help to the Federalists in developing the style of executive pre-emption they used so well toward the end of Washington's administration. Though the people were more aroused by these than by domestic matters, the Constitution still allowed the executive to shape its own course in conjunction with the Senate, which gave the president considerable control over national destiny. Washington was ultimately accountable to the public, and the House might occasionally intrude upon his provenance, but the success of Federalist maneuvering in April 1796 indicated that these factors could be controlled. Unfortunately in 1797 they were forced to abandon this congenial way of working. The coincidence of Washington's retirement with a breakdown in Franco-American relations obliged them once again to become more active in the shaping of public opinion than they would have chosen to be. At the same time, their ability to do this declined, and so they found themselves paralyzed in the midst of a worsening Franco-American crisis. Their inability to act made them apprehensive that a Republican victory in 1800 would bring to power a government owing its life to French influence, which would surely lead to the loss of independence and the subversion of all their previous achievements. By the end of 1797 their old sense of mastery over national destiny had given way to doubt and fear as they faced a crisis of unprecedented proportions.

The Federalists were temporarily reprieved by the arrival of diplomatic dispatches from Paris in March 1798, proving that the Directory meant to humiliate the administration and compromise American neutrality. Their release weakened the foundation of the opposition's popularity and gave the Federalists a chance to turn

137

public opinion to their own account. How great an effect the dispatches produced can best be gauged from the response of the clergy in the older, well-established sects to the president's National Fast on May 9. Hitherto considered unreliable, they now took up the cause of Federalism in no uncertain fashion. In their published sermons, ministers in every section of the country identified the Federalist cause with that of religion. Their intellectual leaders even portrayed events in France as part of a mysterious international conspiracy against all government and religion, a charge which far exceeded the bounds of reason, though it did acquire a brief plausibility when the traditional European world order seemed to be on the verge of disintegration. As a result, during the remainder of the Fifth Congress the Federalists cast off the restraints imposed by the opposition and seized the initiative. Though they dared not go as far as an outright declaration of war, the Alien and Sedition Laws together with the Provisional Army Act allowed them all the power against the opposition which they would have had in that emergency. And the dispatches had made sufficient impression to give them apparent control of the Sixth Congress.

7. *Paralysis*

The events which obliged the Federalists once more to try positively shaping public opinion took them by surprise. They had not expected the treaty to precipitate a crisis with France. Their belief that amity could be preserved, as well as their assurance that the public would follow the government's lead, had enabled them to show greater determination than the opposition in the fight over implementation. This optimism derived in part from the conviction that the treaty was a justifiable expedient for preserving peace and American neutrality. They knew it would not please the French Directory, but then if they could not adjust their differences with one foreign nation because another objected, the United States could hardly be called independent.[1] And they would be able to deal with such grievances as might arise through the ordinary diplomatic channels. Legitimate complaints could be settled by negotiations, and if France tried to press any illegitimate claims Federalist leaders did not doubt that the people would support their own government, particularly after the Jay Treaty was sanctioned by Washington. But they had reason to believe that matters would not come to such a crisis. The remoteness of the United States and the danger of driving her to form an alliance with Britain would surely stop the French from pushing matters to extremes. After all, the concessions the Jay Treaty made to Britain were only temporary and (so many men believed) the European war was drawing to its close.[2]

The initial French response encouraged these comfortable convictions. In contrast to Genêt and Fauchet, his predecessors, French Ambassador Adet had been restrained in all his behavior and was content to be silenced on the subject of the treaty by one note from Secretary of State Edmund Randolph.[3] James Monroe, who had been sent to Paris at the same time as Jay went to London, sounded a warning

139

in the spring of 1796 when he reported that according to Charles De-
lacroix de Constant, the Directory "considered the alliance between
us, as ceasing to exist from the moment the treaty was ratified."
This alarm was echoed in June when French vessels began seizing
property from American shipping along the coast in open retaliation for the treaty.[4] But Monroe's private correspondence and dispatches had given the Federalists the impression that instead of
explaining and justifying United States policies to the French, he
had further inflamed their resentment. Many members of the cabinet
thought that this, together with attempts by the Republican press
to portray French depredations as "the *natural* consequence of the
ratification of the British Treaty," were responsible for French hostility and that the obvious remedy was to send a more reliable
minister to Paris.[5] To this end, Charles C. Pinckney of South Carolina sailed for France at the close of the summer.

As the autumn wore on, it became ever more clear that France
meant to strike at Britain by preying on neutral commerce. Yet the
United States did not seem to be receiving any worse treatment than
the other neutral powers or to be singled out as a special target for
retaliation, until the eve of the presidential elections.[6] Then, in a
letter to Secretary of State Pickering that was simultaneously sent to
the Republican press, Adet confirmed what had so long been rumored. The Directory had equalized the treaties by unilateral action
in a decree directing French ships of war to "treat the flag of neutrals in the same manner as they shall suffer it to be treated by the
English." [7]

This letter, dated October 27, was followed by another on November 15, which threatened the severance of diplomatic relations
between France and the United States, and which appealed to the
people against their government.[8] Though the presidential electors
had already been named, the electoral college would not act until
December 7, so this looked like a naked attempt to influence its decisions.[9] If it was, it backfired. The fear that Adet's appeal would
be "yielded to by the southern states, and produce the alteration in
the systems of national administration, which the Directory wish"
served to unite Federalists east of the Delaware. The result was that
Adams received twelve votes in the South, and Washington two,
but Jefferson gained none east of Pennsylvania.[10] The Federalists

also did well in the elections for the Fifth Congress. Opposition leaders like Madison, Dearborn, and John Page either retired or were defeated, and in New York, Maryland, and Virginia the Federalists gained ground, encouraging many of the leadership to expect a "small majority on the right side" in the next Congress.[11]

Although most of the congressional elections won by Federalists had taken place before Adet's intervention, the results in the electoral college suggested that the people would stand firm against French appeals for them to repudiate their government, and that the Directory would have to make terms with the new Federalist administration. The only thorn in their flesh was Jefferson's accidental election as vice-president. Federalist leaders were particularly upset by this because they thought it gave him a claim to the succession and an opportunity to exert an unpropitious influence.[12] Fortunately their control of the rest of the government would allow them to counteract his presence. Though the last session of the Fourth Congress was a disappointment, it had not been a disaster, and the Federalists had good reason to expect better of the new House. In general they assumed that everything was under control, and that national politics would continue to be the preserve of a Federalist leadership to whose initiative the people always bowed at last, however reluctantly.[13]

I

This happy assurance did not last long. The first blow fell three days after Adams's inauguration, when Pinckney's dispatches arrived reporting that the Directory had refused to receive him as Monroe's replacement. The Directory had also written a letter to Monroe saying that it would neither acknowledge nor receive another minister plenipotentiary from the United States until she had granted that redress of grievances so rightly demanded by the French republic. Nor was this all. Pinckney was denied either a letter of hospitality, without which he was subject to arrest as a common stranger, or a written order to leave France, which would at least have justified him in abandoning his post. With this news, all hope of an easy accommodation with the French vanished on the wind. On March 25, the president summoned Congress to meet in emergency session on May 15. In the meantime, news arrived that France had issued another edict on March 2 clarifying that of July 2, 1796, by declaring the property of all belligerents in neutral vessels to be a lawful prize. The principle of the Franco-American treaty that free ships made free goods was annulled; Americans captured while serving aboard British vessels would be treated as pirates, and all American vessels not carrying a *role d'equipage* (that is, a manifest of passengers and crew certified by the French consul, a document American captains had not formerly needed) were liable to seizure. This made a potential prize of virtually every American vessel on the high seas as well as those in French ports, and French privateers and officials could be expected to make maximum use of their opportunity. The decree was issued with a threatening speech by Paul Barras in reply to Monroe's Valedictory Address. The president of the Directory had appealed to the American people to "weigh, in their wisdom, the magnanimous benevolence of the French people with the crafty caresses of certain perfidious persons who meditate bringing them back to their former slavery." [14]

It might have been expected that this kind of arrogance would play into Federalist hands and rally the people to the support of the government. To some extent it did, but at the same time Washington's retirement had clouded the Federalists' prospects. Even before the crisis of 1793 they had foreseen the problems that would arise with his departure and had urged him to delay it until the European wars ended.[15] It was largely his prestige which had allowed them to assume that the people would acquiesce in any action taken by the government, at least in foreign affairs. Jefferson understood this perfectly when he complained "that the people will support [Washington] in whatever he will do or not do, without appealing to their own reason or to anything but their feelings toward him." And during the Jay Treaty controversy, "Franklin" had accused the Federalists of using the president to protect themselves from popular resentment "as the Sicilians do *Saint Agatha,* to quiet the ragings of Aetna." Before 1797 the Federalists could have relied on Washington's influence to persuade the American people that they must defend their rights against French power.[16] Now he was gone, and all the Federalists had in his place was the rather pompous and crotchety Adams. Although he had been next to Washington in seniority, Adams was conspicuously lacking in the qualities which had made the first president so impressive.[17]

The Federalists certainly were not regretting the loss of Washington as a military leader. They were sure that Britain would remain an enemy to France, and that the Directory would not risk provoking the United States to ally with her. Even if there were to be a war with France, the United States was now more than twice as strong as when she had defeated Britain in the War of Independence. She could also look to the British navy to augment her power still further, and she would be able to seize Florida and Louisiana as hostages.[18] As the Federalists saw it, the real danger was not that France would declare war, but that public opinion might force them to yield to French threats. They might be obliged to annul the Jay Treaty, and perhaps even to join the war against Britain. War with Britain and the disruption of Anglo-American commerce would cause the collapse of public credit, already endangered by a speculative panic at the conclusion of 1796 and by the effect of commercial depredations on the part of both belligerents. In the general loss of confidence that would follow, the French might gain an ascendant influence, and, like Holland and Belgium, once America had submitted to the fraternal embrace of the "terrible Republic," she might never regain her independence.[19]

The altered circumstances of the Federalists immediately influenced their response to Pinckney's rebuff. Men like George Cabot and Oliver Wolcott, Jr., would have preferred to arm and wait for France to make some gesture of conciliation. It appeared to them that if the government allowed France "to dictate what description of men shall be appointed to the foreign courts, our country is undone." Cabot held that to negotiate with France in spite of this insult might be made "the means of recruiting the exhausted strength of the French party within our country." France could achieve this "by profuse promises, which, as they never would be fulfilled, could cost nothing, and by insisting on one or two points, the yielding of which would involve us in new difficulties [with Britain]." [20] But they were forced to compromise. It was imperative to convince the people that everything possible was being done to conciliate the Directory, partly in order to disprove a current rumor (largely the product of Pickering's intemperate language) that the Federalists were itching for war, and partly because they could not rely on Adams to carry the public with him as Washington had done. Therefore, they acquiesced in the President's decision to send a new mission to France composed of John Marshall, Elbridge Gerry, and Pinckney, the presence of Pinckney being an assertion of American independence.[21]

This course of action did not offer much hope of lessening French influence at home. What were those Federalists to do who wanted a strong response to the French challenge so as to counteract any latent tendency in the American public to capitulate to it? The only possible answer was vigorous legislative action. They quickly agreed upon a program for strengthening the navy, recruiting a provisional army, authorizing the arming of merchant vessels, fortifying the major ports, and providing money for defense, but none of these forces would have allowed the nation to wage full-scale war. Their real purpose was to protect commerce and the revenue; to provide defenses against the two forms of reprisal thought to be most likely, raids on American ports and attempts to incite insurrections among the slaves; and most important of all, to counteract "the stupor which every public falls into, when for want of an impression from government, it is left to the anarchy of its own opinions." [22]

This strategy implied a recognition that executive pre-emption was no longer feasible. Ames's statement in the spring of 1797 that "government cannot act without or against Congress" certainly consorted oddly with the way the Federalists had tackled the British crisis in 1794–1796 and sprang from the understanding that with Washington gone, if the House of Representatives should oppose the president and Senate, "they will be followed by many of the people." On the other hand, the Federalists remained confident that "if the House should unite with the other branches, in measures of suitable vigor, the country will go along with the government and support it with constancy." When the emergency session of Congress assembled in Philadelphia on May 15, more attention than usual was fixed on the House reply to the president's address. The Federalist leadership expected some sign of whether or not the new members were going to cooperate with the other branches of the legislature in rallying public opinion against the French threat.[23]

Adam's speech was as firm and decisive as the Federalists could desire. He called the Pinckney rebuff "the denial of a right," and treatment deserved by the United States "neither as allies, nor as friends, or as a sovereign State." Adams charged that President Barras's reply to Monroe's Valedictory Address showed "a disposition to separate the people of the United States from the government . . . and thus produce divisions fatal to our peace." This gave the House an even more clearly marked cue than Washington had provided in 1794 when he had spoken of the societies. The committee charged with drafting a reply came up with one that declared, "We feel the full force of that indignity which has been offered our country in the rejection of the Minister," and expressed indignation at Barras's speech in these words, "An attempt to separate the people of the United States from their Government, is an attempt to separate them from themselves; and although foreigners who know not the genius of our country may have conceived the project, and foreign emissaries may attempt the execution, yet the united efforts of our fellow citizens will convince the world of its impracticability." It ended with a ringing endorsement of the government's conduct as "just and impartial to foreign nations," and an assurance that "the Representatives of the People do not hesitate to declare that they will give their most cordial support to the execution of principles so deliberately and uprightly established." [24]

This was the kind of reply the Federalists had hoped for, but the opposition was not going to accept it without a fight. John Nicholas of Virginia rose at once to propose an amendment that William Laughton Smith thought "went entirely to change the form of the Answer." It construed Pinckney's rebuff as "only intended to suspend the ordinary diplomatic intercourse, and to bring into operation those extraordinary agencies which are in common use between nations," and dismissed Barras's speech with the declaration that "we cannot believe that any serious expectation can be entertained of withdrawing the support of the people from their Constitutional agents." Nicholas's amendment did not rule out enacting the measures recommended by Adams if France should continue to refuse negotiations, but it asked that the executive first show "a disposition on the part of the United States to place France on the footing of other countries by removing the inequalities which may have arisen in the operation of our respective treaties." [25] This touched off a bitter debate in the House, in which the opposition accused the Federalists of having caused the rupture in Franco-American relations by promoting the Jay Treaty and denounced them for proposing so strongly worded and provocative an answer to the president.[26] It consumed more than a quarter of the emergency session and in the end denied the Federalists the vigorous endorsement they had wanted.

The Federalists retorted that the treaty had been more the excuse than the reason for tension between the United States and France. In a brilliant speech on May 29, later published as *Observations on the Dispute between the United States and France*, Robert Goodloe Harper suggested that France's real quarrel with the treaty was not that she was injured by the renunciation of neutral rights, but rather that it had reconciled the United States and Great Britain. Ever since Genêt's first mission, he said, France had been trying to start trouble between them and would never be satisfied until she had. In her efforts to persuade the United States to ban British commerce from American ports, France had played on the people's deep-rooted hostility toward the former mother country, and at the same time had enticed them with the prospect of free admission to the West India trade. Harper concluded that the most important question raised by the French crisis was whether the United States was to be ruled by Americans or by the French.[27]

Despite Harper's eloquence, the House voted to support equalization of the treaties, in effect accepting the conclusion of the Nicholas amendment without the preamble.[28] But the Federalists did not despair. Uriah Tracy wrote to Oliver Wolcott, Jr., that the predominantly Federalist Senate meant to take the initiative in framing defense measures so that if the House obstructed their passage it would have to accept responsibility for the consequences. Furthermore, although the Senate could not originate revenue bills, it could keep the House in session through the heat of a Philadelphia summer until financial provision had been made for the defense of the United States, for as Tracy said, "the House cannot adjourn, but for the space of three days, without our consent." [29]

The aggressive optimism with which they began the emergency session soon dwindled down into despair and frustration. When all was said and done, Congress accomplished nothing of significance beyond providing that $500,000 additional revenue be raised through internal taxes on stamps and salt. The legislation passed for fortifying the ports, increasing the naval armaments of the United States, and authorizing the president to raise money by loans, represented no more than minimal compliance with Federalist desires. The president was authorized to borrow only $800,000 at an interest rate that might be inadequate to secure the funds desired given the current state of the money market. The House had refused to concur in a Senate bill for the arming of merchant vessels to protect American commerce, or in another "empowering the President to employ the naval force of the United States, as convoys to protect the trade thereof," and it had turned down a Senate proposal to raise an additional corps of artillerymen and engineers. Before the session was over, the Senate had shown itself more ready to defer to the House than Tracy had predicted, surrendering its bill for a provisional army in favor of the House bill authorizing the president to muster detachments of state militia.[30]

It is not hard to find the reason for the paralysis that crept over Congress as the emergency session continued into the summer of 1797. From the Federalist standpoint, the European prospect was growing bleak. Since autumn 1796 they had known that the administration's ability to stand firm against France would depend to some extent on the issue of the campaign in Italy and Germany, and the news from Europe that winter told of Jean Baptiste Jourdan and Jean Victor Moreau turned back in Germany, while Bonaparte had been stopped at Mantua.[31] Not until the following June did Americans learn that Napoleon had ultimately triumphed and destroyed much of the Austrian army, leaving the southern flank of the Austrian empire exposed to his forces. It seemed now that Austria would be compelled to make peace with France, leaving Britain isolated.[32] To make matters worse, a rebellion had broken out in Ireland; Britain's banking system had collapsed, forcing the replacement of specie by paper money of dubious value; and the navy, the backbone of British power, mutinied at Spithead and the Nore. It was a disastrous sequence of events that made it certain France would become more difficult to deal with than ever. Either Britain would make terms with her, leaving any other nation with a French quarrel to stand alone, or France would cast off all restraint in her attempt to coerce Britain by preying on neutral commerce.

The Republican opposition was elated by these developments, not because they wanted the Federalists to be chastised by France, but because they could argue that peace was imminent and defense measures were therefore unnecessary if not provocative.[33] The Federalists were correspondingly dismayed, knowing that the Directory had a grudge against them, and would now have more freedom to work it off. Oliver Wolcott, Jr., wrote to his father that "As France approaches peace in Europe, she advances in her threats and insolence to America." [34] Moreover, Federalists could expect French victories to increase Britain's financial, political, and military woes, and consequently the Republicans would be able to charge that the Federalist policy of defying France would leave the United States at best allied to a nation that could not help her, at worst wholly without allies before a victorious France. George Cabot declared that "we resist the French successfully in our own country, but they beat us in Europe. If England *revolves*, our tranquillity must be disturbed." [35] With England's future so doubtful, surely it would have been more prudent to make an accommodation with France rather than oppose her.[36]

II

Time did not improve matters for the Federalists. Britain survived the naval mutiny, the Irish disturbances were temporarily calmed in 1797, and there were signs she could weather her economic crisis, but nevertheless she remained in a precarious state throughout 1797 and much of 1798. France's hegemony over almost all western Europe exccept Portugal made her able to exert substantial pressure on Britain's finances by excluding her commerce from European ports, which increased the strategic importance of Anglo-American trade. There was also at this time a real danger that France would invade England. It was not Britain's command of the seas which had stopped the French from landing at Bantry Bay in December 1796. And there was a possibility that invaders would be welcomed by some, for in both England and Scotland there had been so much opposition to further prosecution of the war with France that the government had been driven to acts of repression. Fervent Federalists like George

Cabot tried to convince themselves that Britain would stand firm despite "the appearance of division and weakness," and even voiced a wish that "it were possible to work up the French to such a frenzy as to attempt an invasion of England. . . . with half a million men, determined to conquer or perish, as I fully believe they would perish, and with them the physical force and the destructive fame of Jacobinism." [37] But for most people, the current state of Great Britain did not inspire confidence. Although the coup of 18 Fructidor made a general peace between Britain and France unlikely, not until the autumn of 1798, when news of Napoleon's Egyptian fiasco was received, were the people at large reassured that France would not be able to carry out her threat of dictating a peace on the banks of the Thames.[38]

As the year progressed, it became more and more difficult for the Federalists to nerve the public mind for resisting French threats to independence. Their predicament was not alleviated by the appearance in April of the first in a long series of "Fabius" letters written by the revolutionary hero John Dickinson. These argued that French excesses were entirely attributable to her opponents; that France as a continental power was bound to triumph over Britain just as Rome had triumphed over Carthage, and that it was in the national interest to preserve the Franco-American alliance.[39] The "Fabius" letters were seconded by Monroe's *A View of the Conduct of the Executive in the Foreign Affairs of the United States,* published at the end of 1797. Monroe reiterated the opposition case that France and the United States were at odds not because the Directory was unreasonable or hostile, but because the Federalist administration had acted unwisely. These attacks were more damaging to the Federalists than abuse in the opposition press, which was usually written by political unknowns, because Monroe and Dickinson commanded great prestige. And no man was in a better position than Monroe to argue the case against the Federalist policy toward France, for he had been on the spot.[40] Federalist attempts to destroy his reputation by blaming him for the rupture and refusing to explain his dismissal only begged the question. Uriah Tracy's "Scipio" letters, which accused Monroe of being "no less servile to the ruling power of France, than disrespectful, if not disobedient, to the Executive of the United States," ought to have had some effect, but they paled to insignificance before the fact that French fortunes were on the rise in Europe. It was this which gave a new cogency to the plea of Monroe and Dickinson that the administration's pro-British foreign policy should be jettisoned.[41]

Yet during the autumn of 1797 the Federalists were by no means ready to give up. They believed events would be more favorable to them during the second session of the Fifth Congress, which re-assembled on November 13. For one thing, they expected news of the Pinckney, Marshall, and Gerry mission to France to remove the ambiguities which had helped paralyze administration sympathizers in the House during the emergency session when the opposition had suggested that Pinckney was rebuffed because his powers were inadequate.[42] Now that three extraordinary ministers had been dispatched to France, a repetition of the incident would be clearly unjustifiable. On the other hand, if these men should succeed in negotiating with France, the crisis would be safely past. Even if France should make an equivocal response, as Cabot feared she would,[43] the Federalists hoped that Pinckney and Marshall would be able to force her to show her true colors while resisting any inclination of Gerry's to connive at the Directory's designs. They had no doubt that if they could present the people with a straight choice between independence and submission to a foreign nation, they and their representatives would choose independence no matter how strong and victorious France appeared. Public sentiment was already turning against her because of continued depredations on American commerce.[44] And the Federalists hoped to take advantage of this by using the second session, while Congress was waiting for news of the negotiations, to put through some of the measures that had been rejected in May. Most promising among them was the proposal to arm merchant vessels, for if Congress continued unwilling to give them official protection, this seemed to be the only alternative to abandoning commerce altogether.[45]

The administration was again to be disappointed in its bid for legislative action. Though there was rising support for such legisla-tion in some of the northern mercantile centers, the opposition was easily able to obstruct it by postponing consideration until the beginning of February.[46] Their argument that such a measure might abort negotiations now going on between the two republics was a good one. Many American vessels were owned either by British subjects or by those who had only become American citizens so as to protect their property under the American neutral flag. In either case, if they were licensed to arm their vessels, they might provoke war by resisting the lawful attempts of French vessels to search or seize. The arming of merchant vessels, said the opposition, was only to be thought of as a last resort should negotiation fail. To do it prematurely would be "placing the peace of the country in the hands of every man who owned a ship." [47] Even such ardent Federalists as Robert Goodloe Harper and Nathaniel Smith were silenced by this argument.[48] Harrison Gray Otis might taunt the opposition by asking "were gentlemen palsied, that such a measure should be thus procrastinated?" [49] Thacher might sneer that a bill directed "against rovers and pirates" could be considered hostile to France only by those who believed that description applied to her, but most Federalists knew that in case there was going to be trouble between France and America, they could not afford to give the opposition any excuse for holding them responsible.[50]

Defeat on the arming of merchant vessels was not hard to accept. It was only temporary, and if it had seemed politically expedient the president could have withdrawn his restrictions on arming at any time, leaving the merchants free to choose how they would act. On both sides, the question of merchant armaments was disposed of with so little fuss that the ensuing session might well have been expected to be uneventful, at least until dispatches should arrive from the envoys. Instead, the tranquillity of the House was violently disrupted by the relatively minor matter of foreign intercourse appropriations. The issue had first arisen at the end of the emergency session. Nicholas had objected to an appropriation of $60,500 for ministers to Portugal, Prussia, and the Barbary powers, and on being informed that the salary of the minister to Berlin was $13,500 he promptly moved that this "be deducted from the $60,500.00 as he knew no possible use that a Minister of Berlin could be of." [51] The motion was a stinging slap in the face of President Adams, who had appointed his son to this office. And it was surely deliberately aimed, for the post was not as meaningless as Nicholas pretended, since the course of the European war had made Berlin a strategic vantage point for diplomatic observation.[52] There was a brief flare-up in the House over Nicholas's motion and its suggestion of constitutional limitation on the executive's power to conduct foreign policy, but the appropriation was passed and the matter dropped.[53] Perhaps the heat of Philadelphia in July and the possibility of another yellow fever epidemic made no one inclined to prolong the session any further.

When the question of appropriations for diplomatic staff reappeared in the next session of Congress, it was a different matter entirely. On January 18, 1798, Robert Goodloe Harper moved that in addition to the standard $40,000 a further appropriation of $28,650 be made to pay for ministers plenipotentiary at the courts of Spain, Prussia, and Portugal.[54] Nicholas promptly countered with a proposal that the diplomatic establishment be reduced to what it had been before 1796; that is, there would be two ministers plenipotentiary, one in London and one in Paris, requiring an appropriation of $9,000 each, while all other envoys would be limited to the lower grade of resident minister at $4,500 a year.[55] Nicholas remarked that he "did not intend . . . that the whole diplomatic establishment should be destroyed at this time," but he added that "the United States would be benefited by having no Ministers at all," that American commerce should be left "to seek its own markets totally disembarrassed," and that any of the routine matters arising from commercial intercourse could be adequately handled by consuls.[56]

If this had been all there was to Nicholas's proposal, there would have been no uproar. But he had prefaced this motion with a diatribe on the dangers of encroaching executive power, declaring: "I do believe there is a tendency in all Governments like ours to produce a union and consolidation of all its parts into the Executive department; and that the limitation and connexion of the parts with each other, as settled in the Constitution would be destroyed by the influence I have mentioned, unless there is constant operation on the part of the Legislature to resist this overwhelming power." [57] What restraint would there be upon a man once he was president, he asked, if "in consequence of a thirst for office majorities were formed by both branches of Congress devoted to the views of the Executive, by which the Executive could hold on with the Legislature a regular and concurrent course to affect any object however hostile to the public good that the President might think proper to pursue?" [58]

Nicholas said he was not charging that this had already happened, but he did go on to attack a new idea of patronage which he said the Adams administration had already adopted. It meant, according to Nicholas, that "no man was hereafter to be admitted into the Administration . . . unless he was willing to sacrifice all independent political opinions and bend at the shrine of Executive wisdom." [59] Striking obliquely at William L. Smith's recent appointment as Portuguese ambassador, Nicholas warned that "when we see the most lucrative offices, the most tempting and most honorable —offices with the greatest attraction—filled by draughts from the Legislative body, and there, too, of one particular class, and that class the believers of the new doctrine," a serious threat to American liberty was raised and "the Legislature should show itself attentive to limit a patronage which was to be exercised in this way." [60]

Nicholas's speech set off a debate which lasted six weeks and made the controversy over implementing the Jay Treaty seem amiable by comparison. Tempers flared and passions rose, as both sides gave vent to all the suspicions and frustrations that had been building up since the spring of 1796. With the international situation so shaky, the last thing the Federalists had wanted was a public display of the divisions that existed at the heart of the national government,[61] yet many were swept irresistibly into the controversy and swelled the flood of anger rather than helping to dam it.[62] Then, in the midst of the debate on the foreign intercourse appropriations, the House was treated to an extraordinary spectacle which interrupted its deliberations for three weeks and dramatized for the world as no mere words could have done the explosive antagonisms that existed in Congress.

The trouble started one morning when Matthew Lyon of Vermont harangued the speaker about the conduct of the Connecticut representatives before the House was in session. Lyon alleged that "they acted in opposition to the interests and opinion of nine-tenths of their constituents . . . that they were seeking offices which they were willing to accept whether yielding $9,000 or $1,000." He went on to boast that "if he should go into Connecticut, and manage a press there for six months . . . [he could] turn out the present Representatives." Roger Griswold, one of the Connecticut representatives, retorted by jeering at Lyon for having been cashiered from the army during the Revolution, taunting him about his "wooden

sword." At this, Lyon spat in Griswold's face. The incident was
turned over to the Committee of Privileges, which subsequently
recommended that Lyon be expelled from the House. But this required a vote of two-thirds of the members, and failed to pass.[63]
Three days later, before the House was called to order, Griswold
went up to the desk where Lyon sat writing and set about him
with a cane. Extricating himself from his seat with difficulty, and
unable to close with his assailant, Lyon at last snatched up the fire
tongs in self-defense. Both men collapsed in a struggling heap on the
floor, and even after they had been separated by other members,
they were with difficulty prevented from going to it again outside
the bar of the House. The next day John Davis of Kentucky proposed
to expel both men from the House, but again the motion failed to
pass.[64] Even these disgraceful scenes, which as one member said
"tended to degrade the members of that House . . . to a level with
the meanest reptile that crawled upon the earth," did not shame
them into toning down the verbal fury of the debate, though they
did thereafter refrain from physical violence.[65]

III

Why should so insignificant a matter raise so violent a storm?
The question becomes more puzzling still when the foreign intercourse controversy of 1798 is compared with the struggle over the
implementation of the Jay Treaty in 1796. The strategic security of
the nation, as well as the future of all former Federalist achievements, had been at issue in the treaty fight, but the appropriations
questioned by the Nicholas amendment would have had no effect
on domestic policy and very little on foreign relations. Admittedly
the same constitutional issue was raised in both, that is, whether or
not the House had discretion in making appropriations touching the
conduct of foreign policy. By 1797–1798, however, the Federalists
might reasonably have been expected to recognize the counter-pro-
ductivity of their claim that exclusive jurisdiction over foreign affairs
belonged to the executive.[66] Certainly there was not the same need
to urge it as there had been in 1796, for they were no longer driven
by circumstances to defy the House. Indeed, the growing importance
of the House to their political strategy should have moderated their
ideas. To have given way on the question of ambassadorial appropri-

ations would have been no more than a temporary concession. They had already received unofficial word that the special mission to France would be as futile as Pinckney's, and they could be reasonably sure that the opposition would soon be denied any grounds for pleading that an honorable accommodation with France was possible.[67] Why then could they not bring to this issue the same wise patience as they had shown in the matter of arming merchant vessels? Why, instead of making light of Nicholas's amendment, did they magnify it out of all proportion by their intemperate response? Their conduct in previous debates bears witness to a calculating self-possession which makes it hard to comprehend their entanglement in this shameful debacle over a minor modification of policy.

Their response to the charge of executive usurpation was particularly revealing. When this had been raised during the Jay Treaty controversy they had succeeded in turning the tables on their adversaries by arguing that the Constitution, the supreme expression of the people's will, had vested the treaty power in the president and Senate, and that both were as much the people's representatives as the House.[68] Washington's great prestige and unanimous elections had made this a safe claim, and had forced the Republicans to spend a good deal of time defending the popular branch of the legislature against counter-charges of encroachment and disorganization.[69] But in 1798 it was no longer possible for the Federalists to use such a strategy. Adams was not nearly so prestigious a figure as Washington had been, and he owed his election to a three-vote margin. Indeed, his majority had been so slender that the opposition questioned whether he was truly the people's choice, insinuating that two of the three ballots to which he owed his victory had been cast by electors whose own majorities had been slight enough to suggest fraud.[70] So the Federalists were bound to be on the defensive when the subject of executive usurpation arose again in 1798. Yet this alone should not have driven them to make statements in defense of the executive which seemed to assert extravagant notions of its power.

For instance, William Craik had said that if "the House of Representatives should be established in the right, which some . . . claimed of exercising, upon all occasions, an unlimited discretion, when called upon to appropriate money, on the acts of the Executive

. . . [it might] take all the powers of the Government into its own hands," which implied that there was no occasion on which this discretion might be properly exercised.[71] Other Federalists unwisely complained that the power of the executive in America was ridiculously weak compared to that of its British counterpart. This together with their charge that anyone refusing to trust absolutely in Adams's conduct of foreign affairs was a "disorganizer"[72] was enough to convince the Republicans that the Federalists wanted to strengthen the executive power. They were not reassured by the hysteria of the Federalist response to what seemed a reasonable motion, subject to none of the objections about breach of national faith that had accompanied the debate over implementing the Jay Treaty.[73]

Nor was this the only cause for Republican concern. There were also attempts to surround the President with royal pomp and circumstance whenever he appeared in public. For instance, as the French crisis had worsened, the Federalists had taken particular pains to provide him with elaborate military escorts whenever he went on journeys and to arrange civic ceremonies in his honor at which it was customary to present him with a congratulatory address. There had been as much if not more of this when Washington was president, but Republicans thought it more offensive since Adams had taken office. Washington had enjoyed an uncontrived popularity which made such occasions seem spontaneous, but as Adams himself knew and the opposition press never ceased to observe, in his case they had an artificial air which made him look absurd.[74] The lengths to which the Federalists would go in bolstering presidential prestige, and how seriously they took their efforts, were not fully revealed until the incident of Luther Baldwin. This insignificant drunk was prosecuted in 1799 for having greeted a sixteen gun salute to Adams as he passed through Newark with the remark, "There goes the President and they are firing at his a[rse]."[75]

Though the indictment and conviction of Luther Baldwin is low comedy to us, it is startling evidence that to the Federalists even a piece of trifling vulgarity could seem a serious threat to the president's dignity and prestige. When a drunken joke could so upset them, it is hardly surprising that Nicholas's assault on the executive power frightened them out of all good sense and restraint. They saw

it as part of a larger design to make an already weak executive still
weaker through legislative censure.[76] This alone would have caused
the Federalists to be touchy about assaults on the executive power,
but what made them unbearably sensitive was the knowledge that
French strategy was still what it had been in Genêt's time: to force
Americans to choose between their government and their sympathy
for France.[77] And whereas they had then been able to set the prestige of a Washington against an isolated diplomat, now they had to
confront the most powerful government in the world with nothing
better than John Adams, an unimpressive man who could not even
command the support of his own government.

It is no wonder that the Federalists behaved so uncharacteristically
during the foreign intercourse debate. The opposition had them
trapped so that no matter what they did, they would lose. As Oliver
Wolcott, Jr., remarked of the Federalist congressmen, "Their situation is humiliating; they can do but little good, and doing nothing,
in the present state of our country, is attended with almost as bad
effects as would result from bad measures." [78] To have tolerated
Nicholas's attack on the executive power would have encouraged
the French in their schemes, yet to assault it dramatized the division
in the government. Caught in this predicament, they were often
driven to make matters worse by lashing out at the opposition and
countering objections to their extravagant claims for the executive
power with the assertion that, on the contrary, it was already too
weak. They had momentarily lost control of their own and the nation's destinies. For men who had been accustomed since 1789 to be
masters of events, it was hard to grow impotent gracefully.

8. *Rally*

From May 1797 until March 1798 it seemed to many Federalists that France held the American republic mesmerized. But although this was frustrating for them, they could look forward to release whenever there should be news from the commissioners in Paris. Continued attacks on American commercial vessels, the coup of Fructidor, and various bits of information from unofficial sources, all combined to strengthen their belief that the French meant mischief, and that this would soon be so clear as to make Republican opposition to defense measures untenable.[1]

I

The long-awaited dispatches from Paris arrived on March 4. They were lengthy and in code, and it was some time before the government knew what they contained. But they were accompanied by a letter which required no deciphering, a letter Adams laid before Congress on March 5 because its contents were "of so much importance [that it should] be immediately made known to Congress and to the public, especially the mercantile part of our fellow citizens." It reported that the Directory had asked for a law, subsequently notorious as the decree of 29 Nivôse, authorizing seizure of "all neutral ships having on board merchandises and commodities, the production of England, or of English possessions," and another providing that "the ports of France, except in cases of distress, shall be shut against all neutral ships which, in the course of their voyage, shall have touched at an English port." As the reconstituted legislature was nothing but a rubber stamp for the Directory, these recommendations were to all intents and purposes already law. The letter concluded with the statement that "there exists no hope of our being officially received by the government, or that the objects of our mission will be in any way accomplished."[2]

This was what the Federalists had been waiting for. They secured passage of the foreign intercourse bill on the very day of the president's message and soon afterwards succeeded in putting through a naval armaments appropriation which would allow three frigates to put to sea, a measure increasing the risk of an armed clash between United States and French warships.[3] Unfortunately, this proved to be the limit of their advantage. When Adams subsequently urged Congress to implement his defense recommendations, at the same time revoking his standing instructions to customs officers "to restrain vessels of the United States from sailing in an armed condition," [4] the opposition was no less prompt in protesting this as a *"war message."* They also made a vigorous attempt to mobilize public opinion against war with France through a set of resolutions introduced by Richard Sprigg, Jr., of Maryland:

Resolved, That it is the opinion of this committee, that under existing circumstances it is not expedient for the United States to resort to war against the French Republic.

Resolved, &c, That provision ought to be made by law for restricting the arming of merchant vessels, except in cases in which the practice was heretofore permitted.

Resolved, &c., That adequate provision shall be made by law for the protection of our sea coast, and for the internal defense of the country.[5]

It was clear that despite the continued degeneration of Franco-American relations, the opposition was still determined to resist the president on the arming of merchantmen and to consider only those means of internal defense which could not possibly provoke war. Petitions received by Congress from late March to late April indicated that a sizeable body of the public supported these objectives.[6]

The Federalists were understandably afraid that Republican intransigence might bring a repetition of the foreign intercourse debacle unless they could gain more influence in the House. They had to end the stalemate that was making them incapable of action, and they chose to do it by releasing the dispatches to Congress. This was a risk for several reasons. No one could know in advance whether they would "electrise the whole American people, *or demonstrate such an utter prostration of national spirit & honor as would shew all hopes of resistance to be vain.*" No one could be sure that publication might not "excite *indignation without bounds against the Commissioners,* if they should be at *Paris,*" and their blood be upon Federalist hands.[7] But something drastic had to be done if the administration were ever to be free of the constraints imposed by the opposition. Therefore they were at last reconciled to a motion by John Allen of Connecticut that the president "communicate to this House the despatches." [8] Access to diplomatic information had been a major opposition objective ever since the Jay Treaty controversy, and they would be sure to rise to the bait. This meant, as Harrison Gray Otis put it, that most Federalists could vote against Allen's motion in the comfortable certainty that it would carry "by means of a few of the federal men who think well of the measure.— The responsibility for any disadvantage resulting from the disclosure of the papers will fall on the right spot, and the advantage arising from the impression would be common to us all." [9]

The dispatches revealed that the commissioners had been treated as badly as Pinckney the year before. Though they were not ordered to leave the country on arrival, Talleyrand would deal with them only by way of intermediaries designated in the published version of the dispatches as X, Y, and Z. These men told the commissioners that reconciliation with France would have to be bought. The price named was a written apology for certain parts of the president's address to the emergency session of Congress; a bribe of 1,200,000 livres to Talleyrand, allegedly for distribution to strategically placed personnel, and a United States loan to France.[10] There was some ambiguity about the first and last of these items. Agent X hinted that the "loan" would consist of the United States making "advances for the payment of debts contracted by the agents of the French Government with the citizens of the United States." [11] And Agent Y, who claimed to have greater authority than X, suggested that the apology could be waived if the United States would assume "thirty-two millions of florins, of Dutch inscriptions, worth ten shillings in the pound . . . at twenty shillings in the pound," this to be repaid by the Dutch government upon the coming of peace.[12] But the principle that the United States would have to pay for an accommodation with France was established beyond doubt.

Only when these humiliating conditions had been met would

France agree "to renew with the United States of America a treaty which shall place them reciprocally in the same state that they were in 1778," except that France would be bound by no stricter terms than were applied to England in the Jay Treaty.[13] Even then, there would be one other difference in France's favor. Though the "nomination of Commissioners will be consented to on the same footing as they have been named in the treaty with England . . . payment which, agreeably to the decisions of the commissioners, shall fall to the share of the French Government, are to be advanced by the American Government itself."[14] Far from showing themselves willing to negotiate grievances, the Directory proposed to dictate terms and to make "demands upon us which had the appearance of our being the aggressing party" before they would receive the American envoys.[15]

The commissioners had rejected these demands, pleading lack of power to comply. The most they would do was send one of their number back to America for consultation with the government, and then only on condition that "the Directory will suspend all further captures on American vessels, and will suspend proceedings on those already captured."[16] Talleyrand would not hear of this offer, however, unless it was accompanied by money.[17] As for disavowing the president's speech, the commissioners said that it was not within their competence to do so, and that

such an attempt could produce no other effect than to make us ridiculous to the Government and to the citizens at large of the United States, and to produce, on the part of the President, an immediate disavowal and recall of us, as his agents; that, independent of this, all America was acquainted with the facts stated by the President; and our disavowing them would not change the public sentiment concerning them.[18]

Indeed, the commissioners did not take this requirement seriously at all, correctly interpreting it as merely a bargaining ploy.[19]

What the Directory really wanted was money. Agent Y had made it plain that money would be the *sine qua non* of any new Franco-American treaty, and this the commissioners had resolutely refused to concede.[20]

If anything could have been worse than the terms proposed to the commissioners, it would have been the way they were treated after they had rejected them. They were threatened with war, a threat made the more believable by the recent conclusion of a treaty between France and Austria which X and Y admitted allowed the Directory to take so uncompromising a line.[21] When the American commissioners suggested that French belligerence would drive the United States into the arms of Britain, the agents replied that the Austrian peace would force Britain to come to terms with France, and the United States would be left isolated. They said that France was gathering a great army to invade Britain, an army whose mere existence would frighten her into ruinous expedients, and "would infallibly destroy [her] Bank and [her] whole paper system." [22] The commissioners were told that if they did not comply with French demands, "the fate of Venice was one which might befall the United States," that she too might "be erased from the list of nations," or returned to the former mother country upon conclusion of a peace in the same way that Venice had been ceded to Austria by the Treaty of Campoformio.[23] On one point there could be no doubt: France was threatening to humiliate if not to annihilate the last free republic on earth.

The commissioners were careful to profess a desire for reconciliation with France, but they firmly refused to compromise American neutrality in achieving it. They declared that "to lend a sum of money to a belligerent Power, abounding in everything requisite for war but money, was to relinquish our neutrality, and take part in the war; to lend this money, under the lash and coercion of France, was to relinquish the Government of ourselves, and to submit to a foreign Government imposed on us by force." They said that America had no interest in the recurring wars between France and Britain, which might continue into the next century. If the United States "now preserved her neutrality and her independence, it was most probably that she would not in future be afraid . . . but if she . . . surrendered her rights of self government to France, or permitted them to be torn from her, she could not expect to recover them, or to remain neutral in any future war." If France was determined either to be paid off or to make war, then, said the commissioners, "even our money would [not] save us; our independence would never cease to give offense, and would always furnish a pretext for fresh demands." They added that "our present situation was more ruinous to us than a declared war could be; that at present our commerce was plundered unprotected; but that if war were declared we should seek the means of protection." And they served notice on the French that their nation "would make at least one manly struggle before we thus surrendered our national independence." [24]

The commissioners spared no pains to show that, unlike the smaller European powers on which France had worked her will, "America was a great, and, so far as concerned her self-defence, a powerful nation." [25] The French, unconvinced, continued to assume that they could play upon what they took to be a division between the government and the people. After two months of fruitless effort, Pinckney had observed to a woman agent of Talleyrand that the commissioners might as well give up and go home; and she had promptly retorted that this "could lead to a rupture, which you had better avoid, for we know we have a very considerable party in America who are strongly in our interest." Y had also tried this method of dissuading the commissioners from breaking off the talks, saying:

Perhaps you believe that, in returning and exposing to your countrymen the unreasonableness of the demands of this Government, you will unite them in their resistance to those demands; you are mistaken; you ought to know that the diplomatic skill of France, and the means she possesses in your country, are sufficient to enable her, with the French party in America, to throw the blame which will attend the rupture of negotiations on the Federalists, as you term yourselves, but on the British party, as France terms you; and you may assure yourselves this will be done.

The commissioners replied that "France miscalculated on the parties in America; that the extreme injustice offered to our country would unite every man against her," but they were not believed.[26]

These documents confirmed every charge the Federalists had made. It was now much harder to deny that France was bent on humiliating the American republic, that opposition activities encouraged her in this, or that the influence of France was a danger to American independence, for the French themselves believed it was. Talleyrand and his agents could have done no more to undermine the Republican position if they had been in the Federalists' pay. And as the Federalists had hoped, the dispatches did have some effect upon Congress. The opposition was obliged to stop criticizing the executive's handling of Franco-American relations, and to abandon Sprigg's first resolution against war with France. Jefferson admitted that to support such a resolution "after we have understood it has been proposed to us to buy peace, would imply an acquiescence under that proposition." [27]

Much to the surprise of the Federalists, however, the Republicans would yield no further. Pickering expressed his disappointment in a letter to King, observing:

There is still an evident opposition on one side of each House, to provide for anything beyond our internal defences; and the exhibition of the dispatches from the Envoys seems not to have produced the proper effect; for while the most inveterate opposers of the Government now acknowledge its sincerity and the propriety and even liberality of its measures to effect an accommodation with France, and add that she has given us abundant cause to declare war against her, they say it is not expedient, and therefore we must not attempt to protect our commerce, because its defense . . . will issue in open war.[28]

Republicans were ready to admit that the dispatches showed Talleyrand as an unprincipled swindler, as might have been expected from the company he kept with Tories when in America, but they said there was no proof that he acted by the orders of his government. Despite the dispatches, the opposition refused to sink their differences with administration supporters in order to present a united front to the French.[29] Their obstinacy boded ill for the future, and threatened continuation of the paralysis which had already pushed the Federalists to extremes of frustration.

It was then that the Federalist leadership decided to release the dispatches to the public, hoping by this means to break the congressional deadlock. They had clearly expected publication to follow Allen's original motion for the papers as a matter of course, but once the Republicans had seen their contents they resolved to oppose any such move. By joining forces with those who feared for the lives of the commissioners if they were still in France they were able to obstruct House action. Thus the Federalist Senate was obliged to take the initiative, though it was able to shrug off some of the responsibility because the content of the dispatches had leaked out to the people beforehand. The tactic was the more appealing as the balance of power in the House was held by four fence-sitters, said by Theodore Sedgwick to be nominally proadministration but "whimsical, kinkish and unaccommodating" in character, so that any measure whose passage depended upon them was always uncertain. Once the dispatches were released, it was hoped that the "indignant voice of the people must irresistibly urge the adoption of efficient measures of defence by sea as well as by land." [30] Republican opposition to publishing the documents had encouraged this hope, and Jefferson had admitted that "their effect on the minds of wavering characters" would be to bring them over to the other party so as "to wipe off the imputation of being French partisans." [31]

Shortly after publication, it looked as if the Federalists had reason to congratulate themselves. William Hindman in a letter to King announced jubilantly that "the Antis in our House count upon 51 on their side, We 55, so that if the Federal members would all attend & be as firm & united as the Opposition, the Power is with Us." [32] And by April 19, Jefferson was complaining to Monroe that "the departure of 4 Southern members, & others going, have given a strong majority to the other party." [33] This change alone did not, however, immediately confer upon the Federalists the advantage they sought. For one thing their new majority resulted from the shift of only a few votes, and as Jefferson pointed out, up to the Provisional Army Act most of the administration measures that had been opposed by the Republican party could have been defeated if all its members had been present.[34] Then the hard core opposition in the House refused to be cowed by publication of the dispatches. These men retorted by repeating in public the questions they had formerly asked behind closed doors: were the propositions made by X, Y, and Z definitely authorized by the Directory, and was it not still possible that Federalist measures might cause an unnecessary war with France? They found more devious ways of obstruction, too. Some Federalists even suspected that when the opposition supported lavish appropriations for internal defense measures, their long-term goal was to deplete the resources the administration had hoped to use for external defense.[35]

Such intransigence served as a constant reminder to the Federalists of how precariously they were situated. If they failed to act at all, the public would not have confidence in them, but if they acted too forcefully public opinion might turn against them.

II

This is why during the spring of 1798 the Federalists watched public response to the dispatches so carefully, and why they were heartened by the avalanche of addresses which descended upon the president. These came from state legislatures, from town meetings, from college students, from societies and masonic lodges, from grand jurors, from military companies, and often from the young men of the larger towns, continuing without interruption late into the autumn.[36] With few exceptions, they endorsed the administration's policy toward France and offered "their property to support, and their lives to defend [the] dear-bought, sacred and inalienable rights" of "national interest, honor, and independence." [37] The addresses were not in themselves a surprise to the Federalist leadership, for its members had often had a hand in drafting and circulating them,[38] but the number and general spirit of them was unexpectedly gratifying. Almost all, but particularly those from young men, college students, and military companies, breathed a martial ardor which the president tried to increase. An address by the Young Men of Boston drew from Adams the exhortation, "to arms . . . to arms especially by sea." In his reply to a Duanesboro address he virtually declared that the nation was at war with France, and he responded to another from the Soldier Citizens of New Jersey by reiterating the opinion that only "the *degraded* and the deluded" opposed administration measures and that in case of a French invasion, French supporters should be "condemned to the severest punishment an American can suffer—that of being conveyed in safety within the lines of an invading enemy." [39] Adams was giving presidential sanction to the idea that the opposition was disloyal, if not traitorous.

This was going further than some Federalists thought prudent. Several began to take exception to the temper of the replies. Hamilton commented that the New Jersey militia reply was "intemperate and revolutionary," adding: "It is not . . . for the government to breathe an irregular or violent spirit." [40] It was also inevitable that in the course of responding to a hundred addresses, all on the same topic, some of the controversial ideas and attitudes expressed in the *Defense of the Constitutions of the United States* and the *Discourses on Davila* should again peep out.[41] In the *Aurora,* "Nestor" objected strongly to the reply to the Young Men of Philadelphia. Adams had said in it that the American Revolution had proceeded "not from a desire of innovation, not from discontent with the government under which we were born and bred, but to preserve the honor of our country, and vindicate the immemorial liberties of our ancestors," and that independence was "not an object of predilection and choice, but of indispensable necessity." "Nestor" denied this vehemently, and insisted that Americans had resisted Britain not just for independence, but for freedom. "To obtain an exchange of masters would not have transported them to hazard fortune and life, it would not have induced them to put at stake everything that was dear and valuable," [42] he said. Another critic, "Senex," remarked that Adams's replies seemed designed to convince the people that democracy was impractical and to reconcile them to monarchy and aristocracy. Certainly his chastisement of the Plymouth addressers for denouncing the British and his frequent references to the French Revolution as a military usurpation were not likely to please many Americans, regardless of the dispatches.[43]

Nevertheless, any ground the Federalists had lost through Adams's replies they more than regained by a new development which seemed to confirm that the dispatches were having the desired effect. In sermons delivered on the National Fast Day proclaimed by Adams for May 9, it became evident that most of the more influential publishing clergy were ready to give active support to the administration in its quarrel with the French Directory.[44] Though only twenty-three such sermons were published, they came from all over the land and represented all the more conservative denominations including the Catholics and the Jews.[45] The Federalists had known all along that the clergy had potential for helping mold public opinion because they were part of virtually every community, enjoying special authority and prestige among their less literate, generally apolitical parishioners. They had exercised their powers before in rallying the people behind the move for independence, and more recently in quashing Shays's Rebellion. And from this time on, the majority of the clergy in the older established sects of the northern and middle states became faithful allies of Federalism. Again and again, in countless sermons preached on local holidays and also in the National Fast Day sermons of 1799, they endorsed the Federalist cause against France.

This active support was the more gratifying to the Federalists because they had hitherto dismissed the clergy as unreliable. The Federalists' one former attempt to mobilize them for political purposes had not been a great success. The occasion had been the National Thanksgiving proclaimed by Washington for February 19, 1795, when the Whiskey Rebellion and the agitation over Jay's mission were still fresh in everyone's mind. The Federalists expected great things from it, and in some respects they were not disappointed. Fisher Ames observed with satisfaction that "the Thanksgiving has helped tone the public mind." [46] A few of the sermons were all that the Federalists desired, roundly condemning the democratic societies and warning against French influence.[47] Most ministers were content to extol the virtues of submission to lawful government, of using only electoral remedies in case of grievances, and of keeping the peace at home by remaining neutral during the European war. Even so tepid an endorsement of these eternal verities was welcome, however, for the sermons usually also eulogized the president, congratulated the administration on preserving the peace, and deplored the growing evidence of party spirit. But the general effect was spoiled by certain jarring notes.[48]

Some of the clergy seemed to show more partiality for France and her revolution than the Federalists cared to see. Federalism did not yet call for the vilification of all things French, but Federalists had come to believe that the principal threat to American neutrality was the people's infatuation with France and they were not pleased with "Jacobinist" reminders of her help in the American Revolution or with assertions that future national security depended on the French republic triumphing over the coalition.[49] They would have preferred that endorsements of the French Revolution be qualified by criticism of its dreadful excesses and reminders that America had done all she could to further the cause of liberty.[50] Worse still was that some of the clergy harangued their congregations on the dangers of British influence.[51] Ebenezer Bradford of Rowley, Massachusetts, had even gone so far as to defend the democratic societies, to damn the president's Thanksgiving Day proclamation for failing to mention Christ or to endorse the French Revolution, and to suggest that the government's policies had been the first cause of the Whiskey Rebellion.[52] David Tappan's attempt to administer a public rebuke to Bradford [53] only provoked him to the still more outrageous charge that Washington's regard for the interests of Christianity was questionable.[54] And the clergy who had used their Thanksgiving sermons to assure the people that the Jay Treaty would make an honorable peace, were so cowed by the uproar that followed disclosure of its terms that (with one notable exception) they were not heard from on this subject again.[55]

The trouble was that the people in general had an overwhelming sympathy for France and all things French, and their ministers shared their feelings. This was why the clergy had hailed the French Revolution with joy and continued to justify it long after its anticlericism, its terror, and its infidelity had become plain to all. Like most Americans, they were gratified to think that France had caught her spark of liberty from their flame, but they were especially delighted because they foresaw the destruction of Catholic idolatry. They did deplore the excesses of the revolution, but believed they were unavoidable and should not obscure the greatness of the cause. Even outrages against religion were tolerated as the understandable response of men whose only acquaintance with it was the irrational superstition of Catholicism.[56]

The clergy had also an economic inducement to partake in their congregation's Francophilia. They had been left very poor by the inflation that accompanied the Revolution and their lot was not improved by the economic development of the 1790's. Most parishes had made only minimal adjustments in ministerial salaries, if any at all. Consequently the clergy were anxious to stay on good terms with their parishioners in the hope that their lot might sometime be ameliorated.[57] This had made them so sensitive to objections raised against their interference in political matters that the Federalists had no reason to think they would ever be politically useful. Until the National Fast of 1798, they regarded the clergy with an indifferent condescension epitomized in John Davis's response to Tappan's "semi-political sermon" just before the dispatches were published: "Dr. Tappan, with great learning and ability, is one of the meekest men in the world." [58]

Tappan's offense had been his failure to pronounce that the causes of religion and Federalism were one, an identity which seemed obvious to Federalist leaders who knew how afraid of infidelity the orthodox clergy had been since Part One of Thomas Paine's *Age of Reason* appeared in 1794. This fear was repeatedly expressed in their published sermons, and it had grown into something like panic by 1797 when they saw that all their exhortations had failed to halt the decline in their congregations and the increasing profanation of the Sabbath.[59] As matters went from bad to worse, some ministers tried to bolster their arguments against infidelity by identifying it with the excesses of the French Revolution. Tappan had been among the first to take this tack, and it seemed to the Federalists that if anyone were to be sensible of the unity of clerical and Federalist interests, it should be he. Since 1793 he had been urging his congregation to shun the French example, and as early as 1795 he had shown himself aware of the implications French political successes would have for the fight against infidelity. In words of censure addressed to Bradford, he had then asked whether

faithful friendship to the cause of Christ and the best interests of man [did not] require the public teachers and defenders of the gospel explicitly to guard their flocks and their country against those sceptical irreligious principles, which come to them recommended by the boastful and fascinating charms of *reason* and *infidelity,* and arrayed in all the splendor of a popular and triumphant Revolution? [60]

And surely he was no less sensitive to the implications of having an "atheist" like Jefferson as president than his fellow clergy, who were attributing the decline of religion to prominent men who "should have been foremost in setting the opposite example" but instead had flaunted "practical contempt of the Sabbath, and neglect of public worship." [61]

Tappan's refusal to be more outspoken may have disappointed the Federalist leadership, but they were to find ample compensation in the published National Fast Day sermons. All were free of the critical note that had been present in 1795, and better still, a significant number explicitly linked the cause of the clergy in their fight against infidelity to the cause of the politicians in their fight against French influence. Jedediah Morse even advanced a preposterous theory that the French Revolution was part of an interna-

tional conspiracy to do away with Christianity and all civil government, a conspiracy which could be traced back to a central European
society of freethinkers called the Bavarian Illuminati, and which was
even now menacing America.[62] Morse was portraying France not
merely as an example to be shunned but as an irreligious threat to
be resisted, hoping thereby to recruit for the political struggle against
her any remaining popular loyalty to the ancient faith. His daring
was appreciated by the politicians, as they proved by their eagerness
to help disseminate his ideas. Morse wrote to Secretary of State
Pickering in early 1799 that "an editn. of 450 of my Sermon and
Appendix is nearly gone—& a second of 800 is in press. A number
of gentlemen in Boston have thought it might be useful to send a
copy to every clergyman in the commonwealth, & have agreed with
the printer to furnish them, & they will be distributed when the
members of the legislature return here." [63] Some lay leaders even
quoted Morse in their Fourth of July orations.[64]

The idea of a conspiratorial Illuminati did not originate with Morse.
He had been reading the anti-Jacobin propaganda of John Robison,
a Scotsman whose *Proofs of a conspiracy against all the religions
and governments of Europe* purported to be an eyewitness account
of Illuminati activities. From this book, Morse had extracted his
"evidence" that a secret organization of infidels had infiltrated European masonry, and through it were trying to "acquire the direction
of education—of church management—of the professional chair and
of the pulpit—to bring their opinions into fashion by every art, and
to spread them among young people by the help of young writers." [65]
Other Americans before Morse had noticed Robison's work,[66] but he
was the first to embrace and even go beyond it in arguing that this
alleged conspiracy threatened America as well as Europe. He saw
in the United States the same "proofs" of their machinations as
Robison had seen abroad. Government and religion "from the most
corrupt to the most pure, are reviled and abused, in a similar manner,
in similar language . . . seemingly by common consent. . . . Have
we not reason to suspect," asked Morse, "that there is one secret plan
in operation, hostile to true liberty and religion, which requires to
be aided by these vile slanders?" [67]

This was, to say the least, tenuous evidence on which to rest a
case. Yet the intellectual leaders of the New England churches were

the men responsible for crediting this theory and undertaking to disseminate it as widely as possible. Morse himself was intellectually renowned, with an international reputation as an American geographer and an honorary degree from the University of Edinburgh. And he was joined by no lesser men than Timothy Dwight, President of Yale College, and later by David Tappan, Hollis Professor of Divinity at Harvard. Their chorus was soon swelled by the voices of Samuel McCorkle of North Carolina and Joseph Lathrop of western Massachusetts, two of the most prolific authors among the publishing clergy.[68] The authority of these five intellectual leaders was seconded by many of the lesser clergy until "Illuminati" became a household word in America.[69] Because these men felt themselves to be singularly responsible for the preservation of the faith, they obviously found it comforting to attribute the inroads of infidelity to some conspiratorial agency beyond their control. But the danger to religion was no greater in July that it had been in April, and the hostility to clerical meddling in politics no less.[70] What impelled men who had been so cautious for so long to display such sudden intellectual and political daring?

A clue may be found in the tone of Federalist polemics. They had begun to move in a direction which made Morse's conspiracy theories seem, if not reasonable, at least within the mainstream of Federalist sentiment. For instance, William Cobbett's scurrilous anti-Jacobin writings, which had been appearing since 1794, ceased to be an isolated extreme. His publication of *The Cannibal's Progress, or the dreadful horrors of French Invasion,* purportedly an account of the French invasion of Germany in 1796, gorged with lurid tales of looting, murder, and rape, began to filter into Federalist Fourth of July orations in 1798.[71] More revealing still was the way the judiciary began to sound like the clergy in their charges to grand juries. The most extraordinary of these was delivered by Judge Jacob Rush to the grand jury of Luzerne County, Pennsylvania, on June 30. Rush hailed the abrogation of Franco-American treaties which was to take place on July 13, and said he hoped that day would thereafter be celebrated like the Fourth of July. He went on to say that, among other reasons, the alliance must be broken if Americans were to be kept free from that moral corruption which had led France to her fearful excesses. All the trouble Europe was currently suffering, he said, could be traced to the success of French reformers and philosophers in disseminating atheism and infidelity, a success linked to their strategy of attacking Christianity through "the sabbath and the laws of marriage" because "some of the strongest propensities of our falen [sic] nature countenance and favor the design." [72]

It is tempting to see this partly as a self-conscious attempt by laymen to ratify the alliance with the clergy that had been projected in the National Fast Day sermons of May. Certainly Rush could have embraced the clerical cause no more warmly than when he observed of the Sabbath that "to the ordinance of public worship, and the knowledge and impressions (particularly of afterlife) disposed by means thereof, we are indebted for that good seed, which produces . . . abundant crops of peace, order, and virtue, in society." There was definitely an element of calculation in the strenuous efforts of political writers and orators to warn the public against the pitfalls of infidelity. William Heth, in *An Infallible Cure for Political Blindness*, June 1798, went out of his way to suggest that impiety in America was one facet of French influence designed to delude the people. And Federalist Fourth of July orations drove home the point that the cause of Federalism and the cause of religion had become one and the same. Dr. Samuel Emerson, haranguing an audience in Kennebuck, Maine, cried: "Let us stand up as one man, rally round our head, and declare to France and all the world, that we will never barter our well-organized Government for their despotic confusion —our trial by jury for their secret daggers or open guillotines—our holy sabbath and heavenly religion, for their sceptical decade and hellish atheism!" [73]

Yet there was more to the politicians' endorsement of the clergy than crude calculation. To many Federalist leaders, developments in Europe after the Treaty of Campoformio in the autumn of 1797 appeared so unprecedented as to suggest that there was some truth in the anti-Jacobin propaganda then being manufactured by refugees like Abbé Barruel as well as by Robison.[74] France was now threatening the traditional European balance of power, a strategic asset on which many Americans had counted even before independence. As long as the great powers were rivals, neither could afford to let the other subdue the young republic. It is true that some Republican thinkers, like the author of *A Caution; or, Reflections on the Present*

Contest, persisted in thinking that a French victory over Britain would mean liberation from the tyrant's yoke.[75] But all responsible national leaders understood that the European balance of power was still essential to American security, and in 1798, when the balance seemed about to tip decisively in favor of France, those whose strategic thinking had been premised on Britain's superiority were badly shaken.[76]

There was nothing to reassure them in the way France treated the smaller European powers. Even before 1797 she had been guilty of excesses, particularly in her conduct toward Holland and Flanders, yet these had seemed at least partially justified by the aggressive coalition formed against her. Beginning with the Treaty of Campoformio however, she embarked on what could only be seen as a series of gratuitous aggressions against her smaller neighbors, including betrayal of Venice, a revolution in Holland, subversion of the Helvetic Confederation, annexation of Geneva, and the capture of Rome, compared to which events the XYZ affair was a minor irritation.[77] The Federalists had still another reason for fearing what would follow from the unprecedented circumstances. They believed their form of government made them as vulnerable to the French style of coercion as those European nations which had fallen under French sway.

Small wonder, then, that in their eyes the future began to assume an apocalyptic aspect. In July 1798 even so level-headed a Federalist as John Quincy Adams could only see great trouble ahead, and early in 1799 he complained to William Vans Murray that the past seven years had shown that "there exists in France a power able and determined to overthrow all government in Europe, and the whole system, religious and political, which has for some centuries governed that quarter of the earth" without desire or means of replacing them. By 1798 there were many who would agree with Samuel Emerson's opinion that "such have been [France's] amazing exertions in the vile project of universal domination, that the only barrier now left, is the powerful English marine, which has hitherto confined her to the continent, and fire and devastation from over-spreading the world." [78]

A mood of grim foreboding hung over the land making Cobbett's hysteria, Rush's accusations, and Morse's Illuminati theory all seem within the bounds of plausibility. Members of Congress conjured up the specter of a "great sectary which has risen up in France" composed of "atheistical philosophers, fanatical politicians, political metaphysicians, and blood-thirsty jacobins" threatening the peace and order of society throughout the world.[79] In vain did the opposition protest that the Federalists were creating and exploiting this alarm to serve their own bad ends.[80] To those who saw Britain as the only security in a world dissolving into chaos, this must indeed have seemed a calamitous time.

III

The addresses and the clergy's leap into politics during the spring of 1798 were signs of a decisive change in public opinion which the Federalists hastened to put to work for them. Well before the National Fast, and before more than a few addresses had been received, the House undertook to consider a proposal (defeated in the emergency session) authorizing the president to procure sixteen armed vessels for convoying American shipping.[81] The opposition promptly denounced it as a war measure, and to drive home the point Albert Gallatin moved an amendment requiring that the vessels "shall not, in time of peace, be employed as convoys to any foreign port or place." [82] This provoked an angry retort from Representative Allen of Connecticut, who accused the Republicans of Jacobinism in obstructing the will of the majority:

I have long considered it as the most prominent feature in the Jacobinic character, the spirit of obstinacy, which knows not to yield: that furious, clamorous spirit, which never acquiesces in measures nor principles, however well settled; which never yields to majorities, but which always seeks, by force or art, to convert minorities into majorities; that spirit which drives men to overset, destroy, or render ineffectual, measures which it disapproves, though adopted by the general consent and approbation of the country.[83]

The Republicans protested that the charge was preposterous, and accused the Federalists in turn of expecting "absolute and unlimited submission to opinions" for which no majority had yet declared.[84] But Samuel Dana retorted with insinuations about the loyalty and patriotism of those who resisted "any measure which had the defence of the country for its object," and the Federalists succeeded in defeating Gallatin's motion while passing their own.[85]

The influence of increasing public support for vigorous defensive measures was even more plain in the debate on the provisional army bill. The bill, which had passed the Senate without difficulty, authorized the president to raise an army of 20,000 and accept volunteer corps into the regular service "whenever he shall judge the public safety shall require the measure."[86] The opposition immediately challenged the necessity for this, arguing that there was no danger of invasion from Europe, and that even if there had been, a force of 20,000 was not sufficient to defend so vast a coastline. The detachment of 80,000 militia authorized by a statute in the emergency session the preceding spring would serve this purpose better.[87] Beyond its necessity, furthermore, the Republicans were suspicious of its tendency to strengthen the executive power. They were able to limit the president's discretion to the "imminent danger of . . . invasion discovered, in his opinion, to exist, before the next session of Congress,"[88] but they were not able to defeat the conditional delegation of authority to raise a provisional army, which would give to the president rather than to the state governors the power to appoint officers. This together with the right to accept voluntary companies into the service would in effect allow the president "to arm one description of men exclusively of others" and to create a partisan military organization which could be directed against the opposition.[89] When Republicans in Congress raised these objections, their Federalist adversaries openly acknowledged that the measures could be used to repress French sympathizers, accusing opposition leaders like Gallatin of traitorous collaboration with France.[90] The force of public opinion as expressed in the addresses was evidently their warrant for going to such extremes.[91]

By late May the people were so up in arms that the Federalist majority felt free to move from defensive measures to more positive forms of retaliation. The crisis of 1797–1798 had convinced an increasing number of them that "an active defensive war" against France was desirable. First of all it would accustom the public to see France as an enemy rather than a friend, making it difficult for her ever again to influence American politics. At the same time it would politically discredit the opposition and justify its repression. For the

Federalists believed that as long as there were Republicans to blame them for every French aggression, so long would the Directory be encouraged to continue its provocations. And if opposition activities should succeed to the point of undermining Federalist ability to resist the French threat, there was a real danger that the people would abandon them for the Republicans and a French alliance.[92] Not all Federalists saw war as desirable, nor were those who did converted all at the same time. The war sentiment grew as the public's increasing exasperation with France seemed to place the objective within reach. The Federalists' course was not made easier by the opposition's perception that war would bring their adversaries certain advantages along with repeated charges of deliberate provocation.[93] Nonetheless, by the end of May public opinion had reached such a pitch that they felt able to override Republican protests. First they authorized naval vessels to take the initiative in capturing French privateers hovering about the coast,[94] and then, on June 1, they proposed a suspension of commercial intercourse with France and her dependencies. The measure resembled Clark's nonintercourse proposal of 1794, and the opposition charged that it would put an end to all negotiations with the Directory.[95]

The boldest step openly taken toward war was the introduction on June 6 of Dwight Foster's resolutions calling for the suspension of the Franco-American treaties, the issuance of letters of marque and reprisal against all French vessels, and the granting of a bounty on guns seized from French armed vessels.[96] On June 8, Foster moved that his resolution be referred to "the Committee for the Protection of Commerce and the Defense of the Country, with power to report by bill." [97] The opposition was quick to observe that reference of the resolutions to the committee was entirely unnecessary as it already had the power to report such bills. There was also the further objection that as soon as the French heard about it they would very likely "seize all the property belonging to our citizens within their power." Lastly, the opposition objected to "measures which must inevitably involve the country in a war" when the last official news indicated that "negotiations were still going on." Certainly this measure, which could not but widen the breach, was "very ill-timed." These objections had a marked effect on the Federalist Joshua Coit, who admitted he was "embarrassed," and thought referral would give the resolutions "a sort of sanction." Though he believed there would be war between the United States and France, "he did not wish to go faster to this state of things than the people of this country, and the opinion of the world, would justify," and he joined a bare majority in defeating reference. For this he was roundly denounced by those who wanted more positive measures.[98]

Coit was not the only Federalist unwilling to be responsible for provoking war, but he incurred special wrath because he made open mention of a constraint that deterred even the extremists. In a government as dependent on public opinion as that of the United States, most Federalists agreed that it would be hazardous in the extreme to assume responsibility for a war until "the mass of our people are convinced that war would be just, necessary and unavoidable." Coit had implied that this was not the case.[99]

Abraham Baldwin immediately hastened to underscore the point, observing that though the people "had endeavoured to fortify their public men on this trying crisis, by assurance of their confidence, and their determination not to appear a divided people," it was still the duty of Congress to "conduct public affairs in such a manner as to merit and receive support so grateful on such occasions." Baldwin thought "it would be wise for the Government not to go too fast for their expectations. Perhaps . . . as much [had] been done . . . as was expected. The people had not said expressly that they are desirous of going into war, as some seem to suppose; we know to the contrary—it is only the worst class of them that are desirous of war." In any case, he added, "will not everyone say that it is desirable . . . adjournment should take place before the question of war is finally determined on? It is the very life of all representative Governments that the representative should have opportunity to see his constituents, more especially on such great occasions; it gives mutual confidence and very much fortifies the Government." [100] Baldwin's words were aimed at Federalist reservations about republican government and helped convince a majority that if there were to be war it would be best if France took the odium on herself.[101]

At the same time as the Federalists were being forced to recognize that they could not take the initiative in driving the nation to war, a sequence of events made it seem more desirable than ever. The first was reliable though confidential information that Gerry had agreed to stay in France, at Talleyrand's request, to work against a final rupture between the two countries. This news, received by the government on June 2, diminished the chances that France would declare war and inspired the attempt to provoke her evident in the Foster resolutions of June 6. It also raised the possibility that Gerry's mission would be as damaging to the Federalists as Monroe's had been in 1796, and that he would "write, a la Monroe, a Book" justifying France and condemning the administration.[102]

These fears were aggravated by the departure on June 13 of George Logan, a man who could be relied upon to tell the Directory that France's belligerent measures were playing into Federalist hands, on what was rightly suspected to be an unauthorized peace mission.[103] The crowning touch was the June 16 publication of a letter Talleyrand had written on the preceding March 18, ostensibly addressed to the commissioners in Paris but actually, like Adet's electioneering note of 1796, an appeal to pro-French sentiments in America.[104] This letter appeared in the *Aurora* before the president had been able to communicate it to Congress, and without the commissioners' reply, which set it before the public in the most flattering possible light. It was a heavy blow, followed after two days by Marshall's return and open confirmation of Gerry's continuance in France, which lent substance to the opposition argument that reconciliation was still possible.[105]

This concatenation of events alerted the Federalists to their vulnerability to that French "diplomatic skill" which Y had vaunted before the commissioners in Paris and which they had already come to know only too well during the first year of Adams's administration. Indeed, the Federalists began to realize that this was more of a problem to them than French pressure, which was rapidly destroying France's influence among the American people. King quickly perceived that the Directory, rather than pressing matters to extremes, would "appear to recede from some of her demands, and send you a soothing and insidious message by Mr. Gerry, who, in vindication of his own conduct, must appear to believe the sincerity of that of France." [106] To prevent the resurgence of French influence in America thus became as vital to the Federalists as demonstrating their ability to counter French aggression.

The president did his part, announcing that by now Gerry should have received instructions to end negotiations, and adding that he would "never send another Minister to France without assurances that he will be received, respected and honored." [107] Even before this, Federalists in the House had decided to seize the opportunity offered by public indignation to amend the Provisional Army Act, giving the president immediate authority to organize and arm volunteer companies. [108] They also passed a Naturalization Act requiring the registration of aliens and drastically restricting access to citizenship. Lastly, the power of the administration to control noncitizens was crowned by an Alien Act giving the president discretionary power to remove dangerous foreigners even in time of peace. [109]

The Federalists insisted that such a power was necessary to protect the nation against the "army of spies and incendiaries scattered through the Continent" through whom France intended to subvert national liberty, much as she had subverted the smaller European nations through her partisans. And William Cobbett's exposure of the United Irishmen in May 1798 tried to make it clear that this danger was not confined to Frenchmen. In his *Detection of a Conspiracy by the United Irishmen with the evident intention of aiding the tyrants of France,* he argued that a fast-growing network of Irish *lumpenproletariat* in French pay was threatening American security, and that prudence demanded a legislative remedy in the form of an alien friends act. [110] These fantasies enjoyed a certain plausibility in Philadelphia, which had the largest alien population of any American city but no protective force, so that a mob of foreigners might physically threaten the federal government. [111] But judging from the fact that the Alien Act was never enforced, its real purpose was more to make aliens afraid of supporting opposition activity than to ensure physical protection for the government. Indeed, some suspected that the Federalists wished to give France still greater provocation than before by deporting from the United States some of her prominent citizens living there. [112]

Yet for all the flurry of legislative activity, war remained the only sure way of making the turn which public opinion had taken against France an irreversible one, and this continued to elude the Federalists. A minority seem to have made another attempt to force the issue at the beginning of July, but with no more success than the Foster resolutions had enjoyed a month before. [113] The closest they came to achieving their goal was in passing a series of measures abrogating the Franco-American treaty and authorizing offensive measures against French armed ships, not only by the United States Navy, but in effect by merchant vessels too.[114] Congress never moved to implement the second Foster resolution for issuing general letters of marque and reprisal against French shipping, which would have led to a full-scale naval war. The Federalists eventually could find no better way to secure the advantage that release of the dispatches had won them in the battle for public opinion than the enactment of a sedition law. And the provisions proposed for this made plain exactly what the Federalists wanted the people to continue thinking about France and the opposition.

The most notorious of these provisions was in a bill James Lloyd put before the Senate declaring "that the government and people of France and its colonies and dependencies . . . [are] enemies to the United States and the people thereof;" that any American who adhered to those enemies, "giving them aid and comfort, within the United States or elsewhere" would be subject to the death penalty; and that any person "having knowledge of the commission of any of the treasons aforesaid" and who concealed it would be guilty of misprision of treason.[115] During a House debate the previous April, Dana had observed that "[w]ere a declaration of war to take place, a man who went from this country to join the French army, would be a traitor, and a man who corresponded with any person in France, would be guilty of treason." [116] Lloyd's bill would secure this advantage to the Federalists without putting them to the trouble of a full-scale war, and would make George Logan liable for trial as a traitor. Other parts of the bill would have made it unlawful to question the constitutionality and policy of governmental measures or "to justify the hostile conduct of the French government to the . . . United States," which would in effect have outlawed the opposition.[117]

Robert Goodloe Harper proposed a slightly different sedition bill to the House which, like Lloyd's, was after bigger game than opposition newspapers. Harper did not fear use of the press to libel the government because "a man's propriety of conduct would always be sufficient to shield him against these slanders," and because the people's failure to rise against their government was proof enough that they were not upset by them.

Whilst this abuse was confined to certain newspapers in the United States, it excited in him, therefore, no alarm; but when he heard a gentleman on the floor of this House [Livingston], whose character and connections gave him weight with the people, pronouncing an invective against the Government, and calling upon the people to rise against the law, the business put on a very serious appearance . . . because this speech may have a very different effect from the filthy streams of certain newspapers; it may gain a credit with the community, and produce consequences which all former abuse has failed to do.

Harper therefore proposed that it be made a crime to "utter or publish any false, scandalous, and malicious words or expressions against the Government of the United States," and to assemble in public or in private for the purpose of conspiring against the peace or laws of the United States, "or with any intent to aid, encourage, or abet any hostile designs of any foreign nation against the United States, their people, or Government; or with intent to establish, hold, or carry on any correspondence with any foreign nation, its agents or people, for any of the purposes aforesaid." Even private correspondence having such objectives would have been made unlawful.[118] Such a law, broadly construed, would have made every activity of the opposition liable to prosecution and would have interdicted the Republican party as effectively as the proposals in the Lloyd bill.

The Federalists were forced to settle for far less than either Lloyd or Harper desired. In the final version, the Sedition Act made it unlawful to attempt or promote a seditious conspiracy, or to "write, print, utter or publish" any lies or scandal designed to defame the government or make it the object of the people's hatred.[119] Even so, the Federalists were not able to gain full legal sanction for suppressing their opponents, being obliged to propose a provision allowing truth as defense against the charge of libel and to accept one vesting the decision in a jury. These qualifications were in part a testimony to the continued strength of the opposition. Theodore Sedgwick complained that because the parties were so evenly divided in the House, successful measures had to be "graduated by the feelings and opinions of the most cool and feeble friends." But it was more significant that behind the Republicans in Congress stood a sizable portion of the public. Alexander Hamilton inadvertently acknowledged how much constraint by public opinion the Federalists still felt, despite their advantage in the government, when he said that Lloyd's sedition bill contained provisions "such as more than anything else may endanger civil war." He went on to declare: "LET US NOT ESTABLISH TYRANNY. Energy is a very different thing from violence. If we make no false step, we shall be essentially united; but if we push things to an extreme, we shall then give to faction body and solidity." [120]

PART V

DEFEAT

Federalist gains made during the spring and summer of 1798 were the result not so much of their own initiatives as of a fortunate conjunction of events they had not directed. They were the beneficiaries partly of the passing fear that the traditional European balance of power was going to be upset, but still more of France's monumental diplomatic blunders. Consequently it remained an open question whether or not they could hold on to their newly won advantage if France should either lose her ascendancy in Europe or attempt to regain her influence in American politics by judicious conciliation. In the autumn of 1798, as it became clear that conciliation would be her strategy, many Federalists felt a desperate need to forestall it. They feared France might be so successful in influencing public opinion as to produce the election of Jefferson in 1800, which they firmly believed would negate all their long and patient efforts to preserve neutrality against French power, and would entangle the young nation in a disastrous war with Britain. They did their utmost to counteract French influence through their control of the federal government, only to have President Adams undermine their work by naming new envoys to France. Rightly perceiving that the pursuit of warlike measures for the sake of manipulating opinion would expose the nation to all the dangers of civil war and Jacobin revolution, he determined to negotiate with France rather than adopt an uncompromising policy that might force the United States into alliance with Britain. This courageous act eventually split the Federalist party and ensured a Republican victory in 1800.

The Federalists realized that their defeat in 1800 was no ordinary setback to be easily recouped. They knew better than anyone else how much the leadership of the wise and good depended on an acquiescent, indifferent populace, and they also knew that their foreign policy was doing as much if not more than the opposition to create a popular politics in which they would be at a permanent disadvantage. This process reached a climax during the war crisis of 1798 when a congressional deadlock drove them to appeal to the people and attempt a Republican-style exposure with the release of the XYZ dispatches. Their success in this had obliged the Republicans, who found that for the first time they were themselves the targets of public opinion, to do as the Federalists had done before them and try to manipulate it. To this end they worked through the most prestigious organs of public authority available to them, the Virginia and Kentucky legislatures. Though they were not immediately as successful as their opponents had been, any unrestrained competition between the two parties was bound to favor the opposition in the long run by further stimulating the people and making it more likely that public opinion rather than intrigue would decide elections.

When it came to competing for public opinion in 1800, the Federalists were at a decided disadvantage. Divisions in their ranks had rendered useless their greatest asset, control of the federal government, and their war measures were unpopular. These could have been passing disadvantages, but their lack of a popular ideology was a more serious and lasting one. Their efforts to compensate by harnessing Protestant piety to serve their ends were unsuccessful, and though they had two other recourses against hostile public opinion, these too disappointed them. The first was to control it punitively through the Sedition Law, which proved self-defeating. The second was to circumvent it through intrigue in the electoral college, which failed and left them in their last moment of power reduced to choosing between Jefferson and Burr in the House of Representatives.

9. Rout

Though some Federalists had misgivings about the actions of Congress during June and July 1798, there was still much that they could be pleased with. They had gained a measure of control over all branches of the federal government, and despite the trammels still set on them by public opinion, they had succeeded in meeting French aggression with a limited naval war. The doubts they had suffered throughout the first year of Adams's presidency about the people's willingness ever to resist France had now been lifted. Indeed, once over this hurdle, many Federalists felt more confident of public support while France continued to pressure the nation than they would have done if she had desisted. They realized that as long as hostilities continued, however limited, this would help purge the people of their Francophilia and discredit the opposition. And as long as France remained supreme in Europe, they felt reasonably certain she would persist in her aggression toward the United States. If she ever did give up what Gallatin called her "egregious folly," [1] however; if she stopped threatening national dignity and independence, and offered to deal with America on equal terms; if she showed some respect for America's neutral rights by repealing the decrees against her commerce and ceasing to prey upon her shipping, might not the people's old affection for France reassert itself? It was impossible to know for sure, though one could confidently say that the longer hostilities lasted, the less vunerable the republic would be to any resurgence of French influence. One thing only was certain: if France could regain her former stature in American eyes, all would be lost.

I

This is why many Federalists were disturbed by official and unofficial reports during the autumn of 1798 that the Directory was interested in reconciliation. Most disquieting of all were the documents arising from Gerry's informal negotiation with Talleyrand after Pinckney and Marshall had gone. The public did not see them all until they were communicated to Congress on January 18, 1799, but Talleyrand had published his July 12 letter to Gerry in the French press, whence it had found its way first into the British papers, then at the beginning of October into the American papers along with Gerry's answer.[2] This letter was in some ways very much like that which had been written on March 18 at the close of negotiations with the three commissioners. Talleyrand tried to pin all blame for the rupture between America and France on the Adams administration. He claimed that Pinckney had been dismissed the first time for lack of adequate powers, and that the mission of the three envoys had been prejudiced by the administration's anti-French statements during the emergency session of 1797. Gerry's reply was a devastating exposure of the inconsistency between Talleyrand's dismissal of Pinckney for inadequate powers and his badgering Gerry to solicit new ones. He pointed out that for him to have negotiated with the Directory by himself would have amounted to transferring executive power from the American government to the French.[3]

Yet Talleyrand's letter of July 12 contained a postscript dated July 15 which was a clear indication that the Directory did not mean to let the United States provoke it into a declaration of war. Responding to the United States laws authorizing the seizure of French warships and the suspension of commercial relations with France, Talleyrand declared that despite these provocative acts, which appeared to leave the Directory "no honorable choice but war," his government confirmed "the assurances which I have given you on its behalf" by limiting reprisal to "a temporary embargo on American vessels." He went on, "It is yet ready, it is as much disposed as ever, to terminate, by a candid negotiation the differences which subsist between the two countries. Such is its repugnance to consider the United States as enemies, that, notwithstanding their hostile demonstrations, it means to wait until it be irresistibly forced to it by real hostilities."[4] What is more, Gerry's suggestion that the Directory should show good will by recalling its privateers and restraining them "by severe penalties to the proper objects of capture" seemed to have been accepted when the Directory issued a series of decrees limiting their

activities in American waters. In a parting note dated July 22, Talleyrand waived "every preliminary respecting a loan, and explanations
on the subject of the speeches delivered," informing Gerry that negotiations could be resumed in Paris with assurance that "every Envoy
who shall unite your advantages cannot fail to be well received." [5]
And in a letter written to the president upon his return to the United
States, Gerry reported that the Executive Directory were eager for
rapprochement if for no other reason than to avoid an alliance of
Great Britain and the United States against France.[6]

Besides the Gerry dispatches, the administration had unofficial
evidence that the Directory wanted peace. At the end of July, Joel
Barlow wrote to his friend James Watson that France was "unequivocal for avoiding a war between the two republics," having officially
declared that

1st. The Directory is ready to name a minister to treat with any that shall
be named on the part of the United States. 2nd. All claims for loans of
money, and all apologies for offensive speeches made by the Executive on
either part, are laid aside. 3rd. All piracies and illegal depredations on
American property are disavowed by the Directory, who have ordered all
commissions given to privateers in the West Indies to be withdrawn, and
new commissions to be issued, in which the proprietors and commanders
of privateers, are to be restricted, under bonds, to the legal objects of
capture.

Barlow concluded, "This is considered here by all parties as a more
pacific overture than was expected, after the irritations that have
been offered on both sides. It is retreating to an open ground that is
quite unsuspicious." But he gave inadvertent support to Federalist
doubts when he added, "A refusal on your part to meet on this
ground, would be considered a declaration of war, and it would be
a war of the most terrible kind." He thought peace with Britain was
inevitable once the negotiations at Rastatt had reached a successful
conclusion, warning that "the ocean will then be left free for the
transportation of French troops, and the two republics left to execute
the projects of the British cabinet, and to disgrace the principles of
both their revolutions." [7]

In mid-August the Directory lifted the embargo on American
vessels which Talleyrand had announced to Gerry in his letter of
July 15 and released the seamen detained by its authority. There

was an offensive preamble claiming that this act would compel the American government to "take measures conformable to the pacific disposition of the French Republic" unless it were "abandoned to the passions of the British Cabinet" or "[un]faithful to the interests of the American nation," and the objectionable decree of 29 Nivôse, making all American vessels in effect lawful prizes, was still in force.[8] Nevertheless, this was a sign that the Directory was mending its ways, and it was followed by others. Richard Codman, a Boston Federalist, wrote from Paris in August to his Harvard classmate, Harrison Gray Otis, urging that the administration should "once more risque sending a minister" because "the moment is extremely favorable for an accommodation." George Logan returned from his mission at the beginning of November bearing official notice of the French government's release of American ships and men. And Joel Barlow wrote to Washington at the beginning of October reaffirming that "the French Directory is at present sincerely desirous of restoring harmony between this country and the United States, on terms honorable and advantageous to both parties."[9] At the same time, French privateering in the Caribbean began to diminish, though this could be attributed to the vigor of American armed vessels in prosecuting the naval war, and letters from American diplomats in Europe, particularly from William Vans Murray at the Hague and John Quincy Adams at Berlin, made it plain that the Directory had abandoned her former policy if not her former intentions.[10]

No Federalist better expressed his misgivings about the Directory's conciliatory posture than James Watson of New York in his reply to Barlow's letter: "You know perfectly well the structure of our government, and that it is impossible that its executive should be long at variance with the wishes of the people." Both the executive and the people wanted peace, he said, but

it must be a fair and honourable peace, not one that invites French anarchists to intermeddle in our elections, to debauch our citizens, and to vilify our government, not one which exposes us to French insults and rapacity at home and abroad, and exhibits us to the world, in the persons of our envoys, as a spectacle for derision. Perceiving that we were recovering from our preposterous predilections for France, that the artifices practiced against us were not sufficiently refined; the Directory condescends to spread new snares for our entanglement."[11]

Watson questioned that France's expressed willingness to name a
new minister who would treat with America, to drop all claims for
loans and apologies, and to restrain her privateers, were true signs
of an honest desire for reconciliation.[12] He concluded with a ringing
declaration that the United States would not be scared out of its
independence by any threat of war from France. On the contrary, he
wrote, "they fear her invasions less than her friendship. The examples
of Holland, Switzerland, and the Italian states are before them, and
they teach them to think of France as the beautiful female figure
which pierced with darts, and crushed the bones of the victims it
embraced." [13]

France's sudden change of face was made the more ominous by
the simultaneous resurgence of the opposition at home, a coincidence
suggesting collusion. From April when the dispatches were published
until the autumn of 1798 the Federalists were kept in the center of
the public stage by favorable addresses and replies, sermons, and
Fourth of July orations. There was an occasional dissenting oration [14]
and several addresses opposing war,[15] but these usually came from
minorities within larger groups which had already endorsed Federalist
policy, and they were drowned by the crescendo of approving voices.
In September, the tide began to turn. The Virginia leadership struck
back through county resolutions in their own state and in Kentucky
culminating in the resolutions passed by the two state legislatures at
the end of the year.[16] This opposition move was not as visible as its
proponents might have wished because the yellow fever epidemic
of 1798 had crippled those newspapers which had national circulation.
Still it began to blaze up just as the first enthusiasm fired by the dispatches was dying down. And the Federalists believed that as long
as the opposition was conspicuous, so long would France continue
to meddle in American affairs.[17]

The close connection between open opposition and French subversion continued to be a serious problem to the Federalists, and the
powers they had arrogated during the war crisis offered no real
solution. If they tried using the volunteer companies in the provisional army to crush the opposition by force, they would run a
grave risk of civil war. Even the Alien and Sedition Laws were only
minor aids. The threat of an alien law had caused the departure
of well-known Frenchmen like Victor Marie Dupont and the Comte

de Volney, the latter an intimate friend of opposition leaders in Philadelphia, and it helped to silence John Daly Burke's *Time Piece*.[18] Nor was it any accident that the first prosecution under the Sedition Law was brought against Matthew Lyon during his campaign for re-election to the House. The Federalists succeeded in convicting and imprisoning Lyon, but this was not a technique they could use against the opposition as a whole. For one thing, the judicial apparatus of the United States was too underdeveloped to handle such a load at short notice. For another, in solidly Republican districts such proceedings would probably provoke some violent challenge to the court's authority. Even a successful prosecution would have no more than a temporary effect, for a determined opposition would always find someone else to carry on the enterprise. The real purpose aimed at in the early sedition prosecutions was intimidation. If this should fail to silence the Republicans, the only other recourse was for the Federalists to try eclipsing them by their own superior visibility.[19]

II

The Federalists set great store by their control of the government because it allowed them to keep their view of the quarrel uppermost in the public mind. To this end, when Congress assembled at the beginning of December the president's address congratulated the nation on "that spirit which has arisen in our country against the menaces and aggression of a foreign nation." Adams went on to put French peace overtures in Federalist perspective. He acknowledged that the Directory "appears solicitous to impress the opinion that it is averse to the rupture with this country" by seeming ready to receive a minister from the United States. But he added:

It is unfortunate for professions of this kind that they should be expressed in terms which may countenance the inadmissible pretension of a right to proscribe the qualifications which a Minister of the United States should possess; and that . . . the existence . . . of a [conciliatory] disposition, on the part of the United States, of which so many demonstrative proofs have been given, should even be indirectly questioned.

Speaking of the Directory's decree limiting her privateers to seizures authorized by French laws, Adams questioned that this would give much relief as "these laws are themselves the sources of the depredations of which we have so long, so justly, and so fruitlessly complained." He singled out the decree of 29 Nivôse "which subjects to capture and condemnation neutral vessels and their cargoes, if any portion of the latter are of British fabric or produce, although the entire property belongs to neutrals," and called it "an unequivocal act of war on the commerce of the nations it attacks." [20] Though Adams's speech concluded with a pledge that the United States would "give no room to infer that we abandon the desire of peace," he said that "to send another Minister, without more determinate assurances that he would be received, would be an act of humiliation to which the United States ought not to submit." Both houses of Congress warmly reiterated these sentiments.[21]

The Federalists did not mean to stop here. When the administration at last released the official Gerry-Talleyrand correspondence, with it was a long letter by Pickering which aimed at accomplishing three objectives. The first was to prove to the American public that Talleyrand's attempt to disown X, Y, and Z was a pretense, so that the opposition would no longer be able to claim that these three men had acted without authorization. This was easily done provided it were allowed that Talleyrand had acted for the Directory. Secondly, he hoped to prove that despite its willingness "to inveigle Mr. Gerry into a separate negotiation," the Directory had no serious intention of resolving Franco-American differences. No government truly desiring negotiation would have rejected the other party's ambassadors, and that France had done so proved she meant rather to dictate treaty terms favorable to herself. Then she could not lose no matter what happened: if the treaty were ratified, all to the good; but if not, the United States would be divided and its defenses against French influence and power weakened. Pickering dismissed as a sham Talleyrand's opening suggestion of May 24 that the United States should put France on an equal footing with Britain in her treaties. When pressed on this, Talleyrand had changed the subject to the Consular Convention, "of all the possible subjects in difference the most insignificant." In any case, if he had ever really intended to make an accommodation he could have done so through the three original commissioners who had been instructed to accept such terms.[22]

Lastly, Pickering dealt with the decrees Gerry and Logan had brought home. He pointed out that even if France repealed all her recent measures against American commerce, the greater part of her depredations would still be authorized under the decree of July 2, 1796. He dismissed the gestures made by France as "a bold imposture" and went on to say that France's conduct with respect to American commerce had been so perfidious that until she agreed to negotiate damages she could not be trusted. What if publication of the dispatches had produced such anger in America that the Directory was now "cowering" before her? As Pickering reminded his fellow countrymen, "the tiger crouches before he leaps upon his prey." [23]

While Pickering labored over his lengthy aspersions of French sincerity, surely without much hope that they could equal the effect produced by the unofficial correspondence, Federalists in the House made their first order of business the outlawing of private diplomacy such as George Logan and Joel Barlow had engaged in. On December 26, Roger Griswold proposed a committee to frame an act that would make it a crime to "usurp the Executive authority of this Government, by commencing or carrying on any correspondence" with foreign governments concerning disputes between them and the United States.[24] This was said to have been made necessary by France's avowed policy of subversion through foreign influence and domestic faction. Edward Rutledge of South Carolina, arguing that many European nations had been subverted by these means, said: "The patriotic party in Holland, previous to their revolution, had their agent in France; and unauthorized individuals had everywhere been employed in the subversion of the old establishments." The United Irishmen had employed agents in France "who instructed the French army where to land, where to find pikes, provisions, and other necessaries, for their work of devastation." [25] And Robert Goodloe Harper asserted that recent events in Europe proved how "republican Governments are especially menaced with destruction" by "the introduction of foreign influence," going on to describe the reasons for this:

Monarchies, despotisms, aristocracies, which, for the most part, depend on the support of a few, may be subverted by foreign force, but popular Governments, unless quite contemptible, in point of extent, cannot be subverted without the aid of internal division. This division is effected by means of foreign influence, which supports, and is supported by, domestic faction; therefore, everything that tends, however remotely, to facilitate the alliance between these two deadly foes, is most carefully to be guarded against.[26]

The Federalists argued that the proposed legislation was a legitimate response to the French threat, but the opposition was not convinced. Gallatin could not deny "that there might be an interference with the executive authority . . . it would be proper to punish by law," or that "men who should attempt to subvert the Constitution by foreign aid, ought to be liable to punishment." He did object, though, to the provision which would make "*any correspondence*" liable to punishment instead of specifying criminal correspondence such as "an invitation of a foreign Power to invade a country." He believed "the nature of the correspondence must constitute the crime, and not the act of corresponding." Nor did he think that such a law was needed. Criminal correspondence was already punishable under existing laws, and it seemed doubtful that any individual could usurp the executive authority in this way.[27] As for the dangers Harper spoke of, the opposition denied that there was any division in America when it came to repelling foreign aggression or changing the nation's form of government. They admitted a division of opinion over government policy, but argued that they were seeking an electoral remedy, not a revolutionary one. Even if there were some men who would have liked to enlist the help of France, they questioned that it could ever be obtained. As Gallatin asked, "Did not our distance from Europe, and the want of naval resources of that nation whose interference was apprehended, secure us from that danger?" [28]

The opposition had more positive reasons for objecting to the proposed law than the lack of necessity for it. They charged that it was part of a system the Federalists were using to crush the opposition, a system of creating alarm and despondency among the people. Nicholas accused the Federalists of perpetually declaiming that "nothing ought to be done, no sentiment offered in opposition to regular Government . . . because it produces divisions in a country." [29] Gallatin pointed out that the bill as drawn would punish expressions of opinion rather than assumptions of power. It seemed to him "a

second edition of the sedition act," extending the government's punitive powers from defamatory publications to speech and private
correspondence.[30] Gallatin said that the French had seen America
as a divided nation, not because of anything the opposition had
done, but because of charges and measures instituted by the Federalists.[31] Nicholas too charged that the only real danger of division
came from Federalist policy, for "so long as the people are not actually oppressed, and they can see in their Government the seeds of
correction, no attempt at dividing or subjugating the people of this
country could be successful." [32] And Gallatin pointed out that French
influence in Europe had subverted only those governments which
were already unpopular.[33]

The Republicans were also afraid that the Federalists intended
this measure to "bring censure on all the acts which can flow from
[Logan's mission], and prevent the people of this country from sus-
pecting the Government of doing wrong in acting so much on party
principles with respect to France." [34] Consequently, the opposition
was as eager to show that Logan's actions were both patriotic and
desirable as they were to prove that a law so obviously drafted in
response to them was unwarranted. Gallatin said that

if a man of his own accord, out of a pure love for his country—out of a
sincere desire for peace, or out of hatred for war—were to go over to
France . . . and to exert his endeavors, however weak they might be, to prevail upon persons in power there to offer such terms of accommodation to
our Government as he is persuaded would be accepted, he saw nothing
either criminal or improper in such a conduct, but the contrary.[35]

And Nicholas avowed that "if he had had any share in sending the
gentleman alluded to to France, he should not be ashamed to con-
fess it—he should not be ashamed or afraid to promote the peace of
his country." At the same time, he agreed that if "any individual
or set of men were bent upon involving the country in war, the
case would be very different." [36]

The Federalists replied that peace was not always preferable
to war. France had shown a disposition to overthrow every government that did not accede to her least demand, and the best safeguard for national independence was to reject her dishonorable terms
at once, without any sign of disunity.[37] Logan's mission had pro-

claimed to the world that the nation was divided because he was the envoy of a party, and as Harper said, "The French government had told us plainly and in so many words, that such a party did exist among us; that they relied on this party . . . and that, although this party could not direct the government, it could so embarrass and fetter it as to disable it from moving hand or foot against France." He did not believe the authors of the mission were prompted by a sense of national injury, for the French had produced this in most Americans long before, while these men had not been moved to act until the whole country was so outraged that the government might be forced to make war on France. Nor did he think this was a genuine attempt to make an honorable peace, but suspected that Logan had been told to persuade France that she should "change her system of menace and blustering for an insidious system, whereby our resentments might be disarmed, and our spirits of resistance lulled to sleep." [38]

What most upset the Federalists about the Logan mission was the fear that despite their strenuous efforts to whip up public opinion, peace was still more popular than war. Dana of Connecticut was giving tacit acknowledgement to this when he countered the objection that no private individual could usurp executive power by observing that the danger was in the capacity of individuals to seduce that public opinion on which America's republican government must rest. [39] James Bayard suggested how a person might do this when he asked, "Can it be right that an individual go and offer terms of peace which could have no other effect than to excite . . . clamor at home . . . by making it appear that there is an unwillingness in the Government to make peace?" Suppose "a Treaty of Peace was negotiated . . . and Government should not approve it, it would be thrown out to the people as a bone of contention" and the result might be "civil war." [40] Harper betrayed the same fear when he introduced a memorial written to the Directory by Richard Codman as an illustration of the way in which individuals might usurp executive authority. The memorial urged France to refrain from uniting Americans against her and driving them into Britain's arms when friendlier conduct would "draw back those wandering affections . . . and leave the true American character to blaze forth in the approaching elections." Harper put the worst possible construction upon these words. "Thus," he proclaimed triumphantly, "a foreign Government is instructed, by the envoy of a domestic faction . . . in the proper method of aiming a successful stab at the vitals of our Constitution, by influencing our elections." [41]

Gallatin was quick to seize on these slips. "The gentleman from Delaware," he said (referring to Bayard), thought it "highly dangerous . . . that an individual might offer terms of peace to a foreign Government which it might be willing to accept; which, when they came to be published in this country, would appear so reasonable to the people, that the refusal of them on the part of our Government, might have the effect to destroy the popularity of the Government." This seemed to rest on the indefensible proposition that the government should refuse terms of peace which were popular throughout the Union. [42] As for the Codman memorial which had upset Harper, Gallatin retorted that the Federalists thought nothing of inviting "further aggressions, nay, an invasion, by assuring France that they have a party here ready to receive them," but they thought it criminal that Codman had spoken of the people's unanimous determination to resist French aggression. Bayard's and Harper's words pointed to the conclusion that the Federalists were apprehensive that France might be led to abandon the outrageous measures which had given the Federalists their justification for repression. [43]

Gallatin's blast silenced Harper, but Bayard returned to the fray six days later with a lengthy speech designed primarily to prove that Codman's memorial was in fact written by Logan. This was an impossible task to start with, and Bayard compounded his difficulties by drawing his proof "from circumstances connected with evidence of the same nature with that on which rested the belief of our holy religion . . . the internal evidence of the work itself." [44] He followed this statement with an argument which inspired confidence in neither his religion nor his politics. No Federalist, he said, could have written what had been produced before the House; Codman was a Federalist, therefore Codman had not written the letter. But he did conclude by restating the Federalist position much more forcefully than he had done before. [45]

Bayard asserted that Logan and his Republican apologists knew that "French popularity was their popularity," and that war with

France would destroy both utterly and for ever.[46] At the same time, they also knew that the people clung to peace. Therefore, if they could make it appear that they were the peace makers while the administration was guilty of warmongering they could "strip the Government of public favor and support, and confer it on a party." If Logan were allowed to succeed, the principle would be established of "allowing a foreign Government to erect a minority in this country into a ruling power, and thereby to establish an influence among us destructive of our independence." [47]

This was a marked improvement on his previous argument, but it was still open to a serious objection. For as Nicholas pointed out, neither Logan nor the Codman memorial had ever suggested that the peace should be made by anyone but the executive of the United States.[48] Bayard's position was untenable. As Nicholas had said earlier on in the debate, because there could be no peace without the administration's consent, "the only possible evil which could arise to the Government from the interference of individuals for the purpose of procuring peace to the country would be that it might be forced to make peace against its will, on terms which it dare not refuse." With heavy irony, he added, "It is not possible . . . that a majority of Congress may have interests distinct from our constituents—an interest which they dare not avow—which may induce them to wish for war." [49] Because the Logan Act made sense only if it were allowed that to pursue peace and avoid unnecessary war were criminal,[50] the debate on it did more than charges in the opposition press could ever do to dramatize before the public how great a stake the Federalists had acquired in preventing a Franco-American *rapprochement*.

III

The large Federalist majority which endorsed the Logan Act, together with Pickering's tedious report on the dispatches, to some extent concealed how badly the Federalists had been mauled in the House. And though this must have been brutally clear to the leadership, they were not as agitated as might have been expected. A development they had long desired was at last taking place, for between July and December 1798, France lost her strategic advantage. As the second session of the Fifth Congress was closing in

July, there came news that she had at last committed her army, apparently to a Mediterranean adventure. At first it was not clear where the large French fleet that left Toulon on May 19 was going: perhaps to Ireland, where revolutionary fervor had reached fever pitch; perhaps even to the West Indies. But by September, Americans heard that Bonaparte had captured Malta on June 12; before the month was out, it was generally thought that Egypt was the French objective, and by the middle of October this was confirmed. Then, toward the end of November, news came that the French fleet had been destroyed at Alexandria.[51] France had overreached herself; her army had been marooned in Egypt by the English navy, and as the shadow of invasion was lifted from Britain it seemed likely that the continental alliance against France would be reborn. Even before Americans heard about the Second Coalition of Russia, Britain, Austria, Naples, Portugal, and the Porte, the newspapers were predicting that the Congress of Rastatt would be abandoned and "those who thought of purchasing a degrading and precarious Peace from France at the risk of Revolution" would now renew the fight against her.[52]

This sudden plunge of French fortunes from the height of triumph caused the Federalists some embarrassment because it removed their justification for war measures. Yet they preferred a beleaguered France to a victorious one, for they believed the potency of French influence bore some rough relation to her military strength. In any case, they could still argue that France had only ventured 35,000 men in Egypt, and even if she lost every one of them she might still be able to raise a new army for fresh foreign adventures. Not until France had suffered the disasters that marked the outset of her struggle with the Second Coalition was it certain that there was no longer any immediate danger, and this news had not yet arrived when the last session of the Fifth Congress adjourned on March 3, 1799. So when the House prepared a report justifying its defense measures at the end of the session it was still possible to cite Egypt as an example, not of American immunity to French aggression, but rather of the French republic's power to reach across the seas. The report urged that "it be candidly considered, whether some of our fertile and flourishing states did not, six months since, present as alluring objects for the gratification of ambition or cupidity, as the inhospitable climate of Egypt." [53] Though it was impossible to claim that the United States was as vulnerable to French invasion now as she had been before, the committee could still argue that the measures taken in the preceding session continued to be necessary, for "so eccentric are the movements of the French Government, we can form no opinion of their future designs towards our country. They may recede from the tone of menace and insolence, to employ the arts of seduction, before they astonish us with their ultimate designs." [54]

Yet the decline of French power caused a dramatic change in the political prospects of the Federalists. For one thing, as Nicholas observed, it put an outright declaration of war entirely out of the question.[55] For another, the restoration of the European balance of power reduced the hysteria which had so helped the Federalists in the summer of 1798, and gave the Republicans a stronger hand in exploiting the potential unpopularity of unnecessary war measures.[56] Most important of all, it impelled the president to appoint William Vans Murray, at that time the resident minister at the Hague, as a new commissioner to negotiate with France. Adams would look back upon this as the bravest deed of his political career, and indeed it was the most controversial. It brought public vilification of him from men who had been his strongest supporters, and eventually caused a rupture within the Federalist party that helped to elevate Thomas Jefferson to the presidency.

Why did Adams make this decision? The question has been argued back and forth ever since. The high Federalists of New England variously attributed it to unstable character, vanity, and the desire to dredge up votes from the ignorant populace in the coming election. It seemed to them a betrayal of everything they had ever done to stiffen the public mind against French power and influence.[57] Some recent writers have generally agreed with the charge that Adams's reasons were primarily political. They note that except within a small clique of frustrated leaders, the president's action was genuinely popular; and except for the New York vote, influenced by Hamilton's shenanigans, Adams was politically stronger in 1800 than he had been in 1796.[58] But to say that a decision made in February 1799 was aimed at an election a year later is to make too great a separation between cause and effect. As long as the United States remained a minor power, the final outcome of the act was still too uncertain. The negotiations might abort (as indeed they almost did). Or there might be yet another French attempt to interfere in American politics, with France holding up negotiations until the election and then making a Republican administration the price of peace.

Adams was thinking of more immediate concerns than the election. For one thing, he was afraid that if the limited war against France intensified the United States might be forced to ally with Britain and remain forever entangled in European quarrels. This made a rift between the president and the Hamiltonians, who were fascinated by the possibility of an Anglo-American coalition against the colonial empires of France and Spain in Latin America and the Caribbean. They thought this might hasten the day when the United States would be a world power impregnable to influence or interference from the outside. Indeed, Adams differed from these Federalists in believing that peace was still the most direct road to the full consummation of independence.[59]

He was also making a sensitive response to political reality. The general public may have been oblivious to the full implications of the debate on the Logan Act, but they could not have escaped the President. He knew that it was politically hazardous to ignore the Directory's peace feelers on the grounds that they were meant to give Americans a false sense of security. An opposition which had continued to insist that Britain was the nation's real enemy and that war with France was unnecessary and unjust, even at the height of the hysteria produced by the dispatches, would surely grow louder and perhaps violent if the Federalists maintained their hard line toward France despite more and more signs pointing toward peace. If he let the nation blunder into a full-scale war with France for which the Federalists were at all responsible, the result would probably be civil war and national dissolution.[60] Much as Adams loathed Barlow, when Washington passed him Barlow's letter asserting France's willingness to make peace, adding a cautious endorsement, Adams felt free to act. As long as Washington lived, he could not now be outflanked by his own party; and no matter how fiercely some members objected to his nomination of a new commission, they could be forced to accept it by his threat of resigning in favor of Jefferson.[61]

The new mission was an implicit acknowledgement of the power of public opinion in the United States and a repudiation of the fantasy that Federalist manipulative techniques could by themselves keep events abroad from impressing the public mind. This was not lost upon the new editor of the *Gazette of the United States,* John Ward Fenno. In a long article appearing on March 4 he effectively acknowledged that the Federalists had been defeated in their efforts to influence opinion, for the imminence of a general conflict had produced nothing but indifference. Fenno went on to question the viability of the republic, pointing to four signs that the polity was diseased: "the imbecility of our frame of government," the increase in moral depravity, the influence of newspapers with a corresponding dearth of real literature, and the absence of national character and public spirit. Fenno objected to the frame of government as a "system of shifts and expedients," and lamented that although everyone agreed "the reins of government [were] too lax . . . the tendency of *every* amendment" had been to emasculate it the more. He deplored the government's apparent inability to declare war and punish traitors, the decentralization of the judiciary, and the absence of a national church which would give the people the moral instruction missing from their newspapers. But most of all he deplored the federal system, which he believed could bring only endless confusion, obstruction, and insurrection. It stood in relation to state governments, said Fenno, like "an old sow with a farrow of pigs, who have so strengthened and encreased on the nourishment she has afforded them, as to be able to insult her authority and resist her controul." Yet all these defects could have been remedied had it not been for the lack of national pride. Fenno devoutly believed that the nation's only hope had been a "long, bloody and obstinate" war with France through which "the government, though feeble, might have had sufficient energy imparted to it for self-preservation, the protection of its friends and the punishment of its enemies; the tide of depravity might then have been turned and the moral character we derived from our ancestors be retrieved." Instead the nation had failed to unite against France, a failure which had let it split into two factions "whose impending collision must produce bloodshed."

Declaring that "the sun of federalism is fast retiring behind the clouds of turbulence and treason," Fenno concluded by resigning his editorship.[62]

Fenno's anxieties were shared by many Federalists who gave them less indiscreet and irresponsible expression.[63] George Cabot used a more measured tone in his letters to Secretary of State Pickering, but his general sentiments were the same. "It has been frequently remarked," he wrote,

that . . . our distance from Europe had saved us from a participation in its calamities, and had given us opportunity to learn wisdom at their expense; and it has been observed, with some pride and great joy, that finally our people (a majority) had acquired such just ideas of the national policy as to approve and support it at every expence and hazard. If this was the case, the blessing is in great jeopardy, if not absolutely lost.

Cabot thought that the president's appointment of a new commission, proclaiming to the world that he believed *rapprochement* with France possible, was likely to revive in American hearts all the old love for the sister republic. But it was not just the subversion of nationalist spirit which disturbed Cabot; there were also strategic risks: "A negotiation with France will necessarily excite the jealousy, if not the resentment, of the coalesced powers," he wrote, and the United States might come "to dread *their* successes as much as we have dreaded those of France." He was particularly pessimistic about the effect of a *rapprochement* on Anglo-American relations. "We have so many men who seek for a quarrel with Great Britain, that no ordinary skill can prevent it," he declared. If the President were driven to brand his old allies as members of a British faction and seek new ones, the newly achieved amity between Britain and the United States might vanish into thin air. This he believed would adversely affect the work of the commissioners who were trying to settle claims under the Jay Treaty (as did happen) and so encourage the people in their latent hatred of Great Britain.[64]

Although things looked bad, Federalists in general did not agree with Fenno that all was lost. The Federalist-dominated Senate did not dare to defy public opinion by opposing the peace mission, but did make the president agree to enlarge it by two members and procured a delay by extracting his promise that they would not leave

America "until they receive assurances from the French government that they will be received." [65] Having once been victimized by events, the Federalists were now playing for time in the hope that there would be news from abroad more favorable to their plans. And though the Republicans claimed Adams's consent to the new commissioners as proof that the crisis had passed, thereby strengthening their case against certain anti-French measures so that some were defeated,[66] the Federalists put up a vigorous show of resistance. They declared that if France had any sincere disposition to negotiate, it was thanks only to the strong measures taken against her; that the president had said no negotiations could begin until France repealed her decree against British manufacturers; and that there was too good reason to fear the French were only pretending to seek conciliation in order to put America off her guard.[67] Indeed, Gallatin suspected the Federalists of sponsoring the Retaliation Law (which allowed capital punishment of French prisoners if France treated captured American seamen as pirates) for the sole purpose of making Americans lose confidence in the negotiations.[68]

In the event, fortune did not favor either the Federalists or the French. Throughout 1799 France's prospects grew steadily worse. By the beginning of September, Cabot was lamenting that "if the disasters of the campaign are not mitigated by some successes to the arms of France, she will probably grant us everything *in promises.*" Her plight was so pitiable that the only reason Federalists could find for not going on with negotiations was the possibility of a monarchical restoration in France which would make any treaty with the Directory a liability and also incur the enmity of the victorious coalition.[69] Extreme Federalists received just one brief encouragement from events in Europe: the mission was temporarily held up by the *coup d'état* within the Directory during June. All but one of its members had been replaced, and it looked as if the reshuffle might mark the beginning of the end for this particular form of government. This made Adams willing to take Pickering's advice and delay the mission for a while.[70] But before long he grew suspicious that some members of his cabinet were hoping to use this as a pretext for aborting the mission altogether. Warned by his two loyal cabinet members, Charles Lee and Henry Stoddart, Adams hurried to Trenton in October where he was alarmed by Hamilton's unwarranted presence at the temporary seat of government. After hearing Hamilton raise objections which had more to do with the risk of a rupture with Britain than with the momentary instability of the French government, and which would have constituted a permanent bar to any negotiations whatever, Adams resolved to dispatch the commissioners at once.[71]

Even if the extremists had succeeded in preventing this departure for France, they would still have sustained irreparable damage from Adams's February initiative. As Cabot observed to Pickering in October 1799, "we cannot recover the high ground on which we stood twelve months ago." Still, when he learned that the commissioners had been ordered to leave for France at the end of October he confessed that it cost him a night's sleep: "My gloomy imagination is too apt to persuade me that the worst which *can* happen *will* happen, or rather that measures of a *tendency* manifestly evil will produce the evil to which they tend." [72] Along with other extreme Federalists, he saw a Jeffersonian triumph in 1800 and a ruinous war with Britain made inevitable. Their only consolation was that the commissioners had been given much stronger instructions than Pinckney, Marshall, and Gerry before them, making the prospect of an early accommodation with France and a rupture with Britain unlikely. If the commission succeeded, unless its success coincided with a general peace in Europe, a break with Britain would be bound to come.[73]

IV

Meanwhile the rift that had first appeared in Federalist ranks when Adams announced the mission was growing ever wider and deeper, until on the eve of the presidential election the whole party was demoralized.[74] This was already apparent to sensitive observers when the Sixth Congress met in December 1799. The Congress, elected during the XYZ furor, was nominally Federalist. But in a letter to Christopher Gore, Cabot admitted:

They are uncemented, and will do less than their precedessors to promote the common weal. You may see by their answer to the speech [of the president] how they are embarrassed. In order to satisfy Mr. Marshall and the Southern Federalists, it was necessary to *appear* satisfied with the mission; and in order to please others, perhaps all true Federalists, it was

necessary to withhold all praise of the measure. Hence an awkward cir-
cumlocutory phraseology resulted, which, while it seemed to approve,
does not *really* approve the step.[75]

The first session showed no will to influence public opinion by
decisive action such as characterized its predecessor. Most of the
time was consumed in warding off the attacks of a numerically weaker
opposition on such unpopular Federalist measures as the army and
the Alien and Sedition Laws,[76] or in defending the president for
having complied with the Jay Treaty in surrendering to British
authorities one Thomas Nash, wanted for mutiny, who claimed to
be Jonathan Robbins, an American impressed into the British
navy.[77] The beleaguered Federalists at first showed a united front
to their attackers, but signs of disunity emerged when they tried
to take the initiative in two important measures.

The first was their attempt to extend the judicial system. Under
the Judiciary Act of 1789, the scope of the federal courts was limited by giving concurrent original jurisdiction to the state courts.
Though the privilege of appealing cases having to do with federal
rights was retained, most of the business coming before the federal
courts was appellate, and Supreme Court justices were required to
serve also as circuit court judges. Added to the diminutive role of
the federal courts this had lowered the judiciary's prestige and made
it difficult to attract the best men. Jay's refusal to be reappointed
chief justice was to prove this in 1800.[78] The Federalist hope was to
reorganize the federal judiciary so as to make it a more efficient
instrument of the central government's power. As Wolcott wrote to
Ames, "It is impossible, in this country, to render an army an en-
gine of government, and there is no way to combat the state opposition
but by an efficient and extended organization of judges, magistrates, and other civil officers." [79] As an opening move the Federalists proposed a national bankruptcy act which the expanding economy
seemed to make attractive and from which political yields were
expected. They believed it would "lessen opposition to the Government by the most active & clamorous description of persons,
debtors finding an interest in its support" and render "an extension
of the judiciary necessary." [80]

Passage of the bankruptcy act was not a foregone conclusion.

As Sedgwick said in a long letter to King, except for Livingston
"who has conflicting motives," all members of the opposition would
resist a measure that promised to confer certain advantages on the
central government. He added that there were "causes which de-
tach several federalists from its support. In New England it will
break in upon our system of attachment laws, which from habit &
education have more favor than their merit entitles them to; and in
Virginia, in one instance will render lands liable to the payment of
debts and may form a precedent for the extension of that principle." [81] To gain their end, Federalist sponsors were obliged to make
substantial concessions in the scope of the bill. They particularly
disliked having to allow "the trial of the question Bankrupt or not,
by jury," which Sedgwick feared would "be found inconvenient,
embarrassing, & dilatory." Even then, passage came so late in the
session that there was not enough time to follow it with the
Judiciary Act, so that the Federalists were defeated in their hope
that this would create judicial patronage in time for the election of
1800 and provide a more efficient means for enforcing the Sedition
Law. Sedgwick blamed the feebleness of Federalist action in the
House on the influence of Marshall. Sedgwick complained that he
"was looked up to as the man whose great and commanding genius
was to enlighten & direct the national councils," but had a weakness
for popularity which led him to defer to public opinion so much that
his "indecision and *an expression* of doubt" immobilized the southern
Federalists.[82]

Marshall's influence and Federalist disunity were nowhere more
apparent than in the matter of a bill for settling disputed presidential
elections. This bill, proposed by Senator James Ross of Pennsylvania,
was specifically intended to resolve a deadlock in the Pennsylvania legislature over selecting presidential electors. The Republican House supported a measure for popular choice of a general
ticket of electors, while the Federalist Senate insisted on a plan
of district elections designed to give them more than their fair
share of electors. By any equitable division of the vote, the Republicans would have come out ahead of the Federalists, so that the
Federalists could do more damage than they would sustain by refusing all compromise and obstructing the casting of any votes by
the state. It was rumored that Governor Thomas McKean would "re-

ject a bill for a district election, and if no law . . . passed, [would] authorize and regulate a general election by proclamation." [83] Ross's bill was aimed at circumventing McKean by giving a joint committee, composed of six senators and representatives with a chairman to be chosen by the Senate, the power to decide upon the validity of the electoral votes cast. Then if McKean tried to initiate an election by issuing a proclamation, or if the people chose Republican electors on their own initiative and the governor passed their votes on to Congress as valid, the committee could disqualify them. It seemed possible that a similar situation might develop in other states,[84] and if enough electoral votes could be disqualified, no candidate would have a majority of the whole. The election would then pass to the House, which would be strongly Federalist when voting by states.

The Republicans saw this as an attempt to snatch the election away from them. Charles Pinckney charged in the Senate that to give one body the power to decide without appeal who was to be the president would tempt minorities in every state to dispute the election whenever they saw that their chosen candidate also had the support of a majority in Congress. This would create ceaseless disputes and make periodic appeals to the people useless, for a majority in Congress would "always be intimately connected with the measures of Administration." [85] After the bill was defeated, even Cobbett allowed that it would have given the Senate complete power over the election of the president.[86] Well before this admission, however, the Republicans had seen their suspicions confirmed when the Senate attempted to proceed against William Duane, the editor of the *Aurora,* for breach of privilege because he had published the text of the proposed bill.[87]

This was the first disaster the Federalists suffered in the Sixth Congress. When the Sedition Law was already inflaming the public, Senate Federalists should have had more sense than to try such a maneuver. In colonial times this kind of action had been commonplace, but it was so opposed to postrevolutionary ideas of judicial procedure and civil liberties that it could not fail to raise a storm. The Federalist defense was that the Senate had a right to protect itself from untruths (and that judicial remedies were not quick enough to save the Senate's reputation), though the only "untruth" they could show in the *Aurora* was an insinuation that the Senate was run by a sinister caucus.[88] It was a feeble effort satisfying no one. Those who were not shocked by the act as a blatant violation of civil liberties were critical of its political implications. Cobbett questioned its wisdom given that this branch of the legislature was already unpopular, and William Bingham blamed his Senate colleagues for letting themselves be dragged into a damaging debate on the Senate's power to punish for breach of privilege. As he tartly observed, "After many tedious preparatory Steps, which seemed to argue a Doubt of the Competency of their Powers, they at length issued their Warrant, & Duane absconded." [89]

In the end all the uproar over the disputed elections bill and Duane's alleged libel came to nothing. The Ross bill never became law, thanks to the action of the House of Representatives. Its defeat proceeded not only from the Republican opposition, which predictably protested it as unconstitutional,[90] but also from the vacillations of John Marshall which Sedgwick said "dissipated our majority." Marshall had first doubted that the legislature was constitutionally qualified to delegate such authority to a committee. Convinced on this point, he then raised another objection, arguing that "altho' the power was not indelegable, yet he thought, in its nature, it was too delicate to be delegated, untill experience had demonstrated that great inconveniences would attend its exercise by the legislature; altho' he had no doubt such would be the result of the attempt." [91] Marshall would only support the bill if the decisions of the grand committee were not final. As a result, when the House did at last pass the bill it was in a form unacceptable to the Senate. The committee was given the power only to enquire and report, and contested votes could not be rejected without the consent of both houses. The outcome was that the bill died of a deadlock, Harper administering the *coup de grâce* on May 10 when he moved that the House adhere to its version.[92]

The demise of the disputed elections bill was probably a blessing for the Federalists. If they had ever tried to use it as anything more than a counterthreat to McKean's proposed line of action, they would in all likelihood have brought down civil war upon their heads. As it was, McKean permitted the legislature to disband without settling on any election law, and the issue was left for resolution by the people in state elections to be held the following October. Because the Federalists still kept control of the Senate despite a smashing Republican victory in the House, and because by that time the only way to name electors was through legislative action, the Federalist minority was able to force a compromise that gave them nearly half of Pennsylvania's electoral vote. Thus they gained their ends as far as they could without exposing themselves any further to the public odium drawn upon them by the election bill.[93]

They paid a price, though. Not only had they given the opposition proof that some of them would pursue party ends without scruple, but they had revealed to the public how deeply divided they were. The *Aurora* reported this as early as mid-February 1800, presumably on the basis of Charles Pinckney's confidential information about the Senate caucus which had been appearing regularly in its columns and had led to disclosure of the Ross bill's text.[94] And the charge was to some extent supported by the critical response of some Federalists when the Senate tried to exercise its privilege. But the strongest confirmation came in early May when James McHenry and Pickering were summarily discarded from the cabinet.[95] It had long been an open secret that they had joined Hamilton and Wolcott in opposing the new mission to France, but that this had caused any serious division within the administration was belied by their continuation in office. These dismissals were accompanied by the abandonment of most Federalist legislative proposals except the bankruptcy bill. The extent of the rout was shown when, after fending off Republican proposals to revoke statutory authorization for an increased army, Harper moved at the end of the session that the president be given a discretion in disbanding it which everyone knew he would use out of hatred for Hamilton.[96] Looking back on the debacle in January 1801, McHenry attributed the adverse state of public opinion equally to "the half measures of Congress, and the false measures of the President." [97]

Still, all was not necessarily lost. What the Federalists sacrificed in unity they had in part regained by the popularity of peace. True, the election was now at the mercy of events in France, and after news of the Battle of Marengo many extreme Federalists were sure she would try another electioneering maneuver like that of 1796. True too that public opinion was turning against them, but the electoral college had been designed to resist momentary popular impulses. So there was still a chance that Jefferson would be excluded from the presidency, if only the party could reunite. The Congressional caucus had agreed that Jefferson would only be beaten if Adams and Charles Cotesworth Pinckney were supported in equal degree, and both wings of the party saw an advantage in adhering to this. Adams Federalists in the northern states knew that if they gave the merest hint of abandoning Pinckney, as some had in 1796, the South might abandon Adams. On the other hand, Pinckney's partisans, not only those in the South but also northern extremists who had lost faith in Adams, knew that the slightest sign of betraying Adams would lose them the benefits of the president's popularity. Cabot saw the irony of the situation, observing: "It is one of the evils incident to popular systems that the best friends of government feel themselves obliged to conceal the defects, and magnify the good qualities of those who administer public offices. A reputation and degree of personal power is by this means acquired, which . . . cannot be suddenly counteracted." Adams's prestige was "in some sort, interwoven with the web of national government," said Cabot, and "every attempt to separate them [would be] ill received." [98] Their only chance, to which they clung until the eve of the election, was to back both candidates equally and hope that Pinckney would pick up extra votes in the South or that in case of a tie the House could be prevailed upon to prefer him.

If the extreme Federalists had unswervingly pursued this strategy they would at least have preserved their reputations. But the behavior of Adams and his supporters during the election provoked them to a rash action. Ever since the inception of the French mission they had suspected Adams of pandering to anti-British sentiment in a craven attempt to curry popular support for the coming election. As the prospect of Franco-American reconciliation led to a cooling of Anglo-American relations, they became acutely sensitive to any references Adams made to revolutionary resentments, particularly his mention in a reply to the address by the citizens of Alexandria of the "injustice and indignities" inflicted on America by Britain.[99] Then as the election approached, perhaps because they knew that Hamilton was busy intriguing to defeat the president, Adams's supporters were more and more open in their attempts to smear his enemies within the party as a "British" faction. This was the last straw for some. As Hamilton observed, "Mr. Adams's personal friends, seconded by the Jacobins, will completely *run us down in public opinion.*[100] And his reluctant partisans were at last persuaded that it was necessary to produce a defense of their actions and a critique of the president's.

This took the form of a pamphlet by Hamilton on *The public conduct and character of John Adams,* in which he argued the untenable proposition that although Adams was incompetent to administer the Federal government, Federalists were still bound to give as much support to him as to Pinckney.[101] If defense of reputation had been Hamilton's only objective, the pamphlet would have contained no electoral advice and would not have been published until after the election. But he could not resist the temptation to influence the election, particularly as a Federalist victory was unlikely unless a deadlock in the electoral college left the Federalist House to make the final choice. He did not want to do this by outright publication of the pamphlet, only by circulation to "men of influence." Unfortunately, a copy fell into the hands of the *Aurora,* and extracts from it were printed and given general circulation. This does not seem to have been planned, for Robert Troup said in a letter to King that Hamilton "was apparently confused" when publication of the letter was first announced to him. But he soon recovered, and in response to Troup's fear that it would do him personal damage and hurt the Federalist cause, he said he had "no doubt it would be productive of good."[102]

He was mistaken. It drew a series of unfavorable comments, not only from Republicans but also from Adams Federalists, calling him too egotistical to subordinate a private grudge to the common cause. And this did more than anything else to draw public attention to the deep divisions within the Federalist party. When these critics went on to blame Hamilton for what had been their greatest liabilities in the campaign of 1800, an expensive, unnecessary army and the Alien and Sedition Laws, their indiscretion was hailed by gleeful opposition writers as an open admission of culpability for ill-advised acts.[103] It is hard to see how the Federalists could have done more to discredit themselves in the people's eyes. To such inartistic blunders had these formerly deft manipulators of public opinion been reduced by events that escaped their control.

10. Competition

The Federalists were not just prey to external events beyond their control. They were also the victims of a competition between the two parties that grew ever more intense and culminated in the war crisis of 1798–1799, driving each to appropriate the other's style. There had been haphazard attempts of the kind even before 1798. The Federalists, in good Republican fashion, had exposed Genêt as a foreigner claiming powers which were compatible neither with neutrality nor with Washington's proper authority. The Republicans in turn had occasionally tried their hands at manipulation, as in December 1795 when the Virginia legislature submitted a series of far-reaching amendments to the other state legislatures. These amendments provided for qualifying the power of the president and Senate to ratify treaties affecting the enumerated powers of the House, prohibiting Supreme Court justices from accepting other federal offices, and modifying the Senate so that its membership would change every three years and it would be denied the power to try impeachments.[1] They were clearly designed to reinforce public hostility to the Jay Treaty as well as to secure changes in the Constitution. Such forays were exceptional, however, and as a rule each party preferred its own distinctive style as being most appropriate to its resources and objectives. Only severe pressure ever produced sustained attempts at emulation, and until the war crisis in 1798–1799 it was not clear which party would benefit most from these competitive incursions. Then the Federalists, rendered desperate by their inability to act, reluctantly took the step of exposing the XYZ dispatches to the public. Their success was so striking that the Republicans were impelled to try a counterattack, using the Federalists' own weapon of manipulation.

I

The strong impact made by the XYZ dispatches was brought home to Republican congressmen in their sadly diminished ability to obstruct Federalist measures by charging that they would provoke a French war and force alliance with and commercial dependence upon Britain.[2] In their eyes, almost every Federalist proposal during the spring of 1798, from the arming of merchantmen and the fitting out of naval vessels to the abrogation of Franco-American treaties, was unnecessarily provocative. They found especially objectionable the Federalist motion authorizing the president to direct that United States vessels should seize French armed vessels committing depredations on American shipping or hovering about the coast for that purpose. The Republicans believed that this measure, which went considerably further in giving official sanction to offensive acts against the French navy than the proposal for arming merchantmen and authorizing convoys which had already passed the House, might tip the scale and provoke France to war. Indeed, it almost did. They protested that as Congress did not know how the Paris negotiations had ended, and as there was still a hope of peace, consideration of the measure should be postponed.[3] Samuel Sitgreaves replied for the Federalists, that according to international law, "when a nation has received aggressions from another nation, it is competent for the injured country to pursue its remedy by reprisal before a declaration of war takes place, and these reprisals shall be perfectly warrantable, whilst they are commensurate with the injuries received, and are not, under such circumstances, justifiable cause of war." [4]

The Republicans saw their chance. Nathaniel Macon of North Carolina moved that the instructions be amended to apply to all nations committing depredations upon United States commerce, which would make them authorize attacks on British naval vessels also.[5] The flabbergasted Federalists tried to argue that France was seizing American vessels within the jurisdiction of the United States, which made a difference, but Gallatin promptly retorted that the president already had all the power he needed to repel such an outrage, so that the new law was clearly unnecessary.[6] Though the Federalists claimed that British seizures conformed to the law of nations, and that both Britain and Spain were observing treaties with the United States which provided a remedy short of war,[7] the opposition had forced them into an open admission that the proposal was belligerent in intent. Nevertheless, encouraged by the vocal support they were receiving in the addresses, the Federalists refused to back away from this measure.[8] It had not been enough to expose the Federalists as warmongers; it was necessary also that the public be unambiguously opposed to war. And the first effect of the dispatches had been to make them more angry than prudent.

It was the same when the Republicans tried to invoke the ideas which had been so effective in defending the democratic and republican societies against congressional censure. The Republicans answered the criticism of their failure to support the president against France by accusing the Federalists of intending to encroach upon the freedom of opinion.[9] This strategy seemed to have momentary effect, for in April 1798 when certain Federalists wanted to reject the critical Magnien petition outright the opposition made them back down by pointing out that to assume the power of accepting one petition and rejecting another amounted to controlling opinion.[10] But when it came to the Sedition Law, the Federalists were impervious to Gallatin's charge that this was their intent, and that "the true object of the law is to . . . have the power to punish printers who may publish against them, whilst their opponents will remain alone and without redress, exposed to the abuse of Ministerial prints." [11]

By the summer of 1798 it was clear that the Republicans could no longer take public opinion for granted, and as a result they found themselves under great pressure to adopt Federalist methods. Unfortunately their options for influencing public opinion were severely limited. For instance, there was no way in which they could acquire such advantages as the Federalists had gained by the addresses to the president and his replies. If they sent critical messages to the president, as some did, this merely gave Adams or his subordinates a chance to censure them.[12] Petitions to the House against the Alien and Sedition Laws did not force the question of their constitutionality to be debated as popular pressure against the Jay Treaty had helped to force the issue of the House's power over treaty appropriations.[13] Instead they were referred to a select committee dominated by Federalists, a tactic which effectively postponed the matter until the end of the session.[14] When the committee did report, as might have been expected it justified the acts and censured the petitioners. Because this report came from a prestigious source and received wide circulation in the newspapers, it had a greater effect upon public opinion than the original petitions.[15]

The Republicans, realizing what an advantage the Federalists had in their control of Congress, attempted to reply in kind through the Virginia and Kentucky Resolutions. In promoting these resolutions, the opposition was using a respected organ of government which they controlled in an attempt to convince a people who had become unreceptive that the Federalists were indeed violating the Constitution. State legislatures acting in concert were the only instruments in their possession that might compare in prestige with the federal government backed by an almost unanimous judiciary. This was not the first time that a state legislature had resolved against the constitutionality of a congressional law, or that one state had called on the others to act. But it was the first time that two states clearly working together had questioned the constitutionality of the federal government's actions, calling on other states to issue similar declarations and to resist encroachment on the rights of the states and people.[16] Moreover, the Resolutions of 1798–1799 did more than present a neutral statement of the opposition's constitutional case.

The Kentucky Resolutions were the most provocative, not only because of their willingness to pronounce the laws "not law," and "altogether void and of no effect," strong language which had been deleted from Virginia's resolutions, but also because of the extreme implications they drew from the Alien and Sedition Laws. These were that

the General Government may place any act they think proper on the list of crimes and punish it themselves, whether enumerated or not enumerated by the Constitution as cognizable by them; that they may transfer its cognizance to the President or any other person who may himself be the accuser, counsel, judge, and jury, whose *suspicions* may be the evidence, his order the sentence, his officer the executioner, and his breast the sole record of the transaction.[17]

And while the Virginia Resolutions settled for a warning that continued federal encroachments would eventually transform the republic "into an absolute, or at best, a mixed monarchy," the Kentucky Resolutions declared that "no rampart now remains against the passions and the power of a majority of Congress, to protect . . . the minority." [18]

All subsequent attempts to clarify the intentions of Virginia and Kentucky have come up against two complicating circumstances. The first and most obvious is that when between 1832–1833 South Carolina attempted to "nullify" a federal tariff, they turned for a precedent to the events of 1798–1799.[19] Recent scholarship has established that Jefferson coined the word "nullification," and in his draft of the Kentucky Resolutions was ready to urge that the states should carry the power "to nullify of their own authority, all assumptions of power by others within their limits." Yet Madison subsequently said that Jefferson meant this to be construed not as a "constitutional right" but rather as a natural one in the event of extreme oppression.[20] It is notable that neither Virginia nor Kentucky followed Jefferson's suggestion that they prevent the execution of obnoxious federal laws within their confines. In Richmond there was even a prosecution under the Sedition Act against James Callender, author of a campaign pamphlet *The Prospect before Us,* and it was conducted without incident or interruption.[21] By contrast, South Carolina thirty-four years later passed a nullification ordinance in a convention specially convened for that purpose, declaring it unlawful "to enforce payment of duties . . . within the limits of this state," ordering the state legislature to pass "such acts as may be necessary to give full effect to this Ordinance," and requiring all state officers elected after the ordinance either to uphold it or to resign their offices. Though the South Carolina legislature temporized over executing this mandate, and avoided penal statutes against federal collectors and collaborating merchants, they did pass a series of laws allowing the population voluntarily to resist the collection of the federal impost. Those who wanted to avoid the duties could plead their unconstitutionality before a state jury and the outcome would not have been in doubt, for that jury together with the judge would have been required to swear to uphold the ordinance.[22] There was a marked difference, then, between South Carolina's response to the tariff of 1828 and the opposition's response to the Alien and Sedition Laws.

The second factor which is apt to make the Virginia and Kentucky Resolutions appear as revolutionary as the South Carolina measures of later times is the Federalist response to them. When James Iredell first saw the resolutions, he wrote to his wife that Virginia was "pursuing steps which directly lead to a civil war." [23] Robert Goodloe Harper was more open in the expression of his feelings. He declared in Congress that the Kentucky Resolutions would bring about "an armed opposition to these laws, and consequently to this Government." [24] The Massachusetts legislature warned that should Virginia "persist in the assumption of right to declare the acts of the national government unconstitutional, and should she oppose successfully her force and will to those of the nation, the Constitution would be reduced to a cypher." [25] Others too believed that if the federal government acquiesced in nullification, "the old republican maxim that the majority must govern" would be exploded, and the republic, lacking coherence, would sink into chaos. Conversely, if the states which valued the union were to join the government in armed opposition to Virginia, the ensuing civil strife would be nothing but a different path to the same destination. It is clear that many Federalists thought Virginia meant to shatter the Union.[26] Indeed, John Nicholas (probably a cousin of the Republican leader) wrote an election letter asserting that the Virginia legislature was organizing her militia for a contest of arms with the federal government.[27]

Since we know what did happen in the nineteenth century, the Federalists' expressions of anxiety have a plausible ring. But they were closing their ears to protestations by proponents of the resolutions that these were appeals to opinion rather than to force, and that a legislature was "pursuing the only possible and ordinary mode of ascertaining the opinion of two-thirds of the states, by declaring its own, and asking theirs." [28] They were also ignoring the fact that the force at Virginia's disposal was hardly commensurate to that of the federal government. "Are the republicans . . . possessed of fleets and armies?" asked John Taylor, sponsor of the resolutions in the House of Delegates. "If not, to what could they appeal for defense and support . . . except public opinion[?] If that should be against them, they must yield." The author of "A Defense of the Virginia Assembly" added, "Nothing can break the union, but a force which can controul the will of the people. . . . To charge the design upon those who have no means to effect it, ought only to induce a suspicion against those who have." [29]

Virginia Republicans thought they had good reason to be suspicious. Some of their loudest accusers surely knew that the decision to establish and stock a state armory, which had attracted Federalist attention, had been made well before the current crisis.[30] And if Virginia's armaments made Federalists elsewhere nervous, Virginians in their turn were thoroughly alarmed by the steadily increasing military power of the federal government. They had not failed to notice ominous remarks that a navy could be used to blockade the Chesapeake and interdict all Virginia's commerce, nor the menace in Pickering's reply to the address from Prince Edward County, where he said that the state should be "humbled in the dust and ashes." [31] This led Virginia Republicans like Taylor to warn that "War or insurrection . . . could not happen" unless a minority should "by the help of the powers of government, resort to force for its defense against public opinion." He added that in pursuing "a system which was only an appeal to public opinion . . . warranted by the Constitution," the legislature of Virginia was giving "an opportunity to the general government to discover whether they would be faithful to the same principle, and thereby establish a precedent, which would both now and hereafter have a strong tendency against civil war." [32]

The Federalists also questioned the constitutionality and propriety of the resolutions. The Massachusetts legislature stated that "the people in that solemn compact, which is declared to be the supreme law of the land, have not constituted the state legislatures, the judges of the acts or measures of the Federal Government." It argued that the power of proposing amendments was vastly different from the power to pronounce on the constitutionality of Congressional Acts, which had been "exclusively vested by the people in the judicial courts of the United States." [33] Others added that the people had chosen their state legislatures only to accomplish "the ordinary purposes of legislation," and had not conferred on them judicial authority over the laws they themselves had passed, let alone those passed by Congress.[34] Furthermore, the decisions of federal judges were more worthy to be respected than those of state legislators who were first of all not usually qualified to deal with such matters, and secondly more liable to be corrupted by the pressure of popular sentiment.[35] Lastly, the Federalists deplored that a part of the people should presume to condemn laws sanctioned by the representatives of the whole, especially as they thought the representatives in the legislature of a state like Virginia where "Two hundred freeholders have the same voice . . . as one thousand" were less pure than representatives in the federal government.[36]

It was not hard for the Republicans to refute these objections. Madison's "Report of the Committee to whom were referred the Communications of the various States" examined every aspect of the question whether the constitutionality of laws should be referred exclusively to the federal judiciary. He noted "first, that there may be instances of usurped power, which the forms of the Constitution would never draw within the control of the judicial department," and secondly "that dangerous powers, not delegated, may not only be usurped and executed by the other departments, but that the judicial department also may exercise or sanction dangerous powers beyond the grant of the Constitution." [37] The danger that judicial authority would be abused was very real to the Republicans. As a member of the Virginia Assembly remarked in December 1798, most of the federal judges "had already pronounced their opinion [of the Sedition Law], either in pamphlets, or political instead of legal charges to [federal] grand juries, thus prejudging a constitutional question, which they knew would be made if ever the law was attempted to be carried into effect." [38] So although Madison would acknowledge the authority of the judiciary as a last resort "in relation to the authorities of the other departments of the Government," he would not do so "in relation to the right of the parties to the constitutional compact." Such a delegation of judicial authority might "annul the authority delegating it; and the concurrence of this department with the others in usurped powers might subvert forever, and beyond the possible reach of any rightful remedy, the very Constitution which all were instituted to preserve." At best, it could not fail to deprive the people of their ultimate sovereignty.[39]

Not all Federalists went so far as to claim that the federal judiciary had exclusive jurisdiction over matters concerned with the constitutionality of federal acts. Some agreed that the people might

arbitrate between federal and state governments when their juris-
dictions clashed, but denied that the state legislatures had any
part in this right. They could propose amendments to the Constitution, or recommend to Congress that a law be repealed, and that
was all. Congress was not subject to the correction of the state
legislatures, but the people only whose decision "was obtainable under the rules of the Constitution in the revolving elections." If it appeared that Congress had encroached upon their rights, they
would have a chance at the next election to show their displeasure.[40]
George K. Taylor even argued that the re-election to the Sixth
Congress of many Congressmen who had passed the objectionable
laws proved that "the people of the United States had decided in
favor of their constitutionality." [41]

The Virginia Republicans replied that elections were not the
best way to decide such issues because "the people often voted
from personal and local attachments; and . . . were not always
apprised of the opinions of the different candidates." [42] They were
not inferring from this that the people should be excluded from
the exercise of their sovereignty, but rather that they should count
on the state legislatures to sound the alarm and give them guidance.
During the trial of the Boston printer who had accused the Massachusetts legislators of perjury when they disclaimed any right to
decide whether or not federal laws were unconstitutional, Abijah
Adams's attorney said:

[S]ociety is diffused, the feeble voice of an individual in any state is
drowned, it is lost in air before it can reach the distant ear of a fellow
citizen in another. How then is the public voice to be heard? We answer,
the departments of government have power alone to articulate the sentiment of the community. . . . With respect to the state legislatures, they
may be denominated *political Telegraphs,* so arranged and connected as
to effect the will of the people from the northern to the southern ex-
tremities of the continent. They are reserved by the constitution itself, as
vigils to the federal system, as the very life-guard to protect the *freedom,*
the *sovereignty,* and *independence* of the states.[43]

These ideas were not the invention of the moment. Their advocates pointed to the *Federalist,* which had argued that state legislatures had the right to warn the people of federal encroachment,
and might even "adopt a regular plan of opposition [to] unite their

common forces for the protection of their common liberty."[44] Republicans in the Virginia House suggested that legislative resolutions were less likely to cause uproar and confusion than letting the people speak for themselves in "tumultuous meetings" where they might rashly decide on a "final and dreadful appeal" to first principles.[45] What the Republicans hoped to achieve by the Resolutions was, in Madison's words, "a change in the legislative expression of the general will, possibly . . . a change in the opinion of the judiciary."[46] Speaking before the Virginia House, John Mercer said that "nothing seemed more likely to produce a temper in Congress for repeal, than a declaration similar to the one before the committee, made by a majority of states." It was hoped that such a remedy would enable the opposition to halt an abuse before it had done irreparable damage.[47]

In their immediate hopes for the Virginia and Kentucky Resolutions, the Republicans were badly disappointed. Most of the legislatures which considered them had either been elected during the war scare of 1798 or were deeply disturbed by it, and regarded the Resolutions as disloyal acts. The Federalists were also the happy beneficiaries of jealousy toward the largest state in the union and her client. Nine state legislatures answered the invitation to speak out on the Alien and Sedition Laws, and they all condemned the Resolutions.[48] New Jersey Federalists secured dismissal of them without even honoring Virginia and Kentucky by any formal communication.[49] In only one state was there any sign of positive support. At the end of January, the *Gazette of the United States* reported that the North Carolina House had resolved that the Alien and Sedition Laws were "a violation of the principles of the constitution," and had instructed their Senators to secure a repeal. But because the Senate did not concur, no official action was taken. Jefferson had originally hoped the North Carolina legislature would adopt the Kentucky Resolutions, but after the election of 1798 this was not feasible.[50] South Carolina, Georgia, and Tennessee seem to have taken no action on them at all.[51]

The Virginia and Kentucky legislatures had nonetheless inflicted considerable damage upon the Federalists. The coincidence of their Resolutions with French overtures for conciliation undercut Federalist efforts to prevent any renewal of pro-French sentiment and made them more afraid than ever of failing in this attempt. That is why many otherwise sensible men panicked and took the resolutions of Virginia, moderate as they were, to be "little short of a declaration of war." [52] The controversies that the resolutions stirred up in many state legislatures certainly more than compensated for the hostile replies they elicited. Indeed, condemnation clearly drew more attention to them than silence would have done. The publicity attending the debates and the prosecution of Abijah Adams in Massachusetts helped to dramatize the issues and awaken the people to an interest in national politics they might otherwise never have felt.[53] Then Madison's authoritative "Report of the Committee" reopened the issue of the Resolutions on the eve of the presidential election, offering systematic rebuttals to all the objections which had been raised to them. Though it is doubtful that his tightly woven constitutional treatise was widely read, it did give authority to the Republican contention that the Alien and Sedition Laws had been unconstitutional, and this at a time when the passing of the war crisis left the people with no compelling reason to think otherwise.[54]

II

If the Federalists were alarmed by the Republican attempts to emulate their style, manifested in the Virginia and Kentucky resolutions, they were also disturbed by their own failure to use the Republican style of exposure successfully. Though the dispatches made French hostility so clear that the Federalists were able for the time being to proceed with their war measures in Congress, they did not prove that the opposition was "in league with France, and ready to support her cause by force of arms." [55] At first, people had been inclined to take the dispatches at face value as indisputable proof of a French party extant in America. On second thought, though, they seemed too candid. When Allen tried to use them for this purpose,[56] Nicholas asked:

Did he suppose that Government, or any other, would authorize persons to inform the Ministers of a foreign country that they were not actuated by principles of justice . . . ? Had not insinuations similar to those now made by the gentlemen from Connecticut been heard in this House almost as often as gentlemen speak? And was it improbable that men of the description of which these agents appear to be should address themselves to the fears which they supposed existed of a factious spirit in this country? [57]

In the hysteria of the moment the Federalists were able to gain their immediate ends by flimsy, circumstantial evidence, but Nicholas's speech had served notice that in the long run they would have to come up with something more substantial.

They thought they saw their chance to do so when Bache's *Aurora* published Talleyrand's letter of March 18, 1798, on June 16, two days before the President released it to Congress but (so Bache said) ten days after it had been received by the government.[58] At once they declared their suspicion that Bache was in direct communication with Talleyrand, a suspicion receiving added support from the disclosure of John Kidder and Samuel M. Hopkins that just before he left France William Lee had been given some letters for Bache, Monroe, and Genêt, bearing the seal of the French Minister for Foreign Affairs. Learning that these were still in the New York post office, Wolcott rushed to New York to intercept them and ask Hopkins directly whether any of the letters had been addressed to Jefferson.[59] Though the packets he found could not possibly have been the source of Bache's acquaintance with Talleyrand's letter, they looked incriminating enough for Wolcott to take them from Lee and send them to Pickering. Bache later speculated that the intention had been to open the packets and publish them if they contained evidence against him, or destroy them if not. The administration wisely decided not to risk it after William Lee, anxious to dissociate himself from the controversy, disclosed in public that he had turned the packets over to the government.[60]

The administration's attempt to expose Bache as "a *hireling* of, and *in correspondence with* the despots of France" was now turned against them. Even before they decided that because of Lee's disclosure they had best give Bache the packets, he went before the mayor of Philadelphia and swore that he had received Talleyrand's letter not direct from France but from a Philadelphian who had probably found it previously published in some foreign newspaper. And after he received the packet from the Secretary of State, Bache staged an elaborate ceremony before the State Department's messenger and two specially summoned witnesses. He opened the packet, and it contained two innocent pamphlets on English affairs written by Bache's friend Pichon, now associated with the French foreign ministry.[61] It is true that this did not prove Bache had not received the Talleyrand letter through Kidder. Lee later admitted that he might have left some letters with Kidder by mistake, and Kidder's statement of his role in delivering them was confused and inconsistent. But when the administration perceived that Lee, who was central to their suspicion of Bache, was no French agent but a harmless commercial agent for Joel Barlow, they wisely decided not to press the matter further.[62]

As the crisis with France began to wane late in 1798, Federalist leaders felt a new urgency to convince the nation that it was threatened not only by France but also by a subversive opposition. Harper was responding to this when he tried to make the Codman memorial demonstrate Republican disloyalty even though the attempt served more to prove opposition charges of Federalist belligerence.[63] And in 1799 the Federalists were lured into two other notorious fiascos.

The first grew out of a report from diplomatic sources that several suspicious persons bearing dispatches from the Directory, concealed in tubs with false bottoms, were aboard a Danish vessel bound for Charleston. When it arrived in South Carolina, the Federalists tracked down these people and found that they were indeed carrying French dispatches concealed as stated. Immediately the Federalists threw them in jail and proclaimed their discovery of a plot to raise an insurrection in the South. When they did pause to decipher and read the documents, these pertained to a conspiracy against Toussaint L'Ouverture which was not even sponsored by the Directory. After promising many exciting revelations, the government could not publish even these disappointing papers for fear of damaging their efforts to reach a commercial agreement with the rebel regime in Santo Domingo. For the rest of the year, they were subjected to derisive taunts about the "Tub-Plot" and other efforts to substantiate the Jacobin conspiracy theory met with equally little success.[64]

An even worse fate awaited Morse's exposition of the conspiratorial Illuminati in America. It was no sooner pronounced than sceptical voices were asking what authority he had for his disclosures, and demanding definite proof.[65] Morse resorted to the dubious expedient of pointing to distinguished intellectual leaders who were also disseminating this theory: Tappan, the two Dwights, and Joseph Lathrop whom he cited as his authority for the existence of such a society in northern Massachusetts.[66] This was somewhat anticlimactic after his projection of a sinister network all over America. Then, in early January 1799, whatever authority Robison's work had acquired was shaken when a letter appeared in the *Columbian Centinel* signed by Augustus Bottinger, described as a German university official, refuting Robison and declaring that the Illuminati had long since disappeared in Germany.[67] To cap all, William Bentley, pastor at the East Church in Salem, made a devastating critique of Robison's *Proofs of a Conspiracy* in a pamphlet showing that he had condemned the very principles on which the American Revolution had been fought.[68] When Morse tried to document the conspiracy in his Fast Sermon on April 25, 1799, he was laughed to scorn.[69] What finished him was his refusal to publish a letter he was known to have received from Professor Ebeling of Hamburg condemning both Robison's book and Robison's character. Bentley had received a similar letter, and this was eventually published in the New London *Bee* as that which had been sent to Morse. Morse protested that his own letter was different, but his refusal to publish it suggested that he had something to hide.[70] From this time on, Morse and the Illuminati theory were discredited in New England, and Alexander Addison met with small success when he tried to revive the conspiracy scare in his charge to the grand juries of Pennsylvania in 1801.[71]

These episodes made it clear that the Federalists' power to expose the Republicans was waning as their adversaries' powers increased. This relieved the Republicans from any compulsive need to emulate Federalist ways with public opinion, particularly as Adams's announcement of a new peace mission had calmed the war hysteria and brought popular feeling back into line with opposition objectives. On the other hand, it left the Federalists no choice but to continue struggling with an uncongenial Republican style. Adams had so alienated extreme Federalists in the administration as to put further aggressive use of the executive out of the question. The Fifth Congress which the Federalists had taken such pains to make a pliant instrument was about to disband, and it was unlikely that the newly elected Sixth Congress, though nominally Federalist, would make the same strenuous efforts as its predecessors to manipulate opinion. The people's longing for a reconciliation with France was clearly irreversible. When Congress did meet most Federalist proposals, such as the expansion of the judiciary and the disputed elections bill, were designed to insulate the government as much as possible from public opinion. Enervated and divided after five years of frenzied maneuvering, they no longer had the resources to continue the heroic manipulations which had become a hallmark of their political style. Yet with an election on the horizon, they could not ignore public opinion altogether. Obviously the style that would best suit their depleted state was exposure, which had recommended itself to the Republicans in the first place because in principle it was as effectively wielded by an anonymous newspaper editor as by a president.

Unfortunately the only factor absolutely essential to the continued effectiveness of exposure was the very one the Federalists lacked: a popular ideology in relation to which the activities of one's opponents were inadmissable. The full extent of their handicap in this respect can best be appreciated by comparing the use each party made of the famous Mazzei letter. In April 1796, Jefferson had written to his Italian friend, Philip Mazzei, about recent political developments in the United States. He observed that the "aspect of our politics has wonderfully changed since you left us. In place of that noble love of liberty, & republican government, which served us so triumphantly thro' the Revolutionary war, an Anglican monarchical, & aristocratic party has sprung up, whose avowed object is to draw over us the substance, as they have already done the forms of the British government." He added that the "main body of our citizens . . . remain true to their republican principles" but that "Against us are the Executive, the Judiciary . . . all the officers of the government, all who want to be officers, all timid men . . . British merchants & American trading on British capitals, speculators & holders in the banks & public funds, a contrivance . . . for assimilating us . . . to the rotten as well as the sound parts of the British model."

The letter was translated into Italian, from the Italian into French, and from the French into English again. When this last English version, three times removed from the original, appeared in American papers, Jefferson was quoted as saying that the other party meant "to impose on us the *substance,* as they have already given us the

form, of the British government." By substituting the singular
"form" for the plural "forms," as Jefferson himself pointed out, he
was made to appear to "express hostility to the form of our government, that is to say, to the constitution itself."

What Jefferson had meant by the "forms of the British government" were the ceremonies with which Washington had surrounded
himself; "the birthdays, levees, processions to parliament, inauguration pompösities" and so on. Yet he could not explain this to the
public "without bringing on a personal difference between Genl.
Washington & myself, which . . . would embroil me also with all
those with whom his character is still popular, that is to say, nine
tenths of the people of the U.S." [72] Consequently Jefferson chose to
remain silent. It was a difficult silence, for the Federalists made
hay with the letter. During the French crisis of 1797–1798 they used
it to neutralize his influence as vice-president by claiming that Jefferson had been instrumental in giving the Directory the idea that
there was a division between the people and their government.[73]
And during the campaign of 1800 they used it to suggest that the
Republicans opposed the form of government rather than merely its
current administration, so that the election of Jefferson would amount
to a revolution.[74]

In the meantime, Jefferson's partisans had seen other possibilities
in the Mazzei letter, and had explored them in a short pamphlet by
Tench Coxe entitled, *Strictures upon the letter imputed to Mr.
Jefferson, addressed to Mr. Mazzei,* published in June 1800. Coxe
capitalized on the currency the Federalists themselves had given to
the charges that they were bent on establishing a monarchy, charges
which still had a certain authority because they proceeded from the
pen of the vice-president. He dwelt at length upon the alterations
which had been made between the original letter and the Federalist
version, tracing this last back to the French translation it had been
taken from, and cataloguing in meticulous detail the "forms" to which
Jefferson had objected. But his best energies were devoted to asking
whether Mr. Jefferson was "right in saying, there was an English
Monarchical Party in this Country." [75] He dredged up a report the
Privy Council had made to the King in 1791 to the effect that *"a
Party in favor of Great Britain* [was] *formed in America."* He hinted
that Adams himself had "entertained the opinion, that *much* British

influence had been used upon our Government in a respectable Appointment to that Court," a reference to a letter Adams had written Coxe in 1792, complaining about the appointment of Thomas Pinckney as his successor to the Court of Saint James. This was doubly embarrassing to Adams, as Pinckney's brother was the other Federalist presidential candidate.[76] Most of all, he took pains to document the charge "that Monarchical Doctrines have been avowed by Citizens holding great Public Trusts and Employments." Coxe reminded his readers that in a reply to an address published on July 3, 1798 Adams had said that *"Republican Government may be interpreted to mean anything";* and that when vice-president he had been heard by two Senators to observe that *"he hoped . . . to see the time, when* [they] *would be convinced, that the People of America could not be happy, without an hereditary Chief Magistrate, and a Senate that should be Hereditary or for life."* Surely, Coxe said, this justified Jefferson in his doubts.[77]

The argument that there was a conflict between Adams's Federalism and revolutionary ideology was much more convincing than the Federalist charge that Jefferson was disloyal to his government, being less dependent on transient circumstances. Between 1797–1798, when France threatened America, to change "forms" to "form" suggested that the nation was in danger not only from a foreign power but also from a disloyal opposition. After Jefferson passed through the crisis of 1798 without ever being identified with any disloyal act (the Republicans studiously refrained from making addresses to him), this suggestion lost its power to alarm. In contrast, the opposition's ability to expose Adams and other Federalist "monarchists" as holding views inconsistent with revolutionary ideology was virtually timeless; and though it had not been enough to outweigh the war hysteria of 1798, all its original force returned with the prospect of peace. By 1800, though the Federalists were under much greater pressure to avail themselves of the Mazzei letter than they had been before, it was more useful to them as support for the notion that Jefferson thought the fundholders were monarchists. This enabled them to play on the resentments and fears of public creditors, yet these still made up a far smaller audience than the Republicans could command for their charges of monarchism.[78]

The Federalists had always known that they were hampered by

the lack of a popular ideology. This had been made clear to them during the 1780's, when every suggestion that an enlightened leadership be allowed to guide the republic had been assailed as an "aristocratic" subversion of liberty, and they had been able to assert themselves only after the state governments had brought the nation to the verge of chaos. During the late 1780's and early 1790's they had developed a theory of popular sovereignty which had served them well in parrying attacks on such unpopular measures as the excise, neutrality, and the Jay Treaty. But the purpose and effect of this theory had been to suppress popular participation rather than to recruit popular loyalty. It was no help when the people were aroused, and threatening to use their power in the one way the Federalists had admitted as legitimate. What they now needed was a popular ideology which would allow them to attack Jefferson as the opposition had attacked Adams on the Mazzei letter.

One thing they could do was appropriate the anti-Jacobinism that the French Revolution had made current amongst the European elite. They had been attracted to this from the start because it agreed with their own view of European developments, and the moral Manicheanism that was one of its distinctive characteristics appealed to their elitism. Ames had invoked this aspect of it in the debate on censoring the popular societies, when he warned that "A Government that protects property, and cherishes virtue, will of course have vice and prodigality for its foes." [79] Nor could the evil be ameliorated by an enlightened administration of government: "Equal laws are the very grievances of these petty tyrants, who combine together to engross more than equal power and privileges. When power is conferred exclusively upon the worthy, the profligate and ambitious are driven to despair of success, by any methods that the worthy would adopt." [80] Its potential for appealing to the people, however, did not lie in its capacity to fortify the Federalist leadership's self-image. Its real value was that it allowed them to call on a popular loyalty which was older and more fundamental even than that felt for revolutionary ideology, the loyalty to Protestant piety.

We have already seen the role played by anti-Jacobinism in luring a reluctant clergy into the Federalist cause in 1798, and it was used again to the same end in 1800.[81] Still no matter how hard the Federalists worked at painting Jefferson as a Jacobin, with all the moral and religious connotations of that title, this would fail to touch the springs of native piety unless the clergy joined in sounding the alarm.[82] The Federalist leadership must have been delighted when in the midst of the election two distinguished New York ministers assailed Jefferson as an infidel if not an atheist, and asked if this should not disqualify him from holding the first office in the land.[83] William Linn's *Serious considerations on the election of a president* and John Mitchell Mason's *The Voice of Warning to Christians, on the ensuing election of a president,* tortuously extracted evidence from Jefferson's own writings, and were not above using hearsay as additional proof of their point. From some cursory Biblical criticism that Jefferson had made in his *Notes on Virginia,* Linn inferred that he rejected the Bible from Genesis to Revelation. Then Jefferson had questioned the usefulness of Bible study for children too young to understand religion, suggesting that instead they should be taught some ancient and modern history together with the first principles of morality, and this was taken as yet another proof of his irreligion. In the same spirit, his famous statement in defense of religious liberty that "It does me no injury for my neighbour to say there are twenty Gods or no God. It neither picks my pocket nor breaks my leg" was adduced as proof of an indifference to religion tantamount to having none at all.[84]

Not content with establishing Jefferson's infidelity, these men went on to make startling inferences. From Jefferson's suggestion that religious freedom be extended to the point where the law would punish men only for doing physical injury to their neighbors, they inferred that Jefferson sanctioned atheism. Mason argued the case in these words:

And that no class or character of abomination might be excluded from the sanctuary of such laws as he wishes to see established, he pleads for the impunity of *published* error in its most dangerous and execrable form. . . . A wretch may trumpet atheism from New Hampshire to Georgia; may laugh at all the realities of futurity; may scoff and teach others to scoff at their accountability; it is no matter, says Mr. Jefferson, "it neither picks my pocket nor breaks my leg." This is nothing less than representing civil society as founded in atheism . . . if it does me or my neighbour no injury, to subvert the very foundation of religion by denying the being of God, then religion is not one of the constituent principles of society, and consequently society is perfect without it; that is, perfect in atheism.[85]

Mason and Linn declared that belief could never be a matter of indifference because it influenced practice. It was not possible, they said, for a man's life to be good regardless of his faith: "If there be no God, there is no law; no future account; government then is the ordinance of man only, and we cannot be subject for conscience sake." Oaths would no longer be sacred and crime no longer inhibited by fear of God's punishment. This was "the morality of devils, which would break in an instant every link in the chain of human friendship, and transform the globe into one equal scene of desolation and horror, where fiend would prowl with fiend for plunder and blood." [86]

These gentlemen did not stop to ask themselves if this was not attributing too much power to a single individual. Their theory, articulated by Mason, was that society would be endangered "if rulers, by adopting atheism, be freed from the coercion of future retribution." He preferred a pious hypocrite to an admitted infidel, for a hypocrite could hurt only himself: "We have a hold of him which it is impossible to get of an infidel. His reputation, his habits, his interests, depending upon the belief of his Christianity, are sureties for his behavior." [87] Both Linn and Mason showed that they were the prisoners of Federalist ideas about the way opinion was formed when they argued that Jefferson would be dangerous as a President, not because he would oppress the people or use force to crush their religion, but because his example would insidiously corrupt them: "Let the first magistrate be a professed infidel, and infidels will surround him. Let him spend the sabbath in feasting, in visiting and receiving visits, in riding abroad, but never in going to church, and to frequent public worship will become unfashionable. Infidelity will become the prattle from the highest to the lowest condition. . . ." [88] And Mason warned that "if you appoint an infidel for your president . . . you will declare, by a *solemn national act* . . . there is no more religion in your collective character than in your written constitution," so drawing God's retribution upon the nation.[89] Some Federalists even interpreted Washington's death in December 1799 as the first warning sign of divine displeasure.[90]

Yet despite the prestigious source of these alarms, it was not hard for the opposition to deflate them. Linn, who was by far the most eminent of the two clergymen, drew three pamphlet replies, one of them purportedly emanating from DeWitt Clinton of the prominent

New York family.[91] Besides defending Jefferson's religious faith, two accused the New York ministers of proposing a religious test contrary to the Constitution, at the same time emphasizing that Jefferson's idea of religious liberty precluded such state regulation. This would appeal to religious minorities in states having orthodox establishments, or those who had left such states for religious reasons.[92] But the strongest Republican defense was to question that Jefferson's religion was even relevant. In *A Solemn Address to Christians and Patriots* Tunis Wortman complained that press and pulpit, combined to serve party ends, were trying to tell the people they must choose between the good of their country and the good of religion. Yet it was not religion that was in danger, but the state. Wortman asked, *"If your civil privileges are once gone, . . . what shall protect your religious ones?"* A monarchical President might subvert the Constitution, but an infidel President could harm neither this nor Christianity, for both would stand on their own merits." [93] The real danger to religion, said the pamphleteers, was its perversion to party purposes.[94] And the author of *Serious facts* commented on the clergy's inconsistency in omitting all mention of Pinckney's deism, observing that to call one man a deist who was not and then to support another who was "shows what lengths unworthy priests will take, when they forsake the altars of God and descend upon the stage of politics." [95]

This Federalist strategy threatened to destroy the reputations of its spokesmen as their part in propounding the Illuminati scare had destroyed the reputation of Morse, Tappan and Dwight. Moreover, religious fears could not be translated into political power as directly as political fears. The exhortations of the clergy would reach only members of the established, conservative denominations, and even then would not necessarily send a man to the polls, or fire him to try exerting his influence on his neighbors and friends, as readily as revolutionary ideology would inflame the political enthusiast. There is also some evidence that church membership and religious interest were disproportionately the province of women, who could not vote except in New Jersey, where the Federalists exploited a legal technicality and used them to win the election of 1800 in certain key areas.[96] As compensation for their lack of a popular ideology this strategy left much to be desired. So did the abusiveness which became typical of Federalism by 1800 and which was an implicit admission of the handicaps they labored under in competing for public opinion.[97]

In the nineteenth century, the distinction between the styles of the
two parties became less sharp. The Republicans were now in control
of the federal government and most of the state governments, and
therefore enjoyed those resources for manipulation which had previously been denied them. While they used this advantage sparingly
and still relied on exposure as their principal weapon, they were not
above occasional attempts to mold opinion, particularly as their
Achilles heel was thought to be the lethargy of the Republican
majority. At the same time, the loss of the national government drove
the Federalists to continue emulating the Republican style, though
their objective remained essentially the same as before: to bend
public opinion in a direction it would not spontaneously have pursued. Although they were still hampered by the lack of a popular
ideology, in one respect defeat had strengthened them. Since Federalism had been transformed from a coalition with national pretensions into a regional sect, its New England leaders, at least, were
given a chance to play on prejudice against other parts of the nation.
The Federalist elite felt their strongest antagonism towards the
western states, but violent popular prejudice could be most easily
excited against the aristocratic plantation owners of the South whom
they portrayed as pushing the eastern states from their rightful place
in the nation's councils through the constitutional inequality in the
three-fifths clause.[98] In 1800 the Federalists could not use this strategy
as much as they would have liked because their only hope of success
was to keep up some semblance of rapport with the South, and particularly with the remnant of Federalism in South Carolina.

III

In 1800, the Federalists still had several options for frustrating the
expression of hostile opinion through the electoral system. One such
"electioneering" device, which had been put into their hands by the
crisis of 1798, was the Sedition Act. The temptation to use it was the
greater because many Federalists believed they were being hurt more
by the opposition press than by divisions in the party or events
abroad.[99] Pickering set in motion all the prosecutions that were made
under the law before he was dismissed, and they were carefully
timed to inflict maximum damage on their opponents' press during
the election. In the end, all but one of the leading opposition papers
were prosecuted, though only three were silenced, and one of those

no more than temporarily.[100] But in the long run these prosecutions did the Federalists more harm than good, as the Republicans had foreseen. The provision in the Sedition Act that the accused could plead truth in his defense led to endless embarrassments. In 1799, Duane threatened to produce Adams's letter to Coxe complaining of Thomas Pinckney's appointment as ambassador to Great Britain. As Pinckney was a member of one of the most powerful Federalist families in the South, the administration chose to abandon the prosecution rather than risk alienating so important an ally.[101] Then, when the President refused to be subpoenaed by Thomas Cooper as a witness for substantiating certain charges he had made, the Republicans declaimed upon the injustice of a law which denied the accused means to procure evidence on his side.[102] The Federalists' determination to override procedural objections bore out the Republican claim that the law was unfair in design. When Callender was prosecuted in Virginia the defense was plainly less interested in protecting the accused than in dramatizing the unreasonableness of the proceedings. The Federalists did themselves infinitely greater harm with these sedition prosecutions than the Republicans suffered by the temporary loss of a few presses.[103]

Yet this did not exhaust Federalist electioneering options. Even with majority opinion against them they might still be victorious if they could concentrate their votes in the electoral college more successfully than their opponents. The complexity of the electoral college, as it was then constituted, worked to the advantage of the Federalists because of their superior ability for concerted action. The events of 1796 were a good example of this. All the states east of the Delaware had delivered their votes for Adams, while those in the South scattered theirs among several candidates. If North Carolina and Virginia had shown the same discipline as New England, Jefferson would have been elected President. The East presented its solid front partly because every state but Massachusetts resorted either to the legislative appointment of its electors, or, as in the case of New Hampshire, to a general ticket. Whichever way they chose, the net result was that minorities had no voice. But in three important southern states—namely Maryland, Virginia and North Carolina—the electors had been chosen by districts, and one vote from each of the two last-named states had been cast for Adams. It is true that even if every state had voted by the unit rule, Adams would still have won the election, as the Republicans would have picked up only two votes for Jefferson while Adams would have gained four additional votes from Maryland. Nevertheless if the district system had been universal, Jefferson might have made greater gains from minority elements in New Jersey, New York and Vermont than Adams could match by minority elements in Pennsylvania. So the Federalist victory in 1796 could be seen partly as the result of the superior discipline and management they had been able to impose on the electoral college in certain areas.[104]

These tactics did not even need the electoral college to succeed. They could be used in any election with equal facility. In 1797 "Republican" had warned the people of Northumberland County, Pennsylvania, that the Federalists had been purposely promoting various popular candidates so as to divide the Republican vote at the same time as they were boosting their own single choice. The obvious defense against such a strategy was nomination.[105] Americans were not unfamiliar with nominations made informally and locally by the friends of a candidate. But this was not a procedure that could be used by just anyone in nominating candidates to be elected from the large constituencies the Federal government had created, where the coordination of many diverse groups was necessary for victory. Rather it played into the hands of cliques who had wide-ranging connections and could achieve agreement by informal means as the Federalist leadership had often done in the first years of the new republic, putting challengers lacking such aids at a distinct disadvantage. If they resorted to nominations through such devices as legislative caucuses or state-wide conventions, they exposed themselves to a charge of violating the traditional freedom of elections, at least in places where this idea still carried weight. If they did not, they risked continuing to lose their battle to the Federalists' divisive tactics and superior resources for concerted action even though the majority was on their side.[106]

Some idea of the obstacles the Republicans had to overcome in openly employing such devices as state-wide nominations can be gathered from the Federalist response when the Virginia legislature tried to prevent unfair advantage being taken of it in the electoral college. Early in 1800, the legislature had repealed a law dating from 1792 that had provided for the district choice of electors, and substituted a new one providing for a general ticket. A block of twenty-one electoral votes was at stake, and several of them might have gone for Adams if the district system had been preserved. Not surprisingly, the Federalists protested the law. One of their reasons was that it violated the freedom of elections by a requirement that each voter list the names of twenty-one men, each one a resident of his district, so that nominations would be vital to those who did not want their votes disqualified. The Federalists said that this interfered with the people's traditional freedom of choice because it forced the electorate to vote for men they could not personally know. And the nominations proceeded from a legislative caucus, whose actions were denounced as the aristocratic dictates of an exclusive minority.[107]

The proponents of the general ticket law replied that without it, and without the nominations it necessitated, Virginia's majority would lose its full influence in the electoral college. As long as other states did not allow minorities a voice through district elections, Virginia could not do so without the risk that her minority, together with Federalist majorities in other states, might gain control of the electoral college. Though the proponents of the bill acknowledged that the general ticket law required nominations by a small minority, they argued that there was no other way to ensure the expression of the majority's will. Without nominations in a general ticket election, victory would go to the most disciplined minority. As for not knowing the candidates, Republican spokesmen said that personal knowledge of electors was not necessary when the only important thing was that they vote for Jefferson! [108]

In 1800, Virginia Republicans were in an unusually good position to trade charges of electioneering with the Federalists, at least compared to their ideological compatriots in other states. They were not unique in being able to expose the Federalists as hypocrites who denounced nominations by the opposition at the same time as they were meeting secretly to make nominations of their own. The opposition in every state could have done that, and could also have revealed that the Federalist aim was to convince some that "their rights have been invaded, and from resentment . . . [that they should] withhold, or throw away their votes" in order that a minority might triumph over the Republican majority.[109] Virginians were better able to make the charge stick, however, since they had more prestige than their opponents, as the Federalists acknowledged when they complained of the "great and imposing names" associated with the Virginia general ticket strategy. In those states where the Republicans found themselves in the opposition on the state level, the situation was different. An exchange of electioneering charges might then have damaged them disproportionately because their efforts to mobilize the public were necessarily more visible than their opponents' more covert forms of influence. So the Federalists often pressed this charge more openly than the Republicans,[110] with the ironic consequence that historians have used Federalist polemics as evidence to support a modern supposition that the Republican victory of 1800 was primarily achieved by superior organization.[111]

When it came to the struggle for the presidential election, any pretense to superior Federalist virtue quickly vanished. Virginia's behavior over the General Ticket Law touched off a mad scramble in which each party tried to seize the advantage by concerted action. In May, Republican and Federalist Congressmen met in caucus at Philadelphia to coordinate electioneering plans throughout the Union.[112] In response to pressures building up in the electoral college, of which the Congressional caucus was merely a symptom, Massachusetts abandoned its old district system and, taking no chances, settled for legislative appointment.[113] New Hampshire also replaced its general ticket system with legislative appointment.[114] In Maryland the issue whether or not district elections should give place to legislative appointment decided the state elections. When the Federalists, hoping to appropriate Maryland's entire block of votes, argued for legislative appointment in this election only, they were overwhelmed by Republican charges that they sought to wrest "from the People their right of suffrage in the appointment of electors to elect the Chief Magistrate of the United States." [115] In Pennsylvania, meanwhile, there was a reversal of roles. The Federalists knew that they were in the minority, and consequently the Federalist Senate insisted on district elections while the Republican House argued for a general ticket.[116] In North Carolina the Federalists, who had briefly captured control of the state during the war crisis of 1798, were in the minority, but they were nonetheless able to enforce a district system which allowed them to win four of the state's twelve votes for Adams and Pinckney.[117] Lastly, in states like New York, New Jersey, and to a lesser extent Connecticut and South Carolina, where legislative appointment was the accepted style, and in Maryland and Pennsylvania, where the election laws were at issue, state elections degenerated into bitter partisan struggles.[118]

By 1800 the framers' original expectations for the electoral college had vanished on the wind. The overriding importance of the presidential election was each party's justification for copying the devices of the other in fighting for control of the electoral college. But competitive emulation played into Republican hands in two ways. First it spelled the end to popular apathy, which was a prerequisite of the kind of factional intrigue at which the Federalists had excelled, and it transformed the Presidential election into a contest for public opinion in which the Republicans could hope to enjoy an advantage.[119] Secondly it brought electioneering into the open so that it became harder for the Federalists to continue making use of the old prejudices against the activity. Thereafter, Republicans did not hesitate to embrace the legislative caucus openly whenever they thought it necessary, though they still had reservations about it.

The Federalists did not always match them in candor. In areas like New England where electioneering was still frowned upon, the Federalists continued to be secretive about their own activity in the hope of turning this prejudice to advantage and conquering the people by dividing them. The result is that although the press of both parties offers insight into Republican party organization, the prime source of documentation for Federalist organizations is to be found in Republican prints which mercilessly assaulted Federalist hypocrisy in this respect.[120]

PART VI

RESOLUTION

When Robert Goodloe Harper acted as valedictorian of the defeated Federalists in *A Letter . . . to his constituents* (1801), he pledged that those who had prided themselves on being friends to the government would support Jefferson as long as he conducted it on rational principles. This turned out to be more of a threat than a promise of help, as could be seen from his warning that the precepts "on which the federalists have acted must be adopted, their plans must be substantially pursued, or the government must fall in pieces." Harper went on to present these in the most flattering light possible, insisting that "The leading principle of their system, as to foreign nations, has been to preserve peace and amity with all . . . but to grant privileges to none, and to submit to indignities from none; to rely for the protection of our rights and honour, not on the friendship the justice or the forbearance of other governments, but on our own strength and resources." This, he said, had enabled them to keep the nation at peace at a time when most of the world was caught up in an unusually vicious war. As for domestic policy, the Federalists had done their best to protect the authority of the federal government against the jealousy of the states, and the executive power against encroachment by the popular branch. They had also seen to it that government office would be well enough paid to attract the best men.[1]

Turning from the precepts of Federalism to the record of administration, Harper said that "the Federalists laid it down as the corner stone of their system, to support cherish and invigorate commerce, as the best and indeed the only effectual means of promoting agriculture and every other branch of industry." The farmer's prosperity depended on commerce, and, more vital still, so did the revenue. This brought him to the "next great object in the plan of the federalists . . . the establishment of a solid and extensive system of revenue;

241

by which the interest of the public debt might be punctually paid, the principal gradually discharged, public credit thus firmly established, the support of the government fully provided for, and ample means of defense furnished against the time of need." Lastly, Harper claimed that the Federalists deserved credit for having seen that the laws were enforced with vigor but clemency, and that the frontiers were properly protected. He believed that some measure of their achievement could be gained by comparing the country as it was when they took office, "without a shilling of permanent revenue; without a system of finance; burdened with a debt arising from the war . . . and without money in the treasury sufficient for the ordinary expenses of government," to its present happy state. Commerce was thriving, the revenue close to nine million dollars, and the nation able to look forward to retiring the national debt by 1824.[2] Harper concluded by affirming his belief that the Federalists had no need to fear being judged on their record, but could "enjoy the secret and sweet satisfaction of knowing that their names will be remembered with affectionate respect, and their services with gratitude, when all the calumnies with which they have been assailed for the purpose of driving them from power, shall have been buried in oblivion." [3]

History has justified his hope, for modern historians concur in his assessment of Federalist achievements. They look back to the Federalist decade as a time when the nation's basic institutions were established and America began to acquire a distinctive identity as a commercial, industrial culture. They feel an instinctive sympathy for the Federalists, and have tended to accept Harper's view that resolution of the tensions existing between the two parties in 1800 depended on the willingness of Jeffersonians to adopt their principles. It was a slow process, requiring the abandonment of many agrarian prejudices, but it received immeasurable impetus from the War of 1812. The exigencies of military conflict taught the Republicans to value such Federalist measures as a national bank and a permanent military establishment, and even led Madison to propose federally-sponsored internal improvements.[4]

Harper's delineation of Federalism left no room for explanation of his party's defeat in the election of 1800. If the Federalists had done so much so well, what possible reason could there be, except unparalleled ingratitude? Indeed, Harper assumed as much, but he saw this as less the people's spontaneous act than the result of their being worked upon by a cabal. In Harper's view, the Republican triumph had been achieved through lies, slander and misrepresentation; in short, by the demonstration of a superior technique for manipulating opinion.[5] This explanation has its appeal in an age which has been altogether too willing to believe that there is no problem for which there is not a technical solution, but it leaves some awkward questions unanswered. Given the tendency of these adversaries to imitate each other in time of stress, why is it that after 1800 the Federalists never came close to regaining power in their own right? They themselves had an answer to this, and modern scholars have recently revived it. They said that among them were men of principle rather than technique, and that because many old-school Federalists refused to abandon principle for manipulation, after 1800 those who were willing to make this adjustment were at a distinct disadvantage.[6] This assumes that before 1800 the Federalists were as innocent of political technique as they claimed to be and also that they represented principles which the people would have embraced had they not been deflected by a series of sinister maneuvers.

Harper's sketch of Federalist principles and policies makes this assumption seem plausible in retrospect, but did the Federalist self-image correspond to the popular view of them in their own time? It is noticeable that Harper says nothing about the most controversial act of the 1790's, the Sedition Law, whose re-enactment as a permanent measure he himself had urged two months before, despite a presidential defeat and decisive Republican gains in the Seventh Congress. To the Republicans, this law was the embodiment of all the dangerous tendencies they feared in their adversaries. The attempt to re-enact it confirmed their worst suspicions, and helped shape their approach to the judiciary in subsequent years. It was in the controversy over this law that the basic ideological issues which had separated the Federalists and Republicans for a decade again became plain, despite the tendency of styles to merge in the late 1790's. Even after the Republican triumph of 1800, when it might have been expected that popular abhorrence of the Federalists would gradually die away, their activities from 1801–1815 kept it alive. Only when the Federalists are seen as most of their compatriots saw them is it possible to understand how and why the first party system came to an end after the War of 1812.

II. Repudiation

Having begun by trying to manipulate public opinion, the Federalists were at last driven to attempt control of it through the Sedition Law. In 1794, when they were in the midst of badgering the popular societies to death, they had shown extreme reluctance to interfere with the press; but now they were desperate. Their ability in 1798 to circumvent all constitutional objections raised by their opponents and to command the almost unanimous support of the judiciary had a lot to do with the war scare, but it was also the result of an ambiguity in a revolutionary tradition which they eagerly exploited. The old tradition which had seen no incompatibility between freedom of the press and restraint provided revolutionary precedent for the curbs which the Federalists now proposed to set on the opposition press.

In prerevolutionary times, every literate American had allowed a distinction between the liberty of the press and licentious abuse of that liberty. Sir William Blackstone had endorsed this precept in his *Commentaries on the Laws of England,* a treatise on which the education of most American lawyers was founded after the Revolution, and which helps to explain why what was essentially a prerevolutionary doctrine should still be current at the end of the century. Blackstone had argued that liberty of the press did not mean freedom from all restraint, but freedom from all *prior* restraint. This argument had won general acceptance before the revolution, not only because it was consistent with opposition ideology, but also because of the uses to which it might be put. At the same time as it could be invoked to assert immunity from executive control, it could also justify the control of any press serving the ends of executive aggrandizement. The standard by which the press was to be judged as making proper use of its freedom or not was compatibility with the public good. And the agency that made the discrimination was in both cases an arm of the people's power. Through the right of a jury to find a general verdict and acquit anyone accused of seditious libel by the executive, freedom of the press could be maintained against oppressive power. But the colonial assemblies, and after them the patriot mobs, felt no compunction about chastising Tory printers for endangering the cohesiveness of the people's power. Following the premises of opposition ideology to their logical conclusion, the people were held to be better judges of public good than the executive.[1]

The controls the colonists imposed on their press seem to us to have been appallingly partisan, but they did not seem so then. The rationale for them was essentially the same as that notion of privilege which Parliament had invoked against Charles I when it asserted its independence of the Crown. This said that Parliament's function was to resist royal tyranny for the people's good, but that if its members could not preserve their own persons or reputations against the Crown they would certainly be unable to safeguard the rights of others. Similar reasoning had prompted the attempt of the colonial assemblies to imprison authors and printers for breach of privilege. The theory was that without the power to control the press, the people would not be able to combine in resisting an overbearing sovereign and public liberty would be forever forfeit. When the welfare of the whole demanded the sacrifice of individual rights, the prerevolutionary American had no doubt that this sacrifice should be made.[2]

I

It was to this tradition that the Federalists turned in 1798 when they sought a justification for the Sedition Law. They argued that without the power to restrain the press, the government could not accomplish the purposes for which it had been elected by the people. Harrison Gray Otis, speaking on the floor of the House of Representatives, said "it must be allowed that every independent Government has a right to preserve and defend itself against injuries and outrages which endanger its existence; for, unless it has this power, it is unworthy the name of a free Government, and must either fall or be subordinate to some other protection."[3] Robert Goodloe Harper asked, "can the powers of a Government be carried into execution, if sedition for opposing its laws, and libels against its officers, itself, and its proceedings, are to pass unpunished?"[4] The Federalist minority in the Virginia legislature contended that "government cannot be thus secured, if, by falsehood and malicious slander, it is to be deprived of the confidence and affection of the people."[5] And in a charge to the grand jury of Barnstable County in Massachusetts, Robert Treat Paine demanded: "How can the Congress protect the people, their constituents, if they are not able to protect themselves?"[6] Once the people had conferred power on a government it was obliged to preserve itself for their sake, which made the Sedition Law "as essential to the rights and privileges of the people as any law upon our code."[7]

Two circumstances helped the Federalists put to use in a republic doctrines which were originally developed for confronting a monarch. The first, oddly enough, was that supervision of the press had largely vanished at the end of the Revolutionary War so that most people had not given much thought to the application of prerevolutionary doctrine to a postrevolutionary state. This does not mean that freedom of the press was taken for granted. The lack of an explicit guarantee in the Constitution had even been used by antifederalists as an argument against ratification. But that freedom had been too integral a part of revolutionary ideology for anyone to dare disavow it, and one of the amendments proposed by the First Congress forbade Congress to abridge "the freedom of speech, or of the press," a provision against which not one recorded objection was brought.[8]

Only in Massachusetts, where some thought the growing licentiousness of the press provoked Shays's Rebellion, were there any widespread proceedings against seditious libels. And once the state had weathered the crisis, press controls disappeared. A pamphlet entitled *Candid considerations on libels* (1789), published in Boston, lamented that libels undermined public confidence in the virtues, abilities, and integrity of prominent men, but argued that libel laws were undesirable on two counts. They were useless in that no court judgment would change an opinion already rooted in the public mind, and potentially despotic in that they might be used to destroy freedom of the press.[9] Although it was generally acknowledged that the press could be abused, most people thought the best guard against this was public opinion.[10] Throughout the rest of the Union, freedom of the press was seldom an issue. As William Claiborne said when the

Sedition Bill was under debate in the House, "the doctrine of libel was very unsettled. . . . Prosecutions of this kind have rarely happened; in some of the States, a cause of this kind had never been tried." [11]

The second helpful circumstance was that the forces threatening the republic in 1798 seemed to parallel those which Americans had faced before and during the Revolution. The notion of controlling the press through the exercise of privilege could be justified only where it was agreed that a benign populace faced a hostile sovereign who tried to exploit divisions among them as a step toward taking away their liberty. But after the Revolution, the power of a legislature to punish libels against itself was no longer defensible and had been challenged on the grounds that a representative body had no more right than an individual to judge a cause in which it was a party.[12] Nevertheless, if France were seen as the leader of an international Jacobin conspiracy, she could be cast in the role taken by the monarch or by Britain in revolutionary times while the Republican opposition would play the part which formerly belonged to ministerial scribblers or loyalists. And if control of the press had been right then, why not during the equally grave crisis of 1798? It might be objected that the Sedition Law protected all the officers of government, whereas only the lower House had claimed the privilege in colonial times, but this could be dismissed with the observation that all the officers of government were now the representatives of the people and bent on defending them against French-sponsored aggression. So long as France appeared threatening, the Federalists could suggest that "libels" by "corrupt partizans and hired presses" were part of the famed diplomatic arsenal with which she had undermined the will of many European nations to resist her.[13]

Federalist sponsors of this law did their utmost to create alarm all the while the Sedition Bill was being considered. Allen of Connecticut charged:

Let gentlemen look at certain papers printed in this city and elsewhere, and ask themselves whether an unwarrantable and dangerous combination does not exist to overturn and ruin the Government by publishing the most shameless falsehoods against the Representatives of the people of all denominations, that they are hostile to free Governments and genuine

liberty, and of course to the welfare of this country; that they ought, therefore, to be displaced, and that the people ought to raise an *insurrection*
against the Government.[14]

Allen was at no loss to document his charges. He pointed to pieces in
the opposition press suggesting that the Federalists were warmongers;
Livingston's rousing speech against the Alien Bill in which his critics
claimed that he had urged the people to resist "unconstitutional"
authority, and an article in the New York *Time Piece* calling the
President "a person without patriotism, without philosophy, and a
mock monarch," whose allegedly free election by the people was
rather "a jostling him into the Chief Magistracy by the ominous combination of old Tories with old opinions, and old Whigs with new."
Allen saw this as part of a Jacobin conspiracy supported by French
power without and disorganizers within which sought through the
press to obtain a powerful influence over "the poor, the ignorant, the
passionate, and the vicious." The danger was all the greater, he said,
because these ideas were known to be sanctioned by prominent men
and even by members of the House.[15]

The opposition was not persuaded by these arguments. Gallatin
spoke for most of them when he demanded: "Would any of them
dare to assert that the time when the Western insurrection took place,
when it was thought *necessary* to call to arms fifteen thousand men,
was not a more dangerous moment for Government, and did not more
forcibly call for a law punishing misrepresentations of the measures or
motives of Government than the present period?" In order to show a
need for such a law, he said, the Federalists would have to prove that
the president and the House could not exercise the powers of government vested in them by the Constitution unless the opposition press
was forbidden to abuse them in any way.[16] Many Republicans would
have added that the question of the necessity of the law should be
subordinated to its constitutionality and that so palpable a breach of
the Constitution, taken in conjunction with other Federalist measures,
suggested the danger of a consolidated government.[17]

The opposition was also alive to the origins of the Sedition Law,
and vigorously protested the application of a monarchical precedent
to the affairs of a republic. In his "Report of the Committee" Madison
pointed out the differences between the two forms of government:

In the British Government the danger of encroachment on the rights of the people is understood to be confined to the executive magistrate. The representatives of the people in the Legislature are not only exempt themselves from distrust, but are considered as sufficient guardians of the rights of their constituents against the danger from the Executive. Hence it is a principle, that the Parliament is unlimited in its power; or, in their own language, is omnipotent. Hence too, all the ramparts for protecting the rights of the people—such as their Magna Charta, their Bill of Rights, &c.—are not reared against the Parliament, but against the royal prerogative. They are merely legislative precaution against executive usurpations. Under such a government as this, an exemption of the press from previous restraint, by licensers appointed by the King, is all the freedom that can be secured to it.

In the United States the case is altogether different. The People, not the Government, possess the absolute sovereignty. The Legislature, no less than the Executive, is under limitations of power. Encroachments are regarded as possible from the one as well as from the other. Hence . . . [t]his security of the freedom of the press requires that it should be exempt not only from previous restraint by the Executive, as in Great Britain, but from legislative restraint also.[18]

Madison added that even in Britain, the press exercised greater freedom in practice than it was allowed in theory. Attacks on the government were occasionally punished, but "The ministry, who are responsible to impeachment, are at all times animadverted on by the press with peculiar freedom, and during the elections for the House of Commons, the other responsible part of the Government, the press is employed with as little reserve towards the candidates." [19]

II

These objections had little effect in the emergency of 1798. The Federalists had succeeded so well in promoting general hysteria that the people would not listen, nor if they had would they have cared whether or not the government was following monarchical precedent. Eventually the passing of the French threat would invalidate the plea of necessity and make the monarchical derivation of the Sedition Law more objectionable, but in the midst of crisis the strongest case Republicans could make against the act was that it struck "at the root of free republican Government" by rendering elections meaningless.[20] Madison's "Report of the Committee" explained how:

[In] competitions between those who are and those who are not members of the Government, what will be the situation of the competitors? Not equal: because the characters of the former will be covered by the Sedition Act from animadversions exposing them to disrepute among the people, whilst the latter may be exposed to the contempt and hatred of the people without a violation of the act. What will be the situation of the people? Not free; because they will be compelled to make their election between competitors whose pretensions they are not permitted by the act equally to examine, to discuss and to ascertain. And from both these situations will not those in power derive an undue advantage for continuing themselves in it, which, by impairing the right of election, endangers the blessings of the Government founded upon it? [21]

This powerful indictment of the Sedition Law did not deter the Federalists. They answered that it was not meant to curb an honest canvass of the government's actions, which they agreed was necessary to the preservation of republican government. It was meant to keep the channels of information pure by stopping the dissemination of falsehood through the press.[22] Was legitimate freedom of the press "abridged by a law to restrain lying?" [23] they asked, adding that far from perverting the freedom of elections, the Sedition Law would help to preserve it. This was why their original proposal had allowed truth as a defense against the charge of libel. They had also proved the purity of their intentions by yielding to opposition pressure in the House for an amendment giving a jury the power to decide both the law and the facts, though some had protested that this was not necessary given the state of American law, and Bayard had even suggested it would work against the accused by obstructing appeals. Dana had observed with heavy irony that "it was not the will of judges—those arbitrary party-spirited characters—that could convict." One man out of twelve could prevent conviction, and "what better [protective] barrier to the liberty of an individual can be presented than this?" The Federalists boasted that given the provision for truth as a defense, and the limitations imposed in sentencing, the Sedition Act was an improvement on the common law which ensured that no man could be penalized for conducting a proper and honest canvass of government.[24]

The opposition was unmoved by these protestations. They retorted that even if juries could ultimately acquit men who were accused, printers would be inhibited from publishing criticism of the government by the fear of prolonged harassment. After all, the law gave the administration the last word on who might be prosecuted. If nothing else, the difficulty and expense of establishing legal proof that their statements were true would deter printers from publishing anything that might draw the government's wrath. What was to prevent a government from using incidental misstatements of fact as a pretext to convict opposition printers?[25] Bayard replied that the Sedition Law did not make a false statement unlawful unless it was malicious in intent,[26] but the Republicans said that to punish the intention of maligning the government was necessarily to silence all comment upon it except praise. Indeed, the more at fault its members were in discharging their duties, the more would be their incentive to punish their critics.[27]

The only possible protection the law afforded an accused man was that a jury could prevent his conviction. According to opposition ideology, the jury was one of the people's first defenses against oppression by the executive. In Britain, juries had sometimes tempered the common law of seditious libel even though they were supposed to have jurisdiction only over the fact of publication, not over the question whether the matter was indeed libel. And when the Federalists tried to censor the popular societies in 1794 for abusing the right of free expression, the Pennsylvania Democratic Society retorted that if there had indeed been such abuses, they might be restrained by a jury.[28] But by the late 1790's the Republicans were beginning to doubt the effectiveness of juries for several reasons. They had long entertained reservations about the impartiality of the federal judicial system, where a judge might be appointed to some lucrative diplomatic post as Jay had been, and where in many parts of the country federal marshals appointed by the President had discretion in choosing jurors. Now they went beyond this and questioned that any jury was competent to decide the matters over which the law gave them jurisdiction.[29]

Gallatin observed that the Sedition Law was directed against the kind of political criticism which would comprise not only facts but also opinions, whose worth could hardly be proved in court by the presentation of evidence. As an example he cited the navy, which some thought was necessary while others thought differently. Because the President had recommended the establishment of a navy, might not "persons writing and speaking against this system, which they ought to do, if they believe the system inimical to the United States . . . be charged with bringing the Congress and President into contempt?"[30] As Nicholas remarked, no jury could determine the truth or falsehood of an opinion, but only "whether or not it is their own." Therefore the Sedition Law's provision for trial by jury and the plea of truth would not protect free expression: "No man will be safe; for though he may have formed his opinion as correctly as possible, if twelve men are to sit upon it, and if it should happen not to be their opinion . . . he will be liable to a severe fine and imprisonment." The chances of such abuse were greater now than ever before, because of the current tendency to let prejudices and passion form opinion. Therefore, if such a Sedition Law were passed, a man might be punished for publishing an opinion considerately formed and honestly held "merely because accident, or design, has collected a jury of different sentiments."[31]

This was a crucial point of disagreement between Federalists and Republicans, one to which the Federalists never fully responded. Though Bayard, running true to form, tentatively suggested that opinions could be as "false, malicious, and scandalous" as facts,[32] Federalists in general argued more prudently that the Sedition Law punished nothing a good man would want to do. In the debate on renewing the Sedition Law in January, 1801, Dana demanded: "How . . . could the rights of the people require a liberty to utter falsehood? How could it be right to do wrong?" And Platt remarked: "To those who took every occasion to show their opposition to the Government, and were accustomed to vilify the conduct of its warmest adherents, this law must be obnoxious; but those who considered the Government a blessing, and worthy the protection of a free people, must approve of the provisions of this law, as one of the most valuable institutions in its support."[33] Such an approach had two merits: it avoided the issue and implicitly questioned the moral character of the Republicans.

Two could play this game. From the start, the Republicans retorted that government did not need to control falsehood because truth would triumph in any free and fair debate. This assumption was behind Thomas Claiborne's observation about some paragraphs abusing the President that "if they are calumnies they will have no weight; and if they are truth, they ought to be published." [34] Strictly speaking, according to the definitions of Gallatin and Nicholas, the supremacy of truth over falsehood was a concept applying to fact but not opinion. Yet in the hands of some Republican ideologues it acquired metaphysical overtones which could not fail to alienate the Federalists. For example, Tunis Wortman and John Thomson in their respective treatises on the liberty of the press defined truth as that which the understanding of man could not resist,[35] giving as examples the triumph of Christianity in antiquity and the progress of science more recently in the early modern world. The triumph of Christianity, culminating in the ideal of religious freedom, proved the uselessness of repressing opinion, while the progress of science demonstrated the benefits to be derived from freedom of inquiry and discussion.[36] If the principle of free debate had such happy results for science and religion, it was surely reasonable to suppose that it would be equally beneficial in other spheres of human life. Thomas Cooper and Thomson eagerly pointed to the role free enquiry had played in the revolution and in shaping the Constitution, two political advances to be matched in significance only by a Republican victory in 1800.[37]

It is not surprising that the notion truth would triumph, supported as it sometimes was by the theory that progress was inevitable, should have little appeal for the Federalists in 1800. Whatever their opinion of eighteenth-century science, most Federalists were appalled by the course world politics had taken since the overthrow of the French monarchy. Instead of bringing about a gradual increase of liberty, the French Revolution seemed to them to have become a symbol of regressive barbarism threatening civilization, a living proof of the evils inherent in democracy if not in republicanism itself. It seemed to show, not the inevitability of progress following on the unrestricted circulation of opinion, but rather the dire peril of exciting the passions and jealousy of the mob. Many Federalists believed that events in France since 1789 proved the people could be roused to destructive fury against the best government they had ever known by a league of clubs, presses and societies.[38] And if the French people had been so induced to destroy the Constitution of 1791, even when the monarchy still had ways of influencing public opinion which were lacking in a republic of equal laws, then certainly republics were even more vulnerable. Nor did Federalist scepticism of political progress derive from the French experience alone. The opposition threat to their hegemony, steadily increasing throughout the 1790's, made the notion of progress laughable to them.

The historical pessimism of the Federalists was not confined to politics. Like their chosen allies, the clergy, when they were obliged to explain the success of infidelity against Christian truth, many lay Federalists were not above thinking that the history of Christianity justified a certain pessimism. James Bayard demanded of the House: "Would the gentlemen say the truth always prevails, when he looked at the state of our holy religion? Near 1800 years had elapsed since its light was abroad, and yet how large a portion of the world remained in darkness and error!" In general, he concluded, history did not verify the intrinsic superiority of truth over falsehood. By such reasoning the Federalists justified their refusal "to be impartial between the principles of truth and falsehood, and to allow them to contend on an equal footing." Alexander Addison argued that the dissemination of falsehoods and slander could distort truth, wryly observing that "listening to error and falsehood is indeed a strange way to discover truth." [39] For the most part, Federalist politicians concurred with Federalist clergymen in distinguishing public opinion from truth. This distinction accorded with the original definition of Gallatin and Nicholas, but it failed to persuade the Federalists that the test of truth was not protection enough for opinions.

There was another flaw in the Republican notion that truth would triumph, and the Federalists hastened to exploit it. This was the assumption that for every falsehood there was a corresponding truth. It had long been a Federalist complaint that falsehoods disseminated by the opposition press went unchallenged in certain remote areas.[40] "Crito" in the *Gazette of the United States* had observed in 1794 that if people in the interior "have no other source of political information, they will believe *all* the evil that is charged upon the government; they will be amazed at the intelligence they receive, but they will not be much the wiser for their wonder." Speaking of the opposition press, "Crito" said that "falsehood of Philadelphia workmanship has been taken up in the distant states and retailed as often as it was necessary for some state demagogue to bespatter a rival that stands in the way. The truth perhaps never begins the chase, or, if it should, the falsehood has got the start." [41] The nation's geographic diffuseness was not the only reason that its intellectual market place was one where the competitors were on less than equal terms. Dana remarked bitterly that lies against the government would always find a newspaper to air them, but there was less eagerness to publish rebuttals. Even when slander was subsequently refuted, the original attack was likely to make a stronger and more lasting impression than the defense.[42]

III

The real issue between the two parties was not whether truth would triumph in some ultimate, metaphysical sense, but whether government could be threatened by the uncontrolled circulation of opinion. The Republicans never denied that there were governments which could be so threatened. The defense in the trial of Abijah Adams had admitted that the monarchical doctrine of libels suited the British government because its principles "were considered to be incapable of bearing the test of scrutiny and investigation" so that it was necessary to punish "as a high *crime* and *misdemeanour,* every effort to analyze the character, or to illustrate the iniquity of any public department." In Britain the truth of a libel increased the offense, because in a government of usurpation "a fair display of its true character would more endanger its existence, than all that malice could invent, or the hundred tongues of slander, falsehood or sedition could propagate." But, so they argued, a republic had no need to fear. "The good sense, the affections of the people who formed it, and whose happiness it was intended to promote, were considered its safe and immovable foundation. . . . In vain might it be assailed by calumny or invaded by faction. Criticism would only tend to exhibit more conspicuously its virtues, and calumny by being reverberated, to lessen the force and influence of its enemies." Such reasoning, designed to challenge the application to the American scene of monarchical doctrines about liberty of the press, revealed their faith in the superior stability of republics.[43]

Needless to say, this faith was not shared by the Federalists. Men like Harrison Gray Otis believed that a monarchy was much better able to tolerate a licentiousness in the press than a republic, because if disorders should arise, the executive possessed means to put them down which were not immediately dependent on the people. In his view, the greater dependence of the American government on the people's good will was an argument for rather than against restraint of opinion. Speaking on another subject, Otis condemned a colleague's disrespectful address to the president because "where the Chief Magistrate is elective, and the dignity of his character is upheld, not like that of a monarch by the splendor of his state, or the compulsive homage of his subjects, but by the esteem of his constituents and the strength of public opinion, it is an incumbent duty to demonstrate, by all ordinary means, our respect for the character and the office." [44] Alexander Addison put the problem neatly: "To mislead the judgement of the people, where they have no power, may produce no mischief. To mislead the judgement of the people, where they have *all* power, must produce the greatest possible mischief." [45]

The belief that republics were fragile because of their dependence on public opinion gave the Federalists an excuse for perpetuating the Sedition Law even after the French crisis had passed. James Bayard first pointed the way to do this in February 1799. Just after Adams had announced Murray's appointment as commissioner to France, he renewed the motion to expel Lyon from the House on the grounds that he was guilty of a "crime . . . of the first political magnitude" which would "go to the subversion of the Government."

This Government . . . depends for its existence upon the good will of the people. That good will is maintained by their good opinion. But, how is that good opinion to be preserved, if wicked and unprincipled men, men of inordinate and desperate ambition, are allowed to state facts to the people which are not true, which they know at the time to be false, and which are stated with the criminal intention of bringing the Government into disrepute among the people? This was falsely and deceitfully stealing public opinion; it was a felony of the worst and most dangerous nature.

Bayard claimed that Lyon had "defamed the President of the United States, with a view of exciting hatred, and stirring up sedition." And the Federalists never gave up the idea that libels might endanger government by leading to violence, or that "the publication of false, scandalous, and malicious matter against the Government . . . tends to produce insurrection and total disrespect for its authority, and that, without the power of preventing these, no Government can exist." [46]

The Republicans were confident that the free circulation of opinion would never disturb the tranquillity of society if only the government were sensitive to it. Thomas Cooper wrote: "The mass of talents, of knowledge, and of respectability will, in every country, from interest as well as principle, be on the side of good order and morality. There can be few who, from ignorance or design, will be tempted publicly to support opinions inimical to the general welfare." [47] Such an assertion did not speak to the Federalist fear that in a government of this sort the public interest would be continuously sacrificed on "the altar of public opinion," which in time might lead to disorder.[48] The Republicans replied that government was always the expression of someone's opinion, and better that this be the people's rather than that of their "superiors." As Cooper put it, "The immediate interest of the people is to discover and promote the general good: that of governors to extend their own power, or preserve it by the continuance of the present order of things." [49] What most Republicans meant when they said true opinions would triumph was that out of unlimited discussion some concept of the general interest would emerge. Cooper gave his idea of how the process would work when he asked, "Should false opinions be propagated, is it probable that the majority of the people . . . will be misled by them, and that persons in power only will have the acuteness and discernment to detect their fallacy? But were even this the case, surely the friends of the existing establishment, with truth on their side, and the collateral aids of wealth and power, will have no difficulty in confuting them." He concluded that free and open discussion would never lead to the deliberate choice of a bad system or the rejection of a good one.

Republican ideologues went beyond arguing that freedom of discussion could not endanger the state to assert that the denial of such freedom was a positive risk. Cooper believed that "restraints imposed on freedom of speech and writing, are evidently calculated to produce the mischief they ostensibly aim to destroy. While one party assumes a right to suppress the opinions of those who differ from them, and the other experiences a degrading and unjustifiable subjection—violence, ill-will, and rancour must subsist." [50] Ever since the controversy over the popular societies, the Republicans had been arguing that to repress discussion would be counterproductive because grievances which could not be voiced would swell in secret until they burst out in rebellious violence. The Republicans attributed most of the excesses of the French Revolution and the Whiskey Rebellion to the ignorance of the people, the proper remedy for which was not coercion but free discussion.[51] Even if the suppression of free discussion did not lead to actual violence, it would arouse the people's jealousy. For just as the clamor against the popular societies had led their proponents to infer their necessity, so a government's unwillingness to submit to examination would lead to the inference that it had something to hide.[52]

The free circulation of opinion and its expression through electoral institutions, on the other hand, would help the government respond with sensitivity to the people's hopes and desires. It would keep representatives informed about the sentiments and feelings of the nation and promote harmony among the people by allowing them to arrive together at a perception of the common good. Last and best, it would produce an enlightened people aware of their rights, a strong deterrent to any rulers who might try to encroach on them. It remained axiomatic among many Republicans that government had a tendency to trespass on popular liberties. This was a tenet of opposition ideology which the experience of Americans in the Revolution and of the opposition in the 1790's seemed to prove true. But as long as the people were vigilant and independent enough to check inroads on their rights, government would avoid giving them occasion to exert themselves against it. And rulers would be led to seek the general good rather than the advantage of a privileged few. Thus free discussion would impart "true republican energy to government," by commanding "the confidence, zeal and prompt cooperation of the people." [53]

There was another sense in which the Federalists felt government and society might be endangered by the free circulation of opinion. This was brought out by Gallatin when he questioned the claim that government depended upon public opinion by observing: "Surely it is not intended to mean whether there shall be a Government or not. It can only relate to the persons who administer the Government." [54] When "Aristides" complained that "[in] our Government it is essential, not only that its measures be correct, but that they be correctly understood," he was in effect arguing that unless the people were told the truth, a good administration might be voted out of office if "the channels of communication between itself and the people became perverted and corrupted" by "misrepresentation" and "falsehood." Suggestions that the Federalists meant to establish monarchy or destroy the Constitution were just the kind of falsehoods they felt justified in controlling.[55]

Again, the Republicans could not agree. Cooper pointed out that "Where respect and confidence are really due from having been earned, the public is never backward in paying them; on the contrary, the people are notoriously apt to err on the opposite side, and to pay an exuberance of homage approaching to adulation, where there exist evidences of public merit." [56] There was certainly no risk that the government's story would not be heard, for as Wortman said, "There are more that will always be ready to vindicate than to censure its measures from selfish or sinister considerations." [57] During most of the 1790's the majority of presses were Federalist, and only in the last years of the decade did this imbalance begin to right itself. Therefore the Republicans felt justified in arguing that "Falsehood cannot make a good administration bad, or a bad administration good. No administration need ever fear false publications, it can always destroy their effects whenever it pleases by publishing truth and truth alone can destroy Governments; nor need any administration fear anything but truth." [58]

The Republicans were not denying that freedom of the press could be abused, or that isolated injustices might arise from its abuse. But they pointed out that it was impossible to repress falsehood by force without the risk that truth would also suffer. It was better to tolerate some abuses "than, by pruning them away, to injure the vigor of those [opinions] yielding the proper fruits." They agreed that if only it were possible to prohibit the publication of falsehoods without obstructing truth, it would also be desirable, but they argued that such questions could not be decided in the federal courts where "the persons who would have to preside in trials of this sort, would themselves be parties." [59] The force of this argument was increased by features of the federal structure. Madison believed that "the peculiar magnitude of some of the powers necessarily committed to the Federal Government; the peculiar duration required for the functions of some of its departments; the peculiar distance of the seat of its proceedings from the great body of its constituents, and the peculiar difficulty of circulating an adequate knowledge of them through any other channel" justified barring the federal government from touching the channel which alone can give efficacy to its responsibility to its constituents.[60] In any case, abusers of this freedom would ultimately harm themselves more than others, for "Falsehoods will always depreciate the press from whence they proceed." [61]

In the end, the Federalist pretense that the Sedition Law was meant only to keep the channels of information pure was belied more by their partisan enforcement of it than by opposition criticism. In the last session of the Sixth Congress, when the Federalists proposed to renew the law, Gallatin observed that he "could not see how this law would correct or render pure the channels of information, if only certain kinds of libels were punished. How . . . has it been executed? Only by punishing persons of politics different from those of the administration." In the original debate on the Sedition Law, Joseph McDowell had complained of Cobbett's *Porcupine's Gazette* "whose paper contains more libels and falsehoods than any other in the United States," and of Fenno's *Gazette of the United States.* Yet neither of these papers was prosecuted, though Cobbett was subjected to a civil action in the Pennsylvania courts for a personal libel of Benjamin Rush. Therefore Gallatin was able to answer the Federalist argument that the law was the only way in which the dissemination of falsehoods could be stopped by pointing out that it "had not prevented the corruption of public opinion, according to the explanation which the gentlemen in favor of the law have themselves given of these words." [62]

The Federalists were seriously embarrassed by the Republican claim that the Sedition Law was incompatible with republican institutions in derivation, principle, and execution. At the same time, their distrust of republics made them reluctant to abandon it even when they were about to lose their power. Harper illustrated their dilemma in his last plea for re-enactment, when he defended it "as a shield for the liberty of the press and the freedom of opinion, as a protection to myself and those with whom I have the happiness and the honor to think on public affairs, should we at any future time be forced, by the imbecility or the mistakes of any future Administration in this country, to commence an opposition against it. . . . When indicted myself, for calmly and candidly exposing the errors of Government and the incapacity of those who govern, I wish to be enabled, by this law, to go before a jury of my country, and say that what I have written is true. I wish to interpose this law between the freedom of discussion and the overbearing sway of that tyrannical spirit, by which a certain political party in this country is actuated; that spirit which, arrogating to itself to speak in the name of the people, like fanaticism arrogating to itself to speak in the name of God, knows neither moderation, mercy, nor justice; regards neither feeling, principle nor right; and sweeps down, with relentless fury, all that dares to detect its follies, oppose its progress, or resist its domination. It is my knowledge of this spirit, sir, of its frantic excesses, its unfeeling tyranny, and its intolerable revenge, that makes me anxious to raise this one mound between its fury and public liberty. . . . This shield . . . will at length . . . be torn away; for the spirit of which I speak, goaded by censorious inferiority, stimulated to madness by the envy of superior talents, reputation, and virtue, knows to brook, no check upon its rise, no censure upon its excess. But I will not sanction my own death by my own voice. I will not yield one barrier to freedom and the right to opinion, while I can defend it." [63]

12. *Vindication*

Harper's fear of Republican persecution had little basis in fact. The only reason the Federalists had to believe that their adversaries were preparing to turn their own weapons against them was the vast amount in punitive damages awarded to Benjamin Rush in his libel suit against William Cobbett. But although the adjudication of this case had undeniable political overtones; although Cobbett was forced to discontinue *Porcupine's Gazette* and leave the country, this was an isolated event.[1] Far from threatening to exact an eye for an eye, Republican writers went out of their way to reassure their opponents that they meant to return good for evil.[2] Even if the Federalists had been unable to believe their declarations that sedition prosecutions would be incompatible with their concept of Republicanism, it should have been some comfort that their own attempts to control opinion in this way had been so futile. The Sedition Law had not improved Federalist prospects. On the contrary, as Davis of Kentucky said in Congress, "If it has ever done any good . . . I believe it has hastened the declension of the Federal sun. Instead of controlling public opinion, as it was intended, the opposite effect has been produced; men have acted up to their opinions, though they were forbidden to speak."[3] And if the sedition prosecutions had hurt rather than helped the Federalists, then should the Republicans disregard the lessons of the past and bring such actions against the defeated party, they in turn would suffer ill consequences.

The Federalists might have replied that the rational tolerance of a few would not guarantee them protection from the vengeance of the many, particularly as the ideological constraints the Republicans claimed to have set upon themselves were equivocal. Though some of their more fervent ideologues like Tunis Wortman, Thomas Cooper and John Thomson, had denied the whole concept of seditious libel, many Republican leaders in Congress had been content to raise merely constitutional objections and to argue that with the state courts already empowered to punish abuse of the press there was no need for the federal courts also to assume jurisdiction. This could be taken to imply that most prominent Republicans did not reject the principle of the Sedition Act but merely quibbled over technicalities.[4]

Even if the jurisdictional issue were the only point of agreement among Republicans, it would still have protected the Federalists against systematic control of public opinion by the government if not against discrete oppressions. The Sedition Law had made it possible for the federal government to proceed simultaneously against opposition presses all over the country, but if such power were strictly confined to each state, total suppression of a political opinion would become impossible. A printer who was chivvied out of one state would surely be able to find another in which he could express his political views.[5] Furthermore, most of those Republicans who had seen a need for state courts to possess some power of acting against libels had also implied that the main function of such prosecutions would be to protect personal reputations from slander. And though they did not always observe this rule to the letter, they did show more respect for the rights of the Federalist press in the state courts after 1800 than the Federalists showed for theirs.[6]

I

Federalists like Harper could be reassured neither by words nor by deeds. Their fears were founded not on evidence, but upon their misgivings about republican government. In their view, history showed that all republics tended to degenerate, and that the experience of France in the 1790's was not the result of unprecedented events but rather the usual course which would be followed by this form of government unless there were resistance by a virtuous minority.[7] The election of Jefferson appeared to them a disastrous yielding of power to those who would acquiesce in this course if not actively encourage it. Though the relaxation of international tensions and Jefferson's conciliatory inaugural had combined to allay their anxieties briefly,[8] they were disturbed anew by Jefferson's appointments policy. It is easy to discount Federalist howls of dismay as their partisans were dismissed from federal office. But in that age before the spoils system had become the rule, and when the Federalists so firmly believed that their appointees enjoyed exclusive merit, the removal of even a few incumbents from minor offices took on grave significance. This was made clear in the controversy over Jefferson's replacement of Elizur Goodrich by Samuel Bishop as collector for the port of New Haven. Noah Webster, Jr., protested that Bishop had reached an age when he was "unqualified to perform the duties to public satisfaction," and that of necessity his son, Abraham Bishop, a man of little talent and disreputable character whose only qualification for office was an inflammatory electioneering pamphlet, would in fact exercise his powers. To the Federalists, this was an ill portent of a new era in which elections would be managed by pandering to needy adventurers, with the same results as had obtained in France.[9]

Jefferson's appointments were not the only sign that things were going from bad to worse. When the Seventh Congress assembled, he recommended a repeal of "all the internal taxes" levied by the Federalists and a review of the judicial system which had been much expanded by the Judiciary Act of 1801.[10] It was now clear that many Federalist political achievements were in jeopardy, and their worst suspicions about Jefferson as an unprincipled popularity seeker seemed to be confirmed. Federalist writers professed to see the latter proposal as "part of the systematic plan for the total subversion of the constitution itself, by means of *legislative construction*" to destroy the independence of the judiciary. This added to the deference shown the legislature in Jefferson's annual addresses seemed to point directly to the establishment of just such an unmixed democracy as they believed had ruined republican France.[11]

The Federalist leadership did not despair, for they still hoped these evils might prove self-correcting. They thought that the departure of the wise and the good from government would be followed by an obvious decline in the fortunes of the republic, and that an indignant people would then turn the Republicans out of office. Some sanguine Federalists saw the prospect of a return to power in the conjunction between the repeal of internal taxes and the trade depression caused by the temporary European peace of 1801–1803.[12] Still others, observing the divisions which soon appeared in the Republican coalition, looked forward hopefully to dividing and conquering their opponents.[13]

But most Federalists quickly saw that the people would not abandon their Republican leaders because of incidental errors, and that the only hope of again commanding the power and influence they had enjoyed before 1800 was that some disaster would shatter popular confidence. They realized that the very divisions within Republican ranks were a sign of the party's secure hold on the loyalty of most people outside the New England states, and that there was no way to exploit them except by allying with the least objectionable wing in the hope of softening the evil tendencies of such a government.[14] The behavior of the Federalists in the late 1790's and their criticism of every measure passed by the new administration did not dispose Republicans to forget and forgive, at least not to the extent of admitting prominent Federalists to office. So long as they remained an insignificant minority, Republican factions could accept their cooperation and occasionally, in states with little other talent, admit them to office.[15] But it was well known that any group making concessions of power which raised the least chance of a Federalist resurgence would be abandoned by all other Republicans uniting to resist any such development.[16]

Short of disaster, then, Federalist prospects were not encouraging. Nor did disaster seem imminent given peace in Europe, Republican success in reducing both debt and taxes without jeopardizing national credit, and the stunning acquisition of Louisiana. Even the resumption of war in 1803 proved a blessing at first by reviving the carrying trade, which had been depressed by peace. By 1804 some leaders of the Federalist party contemplated secession. To those accustomed to command, who had cherished an illusion that Republican mismanagement would soon restore them to power, the future must have looked bleak.[17]

This is not to suggest that Federalist greed for power fathered a conscious attempt to destroy a nation they could not lead in the hope of recreating one they could. Though the secessionist movement of 1804 did reveal a monstrous elitism, their distrust of republican government was what caused it to swell beyond all proportion. It was this distrust which allowed these men to ignore Jefferson's demonstration of respect for national credit and willingness to resist

French power even to the point of alliance with Britain, and to dismiss his dazzling achievements as the prelude to disaster. They believed that just as the collapse of the French republic had begun with the courting of popularity by demagogues and ended in military despotism, so the new Republican administration was taking its first steps along that same path. Jefferson's popularity was not in dispute, but no one could say what use he might make of it. The Louisiana purchase suggested that the Constitution was not an impregnable barrier to usurpation, and the Federalists professed to find in the unrepublican features of its territorial government much that reminded them of French conquests in Europe. They were also alarmed by continued Republican pressure on the judiciary, in the form of impeachment proceedings against several Federalists. This, together with the ratification of the 12th Amendment, convinced them that the Republicans, like the French tyrants before them, were creating a democratic despotism where the Constitution would be made to fit the ruling faction's desires.[18]

After 1804, Federalist fears about the tendency of administration measures found unexpected support from a splinter faction of the Republican leadership called the Tertium Quids. At first, the two groups seemed to have little in common. John Randolph, the prickly leader of the Quids, had taken a major role in the impeachment proceedings against Judges Pickering and Chase, and had even proposed a constitutional amendment to make federal judges removable upon address by both houses of Congress.[19] Moreover, Randolph's dislike of an administration attempt to settle claims arising out of the Yazoo land scandal, which had been the occasion of his parting with the Republican majority, principally threatened the interests of New Englanders in states still under Federalist control. And Randolph accused those who supported the administration's scheme of acting in a "spirit which considers the many as made only for the few, which sees in Government nothing but a job," namely "the spirit of Federalism!"[20]

It soon became clear that insofar as the Quid opposition was ideologically inspired, it too fed on anxieties generated by France's dramatic progression from republicanism to military despotism, a progression which had shaken the faith of some Republicans in the stability of the nation's form of government. This in turn impelled the

Quids to see the foreign policies of Jefferson's second administration as the Federalists did. The first occasion for alliance between the two arose when the administration tried to use the French as intermediaries in the purchase of West Florida from Spain. This looked to Randolph like a dangerous willingness to collaborate with France in her corrupt dealings with other nations, and he feared it as a first step toward subverting republicanism at home. Soon afterward, the administration's efforts to cope with the tightening of British controls over American neutral commerce increased his suspicion that Jefferson was still infatuated with France and meant to commit the nation to a policy of hostility towards Britain which might end in war and the destruction of the republic.[21]

II

The vast majority of Republicans, however, simply did not believe that the American republic would share the sad fate of France. Certainly Federalist fears never enjoyed popular currency. Jefferson had been right to think that most of those who supported the Federalists during the French crisis of 1798 were at heart Republicans who would turn against their leaders once the unrepublican nature of their measures became unmistakable.[22] And though he continued to suspect that some of the Federalist leadership were a threat to the future of the republic, he declared that "as long as we pursue without deviation the principles we have always professed, I have no fear of deviation from them in the main body of republicans." [23] This confidence seemed to be justified after 1801, when the Federalists began to lose strength in their New England strongholds, Connecticut and Massachusetts. Even if there had not been ideological objections, the Republicans would now have had little temptation to use against their opponents those weapons which had been earlier used against them. Jefferson did complain bitterly about the licentiousness of the newspapers and even suggested that "a few prosecutions of the most prominent offenders would have a wholesome effect in restoring the integrity of the presses," but he opposed any such systematic persecution as had been visited upon the Republican press and remained firm in the belief that judicial remedy for abuses must rest with the state courts.[24]

The one exception was a series of prosecutions initiated in the federal circuit court of Connecticut in 1806–1807, against two Federalist presses, the Litchfield *Monitor* published by Thomas Collier, and the *Connecticut Courant* published by Messrs. Hudson and Godwin. At the same time, Judge Tapping Reeve and two clergymen were charged with the common law crime of seditious libel. The Federalist version of these prosecutions, which appeared in *A letter to the President of the United States* (1808) by "Hampden," was that they were part of an electioneering effort by Jacobins to subvert Connecticut's standing order by silencing the Federalist press, and that the grand jury, chosen by a Republican marshal, contained personal enemies of the defendants. "Hampden" suggested that these proceedings had been brought under the common law assumption that truth would be no defense, but that the federal district judge, Pierpont Edwards, had been obliged by the Judiciary Act of 1789 to rule that state laws allowing truth as a defense must also apply to federal prosecutions. Thanks to this ruling none of the prosecutions could be sustained, and all but one, that against the publishers of the *Courant,* were dismissed. "Hampden" even hinted that in the proceedings against the Reverend Azel Backus the prosecution had shown an almost hysterical anxiety to have the case dismissed for fear that certain scandalous details of Jefferson's early life would be disclosed.[25] The end result of these prosecutions was to give the Federalists an excuse for casting themselves as persecuted heroes and the Republicans as hypocritical opressors.

Before we take this Federalist version at face value, we should remember that any conviction in a lower court was subject to reversal in the Supreme Court. In 1806–1807 the Supreme Court was decidedly Federalist, and it would remain so until 1810. Assuming that these suits had been brought with the intention of political suppression, it is still hard to see how the Republicans could have hoped to make a conviction stand when the Federalist majority on the bench would certainly have found a way to strike them down. Judge Edwards had gone out of his way to guarantee the defendants an appeal on the question whether a federal circuit court had a common law jurisdiction.[26] The only possible coercive value would have been the expense and trouble to which defendants were put, which tones down the highly colored picture painted by "Hampden."

It appears in yet another light when viewed in relation to the experience of a Republican paper published by Thomas Ashley and Selleck Osborn, the Litchfield *Witness*, instituted in 1805 under the very eyes of the foremost Federalist oligarchy in the state. Within a month, the editors reported that they had been indicted for libel after writing that in a civil suit in a Litchfield court, *Talmadge and Wolcott* vs. *General Hart*, the jury had made a political decision. Before they had completed four months of publication, they had suffered three physical assaults with countless threats of violence, and were the defendants in another libel suit filed by Julius Deming, a local justice of the peace. Meanwhile the Reverend Dan Huntington was suing the editors of the *American Mercury*, the other leading Connecticut Republican paper, for $1,000 personal damages.[27] There were other signs that the Federalists were waging law against their Republican opponents in Connecticut. According to the *Witness*, *Talmadge and Wolcott* vs. *Hart* was only part of a series of political prosecutions they had instituted against prominent Republicans in the state. The Connecticut sedition actions of 1806–1807, then, begin to look like defensive rather than aggressive acts.[28]

Yet if a Federalist Supreme Court would ultimately draw their teeth, how could they be said to have any deterrent value? It is clear that the Federalists thought them a sham. They responded by increasing rather than tempering their pressure on Connecticut's Republicans. When the *Witness* hinted at a federal prosecution against the *Monitor*, the *Monitor's* publisher, Collier, filed for $2,000 personal damages against Osborn of the *Witness*. Judgment was also executed against the *Witness* and the *Mercury* from previous convictions, and Osborn went to jail for refusing to enter into a recognizance for good behavior. After the first federal indictments were found, the Sheriff of Litchfield, who had become part of a controversy over whether or not Osborn was being mistreated in prison, brought a $3,000 personal libel suit against the editor of the Danbury *Republican Farmer*. At the same time Joseph L. Smith was indicted in the Litchfield courts for seditious libel, his offence being an address he had read at the annual Republican festival celebrated in Litchfield on August 6, 1806, in which he drew attention to Osborn's plight. Though the Republicans promptly indicted the publishers of the

Hartford *Courant* and the Reverend Azel Backus, it was nevertheless clear that their use of the federal courts had not stopped the Federalists.[29]

The Republicans were not merely trading blow for blow. Though some of them undoubtedly hoped that the trouble and cost of defense would have some effect (and it probably did help Collier decide to retire), Pierpont Edwards, who was generally regarded as the author of the Republican prosecutions, was apparently pursuing a more indirect strategy. Judging from his conduct of the trials, he meant to treat the Federalists in the federal courts as they were treating Republicans in the state courts. When the Federalists harassed leading Republican politicians like General Hart, a gubernatorial candidate in 1806, the Republicans indicted Reeve and later Lieutenant Governor Treadwell for obstructing the mails. Actions brought against publicists like Joseph L. Smith were followed by the indictment of Federalist clergymen; actions against newspapers by the indictment of Federalist editors. The defendants were then subjected to the same procedure as the Federalists followed in the state courts. That is why Edwards ruled that Connecticut provisions for pleading truth would apply, and that the federal petit jury should be freshly impanelled according to state practice. Prosecutions were limited to one newspaper editor, probably to save money, and conviction was secured pending a Supreme Court ruling on the jurisdictional issue, explicitly held in abeyance. The Republicans had backed their opponents into a corner where they could not complain about federal court proceedings without effectively condemning their own use of the state courts. At the same time, Edwards had given the high court strong incentives to rule against allowing the federal courts common law jurisdiction, something the Republicans had long desired.[30]

Not to be outdone, the Federalists attempted a maneuver of their own through their representatives in Washington. In the second session of the Ninth Congress, Dana moved that "a committee be appointed to inquire whether prosecutions at common law should be sustained in the courts of the United States, for libellous publications, or defamatory words, touching persons holding offices or places of trust under the United States, and whether it would not be proper, if the same be sustained, to allow the parties prosecuted the liberty of giving the truth in evidence." He seems to have been trying to draw attention first to the Federalist claim that the Sedition Law had ameliorated the common law, and second to the Connecticut prosecutions. His desire to embarrass the Republicans became clear in his refusal to accept their substitute motion made by Eppes that "the common law of England is not a part of the law of the United States . . . and that the prosecution of a person at common law for libel is a violation of the freedom of the press and contrary to the Constitution of the United States." To have agreed would have implied that Dana was prepared to abandon any claims to federal common law jurisdiction which Federalists had long advocated and would have defeated his original aim. With the same end in mind, Dana moved for a report on the costs incurred in the Connecticut prosecutions, hoping to dramatize their expensiveness.[31] But the strategy never bore fruit because a crisis in foreign relations arose simultaneously.

This had been building up ever since Britain's decisive naval victory at Trafalgar, which established her supremacy at sea but left Napoleon still in control of the continent. With each of the two powers supreme in its own sphere yet powerless to strike at the other, the temptation to wage war through commerce became irresistible. Britain started it by interdicting the carriage of indirect trade between French colonies and the mother country in American vessels and by blockading the coast of Northern Europe. France soon followed suit with the continental system, which was designed to exclude British manufacturers from their largest market. Before long each power had made it clear that it would seize any neutral vessel trading with the other. In the midst of these developments, a British ship of war outraged the American warship *Chesapeake* and blockaded Norfolk, Virginia for several days.[32] With many voices raised for war, Jefferson desired to mute all internal divisions and was relieved to hear that most of the Connecticut prosecutions were being dropped.[33] At the same time, the Embargo eased the tension between rival parties in Connecticut by giving the Federalists an issue which made them popular. In the lull that followed the Erskine agreement, when it briefly appeared that Britain might abandon her hostile Orders, they willingly supported Randolph's attempts to embarrass the administration through the prosecutions. By then, though, they had been relieved of local political pressures which had led them to wage law in the first place.[34]

III

By 1809 the Federalists had another reason to second Randolph's agitation against libel prosecutions in the federal courts, for their behavior during the Embargo had invited retaliation. Instead of supporting the administration's policy as at least a good way of gaining time to prepare for war, and at best as a way to protect the nation's rights without war, the Federalists had done all they could to undermine it. They had denounced it from the start as either a failure of statesmanship, or worse as hostile act directed against the nation's commerce.[35] As the months went by, they took pains to dramatize the economic distress caused by the measure, and to organize protests against it. In Massachusetts the Federalist recovery was gradual, and they did not capture the entire state government until May 1809, but that did not stop them using town meetings and county conventions to exert pressure on both state and national governments for repeal of the Embargo. Once they had control of the lower House, they used it in an active attempt to obstruct execution of the law and to censure the Lieutenant Governor, Levi Lincoln, for complying with the Secretary of War's requisition by ordering the militia to assist in its enforcement.[36] In Connecticut, resistance was more direct. After the Embargo, Federalist control of the state was unquestioned and the Governor refused to mobilize the militia to execute the law as requested, an act of disobedience in which he was supported by the legislature.[37]

The Federalists succeeded in destroying the effectiveness of the measure by the rumpus they raised as much as by the violations they encouraged individuals to commit. The ferment in Massachusetts and Connecticut had given visible support to their charge that the Embargo was hurting America more than either Britain or France, and so had nourished the expectation that it would be abandoned quite apart from any concessions the belligerents made to the rights of neutral commerce. When Republicans protested,[38] the Federalists retorted that they were guilty of nothing their opponents had not done to them in the French crisis of 1798.[39] This was not true. The Republicans had never encouraged French aggression, nor had they opposed the actual execution of the law even when they considered it unconstitutional. Indeed, the Federalist response to the Logan mission had shown that their worst offense had rather been to discourage aggression so effectively that Federalist attempts to control the domestic political situation were undermined. But in one respect the Federalists were right to draw an analogy between 1798–1799 and 1808–1809, for the Embargo was a response to the same international pressures as the Federalists had pleaded in justification of the Sedition Law. Until 1808 it had been possible to dismiss Republican tolerance of the opposition as an easy indulgence so long as there were no stresses to make political control seem desirable. After that time, this was no longer feasible.

The Federalists denied that they were shown any indulgence, of course. They saw an attack on their press in Governor Sullivan's warning during his 1808 address to the Massachusetts legislature that Federalist attempts to "furnish powers with whom we are engaged in controversy, with arguments against us; to expose to them our weaknesses . . . is highly criminal." And one Federalist congressman later declared that "tar and feathers" had become a substitute "for common law." But there was a world of difference between a public official's criticism of the opposition, or hostile public opinion, and the institution of prosecutions by the state.[40] It might be argued that Republican pretensions to virtue on this score were much like those of an aging spinster, for no court could prosecute a state legislature. Yet there were sentiments in the Federalist papers with which public figures had refused to associate themselves, and which might legitimately have been prosecuted. For instance, a series of letters signed "Falkland" which appeared in the Columbian Centinel during the autumn of 1808 openly urged dissolution of the union on the grounds that the South was bent on smashing the commerce and power of the eastern states. Those ideas had been in the air since 1804, but the Embargo gave them more prestige than they had ever enjoyed before.[41] It is true that to prosecute such writing might be self-defeating if not impossible given the way in which the Federalist leadership had inflamed New England, but similar factors had not stopped Callender's prosecution in Virginia. At least one Republican later looked back on the Embargo and regretted that the administration had not acted to prevent Federalist presses from disseminating such notions.[42]

There were other provocations. Charges of French influence had been bandied about in the Federalist press ever since the Louisiana purchase, but when the Embargo was imposed, Federalist congressmen and the Federalist legislature of Massachusetts began to suggest that the administration had acted upon orders from France.[43] Only the most flimsy circumstantial evidence was ever offered to support this charge, and such plausibility as it acquired derived largely from its apparent harmony with Napoleon's continental system, imposed by France on her European satellites with the intention of damaging Britain.[44] The Republicans protested that the Embargo affected both powers, and in some ways hurt France more than it hurt Britain,[45] but the Federalists were not to be convinced. They thought they saw evidence of a "hostile disposition" towards Britain in the rejection of the Monroe-Pinkney treaty, the continuation of the ban imposed on British warships in American waters after the *Chesapeake* incident, and the administration's refusal to accept the compensation for that atrocity offered by the British government. And they saw "unwarrantable compliance" with French wishes when the administration acquiesced in the Berlin Decree of November 21, 1806, proclaiming a blockade of Britain and making all her produce lawful prize. America's failure to defend her rights against France justified British retaliation through the Orders in Council of January 7, 1807, prohibiting neutral trade between enemy ports, and those of November 11 and 25, 1807, interdicting neutral commerce with any nation which excluded British ships and goods unless it were licensed by Britain.[46]

On the surface, this seemed to be the same suspicion as Republicans had voiced about Federalist policies in the 1790's. But there was a difference. In the late 1790's no prominent Republican had ever tried to justify French aggression with the blatant disloyalty that Federalist leaders showed when they took the British ministry's part against their own government in 1808–1809. Though Republican congressmen argued that France had a legitimate grievance in the Jay Treaty, enough to justify Pinkney's initial rebuff in 1796–1797; and questioned that Talleyrand's behavior in 1797–1798 had really been authorized by the Directory, they never went so far as Pickering in 1808 when he said that Britain had given the United States "no essential injury." [47] Though they had thought that the Federalist party's foreign policy since 1794 had shown signs of "British influence," they had never said that the only way to prove the purity of its intentions was to oppose Great Britain's pretensions by force.

In the spring of 1809 when war began to be discussed as an alternative to the Embargo, some Federalists in responsible positions did suggest that the only way for the Republican administration to establish its independence from France was to repeal its restrictions on Britain's trade and join her in resisting the French decrees. They warned that the alternatives to this policy were war with Britain and a disastrous alliance with France, or else a confession of national impotence by the abandonment of commerce.[48] This view was stated most plainly in a committee report of the Massachusetts legislature drafted by Christopher Gore, which rejected resolutions condemning both belligerents,[49] but it received indirect Congressional sanction as well. Some Federalists, like Bayard, qualified their assent with the proviso that war should be declared against Britain as well if she subsequently refused to modify her orders against American shipping. But since most Federalists still believed that war with both powers was out of the question, and that war with France would dispose the British to temporize with the United States, this was a meaningless flourish.[50]

Federalist leaders were ready to use the charge of foreign influence as prominent Republicans had never dreamed of doing. The crux of their case, which was that the Berlin Decree justified the Orders in Council, rested upon blindness to some blatant aggressions on Britain's part. Among these were her attempt in 1805 to restrict United States commerce with the colonies of Great Britain's enemies under the Rule of 1756, though she did not pretend to enforce this rule when it came to traffic with her own colonial possessions. Then there was her illegal blockade of the Continent from the Elbe to Brest in May 1806, made no more acceptable by its modification in September 1806. Even if the Berlin Decree had been the first provocation, they hardly justified Britain's Order in Council of January 7, 1807, against United States shipping, for American vessels were at the time exempt from French decrees as far as they applied to the high seas. In any case, France had no naval force with which to enforce her edicts so they were never anything more than an empty menace. As for Britain having done the United States "no essential injury," Republican spokesmen pointed to her impressment of American seamen and the restrictions she imposed on neutral commerce, particularly the requirement that all commerce with European countries under French control pass through Britain and pay duties there. That Britain allowed her own merchants some trade with the enemy while forbidding this to neutrals, and taxed the re-exportation of American commodities from Britain to the Continent, made it appear that she was more interested in tyrannical control of the seas and reduction of the United States to colonial subordination than in retaliating against France.[51]

The Republicans could no more readily justify France's actions. These included a peremptory demand that the United States declare war against Britain or suffer its vessels seized under the Berlin Decree to be condemned, as well as the promulgation of the Milan and Bayonne decrees under which any vessel searched by or even spoken to by the British became a lawful prize. But they had good reason to reject the Federalist suggestion that national independence could be established only by collaboration with Britain. For one thing, the need to rely on any third party in dealing with aggression was fast disappearing. Thanks to unprecedented growth and prosperity in the first years of the nineteenth century, the nation would soon be able by itself to maintain its rights against any power.[52] And since Napoleon's triumph and the establishment of military dictatorship, there was no longer any danger that France might beguile the innocent American people, nor any incentive for the United States to ally with her because she was a republic.[53] Both developments permitted an assessment of national interest less influenced by ideology than had been possible in the 1790's. And for those who were prepared to view the international situation in this new light, it should have been plain that the Louisiana Purchase together with the destruction of French naval power at Trafalgar made France less of a threat to American interests than she had ever been, or than Britain was still. Though she continued to molest American shipping, she could no longer bend American commerce to her will, like Britain, nor embark on military adventures in the New World. These considerations might have persuaded perceptive Federalists that France was now, as John Quincy Adams put it, "the natural ally of the United States," and that the principal threat to the nation's sovereignty lay in Britain's claim to control American commerce and impress American seamen.[54]

In general, though, the Federalists refused to transcend their ideology and be persuaded. Their distrust of republicanism caused them still to believe that the nation was incapable of asserting its rights independently of foreign assistance. When external pressures became so urgent as to demand some sort of response, the strategic advantages of collaboration with Britain seemed irresistible to them. They granted that her commercial restrictions would prohibit trade to European countries dominated by France, but thanks to Napoleon's edicts this trade was worthless anyway. On the other hand, trading subject to British regulations left commerce with the rest of the world open. This prospect was particularly tempting because destruction of the merchant marine in the smaller European countries had created an additional demand for American vessels, and because the Spanish revolution of 1808 promised new commercial opportunities in Spain's overseas empire. As more than one Federalist observed in Congress, if only the Embargo were repealed, the nation could now enjoy a trade which would exceed anything they had previously known, and which would encourage the continued growth of the nation to maturity. To abandon commerce (which was the administration's policy according to the Federalists) would slow down the rise of the United States to the status of a great power.[55] Yet another justification for collaboration with Britain was found in anti-Jacobin ideology which saw Napoleonic France as a force of lawless barbarism and Britain as the last bastion of the civilized world. According to this view the survival of liberty depended on Great Britain's victory and any measure she was forced to pursue in resisting France, from the impressment of American seamen to restrictions on American commerce, were ultimately in the best interests of the republic.[56]

It is clear that the power of the Federalist challenge derived less from the persuasive appeal of their ideology than from economic circumstances. In New England particularly, commerce was one of the few dynamic forces and it had seen an unprecedented expansion from the early 1790's to the Embargo, interrupted only by the temporary peace of Amiens. This boom was the result of an unusual demand for American commodities created by the European war together with neutral interloping in the colonial trade, and New Englanders were reluctant to put an end to it before a peace did. They were particularly reluctant to end it by resisting British regulations, for trade with Britain was safe, lucrative and extensive thanks to her command of the seas. The French trade, on the other hand, had been unpopular even in peacetime and was hazardous in war.[57] So many people had incentives to believe the Federalist leadership's charge that the Embargo had been enacted at the behest of France and was designed to destroy commerce, incentives which grew stronger as the price of American produce rose abroad. Meanwhile Britain did her best to exploit the situation, first by letting it be known that she would receive American vessels in the West Indies without full clearance, and second, when the Spanish revolution broke out, by removing those restrictions on neutral trade with the Iberian peninsula which still applied to the rest of the continent.[58] The Embargo did cause real distress in commercial areas, but for the most part organized protest was led by men moved more by reluctance to miss an opportunity than by personal hardship.[59] Though no one could argue that economic interest should come before national welfare, they could say that commerce vital to the nation was endangered by administration policies which ought therefore to be abandoned.

At last the Embargo fell victim to the fear that trying to enforce it in New England would bring on civil war, or even dismemberment of the Union.[60] War with Britain seemed a better alternative and at least the opportunities for privateering would soften much of the economic distress which the Federalists had used so well against the administration.[61] Submission was unthinkable: in effect it would be a renunciation of independence and an admission that the Republicans were incapable of defending vital national interests.[62] On the other hand, many people were still reluctant to go to war with a powerful monarchy because it would mean putting national institutions to a test better deferred as long as possible.[63] But all attempts to find some viable policy between maintaining the Embargo and war were unsuccessful. The non-intercourse which replaced the Embargo was an obvious capitulation to Britain, as her command of the seas meant that she could easily procure such American produce as she needed

from neutral ports. It had also proved impossible to stop the smuggling of British products into the United States. So the measure,
ineffective as a form of retaliation against belligerent powers, succeeded only in hurting America by forcing disadvantageous terms
of trade upon her producers, by defrauding her revenue, and by
sacrificing the interests of patriotic merchants to smugglers.[64] Yet
another search for an effective solution, conducted in the wake of the
repudiated Erskine agreement, proved abortive; and Congress admitted its bankruptcy with a further capitulation to Britain. Free
trade was proclaimed, qualified only with a pledge which would
appeal to France that the repeal of either's decrees against neutral
shipping would lead Congress to reinstate non-intercourse against
the other.[65]

IV

The government's ineffectuality in dealing with the European
belligerents demoralized the Republican party and changed the nature of its divisions. Hitherto these had been largely the result of
competition for office or concern for the abstract purity of doctrine.
Because they were seen as a sign of strength, they had caused little
concern.[66] Now it was clear that republicanism itself was at stake,
and that should "the present majority . . . fall under the odium of
public opinion against their measures . . . Federalism will again rise
triumphant upon the ruin of the present Republican party & . . . the
cause . . . be lost in the downfall of its quondam advocates." [67] This
fear increased with the growing realization that since the abortion
of all their efforts at commercial retaliation, the only choice left was
between war and submission. To abandon a peace which, however
humiliating, had given the nation time to grow, was to hazard the
future of the republic; and should the issue prove unsuccessful there
was no doubt that its unique political institutions would be repudiated. Most Republicans would not have shied away from the
challenge had it been forced upon them, for this would have united
the nation.[68] But few were willing to initiate a war while the nation
was so deeply divided, not only because of the external threat but
also because they feared a military take-over from within. Even as
it became clear that there was no middle ground, so much hung
upon the issue that the Republicans had difficulty reaching any

agreement about the time of entry or the appropriateness of Madison as a military leader.[69]

Ironically enough, in the end it was the Federalist party which nerved the Republicans for war. That they had been the principal beneficiaries of the Embargo and non-intercourse debacles was clear to all, adding a further dimension to the nation's peril.[70] That they had been the principle cause of the Embargo's failure and were bent on hamstringing the government in its search for workable alternatives was equally clear. As a result, Republicans began to suspect the Federalists of wanting to prostrate the United States before British power in order to show that republican government was impracticable. By rendering ineffectual every Republican measure short of war, they had forced a choice between either sending a divided nation to fight a war against a fully mobilized monarchy, or making a submission which would imply the failure of Republican policies.[71]

Remembering how the opposition had foiled their own efforts to lead the nation to battle in 1798, the Federalists were confident that the Republicans would not be "kicked into a war," believing that those factors which had formerly held them back would now deter their less skilled opponents. The only way the Republicans could unite the country would be to convince the people that the war was necessary and just, and this their opponents thought impossible.[72] If they were mad enough to fight Britain they would surely come to grief, particularly as the war would be fought on offensive principles ill-suited to republics.[73] In either case the Federalists expected to be vindicated in their assessment of republican governments, and probably returned to power.[74]

They had not bargained for the new generation of political leaders. These men had emerged into politics in the late 1790's and the first decade of the nineteeth century. None of them had taken prominent roles in the Revolution, or played any part in shaping the nation's republican form of government, so that unlike their elders they took for granted the unique institutions of their land. During most of their lives they had seen the republic steadily gain in strength, and now they believed she was ready to confirm her destiny by showing that, even though divided, she could defend her honor and independence against any monarchy on earth. Angered by the pusillanimity of the Tenth Congress, which had not only failed to increase

the nation's military power but whose principle achievements were
Macon's Bill Number Two and the dismantling of the Bank, the war
hawks gained a hold on the Twelfth Congress and forced the choice
of war.[75] Their task seemed to be made easier by France's titular
repeal of her decrees, which had allowed Madison to reinstate non-
intercourse against Great Britain. But because France continued her
depredations and severely limited the access of American produce
to continental markets, the Federalists were able to question the au-
thenticity of the repeal.[76] Despite these problems, the new Republicans had resolved that if Britain refused to revoke her orders and
blockades in return for the French concession, they would have to
choose either war or an acknowledgement of national impotence, experience having shown that non-intercourse only depleted the treasury and alienated vital commercial interests. Felix Grundy spoke for
the majority when he said the time had come "to ascertain by actual
experiment how far our republican institutions are calculated to
stand the shock of war." [77]

In pursuing this resolution, the war hawks met with the predictable
obstructionism. Some Federalists resisted all preparations for war,
while others joined nervous Republicans in insisting on a state of
preparedness impossible to achieve. They were probably hoping that
the fiscal burden of maintaining such a defense establishment, made
heavier by their own determination not to subscribe to federal loans,
would undermine the government's political basis much as the direct
taxes of the Adams administration had eaten away Federalist support in 1799–1800.[78] Such a policy would also let them reap the
fruits of the disaster they were sure would follow upon war with
Britain. For at the same time as their urging of defense measures
would testify to their patriotism, it would also leave them free to
oppose a declaration of war on the grounds that the nation was un-
prepared. But they never seriously believed that matters would go so
far. Their estimate of the weakness of the president and the nation's
form of government, their perception of the divisions within the
Republican party, and their ignorance of the war hawks, led them to
think this just another bluff. They could not see how the administration proposed to fight a war with the New England states opposed,
knowing that the South had relied upon them during the Revolution
and that the national government would go bankrupt if they should

withhold their capital. Forced requisitions or conscription would only provoke civil war. The Federalists were sure they could forestall an actual declaration of war,[79] and when it became clear that they could not they tried to dissociate themselves from it as much as possible.

This was done most plainly in *An Address of the Members of the House of Representatives of the Congress of the United States, to their constituents,* signed by the Federalist minority which had voted against the declaration of war. Supposed to have been written by Josiah Quincy, the document acknowledged "that the wrongs of which the United States have to complain . . . [were] in some aspects very grievous to our interests, and, in many, humiliating to our pride . . . [but were such as] either would not justify war, or which war would not remedy." The *Address* went on to say that impressment, the British blockades, and the Orders in Council, were issues which should not have been allowed to lead to a war against the national interest, and asked: "If honour demands a war with England, what opiate lulls that honour to sleep over the wrongs done us by France?" It concluded that the nation was ill-prepared for a war which would expose it "to the vassalage of states serving under the banners of the French Emperor," and questioned that a republic "in no small degree experimental," whose institutions were so immature, and which was clearly divided, should have been precipitated into a contest "calculated to put to trial the strength of the moral bond by which they are united." [80] Such charges were repeated again and again throughout the war, not just by individuals but occasionally in legislative resolves. Their gist was well summarized in the Baltimore *Federal Republican,* which denounced the war as "unnecessary, inexpedient, and entered into from . . . partial, personal . . . motives bearing upon their front marks of undisguised foreign influence." [81]

No matter what their reservations about the war, once the declaration had been made the Federalists might have acquiesced, secure in the knowledge that they would be gainers whatever the outcome. If the war went well, they along with their fellow Americans would benefit from the successful assertion of national sovereignty; if not, they could look forward to vindication and a return to power. Instead, most Federalists tried to fulfill their prophecies of doom by obstructing the war effort in ways that went well beyond questioning its justice and expediency. In Congress, they resisted all administration proposals for strengthening the Army beyond the provisions made before the declaration of war. This was glaringly inconsistent with the conduct of many, but it was excused with the plea that after the repeal of the Orders in Council, news of which had arrived just after the declaration of war, the only outstanding issue between the two nations was impressment, which would be better resolved through negotiation than through hostilities. Though the Federalists were willing to support a naval build-up as a good long-term investment, they argued that a larger army was not necessary to defend the nation and could only be intended for the conquest of Canada. As long as the Republic was not directly threatened by British invasion, the Federalists could dignify their stand against offensive war by observing that to seize Canada would hardly coax concessions on impressment from Britain, and by expressing the fear that a conquering army might go on to subvert liberty at home, as had happened in France. But by the summer of 1814, British invasion had become a reality on more than one front and these arguments were revealed as disguises for obstructionism.[82]

This opposition in Congress was not crucial. The Federalists were always in the minority, and filibustering could be terminated by moving the previous question. Its true significance was the encouragement such visible dissent gave the enemy and the protective coloring it gave to the opposition outside Congress, whose obstructionism was more painfully felt. For instance, when the governments of Massachusetts, Connecticut and Rhode Island refused to comply with federal militia requisitions, the government's military effort was seriously impaired.[83] More crippling still were the informal attempts in the New England states to discourage enlistment and subscriptions to war loans. The first, added to the withdrawal of state militias from federal service, forced the government towards a conscription policy; the second pushed it to the wall financially.[84] And the Boston banks, not content merely to deprive the federal government of funds, were accused of using their position as creditors to other areas to compel large remittances in specie during the first half of 1814 when the government's need was greatest. That the Boston banks were in a position to make such demands was in turn attributed to the wholesale smuggling of British goods in New England and the exemption of her coast from blockade until the spring of 1814. Because Boston merchants enjoyed unrivalled access to British manufactures for the first two years of the war, they were able to make themselves the creditors of all other commercial centers.[85]

The Federalist drive to make their own gloomy predictions come true culminated during the darkest days of the war with the Hartford Convention. After the Battle of Leipzig, it was clear that there was a real danger Britain would be freed from the struggle in Europe and able to turn her awesome power fully upon the American republic. And in April, 1814, when Napoleon abdicated, that danger became a reality. Britain soon showed her intentions by extending her blockade to the entire American coast and intensifying her depredations on American seaports, including assaults on Washington and Baltimore.[86] Coinciding with British operations in the Chesapeake were two invasion attempts from the north, one repulsed on Lake Champlain but the other bringing northern Maine under British control. Although British successes in Washington and the Penobscott area were more than cancelled out by the victories of Macomb and MacDonough at Lake Champlain and the successful defense of Baltimore, it was clear that nothing could be inferred from these events. They were only the first skirmishes in what was a much more ambitious undertaking. Americans had known since July that the possibility of intensifying the war against the United States in the hope of subverting her government and discrediting republicanism had been openly discussed in British government circles. In October, the full scope of British intentions was revealed in the news that the British peace commissioners had been instructed to demand that the United States give up most of the old Northwest so that a permanent Indian buffer state could be erected there to protect Canada.[87]

These demands, coupled with another that the United States unilaterally disarm on the Great Lakes and give to Britain that part of northern Maine which she needed for direct communication between New Brunswick and Quebec, exposed as fiction the Federalist picture of Britain as a passive victim of administration aggression. Yet the Massachusetts legislature produced a series of reports blaming the federal government for provoking a British invasion, accusing it of leaving Massachusetts defenseless, and urging that a state army be raised. There was also a legislative resolution that delegates be ap-

pointed to a convention in Hartford and authorized to confer with
delegates from other states "upon the subject of the public grievances,
. . . upon the best means of defense against the enemy," and lastly
upon "procuring a convention of delegates from all the United States,
in order to revise the constitution thereof." [88] Apart from the propriety
of proposing alterations to the Constitution when the very existence
of the nation was in doubt, the summoning of a New England convention looked like the opening move in just such a plan to sever the
union as had been mentioned in the Henry correspondence, disclosed
just before the declaration of war. The Hartford Convention disavowed secession for the moment, confining itself mostly to proposing
amendments. But its report hinted that dissolution of the union might
eventually be necessary and proposed that the New England states
resist conscription by federal authorities, seeking instead the government's consent to their providing for their own defense with federal
funds. Clearly the stage was being set for the conclusion of a separate
peace between New England and Britain.[89]

From the Embargo on, the Federalists played the obstructionist
role they thought the Republicans had taken against them in the war
crisis of 1798–1799. Their actions hovered on the edge of treason because their estimate of the limitations of republican government
together with their remembrance of Republican success in opposing
them fifteen years before made them believe they would be vindicated by the outcome. They were sure that either the administration
would abandon the war or the nation would be shipwrecked, and that
in either case the people would restore them to power for having been
right.

V

The Republicans would not let the Federalist role of the 1790's be
thrust upon them. In the frustrating years between the repeal of the
first Embargo and the declaration of war, the Republicans never tried
to curb the freedom of the Federalist opposition beyond an occasional parliamentary move to limit the length of the debate in Congress.[90] And the War of 1812 produced no sedition acts, nor (to use
a modern analogy) any internal security measures. To some extent
this was making virtue of necessity, for attempts to control disaffected
elements at this time might have added a civil war to a foreign one.

The Republican administration would have contested any attempt at secession, but so long as they avoided this extreme the governments of Connecticut, Rhode Island and to a lesser extent Massachusetts, were allowed to go their own way throughout the war. The only restraint upon them was the attempt of the United States navy to enforce the restriction against commerce with Great Britain which New England's exemption from the blockade seemed to invite and a brief embargo.

Nevertheless the Federalists complained that they were being muzzled in Congress and that the Republicans were trying to silence their press.[91] The second charge derived principally from two riots that took place in Baltimore during the opening weeks of the war. The first occurred on June 22, 1812, when the offices of the *Federal Republican*, the leading Federalist paper of the middle Atlantic states, was demolished by a mob in response to a particularly strong attack upon the war. This silenced the paper for five weeks. But on July 26th, several prominent Federalists from outlying areas, including General Henry Lee of Virginia, General James M. Lingan, and Alexander C. Hanson as the only Baltimorean in the group, fortified a house in the center of town. From it, on July 27th, they issued a denunciation of the riot of June 22. This alleged that it had been the result of a long-standing conspiracy to destroy the *Federal Republican*, which had the tacit approval if not indeed the active endorsement of the national administration as well as local Republican authorities. The distribution of this paper, together with an ostentatious display of weaponry, produced the predictable mob. Before the militia could intervene between the beseiged and the beseigers, who went to the length of procuring a field piece, there was an exchange of fire and a man was killed in the street. Hostilities ceased on the arrival of the militia, and after prolonged negotiation, twenty-three Federalists surrendered to the authorities on the understanding that they would be taken to the municipal jail and receive protection there.

That afternoon the militia disbanded, fearing that their presence might be provocative and hoping that the populace would remain quiet. But shortly after sundown on July 28, a mob gathered outside the unprotected jail, broke into it, seized the Federalist prisoners, and

beat them horribly. General Lingan died, and eight of the others
were thrown together in front of the jail, supposed to be dead. Those
feigning death then heard the mob arguing about how their bodies
should be disposed. Some wanted to throw them in the sink of the
jail, some to bury them; still others suggested castration, hanging, or
slitting their throats. They were saved by a doctor who urged that
the victims be used for dissection. The suggestion won the rioters'
approval. They carried the bodies back into the jail and then dispersed. The doctor was joined by several other physicians, and together they arranged to smuggle the survivors out of the city.[92]

This appalling event, so like the atrocities of the French Revolution,
confirmed the Federalists in their belief that every democracy tended
to degenerate into a form of mob rule. If they were to use the riots
to support the charge that the administration was silencing the opposition press, however, it was crucial to decide who had been responsible. Although the Republicans could produce several letters which
made it abundantly clear that the supporters of the *Federal Republican* had expected the distribution of their paper in Baltimore to lead
to violence, the Federalists could reply with only the most circumstantial evidence of intentional Republican complicity.[93]

Their most effective point was that local Republican officials were
implicated, for it was undeniable that they had neither stepped into
the initial disturbance nor made any great effort to protect the Federalist prisoners on the night the jail was sacked. The Federalists
charged that the commander of the militia, Brigadier General Stricker,
who had disbanded the companies the afternoon before the attack,
had refused a militia guard for physicians ministering to the beaten
men on the grounds that it was unlikely any of the prisoners were still
alive. Republican officials defended themselves by saying that they
had done all in their power to control the riot, and that Stricker had
disbanded the militia because none but a small minority "inadequate
to the performance of the service for which they were required" had
mustered in response to his commands.[94] It was true that he could
still have undertaken to defend the prisoners in the jail, but the mob
had been clearly uncontrollable and he would most likely have added
to the slaughter without protecting the victims. Undoubtedly, Stricker
had decided that if blood must be shed, better it be the blood of those

whom most Republicans saw as the *provocateurs*. But it was equally unmistakable that public opinion rather than the state had curbed the Federalist press in this case.

No matter how much the Republican leadership might regret the form of expression public opinion had chosen in Baltimore (and it was not the only such outrage during the war),[95] they had never intended freedom of the press to mean immunity from its constraints. On the contrary, they both continually appealed to it as a sanction for the government's actions and encouraged public contempt for what they thought a treasonous attempt to prostrate the republic for a party's vindication and advancement. They did not desire the people ever to resort to violence, but realized that the threat of violence was always their last resort and hoped that those who found themselves on the wrong side of public opinion would fear to provoke use of it. When it became clear that public opinion could not curb Federalist opposition, and that this opposition might defeat the Republican administration at the polls during the war, the Republican leadership made no attempt to suppress the Federalists by force. Republican spokesmen in Congress might call the Federalist leadership traitors,[96] but they did not prosecute them for treason. And though during the war several Americans were tried for giving aid to the enemy, Republican newspapers admitted that it was impossible to procure a conviction in the civil courts, while attempts to put the crime on a *"war establishment"* were effectively blocked by the Constitution.[97]

The Republicans fought the War of 1812 without any of the extraordinary instruments of coercion which had received the sanction of revolutionary usage and which the Federalists in 1798 had assumed were the normal accompaniments to war. This proceeded more from particular necessity than from any abstract desire to show that even in war a republic was a government not of force but of consent. The Republicans never doubted that it could on occasion be necessary to sacrifice the forms of liberty in order to preserve its substance, and if circumstances had so dictated they would have been as ready to make this sacrifice during the War of 1812 as they had been during the Revolution.[98] They were deterred by several considerations. Though the Federalists controlled several New England state governments, they were restrained from outright secession and separate peace with Britain by public opinion in their own section. Revolutionary loyalty alone would have made most people oppose secession. What is more, such action was so clearly irrational that it was doubtful the Federalist leadership could ever have persuaded them to accept it. It did not take much perception to see that New England needed the Union more than the Union needed New England, for as an independent nation her commercial interests could not expect favorable treatment either from British competitors or from what was left of the United States.[99] The Federalist leadership could not have attempted secession unless the administration had forfeited public loyalty through repression, which is why the Republicans quickly abandoned their brief attempt to enforce the embargo.[100] And the enlarged dimensions of the republic made it possible to defend her from Britain not only without the cooperation of New England state governments but even in the face of their active opposition.

VI

That the nation had survived without any attempt to restrain the Federalist opposition paid rich psychic dividends when peace came. For the country's elation on hearing of the Treaty of Ghent was certainly not derived from any success in winning concessions from Britain on the issues which had led to war in the first place. As the Federalists were quick to remark, the peace left the nation with no pledge from her antagonist about the rights of neutral commerce or impressment, so that in their opinion the war had been fought in vain.[101] Yet the lack of these guarantees meant nothing to most people, who saw only that despite Federalist treason the nation had survived Britain's efforts to shatter her republican institutions. For most Republicans, the real point of the war was not to dictate treaty terms to the former mother country but to "determine whether the republican system, adopted by the people, is imbecile and transient, or whether it has force and duration worthy of the enterprise." Looked at in this way, just to have emerged as one had begun and without any loss of territory was a victory. It is true that Americans played down the role of Europe's unsettled state in deterring the British and magnified their own military prowess. But this did not alter the fact that the outcome of the war lifted America's prestige abroad out of the depths to which it had sunk during the years 1808–1812 and restored the confidence of her citizens in her peculiar form of government, a confidence which had been shaken by the events following the Embargo.[102]

The outcome of the war both vindicated the Republicans and forever discredited the Federalists. While hostilities lasted their obstructionism could be defended as true patriotism with the argument that the republic was not yet strong enough to withstand a powerful monarchy and that acquiescence in Britain's wishes, at least until national institutions were more secure, was a better course. The coming of peace stripped them of every defense, and to most Americans they now looked like a traitorous faction which "would have made a common interest with the British during the late war . . . [which] would have raised itself to power on the broken fasces of the union," and whose activities were indefensible. Hezekiah Niles heralded the faction's downfall with a jubilation typical of that felt throughout the nation:

It falls as its country rises—the stability of the republic is *arsenic* to its hopes and wishes. Miserable in the honorable result of the war; miserable that Great Britain did not reduce us to *"unconditional submission"*—miserable, that Mr. *Madison* was not *"deposed"* by a *foreign force;* miserable, that they are despised by the people they would have given soul and body to serve; miserable, that they are laughed at by all who consider them too contemptible for serious rebuke—they drink the very dregs of the cup of mortification.[103]

Although most Federalists understood at once what the consequences of the war would be, there remained some who were able to deceive themselves that diatribes like Niles's were only wishful thinking, and to hope that the administration's failure to achieve any of its war aims conjoined with the enormous debt incurred would at least divide the Republican coalition if not alienate the people. In either event they thought the Federalists would be given another chance for power.[104] They were disabused of this hope once and for all by the elections of 1816. The first disappointment was that a Republican hopeful, William Crawford, agreed to abide by the caucus nomination of Monroe, preventing any split in party ranks which the Federalists could exploit.[105] Their efforts to set up their own independent candidate for the presidency received a decisive setback in the spring of 1816, when Rufus King was defeated for the governorship of New

York. Though Massachusetts, Connecticut and Delaware threw their votes to him the following December, the New York election had already convinced King that the Federalists should abandon their "fruitless struggle." [106]

Federalist candidates continued to be elected by isolated constituencies into the 1820's, but most of the leadership concluded that their party was doomed, and began to disband. Some comforted themselves with the notion that their *raison d'etre* had gone because the Republicans had converted to their views on the broad construction of national powers, but the truth was that after the elections of 1816 they were clearly without a future in national politics unless they could merge with the Republican coalition. They were briefly encouraged to hope for this by Monroe's pleas that party strife give way to national unity. But their wartime activity had convinced Monroe they were dangerous to the state, and he did not mean to make concessions to men who had pursued a traitorous policy of obstruction.[107] Moreover, it was painfully clear that any concession made to Federalists would separate the Republican making it from most of his party. The growing realization that there would be no accommodation with the victorious Republicans did not, however, change the Federalists' resolve to disband. For in the years after the war, continual Republican attacks soon made it clear that only the threat of Federalism held the Republican party together, and that the first party system was on the verge of dissolution.[108]

Epilogue

The war's successful issue attacked the roots of the first party system, and not just by discrediting the Federalists. It was more fundamental than that. Up to now, many Republicans had defended the nation's unique institutions less because they were assured that this form of government was stable than because the alternatives were unacceptable. For most of the revolutionary generation, despite their brave words at the time of trial, republicanism had remained a faith still unproved by experience. Now the nation had shown that it could survive a war undertaken in adverse circumstances, and republicanism had become less problematic.[1] Jefferson's letters show what the implications of this new confidence were. Writing to Lafayette in 1818 he said what no Republican could have said in the 1790's: "Our government is now so firmly put on it's [sic] republican tack, that it will not be easily monarchised by forms."[2] In a letter to Richard Bland Lee, he observed that though "in a new government as ours was, and especially in one somewhat ambiguous in it's [sic] form, it was to be expected that there would be differences of opinion as to the direction in which it should be administered. . . . [Now] time seems to have given it it's [sic] settled shape."[3] As more could be taken for granted, the occasion for ideological disagreement diminished.

Equally important to the growing confidence of the nation was the resolution of the Napoleonic Wars in 1815. Though the outcome of the War of 1812 had reassured the Republicans, there remained a chance that some challenge from abroad would renew that dispute over the stability of republics which had provoked the ideological alliances of Federalists and Republicans in the first place.[4] With Europe generally at peace, this possibility too began to fade. At the time it was not as clear as it is to us now that Europe was settling down to a long period of stability. Many expected war with Britain to be renewed at once when Napoleon returned to the continent, and even after his incarceration on St. Helena some were still afraid that the victorious powers might now turn on America.[5] But during the next few years, Britain's estrangement from her continental allies became ever more clear, guaranteeing the republic against any hostile designs by the Holy Alliance. And when Napoleon died in 1821, the new European order seemed reasonably secure. These changes in the character of international politics meant that the future of the republic was no longer in doubt. Not only had she weathered adversity for twenty-five years, but her unlimited prospects for expansion after the War of 1812 made it virtually certain that before there could be another war in Europe she would be a great power. Consequently the old debate about the stability of republican government became progressively more meaningless.[6]

The new state of affairs soon showed itself in the disintegration of the Republican alliance. The possibility that this would happen had been seen long before. At the beginning of Jefferson's administration, the opposition seemed to be on the verge of disappearing and the president had predicted that the Republican majority would divide into Whigs and Tories as in England.[7] This turned out to be premature. The crisis in Anglo-American relations after 1806 revived the Federalist party, and it continued to be a threat to the Republicans until 1815. As a result, the dominant party was more cautious about giving ground after the War of 1812. On a national level they kept an appearance of cohesion through the election of 1820 despite the absence of any real Federalist party by that time, or even of any issues which the party could focus upon once Massachusetts gave up trying to procure compensation for her wartime expenditures.[8] Between 1821–1824, however, the Republican coalition splintered into several factions competing for the presidential succession. There was no obvious successor for Monroe, but that was only part of the story. Madison had not been a clear-cut choice in 1812, and neither he nor Monroe would have looked obvious in 1808 or 1816 but for the pressures for party unity felt at that time. In 1824 no such pressure was felt, for a Federalist comeback was clearly impossible. The caucus, formerly the principal means of maintaining Republican unity against the Federalists, was largely ignored while five leading contenders made overt attempts to capture a majority of the electoral college.

Without question, a major transformation was taking place in national politics.[9]

It was a transformation which made possible the emergence of a new party system at the end of the 1820's. Parties were no longer to be viewed as lamentable but necessary means to avert some worse evil. They had become legitimate ends in themselves, having the attainment of power as their primary function.[10] Such a development would have been impossible had not old prejudices begun to fade as a consequence of the nation's new circumstances. The fear of political dissolution was removed, and with it went most of the traditional objections to party. They were still heard, but usually from survivors of the Revolution who had found them so full of meaning during the early years of the republic. And as these men yielded to a new generation for whom the old arguments held little meaning when applied to the current chaos of presidential politics, the last inhibitions vanished. For many the transition was made easier by the fiction that Adams's National Republican party and its Whig successor were reincarnations of Federalism.[11] The illusion of continuity was sustained because the question of what limits should be set to the federal government's power, which had played a role in the first party system, became the focus of controversy in the second one, but before 1815 it was not the primary source of disagreement. Its greater importance in the 1820's was symptomatic of a more stable politics in which ideology could be subordinated to the exigencies of electoral machinery.

Party no longer seemed to threaten the life of the republic, but was it not still detrimental to the public good? Whatever else had changed, did not the argument still hold that party jeopardized the quality of leadership and obstructed pursuit of the public interest? Echoes of such patrician opinions would be heard in America until long after the Civil War, but their resonance was diminished by yet another change in national politics, the growing acceptance of a minimal role for the federal government. Republican distrust of power had little to do with this. It resulted from the perception that because of radical expansion and growing agitation over slavery, the Union could be preserved only by the strictest possible construction of the Constitution. John Quincy Adams learned to his cost the liabilities of advocating positive federal action, and though the Whig party followed him in this respect, its promotionalism did not help it form national majorities. Its dismal record shows that there was more popular support for a negative concept of the State than for any positive program.[12] And so long as the government's functions were understood to be limited, the quality of the leadership became less vital. This eventually helped to promote the spoils system, which became important in maintaining the unity of the new parties. It also suppressed disruptive issues. If the Democrats had committed themselves in the 1830's to the controversial issues they were to pursue in the 1840's, the brief interlude of agreement on fundamentals which preceded the Civil War might never have happened.

Abbreviations

A   *Aurora* (Philadelphia, 1794–1820 + successor to the *General Advertiser*).

Annals   *The debates and proceedings in the Congress of the United States; with an appendix, containing important state papers and public documents* . . . (Washington, 1834–1856).

AR   *The American Remembrancer; or, an impartial collection of essays, resolves, speeches, etc. relative, or having affinity, to the Treaty with Great Britain* (Philadelphia, 1795).

ASP:FR   *American state papers, Documents legislative and executive, of the Congress of the United States* . . . (Washington, 1832–1861). The first six volumes pertain to foreign relations.

CC   *Columbian Centinel* (Boston, 1790–1820 +).

GA   *General Advertiser* (Philadelphia, 1790–1794).

GUS   *Gazette of the United States* (Philadelphia, 1790–1804).

IC   *Independent Chronicle* (Boston, 1776–1820 +).

LCK   Charles R. King, ed., *The Life and Correspondence of Rufus King* . . . (New York, 1894–1900).

MAWA   George Gibbs, *Memoirs of the Administrations of Washington and John Adams, edited from the papers of Oliver Wolcott, Secretary of the Treasury* (New York, 1846).

NG   *National Gazette* (Philadelphia, 1791–1793).

NYJ   *The New York Journal & Patriotic Register* or *Greenleaf's New York Journal* and *Patriotic Register* (New York, 1790–1800).

PAH   Harold C. Syrett, ed., *The Papers of Alexander Hamilton* (New York, 1961–).

PMHB   *Pennsylvania Magazine of History and Biography.*

VR   *The Virginia Report of 1799–1800, touching the Alien and*

Sedition Laws, together with the Virginia Resolutions of December 21, 1798, the debates and proceedings thereon in the House of Delegates . . . (Richmond, 1850).

WAH   Henry Cabot Lodge, ed., *The Works of Alexander Hamilton* (New York, 1885–1886).

WGW   John C. Fitzpatrick, ed., *The Writings of George Washington* (Washington, D.C., 1931–1944).

WJM   Gaillard Hunt, ed., *The Writings of James Madison* . . . (New York, 1900–1910).

WMQ   *William and Mary Quarterly*, 3rd series (unless otherwise noted).

WTJ   Paul Leicester Ford, ed., *The Writings of Thomas Jefferson* (New York, 1893–1899).

Notes

Preface

1. This particular definition was suggested to me by George Lichtheim, "The Concept of Ideology," *History and Theory*, IV (1965), 165–6. Though unusual, it is not incompatible with Bernard Bailyn's use of the term "opposition ideology" in *The Ideological Origins of the American Revolution* (Cambridge, Mass., 1967).

Part I. *Division*

1. *PAH*, VI, 65–168.

2. Charles A. Beard, *Economic Origins of Jeffersonian Democracy* (New York, 1915), chs. 5–6; E. James Ferguson, *The Power of the Purse* (Chapel Hill, 1961), Part IV; Whitney K. Bates, "Northern Speculation and Southern State Debts," *WMQ*, XIX (1962), 30–48.

3. *Annals*, 1st Cong., 1930; also 1919, 1937–8.

4. Jacob E. Cooke, ed., *The Federalist* (Cleveland, 1961), 57; Max Farrand, ed., *The Records of the Federal Convention of 1787* (New Haven, 1911), I, 26–7, 48, 108, 135–7, 154; II, 236.

5. Cooke, 63–4, 352–3, 404–5, 425, 428; Farrand, I, 136; II, 273–4; Jonathan Elliot, ed., *The Debates in the several State Conventions on the adoption of the Federal Constitution* (Philadelphia, 1861), IV, 327.

6. Farrand, I, 147; II, 29, 30, 57, 109–10, 114, 119, 500, 501.

7. Cooke, 459–60; Farrand, II, 502.

8. William N. Chambers, "Parties and Nation Building in America," in Joseph LaPalombora and Myron Weiner, eds., *Political Parties and Political Development* (Princeton, 1966), 82–3; William N. Chambers, *Political Parties in a New Nation* (New York, 1963), 123–4; William N. Chambers, "Party Development and the American Mainstream," Richard P. McCormick, "Political Development and the Second Party System," and Paul Goodman, "The First American Party System," in William N. Chambers and Walter Dean Burnham, eds., *The American Party Systems*

(New York, 1967), 20, 93–4, 63–4; Robert A. Dahl, *Political Opposition in Western Democracies* (New Haven, 1966), 10.

9. Richard Hofstadter, *The Idea of a Party System* (Berkeley, 1969), 29–38; see also Caroline Robbins, " 'Discordant Parties': A Study of the Acceptance of Party by Englishmen," *Political Science Quarterly*, LXXIII (1958), 505 ff.

10. Goodman, 57; John P. Roche, "The Founding Fathers: A Reform Caucus in Action," *American Political Science Review*, LX (1961), 799–816; Clinton Rossiter, *1787: The Grand Convention* (New York, 1966), passim; Stanley Elkins and Eric McKitrick, "The Founding Fathers: Young Men of the Revolution," *Political Science Quarterly*, LXXVI (1961), 181–216.

11. Harry Ammon, *James Monroe: The Quest for National Identity* (New York, 1971), 270–7; Gerald Stourzh, *Alexander Hamilton and the Idea of Republican Government* (Stanford, 1970), 103, 185 ff.

12. See for instance Cooke, 475, 168–9; "Tablet," in *GUS*, Mar. 6, 1790; Jefferson to John Taylor, June 1, 1798, in *WTJ*, VII, 264; *Annals*, 5th Cong., 874; David Osgood, *A Discourse, delivered February 19, 1795* (Boston, 1795), 13.

13. John Taylor, *An Enquiry into the principles and tendency of certain public measures* (Philadelphia, 1794), 85; [Donald Frazer], *Party-Spirit exposed, or remarks on the times* . . . (New York, 1799), 5–6; Thomas Day, *An Oration on Party Spirit, pronounced before the Connecticut Society of Cincinnati* . . . *on the 4th of July, 1798* (Litchfield, 1798), 9, 12; John Lathrop, *An Oration, pronounced on the 4th day of July, 1798* (Dedham, 1798), 17; "Tablet," May 20, 1789 and "Constantius," April 13, 1795, in *GUS;* William Wyche, *Party Spirit: an oration delivered at the Hanovian Literary Society* (New York, 1794), 10; Noah Webster, Jr., "The Revolution in France," in *A Collection of Papers on Political, Literary and Moral Subjects* (New York, 1843), 23 ff; see also John Taylor, *A Definition of Parties; or the political effects of the paper system considered* (Philadelphia, 1794), ii. The most thorough historical survey of republican vulnerability to party was John Adams, *Defense of the Constitutions of Government of the United States* (1787–8), in C. F. Adams, ed., *The Works of John Adams* (Boston, 1850–56), IV–VI.

14. *WGW*, XXXV, 228.

15. Jefferson to William Branch Giles, Dec. 15, 1795, in *WTJ*, VII, 43; Archibald S. Foord, *His Majesty's Opposition, 1714–1830* (Oxford, 1964), especially 25–6, 68. For comment on the inflated rhetoric of the first party system, see John R. Howe, Jr., "Republican Thought and the Political Violence of the 1790's," *American Quarterly*, XIX (1967), 147–165.

16. "Farewell Address," in *WGW*, XXXV, 223; Gaillard Hunt, ed., *Disunion Sentiment in Congress in 1794* . . . (Washington, 1905), passim; see also Jefferson, "Anas," in H. A. Washington, ed., *The Writings of Thomas Jefferson* . . . (New York, 1857), IX, 117, 190–1, 197, 203–4; Jefferson to Washington, May 23, 1792, in *WTJ*, VI, 4–5; Christopher Gadsden, *A Few observations on the late public transactions* (Charleston, 1797), 9.

17. In *CC*, Dec. 4, 1793; see also an unsigned piece from the *New York Daily Advertizer*, in *GA*, Dec. 6; Oliver Wolcott, Jr., to Noah Webster, Jr., Aug. 10, in *MAWA*, I, 103–4; Cooke, 142; J. Adams, *Defense of the Constitutions*, in *Works*, V, 473; VI, 216; "Decius," in *AR*, II, 125.

18. Lawrence Stone, "Theories of Revolution," *World Politics*, XVIII (1966), 169–172.

Chapter 1. *Fiscal Policy*

1. *Annals*, 1st Cong., 1196.

2. *Ibid.*, 1192; E. James Ferguson, *The Power of the Purse* (Chapel Hill, 1961), 298–9; "Report on Public Credit," in *PAH*, VI, 79, 87.

3. *Annals*, 1st Cong., 1339–40, 1377, 1378, 1384.

4. Ferguson, 314–17; *Annals*, 1st Cong., 1387–8.

5. Hamilton to Madison, Oct. 12, and Madison to Hamilton, Nov. 19, 1789, Hamilton to Edward Carrington, May 26, 1792, in *PAH*, V, 439, 525–7; XI, 427–8. Madison's draft of the Address to the States by Congress, April 26, 1783, can be found in William T. Hutchinson and William M. E. Rachal, eds., *The Papers of James Madison* (Chicago, 1962–   ), VI, 488–94.

6. Hamilton to Carrington, May 26, 1792, in *PAH*, XI, 428.

7. *Ibid.*, 428–32, 439 ff; [William L. Smith], *The Politicks and views of a certain party* (n.p., 1792), 9, 12, 19, 28, 35.

8. Ferguson, 298; Charles A. Beard, *Economic Origins of Jeffersonian Democracy* (New York, 1952), 51–2; *Annals*, 1st Cong., 1378, 1540; Madison to Edmund Pendleton, March 4, 1790, in *WJM*, VI, 6 n; James Monroe to Madison, July 2 and 25, 1790, in Stanislaus Murray Hamilton, ed., *The Writings of James Monroe* (New York, 1898–1903), I, 208, 215; *Remarks on the report of the Secretary of the Treasury to the House of Representatives of the United States. By a friend to the public* (n.p., 1790), 19–20, 22. For Madison's electioneering see Ralph Ketcham, *James Madison: A Biography* (New York, 1971), 275–7.

9. Hamilton to Carrington, May 26, 1792, in *PAH*, XI, 429–30, 432.

10. Ferguson, 308–10, 321, 322; *Annals*, 1st Cong., 2295–6.

11. Madison to his father, July 31, 1790, in *WJM*, VI, 19 n; *Annals*, 1st Cong., 2243–51.

12. The idea that the bargain which Jefferson and Hamilton struck over the residency was responsible for the passage of funding and assumption has recently been questioned by Jacob E. Cooke, "The Compromise of 1790," *WMQ*, 3d Ser. XXVII (1970), 523–45.

13. Madison to his father, July 31, 1790, in *WJM*, VI, 19 n; Jefferson, "Anas" in H. A. Washington, ed., *The Writings of Thomas Jefferson* . . . (New York, 1857), IX, 92–5; "The Assumption," Feb., 1793, in *WTJ*, VI, 172–4.

14. "Report on Public Credit," *PAH*, VI, 106.

15. Madison to Edmund Randolph, March 14, 1790, in *WJM*, VI, 8 n; "Tablet," in *GUS*, April 24, 1790; "Observer," in *Pennsylvania Gazette*, Nov. 11 and 18, 1789. Parallels were often drawn with the English experience after 1688: see in *GUS*, "Agricola," May 2, and Sir John Dalrymple, "Letter on Public and Private Credit of America," May 16, 1789; Oliver Wolcott, Jr., to his father, March 27, 1790, in *MAWA*, I, 43.

16. *Annals*, 1st Cong., 1895; Jefferson to Madison, April 27, 1785, in Julian P. Boyd, ed., *The Papers of Thomas Jefferson* (Princeton, 1950–   ), VIII, 117.

17. Adam Smith, *An Inquiry into the Nature and Causes of the Wealth of Nations* (London, Everyman's Library Edition, 1938), II, 389–430, quote from 393. Another authority critical of public debts who influenced Hamilton's opponents was David Hume: see his "Of Public Credit," in T. H. Greene and T. H. Grose, eds., *Essays, Moral Political and Literary by David Hume* (London, 1875), I, 360–74; also [George Logan], *Letters . . . on the funding and banking systems* (Philadelphia, 1793), 18.

18. *Annals*, 1st Cong., 1140–2; unsigned, in *GUS*, Oct. 13, 1790; William Maclay, *The journal of William Maclay: United States Senator from Pennsylvania, 1789–1791* new ed. (New York, 1927), 325, 329.

19. *Annals*, 1st Cong., 1271.

20. *Ibid.*, 1261.

21. Jefferson to Washington, May 23, 1792, in *WTJ*, VI, 2, 3; Madison to Henry Lee, April 13, 1790, in *WJM*, VI, 11n; Maclay, 328–9.

22. *Annals*, 1st Cong., 1268.

23. Madison to Randolph, March 14, 1790, and to his father, in *WJM*, VI, 8n, 19n; Jefferson to Madison, May 23, 1792, in *WTJ*, VI, 2; Maclay, 313, 314, 330; [William Findley], *A Review of the revenue system* . . .

(Philadelphia, 1794), 23–5, 29–30, 31–2; in *NG*, "Gaius," Jan. 16, "Sidney," May 24, 1792; *Annals*, 2d Cong., 498.

24. Madison to Edmund Pendleton, March 4, 1790, in *WJM*, VI, 6n; *Annals*, 1st Cong., 1378. Madison's critics thought his proposal contradictory, though: see *Annals*, 1st Cong., 1387–8; Hamilton, "Objections and Answers respecting the Administration of the Government," Aug., 1792, in *PAH*, XII, 238–9.

25. Madison to Monroe, June 17, 1790, in *WJM*, VI, 16n; Maclay, 283.

26. *Annals*, 1st Cong., 1271; [Pelatiah Webster], *A Plea for the poor soldiers* (Philadelphia, 1790), 36. See also Noah Webster, Jr., "To the Public," May 8, 1787, in Harry R. Warfel, ed., *Letters of Noah Webster* (New York, 1953), 65, and "On a discrimination between the original holders and the purchasers of the certificates of the United States," in Webster, *A Collection of essays and fugitiv writings* (Boston, 1790), 378–86; "Equity," in *IC*, Jan. 14, 1790.

27. Maclay, 174–5, 288; *Annals*, 1st Cong., 1094, 1099, 1233; [Pelatiah Webster], 19; *Remarks on the report of the Secretary*, 12–14; "An Advocate of Public Credit," in *IC*, March 4, 1790; David Stuart to Washington, June 2, 1790, in *WGW*, XXXI, 50n; Richard Henry Lee to Patrick Henry, June 10, 1790, in James Curtis Ballagh, ed., *The Letters of Richard Henry Lee* (New York, 1914), II, 524. The animus generated by this speculative activity against the fiscal system did not diminish with time: see in *NG*, "Gaius," Jan. 16, "Brutus," March 5 and April 5, "Sidney," April 16 and May 24, "A Citizen," May 3, 1792; [Logan], *Letters . . . on the funding and banking systems*, 3–4, 24; [Findley], 4, 17–20, 49.

28. *Annals*, 1st Cong., 1221, 1289.

29. *Ibid.*, 1100–1, 1153, 1215, 1219, 1229, 1235, 1238, 1252; see also Maclay, 194.

30. Hamilton to Carrington, May 26, 1792, in *PAH*, XI, 428; Washington to David Stuart, March 28, 1790, in *WGW*, XXXI, 30.

31. James R. Morrill, *The Practice and Politics of Fiat Finance: North Carolina in the Confederation, 1783–1789* (Chapel Hill, 1969), passim; Irwin H. Polishook, *Rhode Island and the Union: 1774–1795* (Evanston, Illinois, 1969), chs. 5–6.

32. Maclay, 280; William L. Smith to Edward Rutledge, Aug. 9, 1789, in George C. Rogers, Jr., ed., "The Letters of William Laughton Smith to Edward Rutledge, June 6, 1788 to April 28, 1794," *South Carolina Magazine of History*, LXIX (1968), 106; *The memorial of the publick creditors, citizens of the state of New Jersey* (Trenton, 1790), 14; "W.O.," in *IC*, April 22, 1790.

33. See Maclay, 194, 195–6.

34. James Jarvis to Hamilton, Feb. 20, 1790, in *PAH*, VI, 257-8; Ames to George Richards Minot, March 23, 1790, in Seth Ames, ed., *Works of Fisher Ames* (Boston, 1854), I, 77; in *MAWA*, I, quote from Chauncey Goodrich to Wolcott, Jr., March 28, 44, and Goodrich to Wolcott, Jr., Feb. 3, 1790, 33; also C. Gore to R. King, May 30, 1790, in *LCK*, I, 388.

35. *Considerations on the nature of a funded debt, tending to show that it can never be considered as a circulating medium* (New York, 1790), 4; [George Logan], *Letters addressed to the yeomanry of the United States* (Philadelphia, 1791), 37; [Findley], 125, 129.

36. Madison to Henry Lee, April 13, 1790, in *WJM*, VI, 11n.

37. *Annals*, 1st Cong., 1894-1902. The Virginia resolutions on assumption and the irredeemability of the debt can be found in *PAH*, VI, 150n.

38. Jacob E. Cooke, ed., *The Federalist* (Cleveland, 1961), 340.

39. *Annals*, 1st Cong., 1898, 1901, 1902.

40. *Ibid.*, 1312, 1313, 1344, 1379-80; Maclay, 209, 226, 230, 243, 258; James Monroe to Jefferson, July 18, 1790, in Boyd, XVII, 231-2.

41. *Annals*, 1st Cong., 1936, 1944.

42. William L. Smith to Edward Rutledge, Aug. 10, 1789, in Rogers, 20-1; Madison to Randolph, March 21, 1790, in *WJM*, VI, 8-9n; also Richard H. Brown, "The Missouri Crisis, Slavery, and the Politics of Jacksonianism," *South Atlantic Quarterly*, LXV (1966), 55-72; James Sullivan, *Observations upon the government of the United States of America* (Boston, 1791), passim; Maclay, 378, 381.

43. Hamilton to Carrington, May 26, 1792, in *PAH*, XI, 443-4; quote from enclosure in Hamilton to Washington, Aug. 18, 1792, in *ibid.*, 252; Noah Webster, Jr., "The Revolution in France," in *A Collection of papers on political, literary and moral subjects* (New York, 1843), 27.

44. *Annals*, 1st Cong., 1944-5; Sullivan, vii, 10-13, 45-47; Maclay, 379; [Logan], *Letters addressed to the yeomanry*, 10, 13, and *Five Letters addressed to the yeomanry of the United States* (Philadelphia, 1792), 20. These ideas had received considerable airing in the ratification controversy: see Jonathan Elliot, ed., *The Debates in the several State Conventions, on the adoption of the Federal Constitution* (Philadelphia, 1861), II, 102, 337; III, 29, 30, 51-6, 216, 263, 279 ff, 323 ff, 589-90, 607, 613-15, 639; IV, 51-2, 115, 135; Paul Leicester Ford, ed., *Pamphlets on the Constitution of the United States, published during its discussion by the people* (Brooklyn, 1888), 13, 14, 17, 63, 101, 102, 121, 127, 129, 282, 286, 289, 294, 298, 299, 320, and *Essays on the Constitution of the United States, published during its discussion by the people* (Brooklyn, 1892), 65, 59, 70, 95, 158, 258, 297; Cecelia M. Kenyon, ed., *The Antifederalists* (Indianapolis, 1966), xi, xiii, 40 ff, 215.

45. *Annals*, 1st Cong., 1891, 1930; Jefferson to Madison, July 10, 1791,

in *WTJ*, V, 350–1; [Logan], *Letters . . . on the funding and banking systems*, 8; John Taylor, *An Examination of the late proceedings in Congress, respecting the official conduct of the Secretary of the Treasury* (Richmond, 1793), 12, and *An Inquiry into the principles and tendency of certain measures* (Philadelphia, 1794), 7–11, 19–20, 32–5, 71–7.

46. The dangers of enhanced executive power were stressed in *Annals*, 1st Cong., 1918–19, 1931, 1959–60; Taylor, *Examination*, 7–11, 13, 27, and *A Definition of Parties, or the political effects of the paper system considered* (Philadelphia, 1794), 11; [Findley], 41. Relevant portions of the act of incorporation are to be found in *Annals*, 1st Cong., 2316, 2317.

47. *Annals*, 1st Cong., 1891, 1917–18, 1935–6; [Findley], 77. See also Jefferson's opinion solicited by Washington, Feb. 15, 1791, in *WTJ*, V, 287.

48. *Annals*, 1st Cong., 1944–5.

49. *Annals*, 2d Cong., 175, 179, 403–4.

50. Though the amendment had been designed to insure the expansion of the House, by 1792 it had become something of a liability to those seeking this end since it called for raising the ratio to 1:40,000 once the House had reached 100 in number. See *ibid.*, 140. This may account for its never being ratified.

51. *Ibid.*, 208–10, 46–7.

52. The plan was first proposed in the Senate on December 7. See *ibid.*, 42.

53. This calculation is made from the table in Jefferson, "Opinion on the bill apportioning representation," April 4, 1792, in *WTJ*, V, 495. It can also be made by comparing the various apportionment bills, see *Annals*, 2d Cong., 208, 540–1, 1359.

54. Washington to the House of Representatives, April 5, 1792, in *WGW*, XXXII, 16–17; also *Annals*, 2d Cong., 539.

55. For a full text of the "Report," see *PAH*, X, 230–340.

56. In *NG*, unsigned, Jan. 12, "Gaius," Jan. 16, and "Brutus," March 22, 1792; [Logan], *Five Letters,* passim.

57. Hamilton to the Speaker of the House of Representatives, Jan. 23, 1792, in *Annals*, 2d Cong., 1063–70.

58. *Ibid.*, 362–396.

59. See the debate over the motion of March 8 directing the secretary of the treasury to report his opinions of the best mode for raising additional supplies, *ibid.*, 437–452, and the debate over permitting additional subscriptions of state debts to a federal loan, *ibid.*, 495–533, 546–7, 595–6. See also the agitation in *NG* against both Hamilton and the fiscal program, Jan. through June, 1792.

60. *Annals*, 2d Cong., 696 ff, 900 ff.

61. *Annals,* 1st Cong., 344 ff; Hamilton, "Address to the Public Creditors," Sept. 1, 1790, in *PAH,* VII, 2; Maclay, 342–3.

62. Hamilton to Jay, Nov. 13, 1790, in *PAH,* VII, 149–50.

63. John Adams, *Defense of the Constitutions of Government of the United States* (1787–8), in C. F. Adams, ed., *The Works of John Adams* (Boston, 1850–56), IV–VI.

64. "A Customer" from the *Poughkeepsie Journal,* May 21 and June 20, 1791, in *NYJ,* July 2 and 13, 1791; "Union," in *ibid.,* Aug. 10, 1793; [John Stevens], *Observations on government . . .* (New York, 1787), 6 ff.

65. Hamilton to Carrington, May 26, 1792, in *PAH,* VI, 438. This was also Noah Webster, Jr's., estimate; see "Revolution in France," 26–7.

66. Hamilton, "Catullus," in *CC,* Oct. 24, 1792; [Smith], *Politicks and views of a certain party,* passim; "Agricola," in *CC,* August 27, 1792; Hamilton's attacks on Freneau and Jefferson in *PAH,* XII, 107, 123–4, 157–64, 188–95, 224, 379–385, 393–401, 498–506, 578–87. There can be no doubt that the opposition bitterly resented the treatment they received from the Federalist prints, see unsigned, in *NG,* Oct. 3, Nov. 10, and Dec. 8, 1792; [Findley], 103; Jefferson to Madison, June 29, 1792, in *WTJ,* VI, 95.

67. "Spirit of Government," *WJM,* VI, 94.

68. "A Candid State of the Parties," *ibid.,* 114–19.

69. *Ibid.,* 118.

70. "Spirit of Government," *ibid.,* 86.

Chapter 2. *Foreign Policy*

1. Jonathan Ogden to Hamilton, March 18, 1793, in *PAH,* XIV, 213; John Steele to Hamilton, April 30, 1793, and William L. Smith to Hamilton, April 24, in *ibid.,* 359, 338–41; see also *Annals,* 1st Cong., 304; 3d Cong., 623–5, 640, 1097, 1116.

2. [George Logan], *Letters addressed to the yeomanry of the United States* (Philadelphia, 1791), 18 ff.

3. John Taylor, *An Argument respecting the constitutionality of the carriage tax; which subject was discussed at Richmond, in Virginia, in May, 1795* (Richmond, 1795); John Wickham, *The Substance of an argument in the case of the carriage duties* (Richmond, 1795); Edmund Pendleton, "Address to the Citizen of Caroline," in David John Mays, ed., *The Letters and Papers of Edmund Pendleton, 1734–1803* (Charlottesville, 1967), II, 650.

4. Norman Risjord, *The Old Republicans: Southern Conservatives in the Age of Jefferson* (New York, 1965).

5. *Annals,* 1st Cong., 103 ff.

6. *Ibid.,* 181, 186–7, 202, 205, 237; Madison to Jefferson, June 30, 1789, in Julian P. Boyd, ed., *The Papers of Thomas Jefferson . . .* (Princeton, 1950–   ), XV, 225–6.

7. *Annals,* 1st Cong., 236, 242.

8. *Ibid.,* 183, 185, 205, 245–6.

9. *Ibid.,* 184, 188, 235, 245.

10. *Ibid.,* 238, 241, 246.

11. *Ibid.,* 238. The best summary of the arguments for a discriminatory tonnage is found in Madison to Jefferson, June 30, 1789, in Boyd, *Papers,* XV, 226–7.

12. Madison to Hamilton, Nov. 19, 1789, in *PAH,* V, 525–6; *Annals,* 3d Cong., 217, 241, 242.

13. William Maclay, *The journal of William Maclay: United States Senator from Pennsylvania, 1789–1791* new ed. (New York, 1927), 94; Julian P. Boyd, *Number 7: Alexander Hamilton's Secret Attempts to Control American Foreign Policy* (Princeton, 1964), 27; Ames to Minot, May 3, 1789, in Seth Ames, ed., *Works of Fisher Ames* (Boston, 1854), I, 35.

14. *Annals,* 1st Cong., 182, 185–6; Madison to Monroe, June 21, and to R. H. Lee, July 7, 1785, in *WJM,* II, 147–8, 151; Boyd, *Number 7,* 31; Merrill D. Peterson, "Thomas Jefferson and Commercial Policy," *WMQ,* XXII (1965), 589 ff; Frederick L. Nussbaum, "American Tobacco and French Politics, 1783–1789," *Political Science Quarterly,* XL (1925), 498–516; see also Samuel Flagg Bemis, *Jay's Treaty: A Study in Commerce and Diplomacy* (New York, 1923), 38.

15. Cf. Hamilton's conversation with George Beckwith, Oct., 1789, in *PAH,* V, 483, also Sept. 26–30, 1790, VII, 73; *Annals,* 3d Cong., 190. A comparison of the British and French colonial systems can be found in Cabot to Hamilton, December 18, 1791, in Henry Cabot Lodge, *Life and Letters of George Cabot* (Boston, 1877), 50–51; see also Paul Warden Bamford, "France and the American Market in Naval Timber and Masts, 1776–1786," *Journal of Economic History,* XII (1952), 21–32; John F. Stover, "French-American Trade during the Confederation," *North Carolina Historical Review,* XXXV (1958), 399–414; Edmund Buron, "Statistics on Franco-American Trade, 1778–1806," *Journal of Economic and Business History,* IV (1931–2), 571–80.

16. *Annals,* 1st Cong., 203. A more comprehensive plan of commercial retaliation was actually proposed in the Senate, but it was never acted upon: see *ibid.,* 57; Madison to Jefferson, June 30, 1789, in Boyd, *Papers,* XV, 225.

308 NOTES TO PAGES 31-35

17. Conversation with George Beckwith, Oct. 1789, in *PAH*, V, 483-4.

18. See Jerald A. Combs, *The Jay Treaty: Political Battleground of the Founding Fathers* (Berkeley, 1970), 49.

19. Conversations with George Beckwith, Sept. 26-30 and Oct. 15-20, 1790, in *PAH*, VII, 74, 114; and Feb. 16, 1791, VIII, 44; Hamilton's "Answers to Questions proposed by the President of the United States to the Secretary of the Treasury," Sept. 15, 1790, VII, 45, 53. Hamilton hinted more cautiously at an alliance in his first recorded conversation with George Hammond, Dec. 15-16, 1791, X, 374.

20. Jefferson, "Anas," in H. A. Washington, ed., *The Writings of Thomas Jefferson* . . . (New York, 1857), IX, 124-5; Hamilton, "The Public Conduct and Character of John Adams . . . ," in *WAH*, VI, 438n, 438-9; Bernard C. Steiner, *The Life and Correspondence of James Mc-Henry, Secretary of War under Washington and Adams* (Cleveland, 1907), 294-5.

21. Combs, 15-28.

22. *Ibid.*, 40; Alexander DeConde, *Entangling Alliance: Politics & Diplomacy under George Washington* (Durham, N.C., 1958), 46-7; Charles A. Beard, *Economic Origins of Jeffersonian Democracy* (New York, 1915), 274 ff; Paul A. Varg, *Foreign Policies of the Founding Fathers* (East Lansing, Mich., 1963), 78; see also Helene Johnson Looze, *Alexander Hamilton and the British Orientation of American Foreign Policy* (The Hague, 1969), 35 ff; Gilbert L. Lycan, *Alexander Hamilton & American Foreign Policy: A Design for Greatness* (Norman, Okla., 1970), 148; Bemis, 33, 36, 38, 189.

23. Jefferson to Monroe, April 17, 1791, in *WTJ*, V, 319-20.

24. DeConde, 75-81; see also Jefferson's Circular, Jan. 1, and Hamilton to Jefferson, Jan. 11 and 13, 1791, in *PAH*, VII, 408, 423-4, 425-6; Jefferson, "Anas," 109-10; Jefferson to Washington, Sept. 9, 1792, in *WTJ*, VI, 103.

25. Conversation with Beckwith, Feb. 16, 1791, in *PAH*, VIII, 44.

26. In *PAH*, conversation with Beckwith, Oct. 1789, V, 484-5, memo of Hamilton to Washington, Sept. 15, 1790, VII, 53; conversation with Beckwith, Sept. 26-30 and Oct. 15-20, in *ibid.*, 73, 74, 114; Jefferson, "Anas," 124, 200.

27. Memo of Hamilton to Washington, Sept. 15, 1790, in *PAH*, VII, 51-2.

28. Memo of Hamilton to Washington, Sept. 15, 1790, in *PAH*, VII, 49-50, 54-6; see also Gerald Stourzh, *Alexander Hamilton and the Idea of Republican Government* (Stamford, 1970), 198.

29. Conversation with Beckwith, July 15, 1790, in *PAH*, VI, 495.

30. Jefferson, "Outline of Policy Contingent on War between England and Spain," July 12, 1790, Jefferson to William Carmichael, Aug. 2, and enclosure, to William Short, Aug 10, and to Gouverneur Morris, Aug. 12, in Boyd, *Papers*, XVII, 109–16, 121–3, 127–8; see also Jefferson, "Anas," 179; Madison to Washington, March 18, and to Jefferson, March 19, 1787, in *WJM*, II, 323–4, 329–30.

31. Jefferson, "First opinion on the question stated in the President's note of August 27, 1790," Aug. 28, 1790, in Boyd, *Papers*, XVII, 129–30.

32. Jefferson, "Report on negotiation with Spain," March 18, 1792, in *WTJ*, V, 460–81, especially 475–6.

33. J. Lynch, "The Iberian States and the Italian States, 1763–1793," *The New Cambridge Modern History* (Cambridge, 1965), VIII, 374–5; Jefferson, "Notes on Spanish Negotiations," Dec. 6 and 27, 1791, and to the President of the United States, May 16, 1792, in *WTJ*, V, 403, 414, 514; Jefferson, "Report to the Senate," Dec. 22, 1791, in *ASP:FR*, I, 130–31.

34. DeConde, 155–61; Jefferson, "Anas," 133, 134, 150–51; Jefferson to the U.S. Commissioners in Spain, March 23, 1793 (draft), in *WTJ*, VI, 206; Lawrence S. Kaplan, *Colonies into Nation: American Diplomacy 1763–1801* (New York, 1972), 208.

35. John Adams, *Discourses on Davila; a series of papers on political history*, in C. F. Adams, ed., *The Works of John Adams* (Boston, 1850–8), VI, 221–403; quotes from Worthington Chauncey Ford, ed., *Writings of John Quincy Adams* (New York, 1913–1917), I, 95, 98.

36. See *NYJ*, 1791, "Agricola" from *IC*, July 6, 9, and 16, and "Review of Burke's Reflections," Aug. 6; "C" from *American Daily Advertiser*, in *CC*, April 3, 1793, and *NG*, March 16, 1793. British distortions of French news were widely recognized: *GUS*, Dec. 30, 1789; "Sidney," in *NG*, Nov. 28, 1792, and April 17, 1793.

37. Memo of Hamilton to Washington, Sept. 15, 1790, in *PAH*, VII, 50–51.

38. Jefferson, "Anas," 111, 128, 99, 163–4.

39. "Aratus," in *NG*, Nov. 14, 1791.

40. Oliver Wolcott, Jr., to his father, Oct. 8, 1792, in *MAWA*, I, 80; "Steady," in *CC*, Aug. 14, 1793; "Alfred," in *GUS*, Dec. 13, 1793; *Marcellus; Published in the Virginia Gazette* (Richmond, 1794), 24; Noah Webster, Jr., "The Revolution in France," *A Collection of papers on political, literary and moral subjects* (New York, 1843), 1–43. For the willingness of Federalist critics to distinguish between France and Republicanism, see "Patriot of the World," in *CC*, June 8 and July 31, and note, June 19, 1793; in *GUS*, 1794, "Americanus" II, Feb. 8, and note Feb. 11.

41. "Reflections on the French Revolution," in *CC*, Nov. 7, 1792; unsigned, in *NG*, Jan. 5, 1793; in *NYJ*, 1793, "Cato" from *Boston Argus*, April 20, "Scaevola" from *NG*, April 24, and "Cursory Thoughts," June 22.

42. Jefferson to Dr. George Gilmer, Dec. 15, to John Francis Mercer, Dec. 19, to Gouverneur Morris, Dec. 30, 1792, and March 12, 1793, to William Short, Jan. 3, to Thomas Mann Randolph, Jan. 7, and to Jean Baptiste Ternant, Feb. 23, 1793, in *WTJ*, VI, 146, 147, 151 and 200, 154, 155, 157, 189–90.

43. Jefferson to Madison, March ?, 1793, in *ibid.*, 192; also Jefferson to Thomas Pinckney, May 7, 242–3; Rufus King's memo, in *LCK*, I, 440–8, especially 442–8.

44. The text of the treaties can be found in Richard Peters, ed., *The Public Statutes at large of the United States of America* (Boston, 1862), VIII, 6–31. The transformed international situation was best analyzed by "A friend to Peace," in *NG*, June 22, 1793, and Hamilton, "Pacificus" VII, in *PAH*, XV, 130–1.

45. "Warren" and unsigned, in *NG*, April 24, 1793; "Democrat" from *IC*, in *NYJ*, May 11.

46. "To Citizens of America" from *GA*, in *NYJ*, April 3, 1793; in *NG*, "An Old Soldier," May 4, "Guillotine," May 15, and "Veritas" II, June 5, 1793. On willingness to acknowledge the superior authority of the French example, see *Remarks occasioned by the late conduct of Mr. Washington, as President of the United States* (Philadelphia, 1797), 38.

47. Jefferson to John Wayles Eppes, May 23, and to Thomas Mann Randolph, June 24, 1793, in *WTJ*, VI, 264, 318. For a detailed account of the civic festivities, see Charles Downer Hazen, *Contemporary American Opinion of the French Revolution* (Gloucester, 1964), 164–76; a hostile account can be found in Rufus Wilmot Griswold, *The Republican Court; or American Society in the days of Washington* (New York, 1867), 347–52. Foreign visitors generally bore witness to the nation's pro-French sentiments: Francois Alexandre Frederic, duc de la Rochefoucault Liancourt, *Travels through the United States of North America* 2d ed., (London, 1800), I, 120.

48. Alexander Moultrie, *An Appeal to the people, on the conduct of a certain public body in South Carolina* (Charleston, 1794), 8; "A Jacobin" from *GA*, in *NYJ*, July 20, 1793; from *NG*, 1793, unsigned, May 25, and "An American," June 12; see also Jefferson to the British Minister, May 15, in *WTJ*, VI, 252 ff, and Washington to Jefferson, June 20, in *WGW*, XXXII, 507.

49. Hamilton, "Pacificus" VI, in *PAH*, XV, 103. An account of French activities in the American Revolution can be found in Samuel Flagg Bemis,

The Diplomacy of the American Revolution (Bloomington, Ind., 1957), 20 ff.

50. Hamilton, "Camillus" II, in *WAH*, IV, 388; Jefferson to Monroe, June 28, 1793, in *WTJ*, VI, 322.

51. Jay to Washington, July 21, 1794, in Henry P. Johnston, ed., *The Correspondence and Public Papers of John Jay* (New York, 1890–93), IV, 33. Jay's proposed draft of the neutrality proclamation would have cautioned the public against inflamatory utterances, *ibid.*, III, 476–7; George Cabot to Samuel Phillips, March 8, 1794, in Lodge, 76; see also Henry Lee to Hamilton, June 23, 1793, in *PAH*, XV, 14–5; unsigned, in *GUS*, March 13, 1794.

52. Jefferson, "Opinion on French Treaties," and to Madison, April 28, 1793, *WTJ*, VI, 223, 232; "An American," in *CC*, Aug. 3 and 7, 1793; see also note, in *NG*, April, 24.

53. Hamilton's conversation with George Hammond, Aug. 2–10, "Cabinet Meeting: Proposed Rules Governing Belligerents," Aug. 3, and "Cabinet Meeting: Opinion on the Fitting Out of Privateers in the Ports of the United States," Aug. 3, 1793, in *PAH*, XV, 163, 168–70; Jefferson to Genêt, June 5 and Aug. 7, 1793, in *WTJ*, VI, 282–3, 365–6, "Cabinet Opinion on 'Polly' and 'Catherine'," June 12, 295–6, and Jefferson to Madison, April 28, 232.

54. Treasury Department Circular to the Collectors of the Customs, May 30, 1793, in *PAH*, XIV, 499. Even Jefferson acknowledged that this was going beyond treaty commitments; Jefferson to Madison, April 28, in *WTJ*, VI, 232. Several feared it might provoke a rupture with Britain: see Henry Lee to Hamilton, and Samuel Smith to Hamilton, June 16, 1793, in *PAH*, XIV, 549, and XV, 1.

55. Rufus King's memo in *LCK*, I, 444–5; Jefferson to Madison, May 19, 1793, in *WTJ*, VI, 260–1; Edward Carrington to Hamilton, April 26, and Hamilton, "Pacificus" III, in *PAH*, XIV, 350, and XV, 65–6.

56. For the text of the proclamation, see *WGW*, XXXII, 430–1. See also "Cabinet opinion on proclamation and French Minister," April 19, 1793, in *WTJ*, VI, 217.

57. In *NG*, Address to Washington, May 15, unsigned, and "A Citizen," May 18, extract from *IC*, May 22, "Veritas," June 8 and 12, "Philo-Veritas," June 26, unsigned, July 10, and "Alcanor," July 7, 1793; in *NYJ*, "No Dissembler," July 3, and "The People," July 24, 1793.

58. Jefferson to Madison, June 23, June 29, and Aug. 11, 1793, in *WTJ*, VI, 315–16, 327–8, 368–9; Jefferson to Monroe, May 5 and July 14, 240, 346; quote from Madison's "Helvidius" II, in *WJM*, VI, 187.

59. Quote from memo of Hamilton and Knox to Washington, May 2,

1793, in *PAH*, XIV, 368; Jefferson, "Anas," 142–3; in *WTJ*, VI, 1793, Jefferson, "Cabinet Opinion on Proclamation and French Minister," April 19, 217; Jefferson to Madison, April 28, 232.

60. Hamilton, "Pacificus" I, in *PAH*, XV, 36.

61. Madison to Jefferson, May 22, 1793, in *WJM*, VI, 130.

62. Hamilton, "Pacificus" I–VI, in *PAH*, XV, 33–43, 55–63, 65–9, 83–6, 90–5, 100–6, 130–5, quotes from 59, 60, 61.

63. Jefferson to Madison, July 7, 1793, in *WTJ*, VI, 338; Madison's, "Helvidius" I–V, in *WJM*, VI, 138–88; quotes from 142, 168, 185.

64. *The Correspondence between Citizen Genet, Minister of the French Republic, to the United States of North America, and the officers of the federal government* . . . (Philadelphia, 1793), 5–7, 11–2. Madison made reference to this possibility in "Helvidus" V, in *WJM*, VI, 185. For the administration's failure to respond to these instructions see Jefferson, "Anas," 171–4.

65. Jefferson to Madison, May 12 and June 2, 1793, in *WTJ*, VI, 251, 278, and Jefferson to Harry Innes, May 23, 266; in *NYJ*, "A Republican," June 15, 1793, and "Cato," Jan. 8, 1794; in *NG*, 1793, unsigned, April 24, "An Old Soldier," May 4, "A Citizen," May 18, "An American," June 12, unsigned, June 15, "Virginius Americanus" and extract from the *Fayetteville Gazette*, July 10, and Letter from New York, Aug. 14.

66. "Address to the Public Security Holders" from *IC*, in *NG*, Sept. 14, 1793.

67. Hamilton, "Americanus" I and II, in *WAH*, IV, 261, 262, 275 ff; Henry Lee to Hamilton, June 15, 1793, in *PAH*, XIV, 550.

68. Hamilton, "Pacificus" III, in *PAH*, XV, 65; Hamilton to Washington, April 14, 1794, in *WAH*, IV, 289.

69. Jefferson to Monroe, May 5 and June 28, and to Madison, June 29, 1793 in *WTJ*, VI, 239, 322, 326; unsigned from *IC*, in *NG*, July 3 and Aug. 7; see also Kersant's speeches before the National Convention, translated and republished in *NG*, March 23 and 27.

70. Hamilton, "Pacificus" VI, in *PAH*, XV, 103; Jefferson, "Opinion on French Treaties," April 28, 1793, in *WTJ*, VI, 219; Memo of Hamilton and Knox to Washington, May 2, in *PAH*, XIV, 379–80, 390.

71. Hamilton to ?, May 18, 1793, in *PAH*, XIV, 475, 476.

72. Hamilton to Henry Lee, June 22, 1793, in *ibid.*, XV, 15.

73. Letter from a gentleman in Philadelphia to his friend in Alexandria, in *GUS*, May 20, 1794; Hamilton to Washington, April 14, 1794 in *WAH*, IV, 290–1.

74. *Ibid.*, 286; Cabot to Samuel Phillips, March 8, 1794, in Lodge, 78.

75. David Ross to Hamilton, July 23, 1793, in *PAH*, XV, 121–2; Wester, Jr., "The Revolution in France," 23 ff.

76. In *NG*, "Freeman" and unsigned, May 4, "Observations on Political and Commercial connections with France" from *IC*, July 31, unsigned, June 15, "A Traveller," Aug. 24, unsigned, Sept. 11, and David Jones, Jan. 26, 1793; Madison to Edmund Pendleton, Feb. 23, 1793, and to Horatio Gates, March 24, 1794, in *WJM*, VI, 125, 209; Jefferson to Tench Coxe, May 1, 1794, in *WTJ*, VI, 507; "Crisis" from *Albany Gazette*, in *Boston Gazette*, May 26.

77. In *NG*, Address to Washington, May 15, and "A Citizen," May 18, 1793.

78. In *NG*, "Crisis" from *IC*, May 8, "An Old Soldier," May 22, unsigned, June 5, and "Callisthenes," Sept. 11, 1793.

79. In *NG*, extract from *IC*, May 22, "Vertias," June 1, and "An American," June 12, 1793; "A Jacobin," in *NYJ*, July 20; Madison, "Helvidius" VI, in *WJM*, VI, 185–6.

80. *Annals*, 3d Cong., 155–6.

81. *Ibid.*, 201, 202, 208; Letter from a person in a neighboring state, in *CC*, March 1, 1794; also Fisher Ames to Christopher Gore, Jan. 28, in Ames, I, 133; R. Troup to King, Jan. 13, in *LCK*, I, 542.

82. *Annals*, 3d Cong., 215, 221, 240, 271, 274, 284, 382.

Chapter 3. *Jay Treaty*

1. In *NYJ*, "Observer," Aug. 24, "Son of Liberty," Aug. 31, and "Argus," Sept. 7, 1793; in *Boston Gazette*, "Seventy-five," Sept. 2, and "America," Nov. 18, 1793; in *GA*, Communciation, Dec. 21, and "A Farmer of the Back Country," Dec. 30, 1793.

2. The addresses began in May, 1790, and continued throughout the remainder of the year, as can be ascertained from any of the major newspapers. The President's refusal to call an emergency session of Congress drew some criticism, though: see "A Citizen," in *NG*, July 27, 1793.

3. Washington to the merchants and traders of the city of Philadelphia, May 17, and to the freeholders and other inhabitants of Salem, June 7, 1793, in *WGW*, XXXII, 460–1; "Taphna," in *NG*, July 13.

4. The Order in Council of June 8 was not officially known of in the United States until the end of August (*NG*, Aug. 31, 1793), though its effects were noticed long before that (*NG*, July 31). For the Algerian pirates, see Edward Church to the Secretary of State, Oct. 12, and Church's "Circular to Citizens of the United States," Oct. 15, 1793, in

Naval Documents related to the United States Wars with the Barbary Powers (Washington, 1939–45), I, 47–51.

5. A. L. Burt, *The United States, Great Britain, and British North America* . . . (New Haven, 1940), 153. For the Instruction see *ASP:FR*, I, 430.

6. Hamilton to Jay, May 6, 1794, in *WAH*, IV, 309–10; "A Spectator from the Galleries," in *GA*, March 29; *Annals*, 3d Cong., 535–6. The statement of the Rule of 1756 is taken from Samuel Flagg Bemis, *The Diplomacy of the American Revolution* (Bloomington, Ind., 1957), 131n.

7. In *NYJ*, New York resolutions, March 5, "Demosthenes," April 12, "Yankee Doodle," March 29, and Resolutions of Chatham County, Ga., May 17, 1794; in *GA*, unsigned, March 18 and 22.

8. Ames to Gore, March 26, 1794, in Seth Ames, ed., *The Works of Fisher Ames* (Boston, 1854), I, 139; Philadelphia resolves, March 18, 1794, in *GA*, March 21; Report of the Secretary of State about Spoilations on Commerce, March 2, in *Annals*, 3d Cong., 1306.

9. Resolves of the New York Democratic Society, in *NYJ*, April 16, 1794; J. Lawrence to R. King, April 3, in *LCK*, I, 558.

10. I rely here on a text printed in the *Boston Gazette*, April 7, 1794, dated New York, March 24.

11. Unsigned, in *GA*, March 31, 1794; Lawrence to King, April 3, in *LCK*, I, 558.

12. Resolutions pertaining to the army can be found in *Annals*, 3d Cong., 500–501. The subject of the navy had previously been raised in connection with the Algerian difficulties, *ibid.*, 432–3 ff.

13. *Annals*, 3d Cong., 535, 561.

14. Ames to Gore, March 26, 1794, in Ames, I, 139; *Annals*, 3d Cong., 505.

15. Ames to Gore, Feb. 25, 1794, in Ames, I, 135; Letter from a gentleman in Philadelphia to his friend in Alexandria, May 1, 1794, in *GUS*, May 20; *Annals*, 3d Cong., 506–22, particularly 506–7, 510, 515.

16. *Ibid.*, 575, 591–2.

17. Hamilton to Washington, April 14, 1794, in *WAH*, IV, quote from 296–7, also 287–8; Ames to Gore, Feb. 25, 1794, in Ames, I, 136; *Annals*, 3d Cong., 572–3, 574, 579; Oliver Wolcott, Sr., to his son, March 17, 1794, in *MAWA*, I, 132.

18. Hamilton to Washington, April 14, 1794, in *WAH*, IV, 295; *Annals*, 3d Cong., 577, 579, 582–3, 587.

19. Hamilton to Washington, April 14, 1794, in *WAH*, IV, 294, 295.

20. *Annals*, 3d Cong., 538, 546, 550.

21. *Annals*, 3d Cong., 554; Hamilton to Washington, April 14, 1794, in

WAH, IV, 292; unsigned, in *GA*, March 29; also see "Federalist" IV, in *AR*, II, 229.

22. Hamilton to Washington, April 14, 1794, in *WAH*, IV, 288; *Annals*, 3d Cong., 578, 593; Thomas Pinckney to the Secretary of State, Jan. 9, 1794, in *ASP:FR*, I, 430; "A Moderate Man," in *GA*, April 8.

23. J. Lawrence to R. King, March 8, 1794, in *LCK*, I, 549; unsigned, in *GA*, June 25; Cabot to Samuel Phillips, March 10, in Henry Cabot Lodge, *Life and Letters of George Cabot* (Boston, 1877), 77–8.

24. See report, in *GA*, April 3, 1794; *Annals*, 3d Cong., 530 ff.

25. *Ibid.*, 602, 606.

26. Hamilton to Washington, April 14, 1794, in *WAH*, IV, 297–8; Washington to Jay, April 19, in Henry P. Johnston, ed., *The Correspondence and Public Papers of John Jay* (New York, 1890–93), IV, 6–7; also Washington to the Secretary of State, April 15, to the Senate, April 16, to Tobias Lear, May 6, in *WGW*, XXXIII, 329–30, 332-3, 356-7. Madison's confidence that the Senate would reject the Clarke motion, in Madison to Jefferson, April 28, *WJM*, VI, 211, was based on knowledge of Jay's appointment.

27. In *NYJ*, from a Philadelphia correspondent, May 10, and Resolves of the Democratic Society of Pennsylvania, May 14, 1794.

28. See ch. 6.

29. Resolves of the Democratic Society of Pennsylvania, in *NYJ*, May 14; unsigned, in *GA*, April 24 and 28; see also Robert R. Livingston, "Cato" IV, in *AR*, I, 167, and "Cinna" III, *AR*, III, 89–90. These charges were refuted by Robert Goodloe Harper, "Address on the Treaty of November, 1794, with Great Britain," *Selected Works of Robert Goodloe Harper . . .* (Baltimore, 1814), 15–16.

30. Madison to Jefferson, May 4 and 25, 1794, in *WJM*, VI, 215, 216; Resolves of the Democratic Society of Washington, Pa., in *GA*, July 26; Resolves of the Democratic Society of Philadelphia, in *NYJ*, May 14; unsigned in *Boston Gazette*, June 2.

31. In *GA*, 1794, Address of the Democratic Society of Wythe Co., Va., Aug. 1, unsigned, June 13, Resolves of Chester Co., Pa., July 14, extract from a Boston paper, July 17; in *Boston Gazette*, 1794, "Resolves of Paper Noblemen and British emissaries," signed Alexander Pacificus, April 28, "Caution," May 5, unsigned, May 19, unsigned from *GA* and "The Funding System," June 16. For British aggressions in the Northwest see *ASP:FR*, I 461 ff.

32. I have used the text of the treaty found in Samuel Flagg Bemis, *Jay's Treaty: A Study in Commerce and Diplomacy* (New York, 1923), 321–43, quotes from 334, 335. See also *Treaty of Amity, Commerce, and*

Navigation, between His Britannic Majesty . . . In which is annexed, A Copious Appendix, 2d ed., (Philadelphia, 1795), 116–7; in *AR,* II, "Decius" I, 118, "Americanus," from *Independent Gazeteer,* 279; A. J. Dallas, *Features of Mr. Jay's Treaty* (Philadelphia, 1795), 5, 12.

33. "Columbus," *Remarks on the Treaty of amity, navigation, and commerce, concluded between Lord Grenville and Mr. Jay . . .* (Philadelphia, 1796), 7. The strategy of bargaining reparations for commercial concessions was suggested in Hamilton to Jay, May 6, 1794, in *WAH,* IV, 309, but it was not part of Jay's instruction, May 6, in *ASP:FR,* I, 472–4; see Bemis, 216.

34. Eleazer Oswald, *Letters of Franklin on the conduct of the executive . . .* (Philadelphia, 1795), 19, 22; Matthew Carey, *Address to the House of Representatives of the United States . . .* (Philadelphia, 1796), 37.

35. Madison to Monroe, Dec. 4, 1794, in *WJM,* VI, 219–20.

36. Boston resolves of July 13, 1795, in *A Volume of Records Relating to the Early History of Boston . . .* (Boston, 1903), XXXI, 407; in *AR,* I, Caesar Rodney, "Speech," 32, Resolutions of the citizens of Petersburg, Aug. 1, 1795, 103–4; Dallas, *Features,* 9, 11; "Columbus," 30; "Constitutionalist," in *The Treaty—its merits and demerits fairly discussed and displayed* (Boston, 1796), 76–80.

37. In *AR,* I, Resolutions of the citizens of Petersburg, Aug. 1, 1795, 104–5, "Caius" to the President of the United States, July 21, 110–111, "Cato" III and IX, 151 and 225–6; in *AR,* II, Proceedings of the town of Lexington, Massachusetts, Aug. 13, 39.

38. In *AR,* I, Charles Pinckney, "Speech," July 22, 1795, 10–11, Resolutions of the citizens of Petersburg, 104, "Caius," 110; in *AR,* II, "Cato" XIV, 4–7; "Decius" I, 122–4.

39. "Atticus" III, in *AR,* II, 220; "Columbus," 8.

40. In *AR,* I, Pinckney, "Speech," 17, "Caius," 110; "Cato" XIV and XV, in *AR,* II, 6–7, 10; Resolutions of Amelia County, Va., 44, Resolutions of Washington District, S.C., Sept. 6, 1795, 286; "Columbus," 11.

41. "Cato" V, in *AR,* I, 169–70; Carey, 36–7. For the opposition's expectations about sequestration, see in *AR,* I, "Cato" XII, 241–4, "Caius," 111; in *AR,* II, "Decius" III, 128–30, Proceedings at Lexington, Aug. 13, 1795, 39–40; "Columbus," 19–20; "Constitutionalist," in *The Treaty,* 98, 101, 105.

42. In *AR,* I, Pinckney, "Speech," 12–13, "Cato" VIII, 219; in *AR,* II, "Decius" V, 136–7, 140; Dallas, 10–11; "Constitutionalist," in *The Treaty,* 85–90.

43. In *AR,* I, "Cato" V, 158–62, Pinckney, "Speech," 12, Report of the

Savannah committee, July 29, 1795, 137; in *AR*, II, "Decius" IV, 134, Proceedings of the citizens of Richmond County, Ga., Sept. 1, 1795, 47–8; Carey, 43; Dallas, 7, 10; "Columbus," 20.

44. In *AR*, I, "Cato" IV and VI, 153–8, 162, "Caius", 108–9; in *AR*, II, Resolutions of Washington District, S.C., 286, "Atticus" III, 223; in *AR*, III, "Cinna" V, 219.

45. In *AR*, I, "Cato" VIII and IX, 221–3, 223–6, Petersburg resolutions, Aug. 1, 1795, 105; "Decius" VI, 157–9, J. Thompson, "Speech," 24, Rodney, "Speech," 33–4; in *AR*, II, Laurens County proceedings, 275–6; in *AR*, III, Virgina memorial and petition from *Petersburg Intelligencer*, Oct. 12, 1795, 6–8; "Columbus," 24, 26–7.

46. Bemis, 336–7.

47. "Cato" X, in *AR*, I, 230–1; "Constitutionalist," in *The Treaty*, 90–3; Boston resolves of July 13, 1795, in *A Volume of Records*, XXXI, 408; in *AR*, II, Proceedings of Lexington, Mass., Aug. 13, 1795, 35–6, Laurens County proceedings, Aug. 12, 275–6.

48. Hamilton, "Camillus" XXXV, in *WAH*, V, 286, 287–8; "Remarks on Charles Pinckney's Speech," in *AR*, II, 170–1.

49. In *AR*, I, "Cato" XI, 236–39, Petersburg resolutions, August 7, 1795, 105; in *AR*, III, Virginia memorial and petition, 6–7; in *AR*, II, "Atticus" I, 210, Williamsburg proceedings, Aug. 5, 1795, 272, Lexington, Kentucky resolves, Aug. 28, 1795, 269; "Columbus," 25; Carey, 39n; Dallas, 16; Oswald, 44, 56–7.

50. In *AR*, II, "Remarks on some of the probable consequences of Mr. Jay's Treaty" from *Boston Chronicle*, 208, "A Republican," 143, "Cato" XI, 237; Oswald, 13–4.

51. Rodney, "Speech," in *AR*, I, 30; in *AR*, II, "A Political Watchman" from *Jersey Chronicle*, 204–5; Oswald, 40; Carey, 17–8; Dallas, 14 ff.

52. Oswald, 12–3.

53. In *AR*, I, "Cato" XI and XII, 235–239, Rodney, "Speech," 32; in *AR*, II, "Americanus" from *Independent Gazetteer*, 280; Carey, 37; Oswald, 24, 30, 37–8; Dallas 20–3.

54. "Camillus" I, II, & V, in *WAH*, IV, 380, 381–2, 421; Noah Webster, Jr., "Vindication of the Treaty of Amity, Commerce and Navigation, with Great Britain," in *A Collection of papers on political, literary and moral subjects* (New York, 1843), 221, hereafter referred to as "Curtius."

55. "Camillus" II, in *WAH*, IV, 379, 387–8; Hamilton to Washington, July 9, 1795, in *ibid.*, 359; "Curtius," 218–221; see also "A Federalist" V and VI, in *AR*, II, 247.

56. "Camillus" V, in *WAH*, IV, 425; also Hamilton to Washington, July 9, 1795, *ibid.*, 362.

57. "Camillus" XXIV, *ibid.*, V, 149–60; Hamilton to Washington, July 9, 1795, *ibid.*, IV, 363; *The Correspondence between Citizen Genet, Minister of the French Republic, to the United States of North America, and the officers of the federal government* . . . (Philadelphia, 1793), 3, 6–7, 11–12, 16.

58. William Vans Murray to Wolcott, Jr., Aug. 29, 1795, in *MAWA*, I, 228; Oliver Wolcott, Sr., to his son, Nov. 23, 1795, 269.

59. Wolcott, Sr., to his son, March 17, 1794, *ibid.*, 132; Wolcott, Jr., to Noah Webster, Jr., Aug. 1, 1795, 222; Hamilton, "Americanus" II, "Horatius," and "Camillus," V, in *WAH*, IV, 273, 366, 423, and Hamilton to Washington, April 14, 1794, 286.

60. Cabot to Wolcott, Jr., August 13, 1795, in Lodge, 85; Oliver Ellsworth to Wolcott, Jr., Aug. 20, 1795, in *MAWA*, I, 226.

61. In *AR*, III, "Cinna" V and VI, 224–33, "Reflections on Mr. Jay's Treaty," 109; Carey, 31, 36; Dallas, 47.

62. In *AR*, II, "A Political Watchman," 206, "Atticus" I, 210–1, "Americanus," 279–80; Oswald, 21–2; Jefferson to Edward Rutledge, Nov. 30, 1795, in *WTJ*, VII, 40.

63. In *AR*, I, "Cato" VI and VII, 168–70, Thompson, "Speech," 26.

64. In *AR*, III, "Atticus" VI, 69–70; in *AR*, I, "Cato" VI, 168–9. On the intentions of the British in signing the treaty, see Dallas, 20; "Columbus," 23–4.

65. "Camillus" I, in *WAH*, IV, 374–5; also his "Horatius," *ibid.*, 364–5; "Curtius," 223–4; "Brief History of the Rise and Progress of the recent Mobs and Riots," *CC*, Sept. 26, 1795.

66. "Camillus" II, in *WAH*, IV, 384; "Curtius," 224.

67. *A Volume of Records*, XXXI, 409; see also Resolutions of Petersburg, Aug. 1, 1795, in *AR*, I, 102–3.

68. Washington to the Boston Selectmen, July 28, 1795, in *WGW*, XXXIV, 253.

69. "Cato" XIII, in *AR*, I, 247.

70. Jefferson to Madison, Sept. 1, 1795, in *WTJ*, VII, 33; in *AR*, I, Thompson, "Speech," 22, "Cato" XIII, 248–50; in *AR*, II, "Observations on Treaties," 114; in *AR*, III, "Atticus" VII, 70, 72, "Address to the citizens of New York," 234; Carey, 38; Michael Leib, *Dr. Leib's Patriotic speech, addressed to the House of Representatives of Pennsylvania, February 24, 1796* . . . (New London, 1796), 8 ff.

71. "The Federalist" IV and V, in *AR*, II, 236–8, 240–43; "Camillus" XXXVI–XXXVIII, in *WAH*, V, 296–332; in *GUS*, "An American," Sept. 2 and 8, William Willcocks, Sept. 4, "Lucian" VI from *Virginia Gazette*,

Oct. 21, extract from *Minerva*, Nov. 3, 1795, Communication, April 8, 1796; *A Review of the Question, In whom has the Constitution vested the Treaty power* (Philadelphia, 1796), 19 ff.

72. For the social implications of antifederalist rhetoric see Gordon S. Wood, *The Creation of the American Republic, 1776–1787* (Chapel Hill, 1969), 483 ff.

73. Marc Egnal and Joseph A. Ernst, "An Economic Interpretation of the American Revolution," *WMQ*, XXIX (1972), 1–32.

Chapter 4. *Sectionalism*

1. Fisher Ames to Thomas Dwight, October 20, 1789, in Seth Ames, ed., *The Works of Fisher Ames* (Boston, 1854), I, 74.

2. Charles A. Beard, *Economic Origins of Jeffersonian Democracy* (New York, 1952); Charles A. and Mary R. Beard, *The Rise of American Civilization*, new ed. (New York, 1939), 336–436; Manning J. Dauer, *The Adams Federalists* (Baltimore, 1953).

3. Paul Goodman, *The Democratic-Republicans of Massachusetts: Politics in a Young Republic* (Cambridge, 1964), 70 ff; Mark D. Kaplanoff, *From Colony to State: New Hampshire 1800–1815* (unpublished Scholar of the House Dissertation, Yale University, 1970), passim.

4. Norman K. Risjord, "The Virginia Federalists," *Journal of Southern History*, XXXIII (1967), 496 ff; Lisle A. Rose, *Prologue to Democracy: The Federalists in the South, 1789–1800* (Lexington, Ky., 1968), 122.

5. Paul Goodman, "The First American Party System," in William N. Chambers and Walter Dean Burnham, eds., *The American Party Systems . . .* (New York, 1967), 68.

6. John A. Munroe, *Federalist Delaware, 1775–1815* (New Brunswick, 1954), 206–7.

7. *Annals*, 4th Cong., 996–1003.

8. Cabot to King, Aug. 4, 1795, in Henry Cabot Lodge, *Life and Letters of George Cabot* (Boston, 1877), 83–4.

9. See ch. 12.

10. Gilbert L. Lycan, *Alexander Hamilton & American Foreign Policy: A Design for Greatness* (Norman, Okla., 1970), 187.

11. David Ramsey, *The History of the Revolution of South Carolina* (Trenton, 1785), II, 372–3.

12. Francois Alexandre Frederic, duc de la Rochefoucault Liancourt, *Travels through the United States of North America*, 2nd ed. (London, 1800), II; also Charles Downer Hazen, *Contemporary American Opinion*

of the French Revolution (Gloucester, Mass., 1964), 165 ff; Benjamin W. Labaree, *Patriots and Partisans: the Merchants of Newburyport* (Cambridge, Mass., 1962), 107 ff.

13. David Hackett Fischer, *The Revolution of American Conservatism* (New York, 1965), 201–2; also William N. Chambers, *Political Parties in a New Nation* (New York, 1963); Noble T. Cunningham, Jr., *The Jeffersonian Republicans* (Chapel Hill, 1957).

14. Ames to George Richard Minot, May 3 and July 9, 1789, in Ames, I, 35, 62; unsigned, in *NG*, January 9, 1793; in *CC*, excerpt from a Connecticut paper, March 9, 1793, "New England," Oct. 3, 1792, and "A Democrat," July 23, 1793, "The Times," in *GUS*, April 30, 1794; *Annals*, 3d Cong., 628; 5th Cong., 961.

15. Jefferson to Madison, Jan. 30, 1787, in Julian P. Boyd, ed., *The Papers of Thomas Jefferson* (Princeton, 1950–   ), XI, 93.

16. *CC*, June 16, 1790.

17. Madison to Monroe, Dec. 4, 1794, in *WJM*, VI, 220–1. For the contrasting sentiments of Massachusetts Federalists and Virginia Republicans on the question of titles and salaries, see "Consistency," "A Spectator," "Cambridge," Massachusetts House Debates, "J," "An American," "A Federalist of 1787," in *Massachusetts Centinel*, Aug. 20, Dec. 31, 1788, Jan. 7 & 21, April 1, July 8, and Aug. 15, 1789; Jefferson to Henry Tazewell, Jan. 16 and to Madison, Jan. 30, 1797, in *WTJ*, VII, 106–7, 116. Richard H. Lee and Ralph Izard, both from the South, were exceptions to the rule.

18. Jonathan Elliot, ed., *The Debates in the several state conventions, on the adoption of the Federal Constitution* (Philadelphia, 1861), III, 397.

19. Max Farrand, ed., *The Records of the Federal Convention of 1787* (New Haven, 1911), II, 222; Elliot, III, 76–7, 192; IV, 283–4; David Ramsey, "An Address to the Freemen of South Carolina, on the subject of the Federal Constitution," in Paul Leicester Ford, ed., *Pamphlets on the Constitution of the United States* (Brooklyn, 1888), 379; Herbert Aptheker, *American Negro Slave Revolts*, new ed. (New York, 1967), 21 ff; *Marcellus; Published in the Virginia Gazette* (Richmond, 1794), 19–20.

20. Aptheker, 209 ff; Winthrop D. Jordan, *White over Black: American Attitudes towards the Negro 1550–1812*, Pelican ed. (Baltimore, 1969), 393 ff.

21. For Gabriel's plot see Aptheker, 219 ff. Pennsylvania's reaction to the Whiskey and Fries's rebellions is best traced in Harry Marlin Tinkcom, *The Republicans and Federalists in Pennsylvania, 1790–1801* (Harrisburg, 1950).

22. William L. Smith to Edward Rutledge, Aug. 9, 1789, in George C.

Rogers, Jr., ed., "The Letters of William Laughton Smith to Edward Rutledge, June 6, 1788 to April 28, 1794," *South Carolina Historical Magazine*, LXIX (1968), 15; see also *Annals*, 1st Cong., 1930.

23. Jefferson to LaFayette, June 16, 1792, in *WTJ*, VI, 78.

24. Oliver Wolcott, Jr., to his father, Jan. 27, 1792 and February 8, 1793, in *MAWA*, I, 85, 86.

25. Ames to G. R. Minot, July 9, 1789, in Ames, I, 62.

26. Enclosure in Ames to Minot, Nov. 30, 1791, in *ibid.*, 103-4.

27. Ames to Minot, July 9, 1789, in *ibid.*, 62.

28. Enclosure in Ames to Minot, November 30, 1791, in *ibid.*, 105.

29. The stereotype did not come into public currency until after 1800. See Labaree, 126-7; *Connecticut Courant*, particularly Feb. 8, 1802 ff; June 1 and July 6, 1803; Feb. 6, 1805 ff.

30. Rochefoucault Liancourt, II, 76-8, 183, 231, 232; Albert Matthews, ed., "Journal of William Laughton Smith, 1790-1791," *Massachusetts Historical Society Proceedings*, LI (1918), 69; also Francois Jean, Marquis de Chastellux, *Travels in North America in the Years 1780-81-82* (New York, 1827), 286.

31. Timothy Dwight, *Travels in New England and New York* (New Haven, 1821), II, 458-9.

32. "Milk" in *CC*, June 21, 1797; "Apology of Mr. Thatcher for not accepting General Blount's challenge," reprinted in the *Middlesex Gazette*, June 30, 1797; John Gardiner to H. G. Otis, March 24, 1798, in Samuel Eliot Morison, *The Life and Letters of Harrison Gray Otis, Federalist, 1765-1848* (New York, 1913), I, 91; Dwight, IV, 334-5; Jack Kenny Williams, "The Code of Honor in Antebellum South Carolina," *South Carolina Historical Magazine*, LIV (1953), 114, 117; Charles S. Sydnor, "The Southerner and the Laws," *Journal of Southern History*, VI (1940), 11-8.

33. Williams, 121 ff; Timothy Dwight, *A Sermon on duelling, preached in the chapel of Yale College* (New York, 1805); Robert Baldick, *The Duel: A History of Duelling* (New York, 1965), 121-2; Lorenzo Sabine, *Notices on Duels and Duelling* (Boston, 1859), 341-6.

34. J. D. Barnhart, *Valley of Democracy: the Frontier versus the Plantation in the Ohio Valley, 1775-1818* (Bloomington, Ind., 1953); L. H. Harrison, "A Virginian Moves to Kentucky, 1793," *WMQ*, XV (1958), 203-13; Thomas P. Abernathy, *Three Virginian Frontiers* (Baton Rouge, 1940), and *From Frontier to Plantation in Tennessee: A Study of Frontier Democracy* (University, Ala., 1967); Robert R. Russell, "The Effects of Slavery upon Non-slaveholders in the Antebellum South," *Agricultural History*, XV (1941), 112-4, 118-21; see also Robert M. Weir, "The

Harmony we were Famous For: An Interpretation of Pre-Revolutionary South Carolina Politics," *WMQ,* XXVI (1969), 482–3.

35. For this interpretation I rely heavily upon Stanley Elkins and Eric McKitrick, "A Meaning for Turner's Frontier," *Political Science Quarterly,* LXIX (1954), 321–53, 565–602; Harry Ammon, "The Jeffersonian Republicans in Virginia: An Interpretation," *Virginia Magazine of History and Biography,* LXXI (1963), 153–4; Dwight, II, 461–2; Albert Laverne Olson, "Agricultural Economy and the Population in Eighteenth Century Connecticut," in *Tercentenary Commission of the State of Connecticut: Committee on Historical Publications,* XL (1935); Lois Kimball Matthews Rosenberry, "Migrations from Connecticut Prior to 1800" and Migrations from Connecticut after 1800," in *ibid.,* XXVIII (1934), LIV (1936); James M. Banner, Jr., *To the Hartford Convention: the Federalists and the Origins of Party Politics in Massachusetts 1789–1815* (New York, 1970), 169–71; Percy W. Bidwell, "Rural Economy in New England at the Beginning of the Nineteenth Century," *Transactions of the Connecticut Academy of Arts and Sciences,* XX (1916), 241–399.

36. William A. Schaper, "Sectionalism and Representation in South Carolina," *Annual Report of the American Historical Association for the Year 1900* (Washington, 1901), I, passim; William W. Freehling, *Prelude to Civil War: The Nullification Controversy in South Carolina, 1816–1836* (New York, 1965), 7–11; Charles Woodmason, *The Carolina Backcountry on the Eve of the Revolution,* Richard J. Hooker, ed. (Chapel Hill, 1953), passim; Richard Maxwell Brown, *The South Carolina Regulators* (Cambridge, 1963), 13 ff.

37. Schaper, 367–8, 379; *An Address to the people of South Carolina, by the General Committee of the representative reform association of Columbia* (Charleston, 1794), 27–8.

38. By far the best account of South Carolina in the revolution is David Ramsay's, *The History of the Revolution of South Carolina,* 2 vols.; I have also relied upon Edward McCrady, *The History of South Carolina in the Revolution 1775–1780* (New York, 1901), and *The History of South Carolina in the Revolution, 1780–1783* (New York, 1902). See also Richard Barry, *Mr. Rutledge of South Carolina* (New York, 1942), particularly 269–302. Some impression of the impact the British invasion had on Carolina society can be gained from Ramsay to Benjamin Rush, June 3, and to Jonathan Elmer, July 15, 1779, in Robert L. Brunhouse, ed., "David Ramsay, 1749–1815: Selections from His Writings," *Transactions of the American Philosophical Society,* new series, LV (Part 4, 1965), 60, 62; also Aedanus Burke to Arthur Middleton, January 25, 1782, in J. L. Barnwell, annotator, "Correspondence of Hon. Arthur Middleton, Signer of

the Declaration of Independence," *South Carolina Historical and Genealogical Magazine*, XXVI (1925), 192.

39. Kenneth Coleman, *The American Revolution in Georgia, 1763–1789* (Athens, Ga., 1958), especially 4–5, 15, 81–3, 179–88, 278–9.

40. Robert W. Barnwell, Jr., "Rutledge the Dictator," *Journal of Southern History*, VII (1941), 244; Edward Rutledge to Jay, November 12, 1786 and May 21, 1789 in Henry P. Johnston, ed., *The Correspondence and Public Papers of John Jay* (New York, 1890–93), III, 217, 368; see also Richard Walsh, ed., *The Writings of Christopher Gadsden, 1746–1805* (Columbia, 1966), 170 ff; Gordon S. Wood, *The Creation of the American Republic* (Chapel Hill, 1969), 367, 482–3; Rogers, 105 n.

41. Malcolm C. Clark, "Federalism at High Tide: The Election of 1796 in Maryland," *Maryland Historical Magazine*, LXI (1966), 229; Dorothy M. Brown, "Maryland and the Federalist: Seach for Unity," *ibid.*, LXIII (1968), 5–6, 9–10, 21; Fischer, 216; Munroe, 147, 199–200, 208, 213, 238–40, 251–4, 261.

42. Walter R. Fee, *The Transition from Aristocracy to Democracy in New Jersey, 1789–1829* (Somerville, N.J., 1933), 19 ff.

43. Kaplanoff, 79–87, 112, 256–7. Connecticut Federalists were quite explicit in appealing to the traditions of the region: see for example, Theodore Dwight, *An Oration delivered at New Haven on the 7th July, 1801, before the Society of the Cincinnati* (New Haven, 1801), and [David Daggett], *Steady habits vindicated: or a Serious Remonstrance to the People of Connecticut, against changing their government* (Hartford, 1805).

44. Risjord, 498, 505–6, 517; Jackson T. Main, "Sections and Politics in Virginia, 1781–1787," *WMQ*, XII (1955), 96–112, and "The One Hundred," *ibid.*, XI (1954), 354–84, and "The Distribution of Property in Post-Revolutionary Virginia," *Mississippi Valley Historical Quarterly*, XLI (1954–5), 241–58; Leonard L. Richards, "John Adams and the Moderate Federalists: The Cape Fear Valley as a Test Case," *North Carolina Historical Review*, XLIV (1967), 14–30.

45. Goodman, *Democratic-Rebublicans*, 86–96; Richard J. Purcell, *Connecticut in Transition: 1775–1818* (Middletown, Conn., 1963), 64; William A. Robinson, *Jeffersonian Democracy in New England* (New York, 1916), 141 ff; L. W. Butterfield, "Elder John Leland, Jeffersonian Itinerant," *Proceedings of the American Antiquarian Society*, N.S., LXII (1952), 207 ff.

46. Goodman, "The First American Party System," 66–7; Fischer, 223–6.

47. *An Address to the People of South Carolina*, ii, 19–21. For the op-

posing point of view see Henry William DeSaussere, *Letters on the questions of the justice and expediency of going into alterations of the representation of South Carolina, as fixed by the constitution* (Charleston, 1795), 10, 14–5; [Timothy Ford], *The Constitutionalist: or, an Inquiry* (Charleston, 1794), 20–2, 37–9, 41–3, 51. Schaper, 408–19 summarizes the controversy.

48. I rely for this interpretation heavily upon John Harold Wolfe, "Jeffersonian Democracy in South Carolina," *James Sprunt Studies in History and Political Science,* XXIV (1940).

49. These developments are best traced in Alfred F. Young, *The Democratic Republicans of New York: The Origins, 1763–1797* (Chapel Hill, 1967), Alvin Kass, *Politics in New York State: 1800–1830* (Syracuse, 1965); Dixon Ryan Fox, *The Decline of Aristocracy in the Politics of New York, 1801–1840* (New York, 1919); Tinkcom; Sanford W. Higginbotham, *The Keystone in the Democratic Arch: Pennsylvania Politics 1800–1816* (Harrisburg, 1952). Population expansion in both states is detailed in *Niles' Weekly Register,* I, 265–6.

50. I rely here on Kaplanoff, Chilton Williamson, *Vermont in Quandary 1763–1825* (Montpelier, 1949), Goodman, *Democratic-Republicans,* and Beverly W. Bond, Jr., *The Foundations of Ohio* (Columbus, 1941), 396 ff, and Barnhart. Population figures are in *Niles' Weekly Register,* I, 264.

51. Purcell, 146 ff; Munroe, 201, 211.

52. I rely here on Edward Field, ed., *State of Rhode Island and Providence Plantations at the End of the Century: A History* (Boston, 1901), I, 287–93; Fee, 119–37; Carl E. Prince, *New Jersey's Jeffersonian Republicans: The Genesis of an Early Party Machine* (Chapel Hill, 1967).

53. Frank A. Cassell, "General Samuel Smith and the Election of 1800," *Maryland Historical Magazine,* LXIII (1968), 343–6.

54. Prince, 170–81; Fee, 150–209; John S. Pancake, "Baltimore and the Embargo 1807–1809," *Maryland Historical Magazine,* XLVII (1952), 181–210; also W. Wayne Smith, "Jacksonian Democracy on the Chesapeake: the Political Institutions," *ibid.,* LXII (1967), 381–2, 392; Williamson, 266 ff; Kaplanoff, 248 ff; Field, 293–300; Goodman, *Democratic-Republicans,* 192 ff; Banner, 284–8.

Part III. *Public Opinion*

1. William N. Chambers, "Party Development and Party Action: the American Origins," *History and Theory,* III (1963–1964), 101; also Richard Hofstadter, *The American Political Tradition* (New York, 1954), 36 ff;

Lee Benson, *The Concept of Jacksonian Democracy* (Princeton, 1961), 232 ff.

2. *Annals*, 3d Cong., 924, 926.

Chapter 5. *Elitism*

1. *Annals*, 1st Cong., 267, 319, 322, 430.

2. *Ibid.*, 427, 428, 429–30, 706; see also Robert A. Rutland, *The Birth of the Bill of Rights, 1776–1791* (Chapel Hill, 1955).

3. *Annals*, 1st Cong., 706, 429, 430–3.

4. "A Candid State of the Parties," in *WJM*, VI, 119.

5. *Annals*, 1st Cong., 437, 1215, 1286; see also "Tablet," in *GUS*, May 6, 1789, June 19 and 30, 1790.

6. Madison, "Charters," in *WJM*, VI, 85; "Government of the United States," *ibid.*, 92.

7. "Public Opinion," "Charters," and "British Government," in *WJM*, VI, 70, 85, 87.

8. Unsigned, in *GA*, Jan. 2, 1792. For the debate on the post office bill, see *Annals*, 2d Cong., 248 ff; "Philanthropes," in *NG*, Feb. 6, 1792; also Madison to Edmund Randolph, Sept. 13, 1792, in *WJM*, VI, 117 n. Noble E. Cunningham, Jr., *The Jeffersonian Republicans: The Formation of Party Organization 1789–1800* (Chapel Hill, 1957), 13–9, gives a detailed account of the founding of the *National Gazette*.

9. Madison, "Public Opinion," in *WJM*, VI, 70.

10. *Maryland Gazette*, Dec. 23, 1790 and *GUS*, Jan. 5 and 28, 1791, report the difficulties the legislatures of Maryland and North Carolina encountered in pursuing Virginia's example. See *GUS*, 1791, for the reception of the Pennsylvania legislature's efforts to resist the excise, "A Pennsylvanian," Jan. 22, the minority protest against the House's action, Feb. 5, and extract from the *Connecticut Courant*, Feb. 19.

11. Benjamin Lincoln to Hamilton, Dec. 4, 1790, in *PAH*, VII, 196; also Jay to Hamilton, Nov. 28, 1790, in Henry P. Johnston, ed., *The Correspondence and Public Papers of John Jay* (New York, 1890–93), III, 410.

12. Edward D. Collins, "Committees of Correspondence of the American Revolution," *Annual Report of the American Historical Association for the year 1901* (Washington, 1902), I, 245–71; Richard D. Brown, *Revolutionary Politics in Massachusetts: The Boston Committee of Correspondence & the Towns 1772–1774* (Cambridge, Mass., 1970); Noah Webster, Jr., "The Revolution in France," in *A Collection of papers on political, literary*

and moral subjects (New York, 1843), 31–2, makes explicit the connection between the revolutionary model and the societies of the 1790's.

13. Eugene P. Link, *Democratic-Republican Societies, 1790–1800* (New York, 1942); see also Margaret Woodbury, "Public Opinion in Philadelphia, 1789–1801," *Smith College Studies in History*, V (Oct. 1919–Jan. 1920), 67–72, 111–20, 123; William Miller, "First Fruits of Republican Organizations: Political Aspects of the Congressional Election of 1794," *PMHB*, LXIII (1939), 118–43. Cunningham, 62–6, gives the most judicious account of the relation of the societies to the Republican leadership in Congress; for a list of the Philadelphia Society's leading officers, see William Cobbett, *Porcupine's Works* (London, 1801), I, 110 n.

14. Brooke Hindle, *David Rittenhouse* (Princeton, 1964), 346.

15. In *NYJ*, "A Republican" from *Boston Chronicle*, Jan. 7, 1795, Constitution of the Democratic Society of Canaan, March 8, Circular of the Massachusetts Constitutional Society to all republican and democratic societies, Sept. 13, 1794, and Address of the Democratic Society of Vermont, March 8, 1795; Link, 6 n; "An American Sans Culottes," in *GA*, April 3, 1794.

16. In *CC*, "B," July 31, "Camillus," Aug. 17 and 24, Address from a real Republican in Boston to Genêt, Sept. 11, "A Republican," Nov. 30, "Columbus," Dec. 4, 1793; and "Americanus," May 10, 1794; in *GUS*, 1794, "Henry" from *Connecticut Courant*, Jan. 15, unsigned, Feb. 4, "A Friend to Representative Government," April 4, "Anti-Club," Dec. 23, and "Facts," Dec. 30.

17. "Z," in *CC*, Aug. 17, 1793; in *GUS*, 1794, "T.T.," Oct. 11, and "E. F.," July 21; see also Webster, Jr., 3, 32.

18. William Miller, "First Fruits," and "The Democratic Societies and the Whiskey Insurrection," *PMHB*, LXII (1938), 141–2, 324–49.

19. Nathaniel Chipman, *Sketches of the principles of government* (Rutland, 1793); Chipman to a friend in Philadelphia, June 9, 1794, in *GUS*, July 14, 1794.

20. "Revolution in France," in *GUS*, Nov. 13, 1794; "A Friend to Government" from *Maryland Gazette*, in *Middlesex Gazette*, Dec. 6, 1794.

21. In *GUS*, 1794, "Review of Robespierre's Report on the Principles of Political Morality" from *Minerva*, Aug. 7, "A Citizen," June 11, and Communication, June 10.

22. In *GUS*, 1794, "E.F.," July 21, "A Citizen" from the *New York Daily Gazette*, Aug. 4, "A Friend to Republican Freedom," April 10, "A Friend to Representative Government," April 4, and "Observations on Democratic Clubs" from *Maryland Journal*, April 23; "Order," in *CC*, Sept. 3; also *Annals*, 3d Cong., 923.

23. Webster, Jr., 28, 35; in *GUS*, 1794, "L.E.," April 19, "A Republican" from *Greenfield Gazette*, Aug. 5, unsigned, Dec. 30, and Correspondent, Jan. 15; "Deodatus," in *CC*, Sept. 27.

24. In *GUS*, 1794, "L.E.," April 19, and extract from *Minerva*, Sept. 29.

25. In *GUS*, 1794, unsigned, Feb. 11, "A Federal Republican," June 18, "A Voter," Sept. 22, and "One of the People," Dec. 29; extract from the *Maine Gazette*, in *CC*, Sept. 6.

26. In *GUS*, 1794, "A Friend to Republican Freedom," April 9, "L.E.," April 19, and extract from *Columbian Mercury*, Sept. 25; Christopher Gore, *Manlius: with notes and references* (Boston, 1794), 51; Webster, Jr., 28.

27. The theme became a favorite with Federalist writers: see in *CC*, 1794, "Vigil" from *Minerva*, May 24, "A Farmer," May 31, and "Deodatus," Sept. 27; in *GUS*, "Unprejudiced," June 17, "A Federal Republican," June 18, "An Observer," Oct. 16, unsigned, Nov. 9, "Anti-Club," Dec. 23.

28. Gordon S. Wood, *The Creation of the American Republic, 1776–1787* (Chapel Hill, 1969), 505, 510 ff; Jacob E. Cooke, ed., *The Federalist* (Cleveland, 1961), 388; Paul Leicester Ford, ed., *Pamphlets on the Constitution of the United States* (Brooklyn, 1888), 41 n, 225; Jonathan Elliot, ed., *The Debates in the several State Conventions on the adoption of the Federal Constitution* (Philadelphia, 1861), IV, 327.

29. [William P. Beers], *An Address to the Legislature and people of the State of Connecticut* (New Haven, 1791), 29, 19; also "Vindex," in *CC*, Jan. 25, 1792; unsigned, in *GUS*, May 13, 1795; Dan Kent, *Electioneering for office defended, with some directions as to the process* (Rutland, 1796), 10 ff.

30. "A Republican," in *CC*, Oct. 19, 1793; also Charles S. Syder, *Gentlemen Freeholders: Political Practices in Washington's Virginia* (Chapel Hill, 1952), ch. IV.

31. See Ch. 1, 8 n.

32. Ames to George Richards Minot, May 31, 1789 and Nov. 30, 1791, to Thomas Dwight, Jan. 7, 1795, and to Pickering, July ?, 1798, in Seth Ames, ed., *Works of Fisher Ames* (Boston, 1854), I, 50, 102, 160, 231; Stephen Higginson to Pickering, May 11, 1792 in J. Franklin Jameson, ed., "Letters of Stephen Higginson, 1783–1804," *Annual Report of the American Historical Association for the Year 1896* (Washington, 1897), I, 798.

33. For New York's electioneering tradition see Milton Klein, "Democracy and Politics in Colonial New York," *New York History*, XL (1959), 221–46; Nicholas Varga, "Election Procedures and Practices in Colonial New York," *ibid.*, XVI (1960), 249–72. For Philadelphia, see J. Philip

Gleason, "A Scurrilous Colonial Election and Franklin's Reputation," *WMQ*, XVIII (1961), 70 ff; Theodore Thayer, *Pennsylvania Politics and the Growth of Democracy* (Harrisburg, Pa., 1953).

34. In *GA*, 1794, Resolves of the Portland Republican Society, Sept. 4, Resolves of the Madison Society of Grenville, S.C., Sept. 5, Address of the Democratic Society of Wythe County, Virginia, Aug. 1, and unsigned, July 21, 1794; in *A*, "Z," Dec. 24, 1794, David Redick to Mr. Scull, Dec. 25, 1794, Jan. 24, 1795. Miller, "First Fruits," 138 ff, makes much of the societies' electioneering, but his case relies almost entirely on Federalist sources. What material he does cite from Republican sources (121–2) does not prove his point because he fails to distinguish between opposing an incumbent, which the societies had no reservations about, and explicitly supporting a nominee at the polls.

35. Cf. "Anti-monoply," in *GA*, Jan. 24, 1792, and "Democrat" from *Maryland Journal*, in *GUS*, April 24, 1794.

36. Richard E. Welch, Jr., *Theodore Sedgwick, Federalist: A Political Portrait* (Middletown, Conn., 1965), 66–70; James M. Banner, Jr., *To the Hartford Convention: The Federalists and the Origins of Party Politics in Massachusetts, 1789–1815* (New York, 1970), 141–2, 179–80.

37. Something of Federalist concern with the growing involvement of the people can be gathered from Ames to Gore, December 17, 1794, to Thomas Dwight, December 7, 1798, and to Pickering, March 12, 1799, in Ames, I, 156–7, 244, 254; also Banner, 131, 177–8; William A. Robinson, *Jeffersonian Democracy in New England* (New York, 1916), 26–7.

38. In *NYJ*, quotes from Address of the Patriotic Society of Newcastle County, Del., Jan. 28, Address of the Canaan Democratic Society of Columbia County, March 18, 1795, and "Cato" from *Newark Gazette*, Dec. 27, 1794; Address of the German Democratic Society, in *A*, Dec. 27, 1794.

39. In *NYJ*, Address of the Republican Society of Baltimore, Dec. 20, "Cato" from *Newark Gazette*, Dec. 27, Declaration of the Democratic Society of New York, May 31, 1794, and "Agis" I & III, Jan. 28 and Feb. 7, 1795; see also in *GA*, 1794, Declaration of the Democratic Society of Philadelphia, Jan. 11, Circular of the Massachusetts Constitutional Society, Nov. 6.

40. In *NYJ*, 1794, Declaration of the Democratic Society of New York, May 31; and Address of the New York Democratic Society, Jan. 17, Address of the Canaan Democratic Society, March 18, "Agis" III and V, Feb. 7 and May 20, 1795; unsigned, in *GA*, Sept. 16, 1794.

41. Address of the German Democratic Society, in *A*, Dec. 27, 1794; in *NYJ*, Address of the Democratic Society of New York, May 31, 1794,

and "A Republican" from *Boston Chronicle*, Jan. 7, 1795, Address of the Democratic Society of New York, Jan. 17, Address of the Canaan Democratic Society, March 18, and "Agis" V, May 20; in *A*, 1795, "Justice," March 13, and Address of the Republican Society at Vauxhall, April 11; Correspondent, in *GA*, March 11, 1794.

42. In *GUS*, 1794, "Order," March 7, and Reply of the citizens of Hanover County, Virginia, to the circular letter of the Democratic Society of Philadelphia, Jan. 15.

43. In *GUS*, 1794, "A Friend to Republican Freedom," April 9, "The Times" X from *Minerva*, May 6, "A Federal Republican," June 18, and "E.F.," July 21; *Annals*, 3d Cong., 923–4.

44. Address of the Vermont Democratic Society to Tracy, Dexter, Sedgwick, Murray, Smith, Ames, and Dayton, in *NYJ*, March 18, 1795. Occasionally Federalists succeeded in capturing control of opposition meetings such as the one called in Boston early in 1794: Miller, "First Fruits," 127; Samuel Eliot Morison, *The Life and Letters of Harrison Gray Otis, Federalist 1765–1848* (Boston, 1913), I, 52–4; Gore to King, March 3, 1794, in *LCK*, I, 547.

45. In *NYJ*, Correspondence committee of the Pennsylvania Democratic Society to the New York Democratic Society, March 25, 1795, and Address of the Democratic Society of New York, May 31, 1794.

46. In *GUS*, 1794, "Unprejudiced," June 17, and unsigned, Dec. 30. The Elizabethtown Constitutional Association was formed by Federalists to oppose the societies, though: in *A*, reports, Jan. 24, and their resolutions Feb. 7, 1795.

47. "Reflections on Mr. Jay's Treaty," in *AR*, III, 129, 131.

48. Washington to the Secretary of State, July 22, 1795, in *WGW*, XXXIV, 244; Cabot to Gore, Jan. 5, 1796, in Henry Cabot Lodge, *Life and Letters of George Cabot* (Boston, 1877), 93.

49. Wolcott, Jr., to Hamilton, Aug. 15, 1795, in *MAWA*, I, 225. For documents surrounding Randolph's resignation, see Washington to the Secretaries of the Treasury and War, Aug. 17–18, 1795, and to Randolph, Aug. 20, 1795, in *WGW*, XXXIV, 275–77; also Edmund Randolph, *A Vindication of Mr. Randolph's resignation* (Philadelphia, 1795); this interpretation parallels that supplied by Madison to Monroe, Dec. 20, 1795, in *WJM*, VI, 259.

50. Washington to Henry Knox, Sept. 20, 1795, in *WGW*, XXXIV, 311.

51. Washington to the Secretary of State, July 29 and 31, and to Alexander Hamilton, July 29, 1795, *ibid.*, 266, 256, 263.

52. Washington to the Boston Selectmen, July 28, 1795, in *ibid.*, 252–53.

53. "Belisarius," in *IC*, Sept. 21, 1795; see also "Strictures on the President's Circular Answer," in *AR*, II, 147–153.

54. "To the Independent Citizens of Virginia" from the *Petersburg Intelligencer*, in *AR*, III, 3.

55. "A Political Watchman," *AR*, II, 206.

56. "Atticus" VI and IX, *AR*, III, 71–2, 151; Address to the citizens of New York, *AR*, II, 235; in *IC*, "Hampden," Aug. 31, 1795, "Belisarius," Sept. 21, 1795 ff, "Pittachus," Oct. 15, 1795 ff; also "Portius," in *GUS*, Sept. 26, 1795.

57. Ch. VI, n 1.

58. "An American," in *GUS*, Sept. 8, 1795.

59. "A Yeoman's Remarks," in *CC*, Aug. 5, 1795; Noah Webster, Jr., "Vindication of the Treaty of Amity, Commerce and Navigation, with Great Britain" in *A Collection of papers on political, literary and moral subjects*, 182; in *GUS*, 1795, unsigned, July 22, 23, and 29; Cabot to King, July 27, 1795, in *LCK*, II, 19; Plymouth protest, Oct. 20, 1795, in *AR*, III, 310.

60. "Fauxbourg de St. Antoine" from *United States Chronicle*, in *GUS*, Sept. 26, 1795.

61. In *GUS*, unsigned, Aug. 13, "Senex" from *Columbian Herald*, Sept. 2, "I," Aug. 18, C. Fitz-James from *Providence Gazette*, Aug. 24, and Presentment of the North Carolina grand jury, Oct. 20, 1795, unsigned from the *Western Telegraph*, April 5, 1796.

62. Excerpt from the *New York Herald*, in *CC*, Sept. 26, 1795.

63. In *CC*, 1795, "An American," Sept. 8, and "A Country Moderate," Sept. 12.

64. "Federalist," in *CC*, July 22, 1795.

65. In *AR*, II, "Mentor," 202, "An Old Soldier of '76," 281–2; "Pittachus," in *IC*, Oct. 29, 1795.

66. Unsigned from a Maryland paper, in *GUS*, Sept. 30, 1795.

67. "An American," in *GUS*, Sept. 8, 1795.

68. "Atticus" V, in *AR*, II, 227.

69. *Ibid.*, 226.

70. *Ibid.*, 226, 227.

71. "A Subscriber" from the *Delaware and Eastern Shore Advertizer*, in *GUS*, Sept. 19, 1795.

72. In *GUS*, unsigned, Aug. 13 and Sept. 7, "Vox Populi," Oct. 12, "A Farmer," Oct. 20, all 1795, and "Civis," Jan. 28, 1796; Fisher Ames to Thomas Dwight, Aug. 24, 1794 in Ames, I, 172; Washington to Knox, Sept. 20, 1795, in *WGW*, XXXIV, 310–1; G. Cabot to King, July 25, and

C. Gore to King, Nov. 19, 1795 in *LCK*, II, 17–8, 32; excerpt from *Minerva*, in *AR*, III, 114 n.

73. In *GUS*, "An American," Sept. 8, 1795, and "Senex," March 28, 1796. For the tally of Senate voting see *Middlesex Gazette*, July 17, 1795.

Chapter 6. *Style*

1. *Annals*, 3d Cong., 580, 588–9.

2. Oliver Ellsworth to Oliver Wolcott, Sr., March 8, Jonathan Trumbull to Oliver Wolcott, Sr., March 9, and Chauncey Goodrich to Oliver Wolcott, Sr., April 1, 1796, in *MAWA*, I, 306, 321, 325–6.

3. The opposition gave this idea currency in their pleas to the President not to sign the treaty: see Eleazer Oswald, *Letters of Franklin on the conduct of the executive* . . . (Philadelphia, 1795), 19, 22.

4. "Monitor," in *GUS*, Aug. 22, 1795.

5. A. Hamilton to R. King, Dec. 14, 1795, in *LCK*, II, 36–7.

6. In *GUS*, 1796, unsigned from the *Virginia Centinel*, Jan. 22, and unsigned, Feb. 9; also reports in *GUS*, and *CC*, late Feb. and early March, 1796. Objections were raised to this practice: see R. Rutherford to the citizens of Frederick and Berkeley Counties, Jan. 15, 1796, in *GUS*, March 5, 1796; and the House defeated a motion for adjournment on Washington's birthday; *Annals*, 4th Cong., 355.

7. *Ibid.*, 400–1, 424; see also Jerald A. Combs, *The Jay Treaty: Political Battleground of the Founding Fathers* (Berkeley, 1970), 174–6.

8. *Annals*, 4th Cong., 426–8.

9. Goodrich to Wolcott, Sr., Feb. 21, 1796; Ellsworth to Wolcott, Sr., March 8, 1796, in *MAWA*, I, 304, 306.

10. Hamilton to Washington, March 28, 1796, in *WAH*, VIII, 386–8; Goodrich to Wolcott, Sr., March 2, 1796, in *MAWA*, I, 305; Combs, 176.

11. Ch. 5 ns 51 and 52. These claims were subsequently made in the House: *Annals*, 4th Cong., 429, 433, 438, 439, 530, 594.

12. Wolcott, Sr., to his son, March 21, 1796, in *MAWA*, I, 322–3.

13. *Annals*, 4th Cong., 518, 479–480, 552, 559, 627, 650; in *CC*, 1796, "Political Investigation," April 16, and "The Echo," May 4; also unsigned, in *GUS*, March 28. These views were, of course, challenged by the opposition: *Annals*, 4th Cong., 653–4; "Harrington" III, in *GUS*, April 2.

14. *Annals*, 4th Cong., 759–60.

15. Goodrich to Wolcott, Sr., April 1 and 9, 1796, in *MAWA*, I, 325–26.

16. Hamilton to King, April 15, 1796, in *LCK*, II, 59.

17. *Annals,* 4th Cong., 970–1; also Noah Webster, Jr., *Ten Letters to Dr. Joseph Priestly in answer to his letters to the inhabitants of Northumberland* . . . (New Haven, 1800), 16.

18. *Annals,* 4th Cong., 1197–8.

19. Wolcott, Jr., to his father, April 18, 1796, in *MAWA,* I, 327; *Annals,* 4th Cong., 1023–4.

20. Hamilton to King, April 15, 1796, in *LCK,* II, 59–60.

21. Goodrich to Wolcott, Sr., April 9 and 23, 1796, in *MAWA,* I, 325–6, 331.

22. *CC,* April 27 and 30, 1796; also *IC,* April 25, 28 and May 5, 1796; *A Volume of Records Relating to the Early History of Boston* . . . (Boston, 1903), XXXI, 429; *Annals,* 4th Cong., 1153, 1228, 1264; Madison to Monroe, May 14, 1796, in *WJM,* VI, 300 n.

23. In *CC,* 1796, "The Echo," May 4, and accounts, April 30 and May 4; *New York Herald,* April 19 and 20, 1796; *IC,* May 2, 1796; *Annals,* 4th Cong., 1003.

24. *Ibid.,* 963, 987, 989, 1170, 1247.

25. *Ibid.,* 989, 1077, 1078, 1124, 1212–13, 1248.

26. *Ibid.,* 1280.

27. *Ibid.,* 991, 1065, 1097–8, 1129, 1199–1200.

28. *Ibid.,* 961–3, 1261–2, 1254; also 949, 1153, 1204.

29. *Ibid.,* 1200, 1238.

30. *Ibid.,* 987 (quote); also 1049, 1097–8, 1156, 1238.

31. *Ibid.,* 1100; also Madison to Monroe, May 14, 1796, in *WJM,* VI, 301 n.

32. Aaron Kitchell to Ebenezer Elmer, March 31, 1796, quoted in Joseph Charles, *The Origins of the American Party System* (New York, Harper Torchbook, ed., 1961), 113. The speaker, Dayton, who was moving towards Federalism, also gave credence to these threats: *Annals,* 4th Cong., 1275, 1277. For the threats, see *ibid.,* 1059, 1262.

33. The absentees were Sherburne, Patten, and Findley: *ibid.,* 1280, 1292; see also Combs, 187.

34. *Annals,* 4th Cong., 1157.

35. The relevant roll calls appear in *ibid.,* 759–60, 768–69, 771, 782–3, 1280, 1289–1292. Several Federalists who had reservations about the treaty voted for it as well, see Irving Brant, *James Madison, Father of the Constitution, 1787–1800* (New York, 1950), 504 n 12.

36. Webster, *Ten Letters,* 16; Wolcott, Jr., to his father, April 18, Goodrich to Wolcott, Sr., April 20 and 23, 1796, *MAWA,* I, 327, 330, 331; also Wolcott, Jr., to Hamilton, April 29, 1796, *ibid.,* I, 334, and Hamilton to King, April 15, 1796, in *LCK,* II, 60.

37. *IC*, May 16 and 19, 1796.

38. The military situation had improved sufficiently by 1795 so that some Federalists were convinced better terms could be secured from Britain: see Samuel Bayard to William Bradford, June 8, 1795, and to Elias Boudinot, July [?], 1795, in David L. Sterling, "A Federalist Opposes the Jay Treaty: the Letters of Samuel Bayard," *WMQ*, XVIII (1961), 414, 415.

39. Madison to Monroe, May 14, 1796, in *WJM*, VI, 300–1n; *Annals*, 4th Cong., 1282 ff.

40. Cf. Ch. V, n 5.

41. Fisher Ames to George R. Minot, May 31 and July 23, 1789 in Seth Ames, ed., *Works of Fisher Ames* (Boston, 1854), I, 51, 66; Noah Webster, Jr., "On the Education of Youth in America," in *A Collection of essays and fugitiv writings* (Boston, 1790), 1–37; in *GUS*, 1796, excerpt from *CC*, March 5, and "E" VII, Aug. 27; David Hackett Fischer, *The Revolution in American Conservatism* (New York, 1965), 4–5, 49.

42. In *NYJ*, 1793, unsigned, June 5, and "Observer," Aug. 24. "Brutus," in *NG*, June 8; also Jay, "Charge to the Grand Jury, Richmond, Virginia," May 22, 1793, in Henry P. Johnston, ed., *The Correspondence and Public Papers of John Jay* (New York, 1890–93), III, 483; Charles Marion Thomas, *American Neutrality in 1793: A Study in Cabinet Government* (New York, 1931), 170–3.

43. An interesting example of Federalist style in this regard was their attempt to suggest that the principal reason for southern opposition to the Jay Treaty lay in its failure to provide compensation for slaves removed by British forces at the end of the war. See in *AR*, II, "No Englishman," 57–9, "The Federalist" II & VI, 67–8, 248–50; Hamilton, "Camillus" V, in *WAH*, IV, 419–20; "Harrington" V, in *GUS*, April 19, 1796.

44. Ch. I, ns 67–70.

45. Cabot to King, July 27, and Gore to King, Aug. 7 and 14, 1795, in *LCK*, II, 19, 22–4.

46. The standard account is Alexander DeConde, *Entangling Alliance: Politics & Diplomacy under George Washington* (Durham, N.C., 1958), 217–23; the best source Hamilton to King, Aug. 13, 1793, in *PAH*, XV, 240–4.

47. Jefferson to G. Morris, Aug. 16, 1793, in *WTJ*, VI, 371–93; Hamilton, "Cabinet Meetings: Proposals Concerning the Conduct of the French Minister," Aug. 1–23, 1793, in *PAH*, XV, 157.

48. Jefferson to Monroe, July 14, and to Madison, Aug. 3, 1793, in *WTJ*, VI, 349, 361; Hamilton to King, Aug. 13, 1793, in *PAH*, XV, 239–41; Hamilton to King, Aug. 13 and 23?, 1793, in *LCK*, I, 457.

49. For the rumors see *Providence Gazette*, Aug. 27, 1793; documents central to the appeal can be found most conveniently in *LCK*, I, 458 ff, though most newspapers carried it: see *NYJ*, Aug. 24, Dec. 4, 11, 1793; see also Donald S. Spencer, "Appeals to the People: The Later Genêt Affair," *New York Historical Society Quarterly*, LIV (1970), 241–67.

50. Jefferson to Madison, Sept. 1, 1793 in *WTJ*, VI, 402; in *ASP:FR*, I, 1793, Jefferson to G. Morris, Aug. 16, 170–1, and Genêt to Jefferson, Sept. 18, 172–4; Genêt to Washington, Aug. 15, 1793, in *Boston Gazette*, Sept. 2, 1793.

51. In *NYJ*, 1793, "One of the People" to Jay and King, Aug. 21, 1793, "A Flatterer" I & II, Aug. 28 and 31.

52. *PAH*, XV, 282–4.

53. King to Hamilton, Aug. 3, 1793, in *LCK*, I, 492–3.

54. Wolcott, Jr., to Webster, Jr., Aug. 10, 1793, in *MAWA*, I, 103.

55. *GUS*, Aug. 14, 1793.

56. *Ibid.*, Aug. 17, 1793.

57. David Ross to Hamilton, July 23 and Aug. 30, 1793, in *PAH*, XV, 121–2, 309–10, and Hamilton's strategy in "No Jacobin" VII, *ibid.*, 268–70. Even in 1794, the Federalists remained aware of the fact that persecution might increase the societies' influence: Correspondent, in *GUS*, June 6, 1794, also *Annals*, 3d Cong., 900, 902.

58. "A Friend to Government" from *Maryland Gazette*, in *Middlesex Gazette*, Nov. 29, 1794.

59. William Findley, *History of the Insurrections in the four western counties of Pennsylvania* (Philadelphia, 1796), 56–7, 214; see also Raymond Walters, Jr., *Albert Gallatin: Jeffersonian Financier and Diplomat* (New York, 1957), 70.

60. Edmund Randolph, *Germanicus. [Letter I–XIII To the citizens of the United States]* (n.p., 1794), 4; Washington to Burgess Ball, Aug. 20, 1794, in *WGW*, XXXIII, 463; Hamilton to King, Sept. 17, 1794, in *WAH*, VIII, 322.

61. Findley, 180; Leland D. Baldwin, *Whiskey Rebels: the Story of a Frontier Uprising* (Pittsburgh, 1939), 112; John Alexander Carroll and Mary Wells Ashworth, *George Washington: First in Peace* (New York, 1957), 198 ff; see also Gilbert L. Lycan, *Alexander Hamilton & American Foreign Policy: A Design for Greatness* (Norman, Okla., 1970), 237–8.

62. In *GUS*, 1794, Reply of the Citizens of Hanover County, Virginia to the circular letter of the Democratic Society of Philadelphia, Jan. 15, and Correspondent, May 24.

63. Noah Webster, Jr., "The Revolution in France," a *A Collection of*

papers on political, literary and moral subjects (New York, 1843), 23, 27, 28, 31–2; in *GUS*, 1794, "A Friend to Representative Government," April 4, "E.F.," July 21, and Correspondent, Dec. 5.

64. *Marcellus: Published in the Virginia Gazette* (Richmond, 1794), 17–9; "The Times" IV from *Minerva*, in *CC*, April 23, 1794.

65. Findley, 56–7; Baldwin, 108–9; Russell J. Ferguson, *Early Western Pennsylvania Politics* (Pittsburgh, 1938), 125 ff; Solon J. and Elizabeth H. Buck, *The Planting of Civilization in Western Pennsylvania* (Pittsburgh, 1939), 468–9.

65. Pennsylvania Democratic Society to the German Republican Society, *NYJ*, April 2, 1794.

67. In *NYJ*, "Agis" IV, March 25, 1795, Declaration of the Pennsylvania Democratic Society, Dec. 27, 1794; "A Democrat," in *GA*, Aug. 4, 1794.

68. Washington to the Secretary of State, Oct. 16, 1794, in *WGW*, XXXIV, 3–4; Carroll and Ashworth, 149–50, 155–7, 179–80; *Annals*, 3d Cong., 788.

69. *Ibid.*, 794.

70. *Ibid.*, 899.

71. *Ibid.*, 900, 901; also in *A*, Address of the Pennsylvania Democratic Society, Dec. 22, 1794, "Argus," Feb. 16, 1795; in *NYJ*, Address of the Democratic Society of New York, Jan. 17, 1795, and "J.M.," Aug. 9, 1794.

72. *Annals*, 3d Cong., 930.

73. *Ibid.*, 901–2, 937; Randolph, 15 ff.

74. *Annals*, 3d Cong., 922, 936; Address to the independent tradesmen and mechanics of Boston, in *CC*, Oct. 29, 1794; William Willcocks, in *GUS*, Feb. 7, 1795; Randolph, 13.

75. In *GUS*, 1794, Correspondent, Oct. 4, unsigned, Nov. 15, and "C," Dec. 8, 1794; Address to the independent tradesmen and mechanics of Boston, in *CC*, Oct. 29, 1794.

76. In *CC*, "Anti-Club," Dec. 23, "E.F.," July 21, "A True Whig," Aug. 20, all 1794, and William Willcocks from *Minerva*, March 7, 1795; *Annals*, 3d Cong., 925; Randolph, 20 ff; Webster, "Revolution in France," 23 ff.

77. "Agis," I and II, in *NYJ*, Jan. 28 and 31, 1795; Address of the Pennsylvania Democratic Society, in *A*, Dec. 22, 1794. The Federalists in pointing to the insignificance of the society's membership had indirectly confirmed this point: see *supra*, Ch. 5, n 26.

78. In *A*, Address of the Pennsylania Democratic Society, Dec. 22, 1794, and Correspondent, March 2, 1795.

79. *Annals*, 3d Cong., 900–1, 903, 922 ff.

80. *Ibid.*, 906, 907, 939.

81. In *A*, "Z" from *Baltimore Daily Advertizer*, Dec. 26, 1794, and

Resolves of the Newark Republican Society, Jan. 3, 1795; "A Republican" from *IC*, in *NYJ*, Jan. 7, 1795.

82. *Annals*, 3d Cong., 912, 917, 934.

83. Fitzsimmons' motion was defeated by amending it to apply only to the four societies that had been implicated in the insurrection, see *ibid.*, 944; then the Republicans defeated an effort to include mention that societies elsewhere had countenanced the rebellion, and the Federalists lost interest in the emasculated version of their original motion, only 19 bothering to vote in its favor: *ibid.*, 944–5; also unsigned in *A*, Nov. 29, 1794.

84. E. P. Link, *Democratic-Republican Societies, 1790–1800* (New York, 1942), 202–3. Support for Link's interpretation can be found in David Redick to Mr. Scull, Dec. 24, 1794, *A*, Jan. 24, and unsigned, Jan. 14 and Feb. 4, 1795.

85. Resolves of the Franklin, or Republican Society of Pendleton County, South Carolina, September 16, 1795, in *AR*, III, 102–14. For the continuing Federalist barrage against them, see in *GUS*, 1795, "Chronus," Aug. 12, William Willcocks, Sept. 4, and excerpts from *Minerva*, Oct. 22 and Nov. 3.

86. In *AR*, II, "Gracchus" I from *Virginia Gazette*, 174; in *AR*, III, "Cinna" III, 95; also *Annals*, 4th Cong., 1200.

Chapter 7. *Paralysis*

1. "An unfrenchified American" from *Hudson Gazette*, in *GUS*, June 30, 1796; *Annals*, 4th Cong., 1660; Washington to Hamilton, May 8, 1796, in *WGW*, XXXV, 40.

2. Gouverneur Morris to Washington, March 4, 1796, in *ibid.*, 38 n; Hamilton to King, Dec. 16, 1796, in *LCK*, II, 126; also King to Pickering, June 1, and Cabot to King, July 24, 1796, *ibid.*, 63, 67; Hamilton to Wolcott, Jr., June 15, and King to Wolcott, Jr., Dec. 12, 1796, in *MAWA*, I, 360, 473.

3. Adet to Randolph, June 30, and Randolph to Adet, July 6, 1795, in *ASP:FR*, I, 594–5, 596; Randolph to King, July 6, 1795, in *LCK*, II, 15.

4. Monroe to Pickering, Feb. 16, 20, March 10, 25, May 2, 1796 in Stanislaus Murray Hamilton, ed., *The Writings of James Monroe* (New York, 1898–1903), II, 454 ff; report from Philadelphia, in *Middlesex Gazette*, June 24; report in *GUS*, July 21; Washington to the Attorney General, July 6, in *WGW*, XXXV, 122–3; Wolcott, Jr., to Hamilton, June 17, in *MAWA*, I, 360–1.

5. Hamilton to Wolcott, Jr., June 15, and Secretaries of Departments to the President, July 2, 1796, in *MAWA*, I, 359–60, 366–8; Cabot to Pickering, Aug. 31, in Henry Cabot Lodge, *Life and Letters of George Cabot* (Boston, 1877), 110; Pickering to King, Aug. 29, in *LCK*, II, 84–5. For the Federalist charge that the opposition press was provoking French actions see in *GUS*, unsigned, July 23, 1796 and Sept. 1, 1795; also Wolcott, Jr., to Washington, July 4, 1796, in *MAWA*, I, 365; Washington to the Secretary of the Treasury, June 24, 1796, in *WGW*, XXXV, 95.

6. Cabot to King, Sept. 24, 1796, in *LCK*, II, 91–2; Wolcott, Jr., to his father, Oct. 17, in *MAWA*, I, 387.

7. Adet to Pickering, Oct. 27, 1796, in *ASP:FR*, I, 576–7.

8. Adet to Pickering, Nov. 15, 1796, in *ibid.*, 582–3.

9. Pickering to King, Nov. 19, Benjamin Goodhue to King, Nov. 27, and William Bingham to King, Dec. 15, 1796, in *LCK*, II, 109, 113, 124; Wolcott, Jr., to his father, Nov. 19 and 27, in *MAWA*, I, 396, 401; Wolcott, Jr., to Hamilton, Nov. 17, in *ibid.*, 395–6.

10. *Annals*, 4th Cong., 2096–7; quote from Wolcott, Sr., to his son, Nov. 28, 1796, in *MAWA*, I, 403; also in *ibid.*, Wolcott, Jr. to his father, Nov. 27, 401–3, Goodrich to Wolcott, Sr., Dec. 17 and 23, 412, 414.

11. Goodrich to Wolcott, Sr., Dec. 17 and 23, 1796, in *MAWA*, I, 413, 414; Wm. Bingham to King, Nov. 29, Benjamin Goodhue to King, Dec. 15, Hamilton to King, Dec. 16, 1796 and April 8, 1797, in *LCK*, II, 113, 125, 127, 168.

12. Cabot to King, March 19, 1797, in *LCK*, II, 161; Wolcott, Jr., to his father, Nov. 19 and 27, Uriah Tracy to Wolcott, Sr., Dec. 6, Goodrich to Wolcott, Sr., Dec. 17, 1796, in *MAWA*, I, 396–7, 402, 407, 412.

13. Hamilton to King, Dec. 16, 1796, in *LCK*, II, 127; *Annals*, 4th Cong., 1667–8; "Americanus," in *CC*, March 18, 1797; also Sedgwick to King, March 12, 1796, in *LCK*, II, 157–8; Wolcott, Jr., to his father, Feb. 20, and James Hillhouse to Wolcott, Sr., March 4, 1797, in *MAWA*, I, 443, 444.

14. Documents pertaining to Pinckney's rebuff are in *Annals*, 5th Cong., 55, 3058 ff and 3076–8; also King to the Secretary of State, April 19, 1797, in *LCK*, II, 172.

15. Goodrich to Wolcott, Sr., May 4, and Wolcott, Sr., to his son, July 4, 1796, in *MAWA*, I, 335, 372; Hamilton to Washington, July 5, 1796, in *WAH*, VIII, 408–9.

16. Wolcott, Jr., to William Heth, June 19, 1796, and Uriah Tracy to Wolcott, Sr., Jan. 24, 1797, in *MAWA*, I, 361–2, 439, Jefferson to Archibald Stuart, Jan. 4, 1797, in *WTJ*, VII, 101; Eleazer Oswald, *Letters of*

Franklin on the conduct of the executive . . . (Philadelphia, 1795), 42.

17. Wolcott, Sr., to his son, March 20, and Jeremiah Wadsworth to Wolcott, Jr., March 26, 1797, in *MAWA*, I, 476, 478.

18. Cabot to Wolcott, Sr., May 15, 1797, in *MAWA*, I, 533; Cabot to King, May 1, 1797, in *LCK*, II, 180-1; Robert Goodloe Harper, *Observations on the dispute between the United States and France* . . . 3rd ed. (Dublin, 1798), 87, 145-6, 157, 159.

19. Wolcott to Cabot, March 27, 1797, in Lodge, 118; Cabot to Wolcott, Jr., May 25, and Hamilton to Wolcott, Sr., March 29, in *MAWA*, I, 533, 482; also Hillhouse to Wolcott, Sr., Jan. 23, Tracy to Wolcott, Sr., Jan. 24, Wolcott, Jr., to Hamilton, March 31, and Wolcott, Jr., to Adams, April 25, in *ibid.*, 437-8, 439, 488, 501; Harper, 66-74.

20. Cabot to King, March 19, and William Smith to King, April 3, 1797, in *LCK*, II, 161-2, 166; Wolcott, Jr., to Hamilton, March 31, Cabot to Wolcott, Jr., April 17, and Wolcott, Sr., to his son, March 20, in *MAWA*, I, 486, 487, 476; Wolcott, Jr., to Cabot, March 27, Cabot to Jeremiah Smith, April 17, and Cabot to Gore, April 17, in Lodge, 117-8, 131-2, 133.

21. Hamilton to Wolcott, Jr., March 30, Cabot to Wolcott, Jr., May 15, and Wolcott, Jr., to Adams, April 25, 1797, in *MAWA*, I, 485, 532, 510; Cabot to Wolcott, Jr., April 17, in Lodge, 129-30; Hamilton to Pickering, March 29 and May 11, to McHenry, March 22, to Wolcott, Jr., and to William Smith, April 5, in *WAH*, VIII, 455, 466-7, 451-2, 458-9, 460. On Pickering's provocative language, see Hamilton to Wolcott, Jr., Nov. 22, 1796, in *MAWA*, I, 398; also Pickering to Adet, Nov. 1, 1796, in *ASP:FR*, I, 578.

22. Quote from Ames to Wolcott, Jr., April 24, 1797, in *MAWA*, I, 498; also Ames to Wolcott, Jr., March 24, Wolcott, Jr., to his father, March 29, and to Hamilton, March 31, *ibid.*, 477, 482, 486; Hamilton to McHenry, March 22, to Pickering, March 22 and May 11, and to King, April 8, in *WAH*, VIII, 451, 453, 467-8, 461; see also *Annals*, 5th Cong., 239.

23. Quotes from Ames to Wolcott, Jr., April 24, Cabot to Wolcott, Jr., April 22, and May 31, 1797, in *MAWA*, I, 496, 499, 540; also Cabot to Wolcott, Jr., April 3 and 17, Washington to Wolcott, Jr., May 29, *ibid.*, 489, 494, 539-40; Cabot to King, April 10, in *LCK*, II, 169-70.

24. *Annals*, 5th Cong., 54-9, 68-9.

25. *Ibid.*, 69-70, 89, 129.

26. *Ibid.*, 74 ff.

27. *Ibid.*, 86, 161; Harper, 26, 43, 46, 48, 55, 63, 95-7, 106, 109, 119-22, 141, 152. Harper's Congressional speech can be found in *Annals*, 5th

Cong., 169–92; the sections relevant to this argument are on 175, 180–89.

28. *Annals*, 5th Cong., 193, 199–200, 210.

29. Uriah Tracy to Wolcott, Sr., May 27, 1797, *MAWA*, I, 537–9; see also *Annals*, 5th Cong., 17, 18, 22, 24.

30. *Ibid.*, 239, 253–383; Hillhouse to Wolcott, Sr., July 10, 1797, in *MAWA*, I, 557; William Bingham to King, July 10, in *LCK*, II, 199.

31. Wolcott, Jr., to Hamilton, Nov. 17, 1796, Tracy to Wolcott, Sr., Jan. 7, 1797, in *MAWA*, I, 396, 415–6. For the reception of this news in America, cf. *CC*, June 7, 1797.

32. Hamilton to Wolcott, Jr., March 30 and April 5, 1797, in *MAWA*, I, 485, 489; King to the Secretary of State, March 5 and April 19, in *LCK*, II, 150–2, 173; in *A*, 1797, reports, Jan. 18 and May 4, and "An American," April 29; reports in *CC*, June 7, 28, July 26, Aug. 2, 5, 9, 1797.

33. *Annals*, 5th Cong., 240 ff; see also Sedgwick to King, June 24, 1797, in *LCK*, II, 192–3.

34. Wolcott, Jr., to his father, July 4, 1797, in *MAWA*, I, 548.

35. Cabot to Wolcott, Jr., June 27, 1797, in *ibid.*, 549; also in *A*, 1797, unsigned, June 17, "Remarks on the situation of the United States," July 17, and "A Republican," July 1; Adams to Wolcott, Jr., Jan. 24, 1798, in *MAWA*, II, 11.

36. *Annals*, 5th Cong., 74; see also Eugene F. Kramer, "Some New Light on the XYZ Affair: Elbridge Gerry's Reasons for opposing War with France," *New England Quarterly*, XXIX (1956), 512.

37. Cabot to Wolcott, Jr., March 26, 1798 in Lodge, 152. See also King's pessimistic reports, King to Wolcott, Jr., April 14, 1797, in *MAWA*, I, 550; King to the Secretary of State, Nov. 12, Dec. 23, 1797, and Feb. 7, 1798, in *LCK*, II, 240–1, 261–2, 280.

38. Americans learned of Fructidor in November: *CC*, 1797, Nov. 15, and "Clarendon," Nov. 25.

39. John Dickinson, "The Letters of Fabius: containing remarks on the present situation of public affairs," *Political Writings of John Dickinson* (Wilmington, 1801), II, 167–286.

40. James Monroe, "A View of the conduct of the executive," in Hamilton, III, 282–457. For other pamphlets in the same vein but by less prominent figures, see Tanguy de la Boissière, *Observations on the dispatches written the 16th January, 1797 by Mr. Pickering* . . . (Philadelphia, 1797); Albert Gallatin, *An Examination of the conduct of the United States towards the French Republic* (Philadelphia, 1797); Richard Beresford, *Sketches of French and English politicks in America, in May, 1797* (Charleston, 1797).

41. Uriah Tracy, *Reflections on Monroe's View, of the conduct of the executive, as published in the Gazette of the United States, under the signature of Scipio* (Philadelphia, 1798), quote from 7. For Pickering's rebuff of Monroe's efforts to get an explanation for his dismissal, see *Annals*, 5th Cong., 3162–71.

42. *Annals*, 5th Cong., 82.

43. Cabot to Wolcott, Jr., and to Gore, April 17, 1797, in Lodge, 129–30, 133.

44. Webster, Jr., to King, May 30, Cabot to King, Aug. 17, 1797, in *LCK*, II, 182, 212.

45. Wolcott, Jr., to James McHenry, Oct. 4, and to Adams, Oct. 16, 1797, in *MAWA*, I, 566, 568.

46. *Annals*, 5th Cong., 764–74.

47. *Ibid.*, 767, 768, 769; also Wolcott, Jr., to Hamilton, June 17, 1796, in *MAWA*, I, 360, for the uses to which American registry might be put.

48. *Annals*, 5th Cong., 765–6, 772–3.

49. *Ibid.*, 765.

50. *Ibid.*, 771.

51. *Ibid.*, 435.

52. Uriah Tracy to Oliver Wolcott, Sr., May 27, 1797, in *MAWA*, I, 538; Robert Goodloe Harper, *Speech of R. Goodloe Harper, Esq. . . . on Friday March 2, 1798 . . .* (London, 1798), 54–5.

53. *Annals*, 5th Cong., 435–6.

54. *Ibid.*, 848–9.

55. For Nicholas' speech, see *ibid.*, 849–52.

56. *Ibid.*, 851.

57. *Ibid.*, 849.

58. *Ibid.*, 850.

59. *Ibid.*, 851.

60. *Ibid.*

61. See Federalist protestations to this effect, *ibid.*, 854–5, 865, 866, 872, 892, 940.

62. *Ibid.*, 854, 855, 870, 872, 868, 873, 1151; Harper, *Speech . . . March 2, 1798*, 32–42, 44.

63. *Annals*, 5th Cong., 961–2, 971–1029.

64. *Ibid.*, 1034, 1036–43, 1048–58, 1063–68.

65. *Ibid.*, 975.

66. Noah Webster, Jr., *Ten Letters to Dr. Joseph Priestly in answer to his letters to the inhabitants of Northumberland . . .* (New Haven, 1800), 16.

67. See James Bayard to Richard Bassett, Dec. 30, 1797, in Elizabeth Dorman, ed., "Papers of James A. Bayard, 1796–1815," *Annual Report of*

the American Historical Association for the Year 1913 (Washington, 1915), 46.

68. *Annals*, 4th Cong., 431, 433, 442, 478, 480, 486, 514–5, 517, 518, 523, 548, 552, 574, 594, 618, 619, 626–7, 643, 644, 650, 659, 672–3, 696, 698, 703.

69. *Ibid.*, 468, 495–6, 513, 608, 625–6, 641, 653.

70. In *A*, 1797, "Brief History of the late Election of electors for the state of Pennsylvania," March 10 and 14, Communication, May 22, unsigned, June 19, and "A Freemen," Oct. 2. The Federalists did not completely foresake this line of argument, though: see *Annals*, 5th Cong., 913, 1204.

71. *Ibid.*, 5th Cong., 898–9, 911, 1106–8, 1153–5; Harper, *Speech*, 19–20.

72. *Annals*, 5th Cong., 892, 898–9; James Bayard, *The Speech of Mr. Bayard on the foreign intercourse bill* . . . (Philadelphia, 1798), 12.

73. *Annals*, 5th Cong., 885, 899–901, 905, 907, 916, 924, 926, 928; Albert Gallatin, *The Speech of Albert Gallatin, delivered in the House of Representatives* . . . *on the first day of March, 1798* . . . (Philadelphia, 1798), 12.

74. In *A*, 1797, "An Old Soldier," Nov. 4 and 13, report, Nov. 7, "No Idolater" and "An Old Whig," Nov. 10, account, Nov. 11, and "Veritas," Nov. 14; see also Adams to Wolcott, Jr., Nov. 7, 1797, in *MAWA*, I, 574; R. Troup to King, Aug. 6, 1798, in *LCK*, II, 391; Stephen Higginson to Pickering, Feb. 22, 1798, in J. Franklin Jameson, ed., "Letters of Stephen Higginson, 1783–1804," *Annual Report of the American Historical Association for the Year 1896* (Washington, 1897), I, 801–2; Page Smith, *John Adams* (Garden City, N.Y., 1962), II, 939, 941–2, 943–5, 950–1, 980, 1006, 1036.

75. The best account of the Baldwin incident is to be found in J. M. Smith, *Freedom's Fetters: The Alien and Sedition Laws and American Civil Liberties* (Ithaca, N.Y., 1956), 270–4.

76. *Annals*, 5th Cong., 855–6, 870, 872, 1145; Bayard, *Speech*, 11–2.

77. John Quincy Adams to John Adams, March 30 and July 7, 1797, in Worthington Chauncey Ford, ed., *Writings of John Quincy Adams* (New York, 1913–17), II, 149, 181.

78. Wolcott, Jr., to Frederick Wolcott, Feb. 27, 1798, in *MAWA*, II, 13.

Chapter 8. *Rally*

1. See Ch. 7, ns 44 and 67.

2. *Annals*, 5th Cong., 516, 1200–1202.

3. *Ibid.*, 1234, 1256–8, 1260, 1264–5.

4. *Ibid.*, 1271–2.

5. *Ibid.*, 1319–20, 1323, 1324, 1333, 1364; Page Smith, *John Adams* (Garden City, N.Y., 1962), II, 957–8.

6. *Annals*, 5th Cong., 1320–1, 1323, 1339; also 1348, 1357, 1367, 1373–4, 1413, 1522.

7. Otis to Jonathan Mason, Jr., March 22, 1798, in Samuel Eliot Morison, *The Life and Letters of Harrison Gray Otis, Federalist, 1765–1848* (Boston, 1913), I, 89, 90; also Wolcott, Jr., to Hamilton, April 5, 1798, in *MAWA*, II, 44–5.

8. *Annals*, 5th Cong., 1358.

9. Quote from Otis to Mason, Jr., March 22, 1798, in Morison, I, 90; see also *Annals*, 5th Cong., 1371.

10. *Ibid.*, 3338, 3339, 3340–1, 3346.

11. *Ibid.*, 3339.

12. *Ibid.*, 3342–3.

13. *Ibid.*, 3341.

14. *Ibid.*, 3339.

15. *Ibid.*, 3344.

16. *Ibid.*, 3343.

17. *Ibid.*, 3352, 3353.

18. *Ibid.*, 3345.

19. *Ibid.*, 3344.

20. *Ibid.*, 3341, 3348.

21. *Ibid.*, 3348, 3349, 3354, 3367.

22. *Ibid.*, 3348, 3354, 3358.

23. *Ibid.*, 3354, 3356.

24. *Ibid.*, quotes from 3348, 3350, 3357; also 3421–3, 3353.

25. *Ibid.*, 3350.

26. *Ibid.*, 3355, 3357, 3364.

27. Jefferson to Madison and to Peter Carr, April 12, 1798, in *WTJ*, VII, 237, 239.

28. Quote from Pickering to King, April 2, 1798, in *LCK*, II, 297, italics removed; also Sedgwick to King, April 9, 1798, *ibid.*, 312.

29. In *A, 1798*, "Sidney" II and III, April 16 and 20, and "Brutus," May 15.

30. In *LCK*, II, 1798, quotes from Pickering to King, April 2, Sedgwick to King, April 9, 297, italics removed, 310, 312–3, and R. Troup to King, June 3, 329.

31. Jefferson to Madison, April 6, and to Monroe, April 19, 1798, in *WTJ*, VII, 236, 240–1.

32. Wm. Hindman to King, April 12, 1798, in *LCK*, II, 314.

33. Jefferson to Monroe, April 19, 1798, in *WTJ*, VII, 241.

34. Jefferson to Madison, May 3, May 10, and May 31, 1798, *ibid.*, 248, 251, 252, 260.

35. *Annals*, 5th Cong., 1433, 1435, 1443, 1510, 1579, 1627–8; Jefferson to Madison, April 12, 26, and May 3, 1798, in *WTJ*, VII, 237, 246, 250.

36. Pickering to King, May 3, Robert Troup to King, June 7, 10, 1798, in *LCK*, II, 321, 329, 345; J. Q. Adams to W. Vans Murray, June 7, 1798, in W. C. Ford, ed., *The Writings of John Quincy Adams* (New York, 1913–17), II, 300.

37. William Austin, ed., *A Selectoin of the patriotic addresses to the President of the United States Together with the President's answers* (Boston, 1798), 21.

38. John Davis to Wolcott, Jr., April 22, Cabot to Wolcott, Jr., April 25, 1798, in *MAWA*, II, 45–6, 48.

39. C. F. Adams, ed., *The Works of John Adams* (Boston, 1850–56), IX, 194, 196. For adverse comment on these addresses: in *A*, 1798, unsigned, May 26, and "A Young Man," June 14.

40. Hamilton to Wolcott, Jr., June 5, 1798, in *MAWA*, II, 50; also William North to Jay, June 6, 1798 in Henry P. Johnston, ed., *The Correspondence and Public Papers of John Jay* (New York, 1890–93), III, 242.

41. In *A*, 1798, "Senex," July 18, and "Nestor" VIII, May 10.

42. The reply is to be found in Adams, IX, 187; "Nestor" IX, in *A*, May 17, 1798.

43. "Senex," in *A*, July 18, 1798; also Adams, IX, 198; Austin, 51–2, 54, 64, 96–7.

44. The idea for a national fast may have originated with Hamilton; Hamilton to Pickering, March 17, 1798, in *WAH*, VIII, 477. None of the published Fast Day Sermons were critical of the Federalist administration, though three of the sermons were either apolitical or at least avoided overt partisan identification: see Jeremy Belknap, *A Sermon, delivered on the 9th of May, 1798* . . . (Boston, 1798); Samuel Miller, *A Sermon* . . . (New York, 1798); Gensham Mendez Seixas, *A Discourse, delivered in the Synagogue in New York* . . . (New York, 1798).

45. John Thayer, *A Discourse, delivered at the Roman Catholic church in Boston, on the 9th of May, 1798* (Boston, 1798); F. Gallagher, *A Sermon preached* . . . *on the 9th of May, 1798* . . . (Charleston, 1798); Seixas. A group of American citizens on the disputed border of Maine listened to a Canadian deliver a sermon: Samuel Andrews, *The True means to avert national judgments. A Sermon upon the solemn fast ordered*

through the states of America, May 9th, 1798 . . . (Boston, 1798).

46. Quote from Ames to Christopher Gore, Feb. 24, 1795, in Seth Ames, ed., *Works of Fisher Ames* (Boston, 1854), I, 168; also Ames to Thomas Dwight, Jan. 7, 1795, *ibid.*, 160.

47. See for instance Samuel Kendal, *A Sermon, delivered on the day of national thanksgiving* . . . (Boston, 1795); Henry Ware, *The Continuance of peace and increasing prosperity a source of consolation and just cause of gratitude to the inhabitants of the United States* . . . (Boston, 1795); John Murray, *The Substance of a thanksgiving sermon, delivered at the Universalist meetinghouse in Boston* . . . (Boston, 1795); Hezekiah Packard, *The Plea of Patriotism. A Sermon, preached in Chelmsford* . . . (Boston, 1795); David Tappan, *Christian Thankfulness explained and enforced* . . . (Boston, 1795); Jedediah Morse, *The present situation of other nations of the world contrasted with our own* . . . (Boston, 1795); David Osgood, *A Discourse, delivered February 19, 1795* . . . (Boston, 1795).

48. In this category might be placed Ezra Sampson, *A Discourse delivered February 19, 1795* . . . (Boston, 1795); John Mellen, *The Great and happy doctrine of liberty* . . . (Boston, 1795); Thomas Baldwin, *A Sermon, delivered February 19, 1795* . . . (Boston, 1795); Joseph Dana, *A Sermon, delivered February 19, 1795* . . . (Newburyport, 1795); John Andrews, *A Sermon, delivered February 19, 1795* . . . (Newburyport, 1795); Thomas Barnard, *A Sermon delivered on the day of national thanksgiving* (Salem, 1795); John Bracken, *The Duty of giving thanks for national blessings* . . . (Richmond, 1795); Samuel Deane, *A Sermon, preached on February 19, 1795* . . . (Portland, 1795); Levi Frisbie, *A Sermon delivered February 19, 1795* . . . (Newburyport, 1795); Pitt Clarke, *On the rise and signalized lot of the united Americans* . . . (Boston, 1795); Ashbel Green, *A Sermon delivered in the second Presbyterian church in the city of Philadelphia* . . . (Philadelphia, 1795); Abiel Holmes, *A Sermon on the freedom and happiness of America* . . . (Boston, 1795); Samuel Eusebius McCorkle, *A Sermon, on the comparative happiness and duty of the United States* . . . (Halifax, N.C., 1795); S. S. Smith, *The Divine goodness to the United States of America* (Philadelphia, 1795); John Tyler, *The Blessings of peace* . . . (Norwich, 1795); Benjamin Wadsworth, *America invoked to praise the Lord* . . . (Salem, 1795); Samuel West, *A Sermon delivered upon the late national thanksgiving* . . . (Boston, 1795); William White, *A Sermon, on the reciprocal influence of civil policy and religious duty* . . . (Philadelphia, 1795).

49. John M'Knight, *The Divine goodness to the United States of*

America . . . (New York, 1795), preface, 12; Ebenezer Bradford, *The Nature and manner of giving thanks to God, illustrated* . . . (Boston, 1795), 35, 18; Joseph Lathrop, *National happiness, illustrated in a sermon, delivered at West Springfield, on the nineteenth of February, 1795* (Springfield, 1795), 19; Thomas Thacher, *A Discourse, delivered at the Third parish in Dedham, 19th February, 1795* . . . (Boston, 1795), 19; Thaddeus Fiske, *Thanksgiving and prayer for public rulers, recommended in a discourse* . . . (Boston, 1795), 9.

50. Dana, 14; Kendal, 10–2; Mellen, 6; Osgood, *Discourse,* 18; West, 19; Baldwin, 21; Morse, *Present situation,* 30; Sampson, 9 ff; Ware, 12.

51. Lathrop, *National happiness,* 18; Bradford, *Nature and manner of giving thanks,* 15.

52. *Ibid.,* 8, 16, 17–8, 19, and *The Nature of humiliation and prayer explained . . . with an appendix, in answer to Dr. Tappan's Remarks on his Thanksgiving sermon* (Boston, 1795), 33.

53. David Tappan, *Christian thankfulness,* 33 ff.

54. Bradford, *Nature of humiliation,* 26, 36–7; see also, *Mr. Thomas Paine's Trial . . . . Dedicated to George Washington* . . . (Boston, 1795), iii ff.

55. Kendal, 22; Holmes, 14; Fiske, 13–14. The one exception was David Osgood, *A Discourse, delivered on the day of annual thanksgiving, November 19, 1795* . . . (Boston, 1795), 22 ff.

56. Charles Crawford, *Observations upon the Revolution in France* . . . (Boston, 1793), 13, 21–2; Joseph Lathrop, *The Happiness of a free government, and the means of preserving it: illustrated in a sermon, delivered in West-Springfield, on July 4th, 1794* . . . (Springfield, 1794), 14; William Linn, *A Discourse, delivered on the 26th of November, 1795; being the day recommended by the governor of the State of New York to be observed as a day of thanksgiving and prayer* . . . (New York, 1795), 22; Fiske, 17 ff; Samuel Stillman, *Thoughts on the French Revolution* . . . (Boston, 1795), 16, 18, 26; M'Knight, 18; Ware, 22; James Malcomson, *A Sermon, preached on the 14th of July, 1794 (being the anniversary of the French Revolution) in the Presbyterian church of Williamsburgh, South Carolina* (Charleston, 1795), 26; Gerry B. Nash, "The American Clergy and the French Revolution," *WMQ,* XXII (1965), 393–9.

57. Bradford, *Nature and manner of giving thanks to God,* 9; David Tappan, *Christian Thankfulness,* 39; Samuel McCorkle, *The Work of God for the French Republic and then her reformation or ruin; or, the novel and useful Experiment of National Deism, to us and all future ages* (Salisbury, N.C., 1798), 40. References to the impact of inflation on the clergy in this period can gleaned from William B. Sprague, *Annals of*

the American Pulpit: or commemorative notices of distinguished American Clergymen . . . (New York, 1857–69), especially I–IV; see also Stephen G. Kurtz, *The Presidency of John Adams* (Philadelphia, 1957), 226–7.

58. Quote from John Davis to Oliver Wolcott, Jr., April 22, 1798, in *MAWA*, II, 46. The sermon that provoked the comment was Tappan's *A Discourse, delivered to the religious society in Brattle-street, Boston . . . on April 5* . . . (Boston, 1798); clerical sensitivity on this score can be seen in William Linn, *Discourses on the Signs of the Times* (New York, 1794), iii–iv; Kendal, 6; A. Green, 20; Henry Cumings, *A Sermon preached at Billerica, June 28, 1795* . . . (Boston, 1796), 17 n; Thomas Worcester, *A Thanksgiving sermon. Delivered November 12, 1795* . . . (Newburyport, 1796), 29.

59. Linn, *Discourse on the Signs of the Times,* 15 ff; A. Green, 19; White, 27; Wadsworth, 30; Mellen, 32; Sampson, 20–1; Tyler, 14–15; Tappan, *Christian thankfulness,* 24, and *A Discourse;* Thacher, 20; Francis Gardner, *A Sermon, delivered on the day of annual Thanksgiving, November 19, 1795* . . . (Leominster, 1796), 15; Belknap, 25–8; James Abercrombie, *A Sermon, preached in Christ Church and St. Peter's, Philadelphia* . . . (Philadelphia, 1798), 27–8; Timothy Dwight, *The Nature and danger of infidel philosophy* . . . (New Haven, 1798), passim; S. E. McCorkle, *A Discourse, on the doctrine and duty of keeping the Sabbath* . . . (Salisbury, N.C., 1798), passim, and *Work of God for the French Republic,* passim; Joseph Lathrop, *God's challenge to infidels to defend their cause* . . . (West-Springfield, 1797), passim; Nathan Strong, *A Sermon, preached on the State fast, April 6th, 1798* . . . (Hartford, 1798); see also Nash, passim.

60. David Tappan, *A Sermon, delivered . . . on occasion of the annual Fast* . . . (Boston, 1793), 27–8, and *Christian Thankfulness,* 38 quote; S. Smith, 34; Sampson, 20–1; see also Bradford, *Nature of humiliation,* 37, for reply.

61. "An Address from the Ministers of the Association in and about Cambridge, at their stated Meeting on the second Tuesday in October, 1796," in *Middlesex Gazette,* Oct. 28, 1796; Abercrombie, 17; McCorkle, *Discourse on the Sabbath,* 8, 9, 30, 41; Asa McFarland, *Duty of people to strengthen the hand of their minister . . . delivered . . . on the 11th of March, 1798* . . . (Concord, 1798), 23–5; Isaac Lewis, *The Political Advantages of Godliness* . . . (Hartford, 1797), 38; Azel Backus, *Absalom's conspiracy; a sermon, preached at the general election at Hartford . . . May 10th, 1798* . . . (Hartford, 1798), 50.

62. Jedediah Morse, *A Sermon, delivered at the new North Church in*

Boston . . . May 9th, 1798, being the day recommended by John Adams . . . (Boston, 1798), 21–2. This identification of the civil and religious struggle was made in less extreme fashion by Abercrombie, passim; S. Andrews, 8-12; Alden Bradford, *Two Sermons, delivered in Wiscasset . . .* (Wiscasset, 1798), passim; Ashbel Green, *Obedience to the laws of God, the sure and indispensable defence of nations . . .* (Philadelphia, 1798), especially 48; William Linn, *A Discourse on national sins . . .* (New York, 1898), 23 ff; John J. Kirkland, *A Sermon, delivered on the 9th of May . . .* (Boston, 1798), 8 ff; Joseph McKeen, *Two discourses, delivered at Beverly . . .* (Salem, 1798), 8 ff; Samuel Osgood, *Some Facts evincive of the atheistical, anarchical and in other respects immoral Principles of the French Republicans* (Boston, 1798), passim; Eliphabet Porter, *A Discourse, delivered at Brookline . . .* (Boston, 1798), 24 ff; John Prince, *A Discourse delivered at Salem . . .* (Salem, 1798), 14, 29 ff; John Wilder, *A Discourse delivered May 9, 1798 . . .* (Wrentham, Mass., 1798), 14, 26. Others contented themselves with making this connection implicitly: Samuel Blair, *A Discourse delivered in the first Presbyterian Church . . .* (Philadelphia, 1798), passim; Gallagher, 10–1; Nathanael Emmons, *National peace, the source of national prosperity . . .* (New York, 1798), 21, 23 ff; James Muir, *A Sermon preached in the Presbyterian church in Alexandria . . .* (Philadelphia, 1798); Samuel Spring, *A Thanksgiving sermon, preached November 29, 1798 . . .* (Newburyport, 1798), 21; see also Robert Gray, *A Sermon delivered at Hopkinton, before the hon. General Court of the State of New Hampshire . . .* (Dover, 1798), 17; Seth Payson, *A Sermon preached at Concord . . . before . . . the Governor . . .* (Portsmouth, 1799), 20; Ezra Weld, *A Discourse delivered April 25, 1799 . . .* (Boston, 1799), 31.

63. Jedediah Morse to Pickering, February 11, 1799, quoted in Vernon Stauffer, *New England and the Bavarian Illuminati* (New York, 1918), 276 n; also 283–4 n, 300–1 n, 303–4, 320.

64. Theodore Dwight, *An Oration spoken at Hartford . . . July 4, 1798 . . .* (Hartford, 1798), 30 n; Zechariah Lewis, *An Oration, on the apparent, and the real political situation of the United States . . .* (New Haven, 1799), 16–7; John Cotton Smith, *An Oration, pronounced at Sharon . . . on the . . . 4th of July . . .* (Litchfield, 1798), 5 ff.

65. John Robison, *Proofs of a Conspiracy against all the religion and governments of Europe, carried on in the secret meetings of free masons, illuminati, and reading societies . . .* 3d ed. (Philadelphia, 1798); Morse, *A Sermon*, 22–3.

66. Timothy Dwight, *Nature and Danger of Infidelity*, 95 n.

67. Morse, *A Sermon*, 18, 20.

68. Timothy Dwight, *The Duty of Americans, at the present crisis, illustrated in a discourse preached on the fourth of July, 1798* . . . (New Haven, 1798), 10 ff; David Tappan, *A Discourse delivered in the chapel of Harvard College, June 19, 1798* . . . (Boston, 1798), 13 ff; Joseph Lathrop, *A Sermon, on the dangers of the times, from infidelity and immorality; and especially from a lately discovered conspiracy, against religion and government* . . . (Springfield, 1798), 14 ff; McCorkle, *Work of God*, iii, 12 ff.

69. See John F. Grimké, *Charge, delivered to the grand juries of Beaufort and Orangeburgh districts* . . . (Charleston, 1798), 4; Joseph Eckley, *A Discourse, delivered on the public Thanksgiving day, November 29, 1798* . . . (Boston, 1798), 18; John Ely, *A Sermon, delivered in the first Presbyterian church in Danbury, November 25, 1798* . . . (Danbury, 1798), 7; Israel Beard Woodward, *American Liberty and independence. A Discourse, delivered at Watertown, on the fourth of July, 1798* . . . (Litchfield, 1798), 19; Alexander Addison, *Rise and Progress of Revolution: A Charge to the Grand juries of the County Courts at the fifth Circuit of the State of Pennsylvania* (Whitehall, Pa., 1801), passim; Peter Eaton, *A Sermon, preached at Boxford, November 28, 1799* . . . (Haverhill, 1799), 12; Payson, 8 ff; Abraham Cummings, *The Present times perilous* . . . (Castine, 1799), 5 ff; Walter Harris, *A Discourse, delivered at Dunbarton, New Hampshire, April 25, 1799* . . . (Concord, 1799), 13 ff; Jedediah Morse, *A Sermon, exhibiting the present dangers and consequent duties of the citizens of the United States of America* . . . (Charlestown, 1799), 15 ff, 36–45; Otis Thompson, *An Oration, urging the necessity of Religion* . . . (Providence, 1798), 7–8.

70. Many of the Fast Day preachers betrayed a sensitivity on this score: Porter, 22; A. Bradford, 2 (second sermon); Linn, *Discourse*, iv; Kirkland, 17–8; Osgood, *Some Facts*, 21; Abercrombie, 4–5; also Samuel Stillman, *A Sermon, preached at Boston, April 25, 1799* . . . (Boston, 1799), 21; Daniel Dana, *Two sermons, delivered April 25, 1799* . . . (Newburyport, 1799), 52; Nathanael Emmons, *A Discourse, delivered on the national fast, April 25, 1799* . . . (Boston, 1799), 12, 17.

71. William Cobbett, *The Cannibal's Progress: or, the dreadful horrors of French invasion, as displayed by the Republican officers and soldiers, in their perfidy, rapacity, ferociousness, and brutality, exercised towards the innocent inhabitants of Germany* (Philadelphia, 1798); Theo., Dwight, 27, 29; J. C. Smith, 14 ff; Josiah Crocker Shaw, *An Oration, delivered July 4th, 1799* . . . (Newport, 1799), 15–6. This was not the first of Cobbett's productions harping on this theme. See *The Bloody Buoy,*

thrown out as a warning to the political pilots of all nations . . . (Philadelphia, 1795), but French atrocities did not occupy a prominent place in Federalist polemics before 1798.

72. Rush's charge can be found in the *Impartial Herald* (Suffield, Conn.), Oct. 16, 1798; Grimké, 8. One oration commemorating the dissolution of the Franco-American Treaty was published in 1799: Edward St. Loe Livermore, *An Oration, in commemoration of the dissolution of the political Union between the United States of America and France* . . . (Portsmouth, 1799); also P. Smith, II, 1106.

73. William Heth, *An Infallible cure, for political blindness, if administered to patients possessing sound minds, honest hearts, and independent circumstances* (Richmond, 1798), 15; Samuel Emerson, *An Oration, pronounced at Kennebunk, on the fourth of July, 1798* . . . (Portland, 1798), 22–3.

74. Abbé Barruel, *Memoirs illustrating the history of jacobinism* . . . (Hartford, New York, Elizabeth-Town, 1799), IV vols.

75. *A Caution; or, Reflections on the Present Contest* . . . (Philadelphia, 1798), attributed to John Dickinson by William G. Sales, "A Reattribution: John Dickinson's Authorship of the Pamphlet 'A Caution' 1798," *PMHB*, LXXVII (1953), 24–31. The pamphlet was answered by "Titus Manlius" IV, in *GUS*, April 19, 1798.

76. Thomas Paine, *Common Sense* . . . (New York, Dolphin ed., n.d.), 31, 51–2; Alexander Hamilton, "Americanus" II, in *WAH*, IV, 277 ff; "A Native American," in *GUS*, March 2, 1798; Strong, 7–8; Heth, 17 ff; *To the Republican citizens of the State of Pennsylvania* (Lancaster, 1800), 7. For Congressional attitudes, see *Annals*, 5th Cong., 1517, 1687–8, 1695–6, 1784.

77. R. G. Harper, *Observations on the Dispute between the United States and France* . . . 3rd ed. (Dublin, 1798), 67 ff; Emerson, 12, 21 ff. France's aggressions against Switzerland generated a refugee literature that was consumed in the American market: David Chauvet, *The Conduct of the government of France toward the Republic of Geneva* . . . (Trenton, 1798), and *Letters of a Genevan* . . . (Philadelphia, 1798); Johann Caspar Lavatar, *Remonstrance, addressed to the executive directory of the French Republic* . . . (New York, 1799); J. Mallet du Pan, *The History of the Destruction of the Helvetic Union and Liberty* (Boston, 1799); Sir Francis d'Ivernois, *d'Ivernois on the downfall of Switzerland* (n.p., 1798). In addition d'Ivernois' earlier *A Short account of the late revolution in Geneva* (1794) was republished in Philadelphia, 1798.

78. John Quincy Adams to William Vans Murray, July 22, 1798, and Feb. 9, 1799, in Ford, II, 343, 386–7; Emerson, 12; Grimké 5; see also

King to Grenville, Jan. 13, and Cabot to King, March 14, 1800, in *LCK*, III, 181, 210.

79. *Annals*, 5th Cong., 1736, 2696–7, 2990, 2992.

80. *Ibid.*, 1744–5, 1995, 2015, 2021–2.

81. *Ibid.*, 334, 1440ff.

82. *Ibid.*, 1466.

83. *Ibid.*, 1476, 1482–6.

84. *Ibid.*, 1495, 1497, 1498, 1501, 1506, 1508.

85. *Ibid.*, 1503, 1521.

86. *Ibid.*, 1631.

87. *Ibid.*, 1537, 1665–6, 1675, 1693, 1756.

88. *Ibid.*, 1683, 1689, 3729.

89. *Ibid.*, 1728, 1729 quote, 1740, 1746, 1760.

90. *Ibid.*, 1732, 1738, 1748, 1751.

91. *Ibid.*, 1735, 1747, 1749, 1755.

92. Fisher Ames to Oliver Wolcott, Jr., April 22, and June 8, and Stephen Higginson to Wolcott, Jr., July 11, 1798, in *MAWA*, II, 47, 51–2, 70; Higginson to Pickering, June 9, 1798, in J. Franklin Jameson, ed., "Letters of Stephen Higginson 1783–1804," *Annual Report of the American Historical Association for the Year 1896* (Washington, 1897), I, 808; Cabot to King, April 16, and King to Hamilton, May 12, 1798, in *LCK*, II, 318, 323; P. Smith, II, 953–5; "Titus Manlius" I & IV, in *GUS*, April 5 and 27, 1798.

93. *Annals*, 5th Cong., 1263, 1365, 1468, 1797.

94. *Ibid.*, 1805 ff.

95. *Ibid.*, 1859 ff.

96. *Ibid.*, 1870.

97. *Ibid.*, 1878.

98. *Ibid.*, 1879–1882, 1886, 1890; Chester M. Destler, *Joshua Coit, American Federalist, 1758–1798* (Middletown, Conn., 1962), 125–6, 128.

99. Quote from Jay to William North, June 25, 1798, in Johnston, IV, 244; [William Pinkney], *A Few remarks on Mr. Hamilton's late letter concerning the public conduct & character of the President . . .* (Baltimore, 1800), 7–8; Wm. Bingham to King, June 5, 1798, in *LCK*, II, 331; see also *supra* ch. III, n. 17.

100. *Annals*, 5th Cong., 1887.

101. Cabot to King, Oct. 6, 1798, in *LCK*, II, 438. Cabot complained that Marshall had reinforced this sentiment with his opinion "that France wou'd declare war as soon as the Dispatches published here shou'd reach Paris." Marshall appears to have played an ambiguous role here: see P. Smith, II, 971, and J. Q. Adams to W. Vans Murray, June 7, 1798, in Ford, II, 301.

102. Pickering to King, June 2, quote from Pickering to King, June 12, 1798, in *LCK*, II, 328, 347; also Jay to North, June 25, 1798, in Johnston, IV, 245.

103. Frederick B. Tolles, "Unofficial Ambassador: George Logan's Mission to France, 1798," *WMQ*, VII (1950), 9.

104. *Annals*, 5th Cong., 3426–33.

105. James M. Smith, *Freedom's Fetters: The Alien and Sedition Laws and American Civil Liberties* (Ithaca, 1956), 58 ff, 193 ff.

106. Quote from King to the Secretary of State, June 6, 1798, in *LCK*, II, 336; also *Annals*, 5th Cong., 2017, 1992.

107. *Ibid.*, 585–6.

108. *Ibid.*, 1916, 1933–54, 3743–4.

109. *Ibid.*, 3739–42, 3744–46.

110. *Ibid.*, 1959–60, 1961, 1969, 1983, 1985, 1986, 1987–9; William Cobbett, *Detection of a conspiracy formed by the United Irishmen . . .* (Philadelphia, 1798), in *Porcupine's Works* (London, 1801), VIII, 197–229.

111. John Adams, "Correspondence originally published in the Boston Patriot," in Adams, IX, 279; P. Smith, II, 977.

112. See comments on the Senate's bill, in Jefferson to Madison, May 31, 1798, *WTJ*, VII, 261–2.

113. Wm. North to Jay, June 22, 1798, in Johnston, IV, 243; Sedgwick to King, July 1, in *LCK*, II, 352; Destler, 127.

114. *Annals*, 5th Cong., 3747–49, 3754–7.

115. A version of the Lloyd bill was published in A, June 28, 1798. John Page felt the Lloyd bill was designed to provoke war with France: *Address to the Freeholders of Gloucester County . . .* (Richmond, 1799), 14, 42; J. M. Smith, 107 ff.

116. *Annals*, 5th Cong., 1504.

117. *Ibid.*, 2116; A, June 28, 1798, and unsigned, Aug. 11, 1798.

118. *Annals*, 5th Cong., 2102–3, 2115–6.

119. The text is in *ibid.*, 3776–7.

120. Sedgwick to King, July 1, 1798, in *LCK*, II, 352; Hamilton to Wolcott, Jr., June 29, 1798, in *MAWA*, II, 68.

Chapter 9. *Rout*

1. *Annals*, 5th Cong., 2539.

2. *Impartial Herald* (Suffield, Conn.), Oct. 9, 1798; R. King to Pickering, Aug. 1, in *LCK*, II, 379.

3. *Annals*, 5th Cong., 3504–9, 3509–10, 3512.

4. *Ibid.*, 3508–9.

5. *Ibid.*, 3513, 3514–6; *Impartial Herald*, Oct. 23, 1798.

6. *Annals*, 5th Cong., 3475–6.

7. Barlow to Watson, July 26, 1798, in *MAWA*, II, 111–2.

8. *Annals*, 5th Cong., 3530–1.

9. Richard Codman to H. G. Otis, Aug. 26, 1798, in S. E. Morison, *The Life and Letters of Harrison Gray Otis, Federalist, 1765–1848* (Boston, 1913), I, 169; Frederick B. Tolles, "Unofficial Ambassador: George Logan's Mission to France, 1798," *WMQ*, VII (1950), 20; Barlow to Washington, Oct. 2, 1798, in Charles Burr Todd, *Life and Letters of Joel Barlow* (New York, 1886), 156–60, quote 157–8.

10. J. Q. Adams to Abigail Adams, Sept. 14, 1798, in W. C. Ford, ed., *Writings of John Quincy Adams* (New York, 1913–17), II, 361; William Vans Murray to Pickering, Sept. 1, and to J. Q. Adams, Sept. 6, 28, Oct. 9, 1798, in W. C. Ford, ed., "Letters of William Vans Murray to John Quincy Adams, 1797–1803," *Annual Report of the American Historical Association for the Year 1912* (Washington, 1914), 463–4, 466–9, 475–6, 480–1. For a summary see James T. Austin, *The Life of Elbridge Gerry* . . . (Boston, 1829), II, 301–2.

11. James Watson to Barlow, Oct. 26, 1798, in *MAWA*, II, 112–3.

12. *Ibid.*, 113–4.

13. *Ibid.*, 114–5.

14. George Clinton, Jr., *An Oration, delivered on the fourth of July 1798* . . . (New York, 1798); Jabez Parkhurst, *An Oration, delivered on the fourth of July, 1798* . . . (Newark, 1798); Thomas Yarrow, *An Oration delivered at Mount Pleasant, New York, July 4, 1798* . . . (Mount Pleasant, N.Y., 1798); also Richard Hillier's oration, in *NYJ*, Aug. 29, 1798.

15. Dissent of a member of the masonic lodge of Orange County, in *NYJ*, Aug. 25, 1798; in *A*, 1798 Address of students of William and Mary College, June 18, Address of the young men of Richmond, June 20, Address of several of the militia of Morris County, June 29, July 14, 1798; and Address of several young men of Newark, July 17; *Annals*, 5th Cong., 1707–8.

16. Report, in *A*, Aug. 1, 1798; in *NYJ*, reports of Aug. 4, and Sept. 4, Instructions of Powhatan County, Va., Nov. 7, Resolves of Dinwiddie County, Va., Dec. 8, Memorial of Essex County, Virginia to the state legislature, Dec. 26, 29, 1798. Some Republicans even insisted on imitating the Federalists by addressing the Republican leader in the House, Gallatin: Addresses of the citizens of Washington and Greene Counties in *ibid.*, Nov. 14, 1798; also Edmund Pendleton, "Address to Citizens of Caroline" [Nov., 1798], in David John Mays, ed., *The Life and Papers of Edmund Pendleton 1734–1804* (Charlottesville, 1967), II, 650–4.

17. King to Pickering, Dec. 7, 1798, in *LCK*, II, 478.

18. Jefferson to Madison, May 31 and June 7, 1798, in *WTJ*, VII, 262, 267; cf. reference, in *NYJ*, Oct. 5, 1799; J. M. Smith, *Freedom's Fetters: The Alien and Sedition Laws and American Civil Liberties* (Ithaca, 1956), 204 ff.

19. *Ibid.*, chap. XI; also Lyon to General Mason, in *NYJ*, Nov. 14, 1798.

20. *Annals*, 5th Cong., 2421.

21. *Ibid.*, 2192–3, 2422, 2438–9

22. *Ibid.*, 3535, 3543 for quotes; these points are made on 3536, 3539, 3544, 3541; Pickering's entire letter runs from 3531–3558.

23. *Ibid.*, 3542–3558, passim, quotes from 3547, 3558. Pickering had actually lifted the last phrase from a letter from King to him, Aug. 17, 1798, *LCK*, II, 392.

24. *Annals*, 5th Cong., 2489.

25. *Ibid.*, 2495, 2504–5.

26. *Ibid.*, 2511–2.

27. *Ibid.*, 2497–8.

28. *Ibid.*, 2518, 2539–40, 2540.

29. *Ibid.*, 2513–4, 2519, 2705.

30. *Ibid.*, 2638, 2641, 2703.

31. *Ibid.*, 2640.

32. *Ibid.*, 2518.

33. *Ibid.*, 2515.

34. *Ibid.*, 2603.

35. *Ibid.*, 2498–9.

36. *Ibid.*, 2495.

37. *Ibid.*, 2501, 2524, 2529–30, 2604.

38. *Ibid.*, 2505, 2507.

39. *Ibid.*, 2615.

40. *Ibid.*, 2605.

41. *Ibid.*, 2624.

42. *Ibid.*, 2641.

43. *Ibid.*, 2640.

44. *Ibid.*, 2710.

45. *Ibid.*, 2711.

46. *Ibid.*, 2715.

47. *Ibid.*, 2716.

48. *Ibid.*, 2719.

49. *Ibid.*, 2516.

50. *Ibid.*, 2495, 2518, 2601.

51. The public's awareness of the progress of Napoleon's expedition can be traced in any newspaper of the period. I have used for this purpose the

CC, July 14, 28, Aug. 8, 18, Sept. 8, 22, Nov. 20, and Dec. 4, 1798; *Impartial Herald*, Oct. 16, 1798.

52. *Impartial Herald*, Dec. 11, 1798; see also J. Q. Adams to Abigail Adams, Sept. 14, 1798 and to W. Vans Murray, Oct. 20, 1798 in Ford, ed., *Writings*, II, 364–5, 376.

53. *Annals*, 5th Cong., 2990–1; see also VR, 128.

54. *Annals*, 5th Cong., 2633, 2992.

55. *Ibid.*, 2494.

56. Most illuminating in this respect was the fight the Republicans were able to put up against the Federalist measure authorizing the President to conclude commercial agreements with France's rebellious colonies in the West Indies, see *ibid.*, 2741–2780.

57. Cabot to Pickering, March 7, 1799, in Henry Cabot Lodge, *Life and Letters of George Cabot* (Boston, 1877), 224; Cabot to King, April 26 and June 2, 1799, in LCK, III, 10, 27.

58. Stephen G. Kurtz, *The Presidency of John Adams* (Philadelphia, 1957), 308, 332–3, 336, 353, 373, 406; Page Smith, *John Adams* (Garden City, N.Y., 1962), II, 1001–2.

59. John Adams, "Correspondence originally published in the Boston Patriot," in C. F. Adams, ed., *The Work of John Adams* (Boston, 1850–56), IX, 268. On the extreme Federalists' desire for alliance with Britain in "liberating" Latin America, see G. Cabot to King, July 2, 1798 and Feb. 16, 1799, King to Pickering, Aug. 17, 1798, and Jan. 10, 1799, in LCK, II, 354, 393–4, 499; Hamilton to King, and to Francisco Miranda, Aug. 22, 1798, and to H. G. Otis, Jan. 26, 1799, in WAH, VIII, 505–7, 524. This subject receives extensive treatment in Manning J. Dauer, *The Adams Federalists* (Baltimore, 1953), ch. XI.

60. Adams, "Correspondence," 278–80, 294; Edmund Pendleton, "An Address of the Honorable Edmund Pendleton of Virginia, to the American Citizens, on the present State of Our Country," in Mays, II, 657–66.

61. Washington to Adams, Feb. 1, 1799, in WGW, XXXVII, 119–20; Barlow to Washington, Oct. 2, 1798, in Todd, 156–60. Adams' feelings about Barlow are revealed in *ibid.*, 161–2; the source of this animosity can be found in *Annals*, 5th Cong., 2962–3; see also *The Second Warning or Strictures on the speech delivered by John Adams, president of the United States of America at the opening of the Congress of said States in November last* (Paris, 1798), attributed to Barlow; Dauer, 238–9.

62. See GUS, March 4, 1799; not content with this indiscretion Fenno followed it with *Desultory reflections on the new political aspects of public affairs . . . since the commencement of the year 1799 . . .* (New York, 1800), Parts I & II. The Republican printer R. T. Rawle promptly repub-

lished Part I in Philadelphia to demonstrate the dangerous nature of Federalist intentions.

63. Cabot to Pickering, March 7, 1799; Sept. 22, 1799, in Lodge, 225–6, 237–8.

64. Quotes from *ibid.*, Cabot to Pickering, March 7, 18, Sept. 5, 1799, 225, 226–7, 234; also Cabot to Wolcott, Jr., and to Pickering, Oct. 16, 245–7, R. King to Pickering, Oct. 11, Dec. 2, in *LCK*, III, 123–4, 151–2.

65. Pickering to Cabot, Feb. 21, 26, and Sept. 13, 1799, in Lodge, 221, 223–4, 235–6, quote from 223.

66. *Annals*, 5th Cong., 2933, 2936, 2944, 3022; Pickering to Cabot, Feb. 21, 1799, in Lodge, 221.

67. *Annals*, 5th Cong., 2933, 2940, 2931, 2877–8, 2947, 2950–1, 2932–3.

68. *Ibid.*, 3046, 3048.

69. Cabot to Pickering, Sept. 5 and Oct. 16, 1799, in Lodge, 234–5, 247.

70. Pickering to Cabot, Sept. 29, 1799, in *ibid.*, 243; also Pickering to Adams, undated, in *MAWA*, II, 265.

71. I rely on Adams' narrative of this event in "Correspondence," 251–3, 271–2, as do other recent accounts: Alexander DeConde, *The Quasi-War: The Politics and Diplomacy of the Undeclared War with France* (New York, 1966), 218–20; P. Smith, II, 1011–7.

72. Cabot to Pickering, Oct. 16 and 31, 1799, in Lodge, 246, 249.

73. George Cabot to Wolcott, Jr., Oct. 16 and Nov. 7, Wolcott, Jr., to Fisher Ames, Dec. 29, 1799, in *MAWA*, II, 284, 286, 314.

74. James McHenry to Washington, Nov. 10, Jedediah Morse to Wolcott, Jr., Nov. 8, Wolcott, Jr., to Fisher Ames, Dec. 29, 1799, in *ibid.*, 232, 287, 314–5.

75. Cabot to Gore, Jan. 21, 1800, in Lodge, 268; also Wolcott, Jr., to Fisher Ames, Dec. 29, 1799, in *MAWA*, II, 314.

76. *Annals*, 6th Cong., 247–506.

77. *Ibid.*, 542–619.

78. See Kathryn Turner, "Federalist Policy and the Judiciary Act of 1801," *WMQ*, XXII (1965), 4–6; John C. Miller, *The Federalist Era, 1789–1801* (New York, 1960), 28–9, 179–80; Jay to Adams, Jan. 2, 1801, in Henry P. Johnston, ed., *The Correspondence and Public Papers of John Jay* (New York, 1890–3), IV, 285.

79. Wolcott, Jr., to Ames, Dec. 29, 1799, in *MAWA*, II, 316. A good secondary account of the Bankruptcy Act can be found in Morton Borden, *The Federalism of James Bayard* (New York, 1955), 62–72.

80. Sedgwick to King, Feb. 6, 1800, in *LCK*, III, 189.

81. *Ibid.*, 189–90.

82. Sedgwick to King, May 11, 1800, in *LCK*, III, 236, 237.

83. For background on the situation in Pennsylvania see Harry Marlin Tinkcom, *The Republicans and Federalists in Pennsylvania, 1790–1801* (Harrisburg, 1950), 244–5; also reports in A, Jan. 27, March 18, 1800; Wolcott, Jr., to Ames, Dec. 29, 1799, in *MAWA*, II, 316.

84. See reports in A, Jan. 17 and 27, 1800; a text of the bill can be found in William Cobbett, *Porcupine's Works* (London, 1801), XII, 35–41; also A, Feb. 19, 1800.

85. *Annals*, 6th Cong., 129, 134–5, 146; also see A, March 11 and 18, 1800.

86. Cobbett, XII, 41.

87. For the Senate's efforts to punish Duane for breach of privilege cf. *Annals*, 6th Cong., 63, 68–96; A, Feb. 21, March 10, 25, 27, 28, and April 1, 1800.

88. For the Federalist defense see *Annals*, 6th Cong., 85–7; the Federalists should have been aware after the Keteltas case in New York that such proceedings would be viewed with intense suspicion. See Alfred F. Young, *The Democratic Republicans of New York: The Origins, 1763–1797* (Chapel Hill, 1967), 482–493; also the warnings of the opposition in *Annals*, 6th Cong., 68, 80, 83.

89. The civil libertarian objection was made strenuously by the opposition in *ibid.*, 69–84; Federalist reservations can be found in Cobbett, XII, 42–4, and Bingham to King, Aug. 6, 1800, in *LCK*, III, 284–5.

90. *Annals*, 6th Cong., 673, 678, 692; A, March 22 and April 1, 1800.

91. Sedgwick to King, May 11, 1800, in *LCK*, III, 237–8.

92. Cf. *Annals*, 6th Cong., 176–7, 179, 670, 691–2, 713; also [Henry W. DeSaussere], *Answer to a dialogue between a Federalist and a Republican* . . . (Charleston, 1800), 28.

93. Tinkcom, 245–54.

94. A, Feb. 15 and 19, 1800.

95. *Ibid.*, May 13, 15 and 16.

96. *Ibid.*, Feb. 17, 1800; James McHenry to John McHenry, May 20, 1800, in *MAWA*, II, 314–5, 347; Gore to King, May 5, in *LCK*, III, 232; [Tunis Wortman], *A Solemn address to Christians and patriots, upon the approaching election of a president of the United States* . . . (New York, 1800), 31–2; *Annals*, 6th Cong., 704.

97. James McHenry to Wolcott, Jr., Jan. 22, 1801, in *MAWA*, II, 469.

98. Cabot to Wolcott, Jr., June 14, 1800, in *MAWA*, II, 370; see also Ames to Goodrich, June 12, Richard Stockton to Wolcott, Jr., June 27, and Cabot to Wolcott, Jr., Aug. 23 and Nov. 28, *ibid.*, 366–7, 375, 406,

449–50; Pickering to King, May 7, Ames to King, Aug. 19 and 26, in *LCK*, III, 232, 295–6; Cabot to Hamilton, Aug. 23, in Lodge, 286. Hamilton had reservations about this strategy from the beginning: see Hamilton to Sedgwick, May 10, in *WAH*, VIII, 552, in which Wolcott, Jr., concurred; Wolcott, Jr., to Ames, Aug. 10, in *MAWA*, II, 401. For secondary accounts of this friction see Kurtz, 392 ff, and Dauer, ch. XVI.

99. Wolcott, Jr., to Goodrich and Cabot to Wolcott, Jr., July 20, 1800, in *MAWA*, II, 382, 383–4; Ames to King, Aug. 26, in *LCK*, III, 297. For the Alexandria Address and Reply of June 11, 1800, see *Middlesex Gazette*, June 27.

100. Hamilton to Wolcott, Jr., July 1, Ames to Wolcott, Jr., Aug. 10, 1800, in *MAWA*, II, 376, 400–1; Hamilton to Wolcott, Jr., Aug. 3, and Sept. 26, in *WAH*, VIII, 558, 563.

101. Hamilton, "The Public Conduct and Character of John Adams, Esq., President of the United States" (1800), *WAH*, VI, 391–444; the pages which make the above point are 392, 442–4.

102. Adams, "Correspondence," 293; John Quincy Adams thought Hamilton was trying to influence South Carolina in naming electors; see "Reply to the Appeal of the Massachusetts Federalists," in Henry Adams, ed., *Documents relating to New England Federalism* (Boston, 1877), 151. Also Hamilton to Wolcott, Jr., Sept. 25, 1800, in *WAH*, VIII, 563–4; Troup to King, Nov. 9, in *LCK*, III, 330–1.

103. For the Republican reaction to this controversy see James Cheetham, *An Answer to Alexander Hamilton's letter concerning the public conduct and character of John Adams . . .* (New York, 1800); Federalist dissent was registered in [William Pinkney], *A Few remarks on Mr. Hamilton's late letter, concerning the public conduct & character of the President . . .* (Baltimore, 1800); *A Reply to Alexander Hamilton's letter concerning the public conduct and character of John Adams . . . By a Federal Republican* (New York, 1800); [Noah Webster, Jr.], *A Letter to General Hamilton, occasioned by his letter to President Adams. By a Federalist* (New York, 1800).

Chapter 10. *Competition*

1. *GUS*, Dec. 23, 1795.

2. *Annals*, 5th Cong., 1256 ff, 1350, 1352, 1470; see also Edmund Pendleton, "Address to the Citizens of Caroline," [Nov. 1798], in D. J. Mays, ed., *The Letters and Papers of Edmund Pendleton, 1734–1803* (Charlottesville, 1967), II, 652.

3. *Annals*, 5th Cong., 1797–8, 1800–2.

4. *Ibid.*, 1803.

5. *Ibid.*, 1815.

6. *Ibid.*, 1817, 1820, 1828, 1831.

7. *Ibid.*, 1802, 1807, 1809, 1815 ff.

8. *Ibid.*, 1827–35.

9. *Ibid.*, 1500–1, 1508.

10. *Ibid.*, 1712.

11. *Ibid.*, 2162.

12. Address of the freeholders of Prince Edward County, Virginia, in *Impartial Herald* (Suffield, Conn.), Nov. 6, 1798, and Pickering's reply of Sept. 29, in *GUS*, Oct. 9, 1798.

13. *Annals*, 5th Cong., 2885.

14. *Ibid.*, 2886, 2887, 2891.

15. *Ibid.*, 2985–93, esp. 2986–91.

16. Virginia Resolutions of December 21, 1798, in *WJM*, VI, 330–1; Ethelbert Dudley Warfield, *The Kentucky Resolutions of 1798: An Historical Study*, 2d ed. (New York, 1894), 82, 84–5.

17. Quotes from *ibid.*, 78, 82–3; see also 79, 80, and *VR*, 150.

18. *VR*, 23; Warfield, 83.

19. Madison to Hayne, April 3 or 4, 1830, in *WJM*, IX, 383–94 n; James Morton Smith, "The Grass Roots Origins of the Kentucky Resolutions," *WMQ*, XXVII (1970), 222; William W. Freehling, *Prelude to Civil War: The Nullification Controversy in South Carolina, 1816–1836* (New York, 1966), 207–10.

20. Adrienne Koch and Harry Ammon, "The Virginia and Kentucky Resolutions: An Episode in Jefferson's and Madison's Defense of Civil Liberties," *WMQ*, V (1948), 157 ff; Jefferson's draft of this part of the resolutions can be found in *WTJ*, VII, 301; see also Freehling, 208–9; Smith, "Kentucky Resolutions," 239; Madison to Everett, Sept. 10, 1830, in *WJM*, IX, 395 n.

21. A bill to protect the people of Kentucky in the exercise of their constitutional rights" was voted down by the state legislature. See Smith, "Kentucky Resolutions," 241, 244, 245. The best account of the Callender trial is in his *Freedom's Fetters: The Alien and Sedition Laws and American Civil Liberties* (Ithaca, N.Y., 1956), 334–58.

22. Freehling, 260–75.

23. Iredell to his wife, Jan. 24, 1799, in Griffith J. McRee, *Life and Correspondence of James Iredell . . .* (New York, 1851), II, 543; see also extract from a Richmond letter, in *GUS*, Jan. 26, 1799; *VR*, 103.

24. *Annals*, 5th Cong., 2430; see also *VR*, 30.

25. *VR*, 171.

26. *Ibid.*, 30, 103, 104, 107, 140; [Henry Lee], *Plain Truth: addressed to the people of Virginia* . . . (Richmond [?], 1799), 2, 12–3, 15; Alexander Addison, *Analysis of the report of the committee of the Virginia Assembly on the proceedings of sundry of the other States in answer to their resolutions* (Philadelphia, 1800), 8.

27. Koch and Ammon, 163; see also Manning J. Dauer, "The Two John Nicholases: their relationship to Washington and Jefferson," *American Historical Review*, XLV (1940), 338–48, though a conclusive identification is impossible on the basis of the evidence available.

28. *VR*, 113; also Madison, "Report," in *WJM*, VI, 402–3.

29. *VR*, 113; also "Defence of the Virginia Assembly against the Charges of 'Plain Truth,'" VI, from *Richmond Enquirer*, reprinted in *NYJ*, May 11, 1799.

30. Philip G. Davidson, "Virginia and the Alien and Sedition Laws," *American Historical Review*, XXXVI (1931), 339–42.

31. "Defence of the Virginia Assembly against the Charges of 'Plain Truth'" V, in *NYJ*, April 17, 1799; *Annals*, 5th Cong., 2802; George Nicholas, *A Letter from George Nicholas of Kentucky, to his friend in Virginia, Justifying the conduct of the citizens of Kentucky* . . . (Philadelphia, 1799), 29–30; Hamilton's intentions toward Virginia were made plain in Hamilton to J. Dayton [?], 1799, in *WAH*, VIII, 521.

32. *VR*, 113, 114.

33. *Ibid.*, 170; Addison, *Analysis*, 16.

34. *VR*, 71.

35. Addison, *Analysis*, 8; *Observations on a letter from George Nicholas; of Kentucky; to his friend in Virginia* (Cincinnati, 1799), 27–8.

36. *VR*, 76, 80.

37. Madison, "Report," in *WJM*, VI, 351.

38. *VR*, 95; also 114, 152.

39. Madison, "Report," in *WJM*, VI, 352; see also unsigned from the *Albany Register*, in *IC*, Feb. 21, 1799.

40. *VR*, 81, 108, 141.

41. *Ibid.*, 38, 173.

42. *Ibid.*, 53.

43. Report of the trial of Abijah Adams, in *IC*, April 25, 1799; *VR*, 55.

44. *Ibid.*, 43; also Jacob E. Cooke, ed., *The Federalist* (Cleveland, 1961), 169, 179–80, 199, 305, 359, 582–3; Madison, "Report," in *WJM*, VI, 405.

45. *VR*, 98, 121; also 41, 54, 93.

46. Madison, "Report," in *WJM*, VI, 402–3.

47. *VR*, 42, 97, 114.

48. Warfield, 111–5; seven state replies appear in *VR*, 168–77; they should be supplemented by those in Frank Maloy Anderson, "Contemporary Opinion of the Virginia and Kentucky Resolutions," *American Historical Review*, V (1899–1900), 245–9.

49. Carl E. Prince, *New Jersey's Jeffersonian Republicans: The Genesis of an Early Party Machine, 1789–1817* (Chapel Hill, 1967), 35.

50. *GUS*, Jan. 29, 1799; also *IC*, Feb. 7, 1799; Governor Johnston to Iredell, Dec. 23 and 30, 1798, in McRee, II, 542; Koch and Ammon, 155, 167; see also Madison to Jefferson, Dec. 29, 1799, in *WJM*, VI, 343 n.

51. Anderson, 236.

52. The phrase is taken from Sedgwick to King, Jan. 20, 1799, in *LCK*, II, 518.

53. Anderson, 45–63, 225–44; also the series "Defence of the Virginia Assembly against the Charges of 'Plain Truth,'" in *NYJ*, April 17, 1799 ff; Prince, 34–5.

54. Addison, 4.

55. The phrase is Gallatin's from *Annals*, 5th Cong., 2514.

56. *Ibid.*, 1482 ff.

57. *Ibid.*, 1497, 1501, 1506.

58. *A*, June 16 and 22, 1798; also "Truth," in *CC*, July 7, 1798.

59. *GUS*, June 16, 18, and 22, 1798; *Annals*, 5th Cong., 1972–3; Stephen Higginson to Pickering, June 25 and 26, 1798, in J. Franklin Jameson, "Letters of Stephen Higginson, 1783–1804," *Annual Report of the American Historical Association for the Year 1896* (Washington, 1897), I, 812–3, 814; a good secondary account is to be found in Smith, *Freedom's Fetters*, 194–5.

60. See Bache's account in *A*, June 25, 1798; Smith, *Freedom's Fetters*, 196.

61. *Ibid.*, 196–9; quote from William Cobbett, *Porcupine's Works* (London, 1801), VIII, 245.

62. See Stephen Higginson to Wolcott, Jr., July 11 and 13, 1798, in *MAWA*, II, 70, 72.

63. See ch. IX, ns, 41–3.

64. I have relied here on the account of Alexander DeConde, *The Quasi-War: The Politics and Diplomacy of the Undeclared War with France* (New York, 1966), 189–90; see also Benjamin Austin, Jr., *Constitutional Republicanism in opposition to fallacious federalism . . .* (Boston, 1803), 70.

65. Vernon Stauffer, *New England and the Bavarian Illuminati* (New York, 1918), 241–2, 254–5.

66. *Ibid.*, 258–9, 268; see also Joseph Lathrop, *A Sermon, on the*

dangers of the times, from infidelity and immorality; and especially from a lately discovered conspiracy against religion and government . . . (Springfield, 1798), 24.

67. *CC,* Jan. 5, 1799; Stauffer, 278–9.

68. William Bentley, *Extracts from professor Robison's "Proofs of a Conspiracy"* (Boston, 1799), 4, 6, 10, 11, 20.

69. Jedediah Morse, *A Sermon, exhibiting the present dangers, and consequent duties of the citizens of the United States of America . . .* (Charlestown, 1799); Stauffer, 289 ff. The scorn with which Morse's effort was received can be gauged from Austin, Jr., 74–9; and in *IC,* "Credulity," May 16, and "A friend to a Real Clergyman, and Enemy to Bigotry," May 27 and 30, 1799.

70. This episode is recounted in full by Stauffer, 313–8; Austin, Jr., 117–21.

71. *Ibid.,* 72 ff; Alexander Addison, *Rise and progress of revolution: a charge to the Grand Juries of the County Courts of the Fifth Circuit of the State of Pennsylvania, at December sessions, 1800* (Whitehall, Pa., 1801); John Wood, *A Letter to Alexander Addison . . . . In answer to his Rise and progress of revolution . . .* (Philadelphia, 1801).

72. Jefferson to Mazzei, April 24, 1796, and to Madison, Aug. 3, 1797, *WTJ,* VII, 74–6 and n, 165–6; Tench Coxe, *Strictures upon the letter imputed to Mr. Jefferson, addressed to Mr. Mazzei* (n.p., 1800), 4; the various texts are reproduced in Howard R. Marraro, "The Four Versions of Jefferson's Letter to Mazzei," *WMQ,* 2d Ser., XXII (1942), 18–29.

73. The letter first appeared in the American papers in May 1797, with an invitation to Jefferson to disavow it as a forgery, *CC,* May 10, 1797; for subsequent comment see *ibid.:* unsigned and "One of the American People," May 31, Communication, July 26, "One of the People," July 29, 1797; unsigned, in *GUS,* Jan. 16, 1798; Marraro, 20–2.

74. For reference to the Mazzei letter in the campaign of 1800, cf. Claudius Herrick, *An Oration, delivered at Deerfield, on the fourth of July, 1800 . . .* (Greenfield, Mass., 1800), 7–9; "Decius" VII, in *CC,* July 26, 1800; *GUS,* July 3 and Aug. 14, 1800, as referred to in Marraro, 22–3; Henry William DeSaussere, *Answer to a dialogue between a Federalist and a Republican . . .* (Charleston, 1800), 17–20, and *Address to the citizens of South Carolina, on the approaching election . . .* (Charleston, 1800), 10–13; also Charles O. Lerche, Jr., "Jefferson and the Election of 1800: A Case Study in the Political Smear," *WMQ,* V (1948), 477–9.

75. Coxe, 4–6.

76. *Ibid.,* 7–8; a copy of Adams to Coxe, May 1792, is in *MAWA,* II, 424; see also in this connection Adams to Thomas Pinckney, Oct. 27, 1800,

in *ibid.*, 425-6; *To the Republican citizens of Pennsylvania* (Lancaster, Pa., 1800), 16.

77. Coxe, 7 ff; also [Jonathan Russell], *To the freemen of Rhode Island* (Providence, n.d.), 3; *To the people of Cecil* (Wilmington, 1800), II, 4-5; the idelogical case against Adams was further strengthened after the publication of Coxe's *Strictures* by an incident in New Haven, where he had been heard to say that "he did not believe the United States could exist as a nation, unless the Executive was hereditary"; Timothy Phelps to Wolcott, Jr., Sept. 18, 1800, in *MAWA*, II, 419; *To the Republican citizens of Pennsylvania*, 7.

78. "Decius," XIII, in *CC*, Aug. 27, 1800; DeSaussere, *Answer to a Dialogue*, 21-2; also Gouverneur Morris to King, June 4, 1800, in *LCK*, III, 252.

79. *Annals*, 3d Cong., 924.

80. *Ibid.*, 926.

81. See "Aristides," from the *Connecticut Courant*, in *Middlesex Gazette*, Oct. 3, 1800; "An Enemy to Sedition," in *ibid.*, Sept. 12, 1800.

82. For Federalist efforts in this direction see *The Claims of Thomas Jefferson to the presidency, examined at the bar of Christianity—By a Layman* (Philadelphia, 1800); also Henry Lee, *Funeral oration [on the death of Washington, delivered December 26, 1799, and published by order of Congress]* (Philadelphia, 1800); Herrick, 13, 19; David Hale, *An Oration, pronounced before the honorable justices of the Supreme Judicial Court . . . and the citizens of Portland . . . July 4, 1800 . . .* (Portland, 1800), 13; Cushing Otis, *An Oration, pronounced at Scituate, July 4, 1800 . . .* (Boston, 1800), 16; Benjamin Parsons, *An Oration, delivered at Chesterfield, on the 4th of July, 1800* (Northampton, Mass., 1800), 9-11; Luther Richardson, *An Oration, pronounced July 4, 1800, at the re-request of the inhabitants of the town of Roxbury . . .* (Boston, 1800), 12; "The Creed of a Full Blooded Jacobin," in *CC*, Aug. 27, 1800.

83. William Linn, *Serious considerations on the election of a president; addressed to the citizens of the United States* (New York, 1800); John Mason, *The Voice of warning, to Christians, on the ensuing election of a president of the United States . . .* (New York, 1800); see also the less widely circulated orations of clergymen: Chauncey Lee, *The Tree of knowledge of political good and evil . . . Delivered at Colebrook [Conn.] . . . July 4, 1800* (Bennington, 1800); Robert Fowle, *An Oration delivered at Plymouth, in New Hampshire . . . July 4th, 1800 . . .* (Concord, 1800).

84. Linn, 5-13, 14-17; Mason, 8-17, 19-20, 22.

85. Mason, 19; Linn, 17.

86. Linn, 19; Mason, 20.

87. Mason, 20, 29; Linn, 33; also *Claims of Thomas Jefferson to the presidency*, 36–39.

88. Mason, 20; Linn, 25–6; *Claims of Thomas Jefferson to the presidency*, 45, 47; Federalist assumptions about the way public opinion was formed were most clearly outlined by Joseph McKean, *A Sermon, preached before the . . . Council . . . of Massachusetts, May 28, 1800, being a day of general election . . .* (Boston, 1800).

89. A public party given for Jefferson one Sunday in July, 1798 at Fredricksburg provided some basis for these anxieties, and was given considerable publicity by the Federalists. Mason, 31–2, Linn, 28; "Censor Morum," in *Middlesex Gazette*, Oct. 3, 1800.

90. John Smalley, *On the evils of a weak government, A Sermon, preached on the general election at Hartford, in Connecticut, May 8, 1800* (Hartford, 1800), 39–40.

91. DeWitt Clinton, *A Vindication of Thomas Jefferson; against the charges contained in a pamphlet entitled, "Serious Considerations" . . .* (New York, 1800); Tunis Wortman, *A Solemn address, to Christians and patriots, upon the approaching election of a president of the United States: in answer to a pamphlet, entitled, "Serious considerations" . . .* (New York, 1800); *Serious facts, opposed to "Serious Considerations": or, the voice of warning to religious Republicans . . .* (n.p., 1800); also Samuel Knox, *A Vindication of the Religion of Mr. Jefferson . . .* (Baltimore, 1800).

92. Clinton, 18–21, 34; Wortman, 27–8; Knox, 4–7, 8, 11 ff; *To the Republican citizens of Pennsylvania*, 6; *To the People of Cecil*, II, 5–6. The issue was raised in the Kentucky Resolutions of 1798; see Warfield, 77–8. See also Ch. IV, n 45.

93. Wortman, 3, 11, 12, 13, 35.

94. *Ibid.*, Introduction, 5–8; Clinton, 4, 41–2; Knox, 15 ff.

95. *Serious facts*, 10; the author of this pamphlet also insinuated that Adams was a deist, *ibid.*, 14; Clinton, 12, went on to point out the inconsistency between Linn's association with Hamilton, a confessed adulterer, and his condemnation of Jefferson.

96. In this connection I have found Cedric B. Cowing, "Sex and Preaching in the Great Awakening," *American Quarterly*, XX (1968), 624–44 particularly suggestive; see also Prince, 9.

97. Lerche, passim; James M. Banner, Jr., *To the Hartford Convention: The Federalists and the Origins of Party Politics in Massachusetts, 1789–1815* (New York, 1970), 23; Linda K. Kerber, *Federalists in Dissent: Imagery and Ideology in Jeffersonian America* (Ithaca, 1970), 13–5; also

Malcolm C. Clark, "Federalism at High Tide: The Election of 1796 in Maryland," *Maryland Historical Magazine*, LXI (1966), 220.

98. Banner, 13, 45–6, 99 ff; for the attitude of the New England elite toward westward migrants see Purcell, 91. The success of the Federalists in appealing to local prejudices against other areas was enhanced by the notion that New England was under attack from the rest of the nation; see Theodore Dwight, *Oration delivered at New Haven on the 7th of July, 1801* (Suffield, Conn., 1801), 6 ff. A variant on this theme was to persuade the smaller states they were threatened by the larger ones in the election of 1800; see *Address to the citizens of the county of Morris* (Morristown, 1800), broadside listed as Evans 36770.

99. J. W. Fenno, in *GUS*, March 4, 1799; and Sedgwick's bitter comments on the press in his "Farewell Address of Sedgwick to his constituents," in *A*, June 20, 1800. For a retrospective view see Ezra Witter, *Two Sermons on the party spirit . . .* (Wilbraham, Mass., 1801), Sermon I, 8–10; also Donald A. Stewart, *The Opposition Press of the Federalist Period* (Albany, 1969).

100. The best account of the enforcement of the Sedition Act during the election of 1800 is in Smith, *Freedom's Fetters*, 277–417.

101. *Ibid.*, 284–6.

102. *Ibid.*, 316–7; this incident received unusual publicity thanks to the publication of *An Account of the Trial of Thomas Cooper, of Northumberland; on a charge of libel against the President of the United States . . .* (Philadelphia, 1800); see also *Annals*, 6th Cong., 922, 930; Wortman, 30.

103. Smith, *Freedom's Fetters*, 346–54; *Annals*, 6th Cong., 952, 965–6.

104. The ballots cast by the electoral college in the election of 1796 are reported in *Annals*, 4th Cong., 2096–7; *A Vindication of the general ticket law, passed by the Legislature of Virginia, on the 18th day of January, 1800 . . .* (Richmond, 1800), 7, 9 n; Letter of two county representatives in Virginia to their constituents, in *A*, February 24, 1800.

105. "Republican," in *A*, September 20, 1797; unsigned, in *ibid.*, July 19, 1797; Prince, 43.

106. On early nomination procedures cf. George D. Luetscher, *Early Political Machinery in the United States . . .* (Philadelphia, 1903), 63–67; Frederick W. Dallinger, *Nominations for Elective Office in the United States* (New York, 1897), 4–5, 12. On the advantages cliques had in enlarged constituencies cf. Prince, 8. The ideal of free elections did not have that much force in Pennsylvania, see the election circular of 1796 reproduced in Noble E. Cunningham, Jr., *The Jeffersonian Republicans: The Formation of Party Organization* (Chapel Hill, 1957), 112.

107. These objections are taken from the Federalist broadside, *An*

Address to the voters for election of President and Vice President (Richmond?, 1800), listed in Evans as 36773; also *A Vindication of the general ticket law,* 10 ff.

108. Letter of two county representatives in Virginia to their constituents, in *A,* February 24, 1800; *Vindication,* passim. John Nicholas, a Virginia member of the House of Representatives, did propose a constitutional amendment that would have made the district election of Presidential electors uniform throughout the nation, see *Annals,* 6th Cong., 627–8; Projections of what the results of such an election would have been in 1800 can be found in *To the People of Cecil,* III, 3–5; [Robert Goodloe Harper], *Bystander; or a series of letters on . . . the "legislative choice" of electors in Maryland: in which the constitutional right to a legislative choice in that state, and the necessity of adopting it . . . in order to counter act a president from being elected by the minority . . .* (Baltimore, 1800), 9–14.

109. *Vindication,* 15; see for instance *The Honourable Mr. Sedgwick's political last will and testament . . .* (From a Republican press, Stockbridge[?], 1800), 3, 7.

110. *An Address,* Evans 36773; "A Federalist," in *CC,* March 22, 1800; "'Laocoon" I, from *Boston Gazette,* in Seth Ames ed., *Works of Fisher Ames* (Boston, 1854), II, 115–6; in *MAWA,* II, 403, 418, Ames to Wolcott, Jr., Aug. 10, Wolcott, Jr. to Hamilton, Sept. 3, 1800. The most graphic example of the disadvantages under which Republican challengers were forced to work in the election of 1800 came in the case of New Jersey, where their foothold in the state legislature was too slim to be useful and where to coordinate activities for state and Congressional elections they had laboriously to construct local organizations from the grass roots and to call a state nominating convention to hold their insecure organization together as well as to give their candidates publicity; see Prince, 27–8, 58 ff. The disadvantage could be reversed, as it was briefly in Massachusetts by the indiscreet disclosure of the Federalist congressional caucus in an effort to hold New England Federalists to an Adams-Pinckney ticket; see Austin, Jr., 87–9.

111. The historian who makes this inference most explicitly is Edward G. Roddy, "Maryland and the Presidential Election of 1800," *Maryland Historical Magazine,* LVI (1961), 249. The notion that the Republican victory in 1800 was largely due to technique became central to Federalist mythology because it not only offered an attractive explanation for Federalist failures but provided the excuse for the unscrupulous resort to countertechnique after the election of 1800; see Dwight, 5. This Federalist pretense has deeply colored the interpretations of the struggle between Fed-

eralists and Republicans, though in different ways, in such recent works as David Hackett Fischer's *Revolution in American Conservatism* . . . (New York, 1965); and Stewart, *Opposition Press.*

112. Dallinger, 14–16; Cunningham, 162 ff.

113. Banner, 226–7. There was pressure for this action long before the congressional caucus: see *CC,* Feb. 8, 1800.

114. Cunningham, 147.

115. Wolcott, Jr., to Ames, Aug. 10, 1800, in *MAWA,* II, 404; quote from *Address to the citizens of Kent, on the approaching elections* . . . (Wilmington, Del., 1800), 11; [Harper], passim; *To the people of Cecil* . . . , passim; also Roddy, 252 ff; Frank A. Cassell, "General Samuel Smith and the Election of 1800," *Maryland Historical Magazine,* LXIII (1968), 343, 345.

116. Ch. IX, n 83.

117. Delbert H. Gilpatrick, *Jeffersonian Democracy in North Carolina: 1789–1816* (New York, 1931), 122.

118. Cassell, 343–5; Prince, 41–2, 54; Bingham to King, March 5, 1800, in *LCK,* III, 205; Harry Marlin Tinkcom, *The Republicans and Federalists in Pennsylvania, 1790–1801* (Harrisburg, 1950), 245 ff; Purcell, 149–52; John H. Wolfe, "Jeffersonian Democracy in South Carolina," *James Sprunt Studies in History and Political Science,* XXIV (1940), 140 ff; also *To the citizens of the United States, and particularly to the citizens of New York, New Jersey, Delaware and Pennsylvania, Maryland and North Carolina, on the propriety of choosing Republican members to their State legislatures* . . . (New York, n.d.).

119. Ch. V, n 37; also Ames to Wolcott, Jr., Aug. 10, 1800, in *MAWA,* II, 404.

120. William A. Robinson, *Jeffersonian Democracy in New England* (New York, 1916), 38, 54–5, 57, 58, 64; Fischer, 69, 86, 90; Banner, 250. This Federalist strategy proved counter-productive in a state like New Jersey, see J. R. Pole, "Jeffersonian Democracy and the Federalist Dilemma in New Jersey 1798–1812," *Proceedings of the New Historical Society,* LXXIV (1956), 260–92.

Part VI. *Resolution*

1. Reprinted as, "A Letter, containing a short view of the political principles and systems of the Federalists, and of the situation in which they found and left the government," *Selected Works of Robert Goodloe Harper* . . . (Baltimore, 1814), I, 325 ff.

2. *Ibid.*, 335, 337, 339.

3. *Ibid.*, 326, 350.

4. This assessment of the Federalist achievements has been advanced by John C. Miller, *The Federalist Era: 1789–1801* (New York, 1960), esp. 227–8; also Shaw Livermore, Jr., *The Twilight of Federalism: The Disintegration of the Federalist Party 1815–1830* (Princeton, 1962), viii–ix, 14–6. Recently a new twist has been given to the convergence theory by David Hackett Fischer, *The Revolution of American Conservatism: The Federalist Party in the era of Jeffersonian Democracy* (New York, 1965); and Marshall Smelser, *The Democratic Republic: 1801–1815* (New York, 1968), 321–2; both of whom suggest that instead of the Republicans emulating the Federalists, it was the Federalists who emulated the Republicans.

5. Harper, 325.

6. Livermore, 8; Fischer, 16, 19, 25, 31 ff.

Chapter 11. *Repudiation*

1. William Livingston et al., *The Independent Reflector; Or Weekly Essays on Sundry Important Subjects More Particularly Adopted to the Province of New York*, Milton M. Klein, ed. (Cambridge, Mass., 1963), 336–42, for a summary of colonial attitudes about the press; also Sir William Blackstone, *Commentaries on the Laws of England* (Philadelphia, 1771–2), IV, 151–3. I have analyzed colonial notions about the function of juries in my "Studies in the Political Ideas of the American Revolution" (unpublished Ph.D. thesis, Harvard, 1962), 124–40; on legislative and mob control of the press I draw on my "Freedom of the Press in Revolutionary Thought," a paper presented at the OAH, Kansas City, April 1965. See also Harold L. Nelson, "Seditious Libel in Colonial America," *American Journal of Legal History*, III (1959), 163–4; Alden Bradford, ed., *Speeches of the Governors of Massachusetts from 1765 to 1775* (Boston, 1818), 119.

2. The inconsistency of the colonists in this regard has been stressed by Leonard W. Levy, *Legacy of Suppression: Freedom of Speech and Press in Early American History* (Cambridge, Mass., 1960), vii, 16, 18–87 *passim;* on privilege see Mary Patterson Clarke, *Parliamentary Privilege in the American Colonies* (New Haven, 1943), and [John Hatzell, ed.], *Precedents and Proceedings in the House of Commons with observations,* 3d ed. (London, 1796), I.

3. *Annals*, 5th Cong., 2146.

4. *Ibid.*, 2167; see also 2988; Alexander Addison, *Liberty of speech and of the press. A Charge to the grand juries of the County Courts of the fifth circuit of the State of Pennsylvania* (Albany, 1798), 8.

5. *Address of the fifty-eight Federal members of the Virginia legislature to their fellow citizens, in January, 1799* (Augusta, Me., 1799), 25.

6. *IC*, June 6, 1799.

7. *Annals*, 5th Cong., 2892; *Observations on the Alien and Sedition Laws of the United States* (Washington, Pa., 1799), 8–9; VR, 105, 133, 134.

8. Paul L. Ford, ed., *Pamphlets on the Constitution of the United States, published during its discussion by the People* (Brooklyn, 1888), 9, 48, 76, 113, 156, and *Essays on the Constitution of the United States, published during its discussion by the people* (Brooklyn, 1892), 164, 239; *Annals*, 1st Cong., 731 ff.

9. Massachusetts sedition prosecutions in connection with Shays's Rebellion are referred to in *IC*, April 11, 1799; *Candid considerations on libels* (Boston, 1789), 5, 13, 14–5, 18, 20.

10. *Ibid.*, 17 ff; *Annals*, 3d Cong., 915, 932, 940; 5th Cong., 2109, 2133–4, 2143, 2164; 6th Cong., 923; James Ogilvie, *A Speech delivered in Essex County in support of a Memorial presented to the citizens of that County and now laid before the Assembly, on the subject of the Alien and Sedition acts* (Richmond, 1798), 6, 8.

11. *Annals*, 5th Cong., 2135.

12. Leonard W. Levy, ed., *Freedom of the Press from Zenger to Jefferson* (New York, 1966), 158–70; also Alfred F. Young, *The Democratic Republicans of New York: Origins, 1763–1797* (Chapel Hill, 1967), 480–9. These same objections were raised against the Senate's efforts to punish Duane for breach of privilege; see *Annals*, 6th Cong., 68 ff, esp. 81.

13. Analogies with the revolutionary period were made by [Thomas Evans], *An Address to the People of Virginia, respecting the alien and sedition laws* (Richmond, 1798), 47, Appendix, ii; also *Annals*, 5th Cong., 2096, 2146, 2164–71, 2992. Such analogies were challenged by the Republican writer St. George Tucker, *A Letter to a member of Congress, respecting the Alien and Sedition Laws* (n.p., 1799), 38.

14. *Annals*, 5th Cong., 2093–4.

15. *Ibid.*, 2094–6, 2097, 2098, 2100.

16. *Ibid.*, 2161–2; VR, 50.

17. *Ibid.*, 2153–4; see also Virginia Resolutions of 1798, Address of the General Assembly to the People of the Commonwealth of Virginia, and Madison, "Report," in *WJM*, VI, 327–8, 333–4, 335, 352–9; Kentucky Resolutions, in *WTJ*, VII, 289–309; Tucker, 2 ff; "Philademos," *An En-*

quiry whether the Act of Congress, "In addition to the Act, entitled . . . for the punishment of certain crimes against the United States" generally called the Sedition bill, is unconstitutional or not (Richmond, 1798).

18. In *WJM*, VI, 386–7.

19. *Ibid.*, 388; *Annals*, 5th Cong., 2145.

20. *Annals*, 5th Cong., 2104.

21. In *WJM*, VI, 397–8; *Annals*, 5th Cong., 2110, 2144, 2996, 3003, 3006–7, 3014; 6th Cong., 406, 964.

22. *Annals*, 5th Cong., 2097, 2103, 2960–1.

23. *Ibid.*, 2112.

24. *Ibid.*, 2112, 2904, 2989; 6th Cong., 925; Addison, *Liberty of speech and press*, 7, and *Analysis of the report of the committee of the Virginia Assembly, on the Proceedings of sundry of the other States in answer to their resolutions* (Philadelphia, 1800), 49; Charles Lee, *Defence of the alien and sedition Laws, shewing their entire consistency with the Constitution of the United States, and the principles of our government* (Philadelphia, 1798), 30, 36–7; *Observations on the Alien and Sedition Laws*, 42; [Henry Lee], *Plain Truth: addressed to the people of Virginia . . .* (Richmond, 1799), 48.

25. *Annals*, 5th Cong., 2140–41. It was also pointed out that the Sedition Act extended the common law by making more actions punishable than writing and publication. Tucker, 39–40.

26. *Annals*, 6th Cong., 408.

27. Madison, "Report," in *WJM*, VI, 396–7; also Thomas Cooper, *Political essays, by Thomas Cooper, Esq. of Northumberland*, 2d ed. (Philadelphia, 1800), 65.

28. Pennsylvania Democratic Society to fellow citizens throughout the United States, in *A*, Dec. 22, 1794; the development of the English law of libel is best traced in Sir William Holdsworth, *A History of English Law* (London, 1922–66), VIII, 336–46; X, 672 ff.

29. *Annals*, 5th Cong., 2105, 2140, 2163–4; Ogilvie, 8; *Annals*, 6th Cong., 35–41, 97–102.

30. *Annals*, 5th Cong., 2108, 2162, 2969, 2970.

31. *Ibid.*, 2113, 2963–4, 3005, 2006; Nathaniel Pope, *A Speech, delivered . . . in support of the resolutions . . .* (Richmond, 1800), 21.

32. *Annals*, 5th Cong., 2967.

33. *Annals*, 6th Cong., 916–7, 921, 924; 5th Cong., 2112.

34. *Ibid.*, 2134, 2143; Tunis Wortman, *A Treatise, concerning political enquiry and the liberty of the press* (New York, 1800), 59, 121, 122, 123, 142; Address of the Democratic Society of New York, and "Agis," III, in *NYJ*, Jan. 17 and Feb. 7, 1795; John Thomson, *An enquiry, concerning*

the liberty, and licentiousness of the press, and the uncontroulable nature of the human mind (New York, 1801), 6, 23, 69, 74–5, 83.

35. Wortman, 32, 34–5; Thomson, 11–3, 16–7, 23.

36. Thomson, 15, 19, 69 ff, 80; Wortman, 44–5.

37. Thomson, 19; Wortman, 41, 128–9; Ogilvie, 9; Cooper, 67.

38. "A.B." from *CC*, in *GUS*, Jan. 1, 1798; "Plain Truth" from the *Farmer's Weekly Museum*, in *ibid.*, Feb. 5, 1798; Addison, *Liberty of speech and press*, 12–3; *Annals*, 5th Cong., 2098.

39. *Annals*, 6th Cong., 409; Addison, *Liberty of speech and press*, 15, and *Rise and progress of revolution: a charge to the Grand Juries of the County Courts of the Fifth Circuit of the State of Pennsylvania, at December sessions, 1800* (Whitehall, Pa., 1801), for a forceful statement of Federalists' historical pessimism.

40. Alexander Addison, *An Oration on the rise and progress of the United States . . . to the present crisis; and on the duties of the citizen* (Philadelphia, 1798), 20; in *GUS*, unsigned, Nov. 10, 1798, extract from a Massachusetts letter, Nov. 18, 1794, and "C," Dec. 8, 1794.

41. "Crito," in *ibid.*, June 21, 1794; also *Annals*, 6th Cong., 87.

42. *Ibid.*, 925.

43. *IC*, April 8 and 15, 1799; *Annals*, 5th Cong., 3007, 3009; John Page, *Address to the freeholders of Gloucester County . . .* (Richmond, 1799), 17–18.

44. *Annals*, 5th Cong., 2150; 6th Cong., 471.

45. Addison, *Analysis of the report*, 42.

46. *Annals*, 5th Cong., 2960, 2961; 6th Cong., 967.

47. Cooper, 64.

48. "Fabricus" I, in *GUS*, May 24, 1798; see also Ch. V.

49. Cooper, 64; Thomson, 6.

50. Cooper, 64–5, 66, 67.

51. Cooper, 66–7, 84; Wortman, 26–7; see also in *A*, Governor Mifflin's Address to the Pennslyvania Legislature, Dec. 9, Pennsylvania Democratic Society to fellow citizens throughout the U.S., Dec. 22, "Z" from *Baltimore Daily Advertizer*, Dec. 26, 1794; in *NYJ*, "Agis" III, Feb. 7, 1795.

52. Wortman, 163; Cooper, 67–8, 78; *Annals*, 5th Cong., 2105, 2156; unsigned, in *GA*, Jan. 28, 1794.

53. In *NYJ*, "Democritus," Jan. 31, "Justice," March 13, Address of the Canaan Democratic Society, March 18, "Agis" V, May 20, 1795; also, in *A*, "Speech," Nov. 26, "Columbus," Dec. 31, 1794; Cooper, 84–5.

54. *Annals*, 6th Cong., 952.

55. "Aristides," in *Middlesex Gazette*, Oct. 3, 1800; *Annals*, 6th Cong., 931, 412, 956, 961.

56. Cooper, 79.

57. *Ibid.*, 80–1, 86; Wortman, 162.

58. *Annals,* 6th Cong., 964.

59. Madison, "Report," in *WJM,* VI, 289; Cooper, 78; *Annals,* 5th Cong., 2140; Page, 15 n.

60. Madison, "Report," in *WJM,* VI, 392–3.

61. *Annals,* 5th Cong., 2143; 6th Cong., 923.

62. *Annals,* 5th Cong., 2107; 6th Cong., 93, 922, 952; Ogilvie, 7. At one point, in 1797, the Federal authorities had initiated proceedings against Cobbett for libel; see his *The Republican Judge; or, the American Liberty of the Press* (1798), in *Porcupine's Work* (London, 1801), VII, 332–3.

63. *Annals,* 6th Cong., 939–40. This speech made something of a sensation in Congress; see Randolph's sarcastic reference to it in 11th Cong., 1st Session, 75.

Chapter 12. *Vindication*

1. The best short account of this episode is to be found in Lyman H. Butterfield, ed., *Letters of Benjamin Rush* (Princeton, 1951), II, 1213–18; see also *A Report of an action for a libel, Brought by Dr. Benjamin Rush, against William Cobbett, in the Supreme Court of Pennsylvania, December Term, 1799* (Philadelphia, 1800); William Cobbett, "The American Rush-light," in *Porcupine's Works* (London, 1801), XI, 209–434.

2. "Remarks," in *A,* May 12, 1800; *Annals,* 6th Cong., 918.

3. *Ibid.*, 919.

4. Nathaniel Pope, *A Speech, delivered . . . in support of the resolutions . . .* (Richmond, 1800), 18; [George Hay], *An Essay on the liberty of the press . . . By Hortensius* (Philadelphia, 1799), 19–20; *Annals,* 5th Cong., 2142, 2153–4; also Leonard W. Levy, *Jefferson and Civil Liberties: The Darker Side* (Cambridge, 1963), 42–69.

5. Only one Republican explicitly rejected the notion that the federal courts had no jurisdiction over libels, though he argued that personal libels against the president such as had been the basis of most of the prosecutions under the Sedition Act should be prosecuted in the state courts: James Sullivan, *A dissertation upon the constitutional freedom of the Press in the United States of America* (Boston, 1801), 31 ff.

6. George Hay, *An essay on the liberty of the press, shewing, that the requisition on security for good behavior from libellers, is perfectly compatible with the constitutional laws of Virginia* (Richmond, 1803), 4, 28–9, 35, 41; James Madison, "Report," in *WJM,* VI, 393; see also Sullivan,

passim; Thomas Seymour *et al.* to Jefferson, Dec. 20, 1806, in W. C. Ford, ed., *Thomas Jefferson Correspondence, Printed from the originals in the collection of William K. Bixby* (Boston, 1916), 138–40. I am aware of only two or possibly three prosecutions for seditious libel by Republican state authorities against Federalist editors after 1800, while there were at least this number initiated by Federalists in Massachusetts and Connecticut alone, quite apart from politically motivated personal libel actions against Republican editors; see *American Mercury,* March 17, 1808; Litchfield *Witness,* March 5 and Sept. 9, 1806; *A report of the trial of Andrew Wright, printer of the Republican spy on an indictment for libels against Governor Strong* . . . (Northampton, 1806). The better known Republican prosecutions are tabulated in Levy, 59.

7. These assumptions were most candidly expressed in private letters, e.g., Ames to King, Oct. 27, and Cabot to King, Nov. 6, 1801, in *LCK,* IV, 5, 11–2; Cabot to Gore, April 10, and to Wolcott, Jr., Aug. 3, 1801, Cabot to Pickering, Feb. 14, and to John Lowell, Jr., July 18, 1804, in Henry Cabot Lodge, *Life and Letters of George Cabot* (Boston, 1877), 318, 322, 342–3, 348–9. But they are also quite evident in much of the Federalist literature of the period, for example [Thomas Evans], *A series of letters, addressed to Thomas Jefferson* . . . *By Tacitus* (Philadelphia, 1802), 25 ff, esp. 89–95; also extract from the *Boston Repertory* in *Connecticut Courant,* July 16, 1806. A more oblique way of articulating the same sentiments was pursued by Theodore Dwight, *An Oration, delivered at New Haven on the 7th of July, A.D. 1801, before the society of the Cincinnati* (Hartford, 1801), 6–7, 22–3.

8. Unsigned extract from *GUS,* in *Middlesex Gazette,* April 3, 1801; Sanford W. Higginbotham, *The Keystone in the Democratic Arch: Pennsylvania Politics, 1800–1816* (Harrisburg, 1952), 35; Robert Goodloe Harper, "A Letter containing a short view of the political principals and system of the Federalists," *Selected Works of Robert Goodloe Harper* . . . (Baltimore, 1814), 324.

9. Noah Webster, Jr., to Madison, July 18, 1801, in Harry R. Warfel, ed., *Letters of Noah Webster* (New York, 1953), 233–4. Remonstrance of the merchants of New Haven, on the appointment of Samuel Bishop, and the president's reply, July 12, 1801, appear in the *Middlesex Gazette,* July 31, 1801; see also Lucius Junius Brutus, pseud., *An Examination of the President's reply to the New Haven remonstrance* . . . (New York, 1801), 13–7; the Brutus pamphlet provoked a reply from Tullius Americus, pseud., *Strictures on a Pamphlet* . . . (Albany, 1801), which ridiculed Federalists whose "patriotism is profit," 32; also Abraham Bishop, *Connecticut Republicanism, An Oration on the extent and power of political delusion* (New Haven, 1800).

NOTES TO PAGES 264–266   373

10. Jefferson, First Annual Message, Dec. 8, 1801, in *WTJ*, VIII, 119, 120, 123–4.

11. For the Federalist response to Jefferson's tax proposals, see "Steady," from *CC* in *Middlesex Gazette*, Feb. 15, 1802; "A Farmer," from *Poughkeepsie Journal* and "Phocion" from the *Litchfield Monitor*, in *ibid.*, Feb. 22, 1802; for their response to the repeal of the Judiciary Act of 1801, see "L. J. Brutus," from the *Washington Federalist* in *ibid.*, Jan. 18, 1802; and unsigned, from the *Washington Federalist* in *ibid.*, March 15, 1802; for the fear of undermining the constitutional balance, see [Evans], 30 ff, esp. 89–90; also Ames to King, Dec. 20, 1801, in *LCK*, IV, 40; Wolcott, Jr., to Cabot, Aug. 28, 1802, in Lodge, 325.

12. [Evans], 13; Sedgwick to R. King, Feb. 20, 1802, Vans Murray to King, April 5, Troup to King, April 9 and May 6, and J. Q. Adams to King, Oct. 8, 1802, in *LCK*, IV, 74, 95, 103–4, 121, 177.

13. See "The Faction Splitting" from *CC*, in *Middlesex Gazette*, Aug. 23, 1802; Vans Murray to King, April 5, 1802, Hamilton to King, June 3, 1802 and Feb. 24, 1804, in *LCK*, IV, 95, 133, 352.

14. J. Q. Adams to King, Oct. 8, 1802, Troup to King, Jan. 6 and 27, 1807, in *LCK*, IV, 176–7; V, 4–5, 7; Cabot to Wolcott, Jr., Aug. 3, 1801; Wolcott, Jr., to Cabot, Feb. 7, 1803, in Lodge, 322, 330.

15. Cf. Jefferson to Dickinson, July 13, 1801, to Barlow, May 3, 1802, to W. C. Nicholas, March 26, 1805, in *WTJ*, VIII, 76–7, 149–50, 348–9; Walter R. Fee, *The Transition from Aristocracy to Democracy in New Jersey, 1789–1829* (Somerville, N.J., 1933), 139.

16. Jefferson to George Logan, May 11, 1805, in *WTJ*, VIII, 352–3; Troup to King, Feb. 17, 1807, in *LCK*, V, 9–10; also Higginbotham, 25, 32–4, 37–8; Dixon Ryan Fox, *The Decline of Aristocracy in the Politics of New York*, ed. Robert V. Remini (New York, 1965), passim, 1–120; and the Republican strategy in New York of proclaiming the danger of a Federalist victory as reported in *CC*, May 14, 1808.

17. Pickering to Cabot, Jan. 29, Cabot to Pickering, Feb. 14, and Cabot to King, March 17, 1804, in Lodge, 337–348; cf. also *LCK*, IV, 353 ff.

18. The most succinct published statement of Federalist fears about the tendency of Republican measures is to be found in George W. Stanley, *An Oration delivered at Wallingford, August 18, 1805* . . . (New Haven, 1805), particularly 3–10; see also James Elliot's letters to his constituents published in the *Connecticut Courant*, April 17, April 24, May 7, June 12, and June 26, 1805; and unsigned, in *ibid.*, Aug. 21, 1805; Pickering to King, March 3 and 4, 1804, I. Allen Smith to King, Jan. 22, 1805, in *LCK*, IV, 360–62, 364–5, 438; also Pickering to Cabot, Jan. 4 and 29, 1804, Cabot to King, March 17, in Lodge, 335, 338, 345; fears about Louisiana's proposed form of government can be found in [William

Plummer], *Address to the Electors of New Hampshire* (n.p., 1804), 7–8, and were shared by some Republicans, cf. *Annals,* 8th Cong., 1st Session, 1054–1079. For the struggle over the judiciary see Richard E. Ellis, *The Jeffersonian Crisis: Courts and Politics in the Young Republic* (New York, 1971), 68–107.

19. *Annals,* 9th Cong., 1st session, 446, 500.

20. *Ibid.,* 8th Cong., 2d session, 1032.

21. *Ibid.,* 9th Cong., 1st session, 555–74, 592–605, 790–93, 875–7, 946–49, 959–62, 981–85. Joseph I. Shulim, *The Old Dominion and Napoleon Bonaparte: A Study in American Opinion* (New York, 1952), 166, 322–4, 266–7; Norman K. Risjord, *Old Republicans* (New York, 1965), 41 ff.

22. Jefferson to Dickinson, March 6, to Monroe, Feb. 7, to Henry Knox, March 27, to Elbridge Gerry, March 29, 1801, in *WTJ,* VIII, 7, 9–10, 36, 41.

23. Quote from Jefferson to Caesar A. Rodney, March 24, 1806 in *ibid.,* 436; also Jefferson to Horatio Gates, March 8, to Gerry, March 29, to Levi Lincoln, July 11, and to John Dickinson, July 23, 1801, in *ibid.,* 11–12, 43, 67, 76–7.

24. Jefferson to Gideon Granger, May 3, 1801, to Caesar Rodney, April 24, to Joel Barlow, May 3, to Robert R. Livingston, Oct. 10, and to Levi Lincoln, Oct. 25, 1802, to Thomas McKean, Feb. 19, 1803, Second Inaugural Address, March 4, 1805, to James Sullivan, May 21, 1805, in *ibid.,* 48, 147, 149–50, 173–4, 175, 218–19, 346–7, 355.

25. "Hampden," *A letter to the President of the United States, touching the prosecution, under his patronage, before the circuit court in the district of Connecticut* (New Haven, 1808), particularly iii–iv, 8–12, 17–18, 26; Levy, *Jefferson and Civil Liberties,* 61–66 restates the "Hampden" case with some additional details; for Jefferson's account of the scandal, see Jefferson to Robert Smith, July 1, 1805, in Ford, ed., *Jefferson Correspondence,* 115.

26. "Hampden," 14; Litchfield *Witness,* May 6, 1807; also *Annals,* 11th Cong., 1st Session, 78.

27. The suits were over articles appearing in the Litchfield *Witness,* Aug. 21, Sept. 4 and Oct. 9, 1805; for reports on developments, see *ibid.,* Sept. 25, Oct. 30, and Dec. 4, 1805; Jan. 8, Jan. 15, March 5, March 12, March 19, 1806.

28. Litchfield *Witness,* March 15 and Sept. 17, 1806; Richard J. Purcell, *Connecticut in Transition: 1775–1818* (Middletown, Conn., 1963), 175 n; the retaliatory nature of the prosecutions was made clear in Thomas Seymour et al. to Jefferson, Dec. 20, 1806, in Ford, ed., *Jefferson Correspondence,* 137–140.

29. Litchfield *Witness,* March 5, Aug. 27, Sept. 3, Sept. 17, Oct 1, Dec. 10, 1806.

30. *Ibid.,* May 6, 1807; the Supreme Court ultimately ruled against the federal common law jurisdiction in 1812, see *U.S. v. Hudson and Goodwin,* 7 *Cranch* (U.S.) 32 (1812); Edward's role in the trials is mentioned in Jefferson to W. C. Nicholas, June 13, 1809, in *WTJ,* IX, 254.

31. *Annals,* 9th Cong., 2nd Session, 247, 251, 378, 427.

32. These strategic developments are summarized by Marshall Smelser, *The Democratic Republic: 1801–1815* (New York, 1968), 138, 145.

33. Jefferson to Madison, Sept. 18, 1807, in *WTJ,* IX, 139.

34. Dana mentioned the prosecutions in passing in *Annals,* 10th Cong., 2nd session, 1328; the revival of the subject by Randolph in 1809, see *Annals,* 11th Cong., 1st session, 75 ff, caused Jefferson some embarrassment, see Jefferson to W. C. Nicholas, June 13, 1809, in *WTJ,* IX, 253–5; cf. also "Veritas," in *National Intelligencer,* July 21, 1809; Jefferson to Gideon Granger, January 24, 1810, in Andrew H. Lipscomb and Albert Ellery Bergh, eds., *The Writings of Thomas Jefferson* (Washington, 1904–5), XII, 353.

35. Pickering argued that the Embargo was unnecessary in his *A Letter from the Hon. Timothy Pickering . . . to His Excellency James Sullivan . . .* (Boston, 1808), republished in the *CC,* March 12, 1808; see also in *CC,* 1808, "An American" and "What think ye of Congress now," Jan. 6, Retrospect and "An American," Jan. 9, unsigned, May 11, "Themistocles," June 11, "An American," Aug. 3; see also "Letter to the editor of the U.S. Gazette," in *Middlesex Gazette,* Jan. 21, 1808.

36. Extract from the *GUS,* in *Middlesex Gazette,* Jan. 14, 1808; in *CC,* Memorial signed by 110 unemployed seamen in Boston, Jan. 23, and "A Friend," March 2, 1808; agitation in the Massachusetts towns was noticeable during the spring in anticipation of the state elections, see *ibid.,* March 23, March 30, and April 16, but only gained real momentum in the late summer, see *ibid.,* Aug. 10, 1808 ff; also *The patriotic proceedings of the legislature of Massachusetts, during their session from January 26 to March 4, 1809 . . .* (Boston, 1809); a good behind-the-scenes account of the agitation in Massachusetts can be gathered from William Bentley, *The Diary of William Bentley . . .* (Gloucester, Mass., 1962), III, 336 ff; distress caused by the Embargo was not all fabricated, see the hate letter of John Lane Jones to Jefferson, Aug. 8, 1808, in Ford, ed., *Jefferson Correspondence,* 166–7.

37. Connecticut's actions are reported in the *Middlesex Gazette,* March 2 and 9, 1809.

38. For Federalist charges see "An American," in *CC,* Jan. 1, 1808; *Annals,* 10th Cong., 1st session, 1655, 1703, 1705–6, 1852–3, 2109, 2122–

3, 2207-8, 2210; 2d session, 20-23, 31-4, 35, 52-3, 58, 59, 60, 1239, 1304-5; for Republican protests about the tendency of such activities, see *ibid.*, 1st session, 2116, 2129; 2d session, 61, 1303, 1306, 1307, 1308, 1309, 1368; Joseph Story to Joseph White, Jr., Dec. 31, 1808, to Samuel P. P. Fay, Jan. 9, 1809, in William W. Story, *Life and Letters of Joseph Story* . . . (Boston, 1851), I, 173, 180; Jefferson to Thomas Leib, June 23, 1808, in *WTJ*, IX, 196; also [Matthew Carey], *The olive branch: or Faults on both sides*, 7th ed. (Philadelphia, 1815), 141 ff; for Federalist replies to such charges cf. Report on a Boston Town Meeting, in *CC*, Aug. 13, 1808.

39. In *CC*, 1808, editor's comment on Sullivan's speech, Jan. 9, "Algernon Sidney," Jan. 30, "Falkland" and "Hampden," Sept. 10; *Annals*, 10th Cong., 2d session, 173, 1261-2; for Republican replies see *ibid.*, 1269, 1320, 1408, 1444-5; also J. Q. Adams, *American principles: A review of the Works of Fisher Ames* . . . (Boston, 1809), 41.

40. Sullivan's speech appears in *CC*, Jan. 9, 1808; see also Levi Lincoln's speech in *The patriotic proceedings*, 16; adverse comment is to be found in *CC*, "Algernon Sidney," Jan. 30, and "Livy," March 19 and March 23, 1808; Cabot to Pickering, Jan. 20, 1808, in Lodge, 375; see also *Annals*, 10th Cong., 2d session, 1512.

41. The "Falkland" pieces began in the *CC*, Sept. 10, 1808, under the bold heading "A Separation of the States and its consequences to New England"; but before long under the pressure of Republican denunciation had to disavow this intent, claiming lamely that it was Virginia that would secede once commerce was fully protected, cf. *ibid.*, September 24, 1808; Cabot to Pickering, October 5, 1808, in Lodge, 398.

42. [Carey], 60-1.

43. *Annals*, 10th Cong., 1st session, 1653-6; 2d session, 194, 431; [Henry Lee], *A Cursory sketch of the motives and proceedings of the party which sways the affairs of the union* . . . (Philadelphia, 1809); passim; Pickering's *Letter*, in *CC*, March 12, 1808; *The patriotic proceedings*, passim. For Republican sensitivity to this charge, see *Annals*, 10th Cong., 1st session, 1251, 1658, 1660-1, 1668-9, 1674-5; 2d session, 95-6, 222; unsigned, in *National Intelligencer*, April 17, 1809.

44. *Annals*, 10th Cong., 2d session, 194, 430-1, 1106, 1108.

45. *Ibid.*, 1st session, 1671; 2d session, 110-1, 149, 2132.

46. Quotes from *The patriotic proceedings*, 44, 112; see also [Lee], 25 ff; *Annals*, 10th Cong., 2d session, 132, 193, 390 ff, 822 ff, 1460-1; Canning played up to this sentiment in his note to Wm. Pinkney, Sept. 23, 1808, in *ibid.*, 1629-30.

47. The phrase comes from Pickering's *Letter*, in *CC*, March 12, 1808;

it was the subject of considerable animadversion on the part of the Republicans. See Resolves of the Republican conventions of Essex Co. and Hampshire Co., Address of the Officers of the Third Militia Division to Levi Lincoln, Resolves of West Cambridge, Resolves of Worcester town meeting, in *IC*, March 2, 9, 16, 20, 27, 1809.

48. *The patriotic proceedings*, 42, 44–5, 107–8, 123–4; *Annals*, 10th Cong., 2d session, 35, 420–1, 860–1, 1364–5, 1373–4.

49. *The patriotic proceedings*, 63; for the Republican response, see in *IC*, 1809, "Dion," March 9, "Hancock," March 13, Resolves of West Cambridge, March 20, Resolves of Worcester town meeting, March 27.

50. *Annals*, 10th Cong., 2d session, 408, 419, 851, 170–1, 175, 860, 882–3; some Federalists advocated arming merchant vessels, presumedly under the assumption that since the French decrees had made trade with Europe so risky, those exercising the privilege would be trading within the British empire and would only use their armaments against French cruisers, see *ibid.*, 138, 171, 1341–2; but the Massachusetts legislature pointed to the risks in such a policy, see *The Patriotic proceedings*, 102.

51. *Annals*, 10th Cong., 1st session, 2135–7; 2d session, 61–2, 124–5, 158, 220, 223, 225, 368, 371, 1369, 1372, 1403–4; John Quincy Adams, *A Letter to the Hon. Harrison Gray Otis . . . on the present state of our national affairs with remarks upon Mr. Pickering's letter to the Governor of the Commonwealth* (Boston, 1808); see also James Madison, "An Examination of the British Doctrine, which subjects to capture a neutral trade not open in time of peace," in *WJM*, VII, 204–375.

52. See Jefferson, Second Inaugral Address, March 4, 1805, in *WTJ*, VIII, 343–4; also Jefferson to Madison, Oct. 23, 1805, in *ibid.*, 380 n; Jefferson was unclear on when this moment would arrive, though. See Jefferson to Madison, August 4, 1805 and March 11, 1808, and to Monroe, January 28, 1809, in *ibid.*, VIII, 374; IX, 183–4, 243.

53. Joseph I. Shulim, *The Old Dominion and Napoleon Bonaparte: A Study in American Opinion* (New York, 1952), passim and especially 295–7; also [Gideon Granger], *An address to the people of New England* (Washington, 1808), 3–4; Smelser, 139, 154, 201.

54. J. Q. Adams, "Reply to the Appeal of the Massachusetts Federalists," in Henry Adams, ed., *Documents relating to New England Federalism 1800–1815* (Boston, 1877), 148, 193; see also 74–5, 114–15; *Annals*, 10th Cong., 2d session, 357, 1320, 1406; 11th Cong., 2d session, 1146; Smelser, 164.

55. *Annals*, 10th Cong., 1st session, 1852–3; 2d session, 26, 183, 420, 1412–13, 1418–20; Cabot to Pickering, March 12, 1808, in Lodge, 383.

56. In *CC*, Pickering's *Letter*, March 12, and "Candidus," April 20 and

23, 1808; *Annals*, 10th Cong., 1st session, 1853; 2d session, 30, 852, 1461; *The patriotic proceedings*, 110; [Lee], 21 ff.

57. *Annals*, 10th Cong., 2d session, 26, 181-3, 185, 1391.

58. *Annals*, 10th Cong., 2d session, 86, 105-6, 109, 68-9; Madison to Pinckney, July 18, 1808, in *WJM*, VIII, 34; CC, July 2 and Aug. 6, 1808.

59. *Annals*, 10th Cong., 2d session, 90, 96, 100, 1308, 1310.

60. J. Q. Adams, "Reply to the Appeal," 113; J. Q. Adams to Ezekiel Bacon, Dec. 21, 1808, in W. C. Ford, ed., *Writings of John Quincy Adams* (New York, 1913-17), III, 277-8; Monroe to John Taylor, Nov. 19, 1810, in Stanislaus Murray Hamilton, ed., *The Writings of James Monroe* (New York, 1898-1903), V, 154-155; see also Story, I, 185; civil war within New England seems to have been a real possibility, cf. Bentley, III, 405, 409.

61. Some Federalists agreed, cf. *CC*, June 29, 1808, though others objected that privateering was not feasible given British convoying, cf. *Annals*, 10th Cong., 2d session, 1361, 421.

62. *Annals*, 10th Cong., 2d session, 62, 70, 113-4, 124-6, 142, 225-6, 1320-1.

63. *Annals*, 10th Cong., 2d session, 354, 421; 11th Cong., 2d session, 1649-50.

64. *Annals*, 10th Cong., 2d session, 387; 11th Cong., 2d session, 1163, 1164, 1168, 1176-7, 1184, 1231, 1236, 1493, 1638, 1642, 1651-2, 1678.

65. Madison to Jefferson, May 25, 1810, in *WJM*, VIII, 102; this was Macon's Bill No. 2.

66. Jefferson to Barlow, May 3, 1802, and to W. C. Nicholas, March 26, 1805, in *WTJ*, VIII, 150, 348. This did not prevent Jefferson from perceiving the danger inherent in such developments, see Jefferson to Granger, August 29, 1802, to George Logan, May 11, 1805, to Monroe, May 4, 1806, to Andrew Ellicott, November 1, 1806, in *ibid.*, 170-1, 352-3, 447-8, 479-80. The early intramural disagreements are chronicled in Noble E. Cunningham, Jr., *The Jeffersonian Republicans in Power: Party Operations, 1801-1809* (Chapel Hill, 1963), ch. IX; Raymond Walters, Jr., *Albert Gallatin: Jeffersonian Financier and Diplomat* (New York, 1957), ch. XIII; also Risjord, passim.

67. L. W. Tazewell to Monroe, February 13, 1811, and Monroe to Richard Brent, February 25, 1810, in Hamilton, V, 175 n, 179.

68. The Federalists played on this fear, cf. *Annals*, 10th Cong., 2d session, 1362; see also *ibid.*, 1315-16, 1317; 11th Cong., 1st session, 1238, 1277.

69. *Annals*, 10th Cong., 2d session, 354, 433; 11th Cong., 1st session, 1189; also Randolph's speech reported in *Niles' Weekly Register*, I, 315 ff;

and Sheffey's in *ibid.*, 349. The Federalists understood the Republicans' reluctance about war, cf. *Annals*, 10th Cong., 1st session, 421, 1355–6; and suspected them of wanting to provoke Britain to a declaration, Pickering to King, Feb. 5, 1810, in *LCK*, V, 194, 195, also 269; Roger H. Brown, *The Republic in Peril: 1812* (New York, 1964), passim, particularly 66 ff.

70. Monroe to John Taylor, Jan. 9, 1809, and Nov. 19, 1810, in Hamilton, V, 89–90, 154.

71. [Carey], 235–39; also Monroe's warning that republicanism was facing a crisis, Monroe to John Randolph, February 13, 1811, in Hamilton, V, 171–2, 183; *Annals*, 11th Cong., 1st session, 1231; Royall Tyler to James Fisk, May 13, 1812, in Roger H. Brown, "A Vermont Republican Urges War: Royall Tyler, 1812, and the Safety of Republican Government," *Vermont History*, XXXVI (1968), 16–17. While Federalists in Congress obstructed administration measures, those outside like Governor Griswold of Connecticut complained of national degradation, see in *CC*, Address to the Connecticut Legislature, October 16, 1811, and the series "Present and Future state of this disgraced and degraded Nation," October 23, 1811 ff.

72. Cf. *Annals*, 10th Cong., 2d session, 93, 1342, quote from Eppes' paraphrase, 1525, of Quincy, 1112; 12th Cong., 2d session, 661; see also [Carey], 235.

73. Federalists were making this point during the repeal of the Embargo. See *Annals*, 10th Cong., 2d session, 1323, 1355, 1413; also Sheffey's speech, in *Niles* [1] *Weekly Register*, I, 348; excerpt from *CC* and Memorial of the Representatives of Masachusetts to Congress, in *ibid.*, II, 207–8, 259.

74. Excerpt from the *Federal Republican*, in *Niles' Weekly Register*, I, 252; Troup to King, Jan. 23, 1810, in *LCK*, V, 187–8.

75. On the pusillanimous character of the 10th and 11th Congresses, see *Niles' Weekly Register*, I, 250; II, 208; Irving Brant, *James Madison: The President 1809–1812* (New York, 1956), 251, 260, 433, 443–4; also Norman K. Risjord, "1812; Conservatives, War Hawks, and the Nation's Honor," *WMQ*, XVIII (1961), 196 ff.

76. In *CC*, "Impartial Enquirer," Jan. 2 and 5, 1811, and reports, Feb. 9 and 20, April 24, 1811; J. Trumbull to King, Aug. 25, 1810, R. King to John Porter, Dec. 10, 1811, in *LCK*, V, 221–2, 253; and Pickering's *Letter* from the *Boston Repertory*, in *Niles' Weekly Register*, II, 155.

77. Britain's rejection of any accommodation with the United States became evident in the Monroe-Foster correspondence of the late summer and then in the Prince Regent's declarations in the spring of 1812, see *Annals*,

12th Cong., 1st session, 1770–1775, 1781 ff; also Madison to J. Q. Adams, Nov. 15, 1811, in *WJM*, VIII, 166; Address of the Governor of South Carolina, Nov. 26, 1811, in *Niles' Weekly Register*, I, 276; for the unpopularity of the non-intercourse, see in *CC*, report, March 10, and "Massachusetts Yeoman," Sept. 14, 1811. The determination of the war hawks is best seen in their speeches, see especially Grundy's and Clay's in *Niles' Weekly Register*, I, 313, 332–4; Niles' editorials also reflected this spirit, cf. *ibid.*, I, 352–3; II, 29–30, 85–6, 362.

78. Federalist strategy in the emergency session of the 12th Cong., was analysed in Monroe to John Taylor, June 13, 1812, in Hamilton, V, 207–9; Brant, 398. See also Edmund Quincy, *Life of Josiah Quincy of Massachusetts* (Boston, 1868), 239–40.

79. Federalist contempt for Madison clearly expressed itself in such papers as *CC*, July 13 and Nov. 6, 1811, and "War," May 20, 1812; see also *Niles' Weekly Register*, I, 348; [Carey], 236–7; Brant, 431, 433.

80. *An Address of the members of the House of Representatives of the Congress of the United States, to their constituents, on the subject of war with Great Britain* (New York, 1812), quotes from 6, 27, 28; see also *Niles' Weekly Register*, II, 303; Samuel Taggart's Speech, in *Annals* 12th Cong., 1st session, 1638–1679.

81. *Niles' Weekly Register*, II, 379; also Address of the House of Representatives to the People of Massachusetts, in II, 417–18; Resolves of New England towns, in *CC*, September 12, 1812; Massachusetts Remonstrance, in *Annals*, 13th Cong., 1st session, 333–41; Maryland Memorial from the House of Delegates, *ibid.*, 1204–9; Bentley, IV, 102; also Declaration of the Connecticut General Assembly, in *Niles' Weekly Register*, III, 24–5; Resolves of the Massachusetts Senate, June 15, 1813, in IV, 287; Maryland House of Delegates to R. King, January 2, 1815, in VII, 326–7; William Ellery Channing, *A sermon, preached in Boston, July 23, 1812; the day of publick fast, appointed by the executive of the commonwealth of Massachusetts . . .* (Boston, 1812), 7 ff.

82. The Federalist position on the war in Congress is best traced in the debates on the bill for an additional military force; *Annals*, 12th Cong., 2d session, 459 ff, and on the proposal for a militia draught in *Annals*, 13th Cong., 3d session, 73 ff, 775 ff; some Federalists changed their tune as the war became clearly defensive; see King's Memorandum, Oct. 1814, in *LCK*, V, 422–4.

83. *Niles' Weekly Register*, II, 288–9; III, 4–5, 22–4, 179–80, 273, 343; VII, 113–14, 148–152; *Annals*, 12th Cong., 2d session, 483; Bentley, IV, 108; Madison's Fourth Annual Message, November 4, 1812, in *WJM*,

VIII, 224–5; Samuel Eliot Morison, *The Life and Letters of Harrison Gray Otis, Federalist, 1765–1848* (Boston, 1913), II, 63–64; most of the important documents connected with state resistance to militia requisitions are to be found in Herman V. Ames, *State Documents on Federal Relations: the States and the United States* (Philadelphia, 1906), nos. 28–32.

84. *Niles' Weekly Register,* II, 418; [Carey], 301–8; Morison, II, 66–7; John Lowell to Otis, February 25, 1823, in *ibid.,* 75–6.

85. [Carey], 308–315; some evidence to confirm the existence of such a conspiracy can be found in *Niles' Weekly Register,* V, 380; VI, 119; VII, 194–6; see also C. Gore to R. King, July 28, 1814, in *LCK,* V, 403. Subsequent historians have been more charitable about the creditor position of the New England banks. See J. T. Adams, *New England in the Republic, 1776–1850* (Boston, 1926), 284–5.

86. *Niles' Weekly Register,* V, 218, 220, 240, 280–1, 295–6, 305–6, 317, 368–9; VII, 51–2.

87. *Ibid.,* VI, 307–310; VII, 70–76; Americans had also long known of British designs on New Orleans, *ibid.,* IV, 148; V, 250; VII, 356, 361.

88. *Ibid.,* VII, 149–153.

89. For the Henry correspondence see *ibid.,* II, 20–27; VII, 185–9. For the activities of the Convention, see Theodore Dwight, *History of the Hartford Convention: with a review of the policy of the United States Government, which led to the war of 1812* (Boston, 1833), 352–379.

90. *Annals,* 11th Cong., 1st session, 1209 ff; *Niles' Weekly Register,* II, 259–267; also Clay's Reply to John Randolph's pamphlet attack, June 17, 1812, in James F. Hopkins, ed., *The Papers of Henry Clay* (Lexington, 1959–), I, 668–674 and Randolph's reply to Clay's public letter, July 2, 1812, *ibid.,* 686–694.

91. *Niles' Weekly Register,* II, 309; *Interesting papers relative to the recent riots at Baltimore* (Philadelphia, 1812), i.

92. Documentation on the riots is to be found in *Interesting papers,* passim; *Niles' Weekly Register,* II, 373–380.

93. *Interesting papers,* 7–8; for the uses to which the Federalists tried to put this incident, see the unnumbered pages of the introduction, and Resolves of Gorham, Mass., in *CC,* September 19, 1812; L. H. Stockton, *An address delivered before the convention of the Friends of peace of the state of New Jersey, July 4, 1814 . . .* (1814), 21.

94. *Niles' Weekly Register,* II, 405.

95. D. H. Fischer, *The Revolution in American Conservatism* (New York, 1965), 168–9; Baltimore's reputation suffered seriously as a consequence of the riots, see *Niles' Weekly Register,* III, 45–7; IV, 143.

96. See Robert L. Meriwether, *The Papers of John C. Calhoun* (Columbia, 1959–   ), 195, 198–200; Annals, 13th Cong., 1st session, 225–6.

97. I have found report of only one treason trial in the state courts, *People* vs. *Lynch* (New York, 1814); and three in the federal courts *U.S.* vs. *Pryor* (1814), *U.S.* vs. *Lee* (1814), and *U.S.* vs. *Hodges* (1815), none of which led to conviction. The most comprehensive contemporary discussion of treason I have encountered is Judge Peter's charge in the Circuit Court of the United States, Pennsylvania District, Oct. 7, 1813, in *Niles' Weekly Register*, VII, 187–8. Complaints against the ineffectualness of the treason laws are to be found in IV, 177, 209, 322; VII, 170, 270; I have found notice of only one execution for treason levied by a military court, cf. IV, 66; attempts to expand the jurisdiction of military courts over the crime came to nothing, see *Annals*, 13th Cong., 1st session, 881–889; similarly, the attempt to have Governor Chittenden prosecuted for treason by resolution of the House of Representatives aborted, *ibid.*, 859–61.

98. Gerry at one point recommended the seizure of Federalist printers in Massachusetts, Morison, II, 57; also Jefferson to John B. Colvin, September 20, 1810, in *WTJ*, IX, 279–80; Madison bitterly complained about Federalist activity throughout the war, Madison to Jefferson, August 17, and to S. Spring, September 6, 1812, and to W. C. Nicholas, November 26, 1814, in *WJM*, VIII, 210–11, 215, 319.

99. Madison to David Humphreys, March 23, 1813, in *WJM*, VIII, 241; *Niles' Weekly Register*, II, 396; VII, 187–8, 258.

100. See Jefferson to Lafayette, Feb. 14, 1815, in *WTJ*, IX, 509; Henry Adams, *History of the United States of America* . . . (New York, 1891–3), VII, 379.

101. The peace treaty can be found in Richard Peters, ed., *Statutes at Large: Foreign Treaties* (Boston, 1862), 218–223; Shaw Livermore, Jr., *The Twilight of Federalism: The Disintegration of the Federalist Party, 1815–1830* (Princeton, 1962), 12–13.

102. Quote from E. Gerry, Address to the Senate, May 24, 1813, in *Annals*, 13th Cong., 1st session, 11; see also *Niles' Weekly Register*, II, 362; Madsion, Second Inaugural Address, March 4, 1813, Special Message to Congress, Feb. 18, 1815, Seventh Annual Message, Dec. 5, 1815, in *WJM*, VII, 236, 324, 343; Henry Clay, "Reply to a toast at a Lexington Banquet," Oct. 7, 1815, in Hopkins, II, 69–70. Though the question of impressment had not been resolved, it could always be taken up again, see Jefferson to Lafayette, Feb. 14, 1815, in *WTJ*, IV, 511.

103. *Niles' Weekly Register*, IX, 2–3.

104. King understood immediately what the war had done to the Federalists, see King to Gore, March 21, 1815, in *LCK*, V, 475; for Federalist

optimism see Wm. Duer to Wm. Henderson, Feb. 16, and S. Van Rensselaer to King, Feb. 29, 1816, in *ibid.*, 517, 521–2; Livermore, 27, 30.

105. Livermore, 31.

106. King to Gore, May 15, 1816, in *LCK*, V, 535; Livermore, 43–4.

107. For Monroe's conciliatory pronouncements see Inaugural Address, March 4, 1817, in Hamilton, VI, 13; for his private estimate of the Federalists see Monroe to Madison, July 7, 1816, in *ibid.*, V, 343, 344–5, 346.

108. Livermore, passim.

Epilogue

1. *Niles' Weekly Register*, XIII, 1–2.

2. Jefferson to Lafayette, November 23, 1818, in W. C. Ford, ed., *Thomas Jefferson, Correspondence, Printed from the originals in the collection of William K. Bixby* (Boston, 1916), 243.

3. Jefferson to Richard Bland Lee, August 11, 1819, in *ibid.*, 250.

4. Cf. Monroe's caution in his Inaugural, March 4, 1817, in Stanislaus Murray Hamilton, ed., *The Writings of James Monroe* (New York, 1898–1903), VI, 10; *Niles' Weekly Register*, XII, 33; XIII, 46.

5. *Ibid.*, XI, 32, 205, 220.

6. *Ibid.*, XV, 1–2; the possibility that Napoleon might return to the Continent was seriously entertained, cf. *ibid.*, XI, 33–4.

7. Jefferson to Joel Barlow, May 3, 1802, in *WTJ*, VIII, 150.

8. The compensation controversy grew out of an effort on the part of Massachusetts to claim compensation for troops sent out of the state. The administration refused to sanction such a proposal on the grounds that Massachusetts had failed to place the militia under Federal authority, cf. James Lloyd and William H. Sumner to the Secretary of War, February 3, 1817, and reply in *Niles' Weekly Register*, XII, 8–12; the Republicans managed to keep the issue alive as long as possible in Congress by continually postponing its consideration, see *ibid.*, XIII, 372–3, 374, 413–4; XV, 326.

9. On the caucus see Frederick W. Dallinger, *Nominations for Elective Office in the United States* (New York, 1897), 7–21; *Niles' Weekly Register*, XXV, 137–9.

10. The most detailed study of this transition is to be found in Michael Wallace, "Changing Concepts of Party in the United States: New York, 1815–1828," *American Historical Review*, LXXIV (1968), 453–491; see also Richard Hofstadter, *The Idea of a Party System: The Rise of Legitimate Opposition in the United States, 1780–1840* (Berkeley, 1969), ch. VI.

11. *Niles' Weekly Register*, XXV, 49 ff; Martin Van Buren, *Inquiry into the Origin and Cause of Political Parties in the United States* (New York, 1867).

12. For this characterization of Whig ideology I rely on Lee Benson, *The Concept of Jacksonian Democracy: New York as a Test Case* (Princeton, 1961), passim; the survival of antipartyism as well as the failure of the Whig party are treated in Ronald P. Formisano, "Political Character, Antipartyism and the Second Party System," *American Quarterly*, XXI (1969), 683–709.

Index

Securing the Revolution

Designed by R. E. Rosenbaum.
Composed by Vail-Ballou Press, Inc.,
in 10 point linotype Caledonia, 3 points leaded,
with display lines in Caslon 337 and 3371.
Printed letterpress from type by Vail-Ballou Press
on Warren's 1854 text, 60 pound basis,
with the Cornell University Press watermark.
Bound by Vail-Ballou Press
in Holliston Roxite B book cloth
and stamped in All Purpose foil.

Library of Congress Cataloging in Publication Data
(For library cataloging purposes only)

Buel, Richard, date.
  Securing the revolution.

  Includes bibliographical references.
    1. Political parties—United States—History.
  2. United States—Politics and government—1789–1815.
  I. Title.
  JK2260.B8   329'.02   74-38120
  ISBN 0-8014-0705-2